Construction Equipment Management

John E. Schaufelberger

University of Washington

Prentice Hall
Upper Saddle River, New Jersey   Columbus, Ohio

Library of Congress Cataloging-in-Publication Data

Schaufelberger, John E.
    Construction equipment management / John E. Schaufelberger.
      p. cm.
    Includes index.
    ISBN 0-13-716267-7
    1. Construction equipment—management.   2. Engineering—Equipment
and supplies—Management.   3. Construction industry—Management.
I. Title.
TA213.S34   1999
690'.028'4—dc21   98-38289
                                                        CIP

Cover photo: © Frank Grant, International Stock
Editor: Ed Francis
Production Editor: Christine M. Harrington
Production Coordination: Custom Editorial Productions, Inc.
Design Coordinator: Karrie M. Converse
Text Designer: Custom Editorial Productions, Inc.
Cover Designer: Jason Moore
Production Manager: Patricia A. Tonneman
Marketing Manager: Danny Hoyt

 © 1999 by Prentice-Hall, Inc.
Pearson Education
Upper Saddle River, New Jersey 07458

Printed in the United States of America

ISBN: 0-13-716267-7

Prentice-Hall International (UK) Limited, *London*
Prentice-Hall of Australia Pty. Limited, *Sydney*
Prentice-Hall Canada, Inc., *Toronto*
Prentice-Hall Hispanoamericana, S. A., *Mexico*
Prentice-Hall of India Private Limited, *New Delhi*
Prentice-Hall of Japan, Inc., *Tokyo*
Simon & Schuster Asia Pte. Ltd., *Singapore*
Editora Prentice-Hall do Brasil, Ltda., *Rio de Janeiro*

To my parents

Preface

Knowledge of construction equipment, its use, and management considerations are critical skills for construction professionals. This book was written to provide readers with this knowledge in an easy-to-read format using numerous examples to illustrate major concepts. It is intended to be used as a text in undergraduate civil engineering, construction, or construction management courses. It also is suitable as a reference for professional construction managers.

The book starts with a description of techniques for estimating equipment ownership and operating costs. Next, students are introduced to site work estimating and scheduling using equipment productivity and cost data. Specific types of equipment are then introduced, and techniques for estimating productivity are presented. The book concludes with a discussion of major equipment management issues. The appendixes include a glossary, common conversion factors, and tables of interest factors.

The book was developed on the premise that readers have a basic understanding of the construction process but limited knowledge of construction equipment. Coverage includes all major types of equipment typically used on commercial construction projects. The operational capabilities of each type of equipment are described and illustrated with numerous figures. Equipment selection considerations are discussed, along with techniques for estimating equipment productivity and costs. Concise explanations of concepts are followed with detailed example problems to illustrate major teaching points. Sample manufacturers' technical data are provided to illustrate the use of each type of equipment. Realistic exercises are included at the end of each chapter to reinforce the concepts discussed. An instructor's manual containing solutions to all exercises is also available.

This book could not have been written without the help of many people. I wish to express my deep appreciation to the many construction associations and equipment manufacturers who graciously permitted publication of the photographs and technical data contained in the book. I also want to thank the following reviewers of the manuscript for their helpful comments: Thomas R. Dunn, University of Cincinnati; and Jerry Householder, Louisiana State University.

John E. Schaufelberger
Department of Construction Management
College of Architecture and Urban Planning
University of Washington

Contents

Introduction

1.1   Construction Equipment Management

Equipment is a critical resource in the execution of most construction projects. The equipment fleet may represent the largest long-term capital investment in many construction companies. Consequently, equipment management decisions have significant impacts on the economic viability of construction firms. Equipment must pay for itself by earning more for the contractor than it costs to purchase, own, and use it. Idle equipment is a drain on income—*operating* costs incur only when the equipment is used, but *ownership* costs incur irrespective of frequency of use. Contractors must continually evaluate their equipment fleets to determine when to acquire additional items, when to replace items, and when to dispose of items that are underutilized.

One of the key decisions in planning and executing a construction project is the selection of equipment to use on the project. The type of equipment chosen will determine how the work will be done, the time required to complete the work, and the cost of construction. Therefore, it is important that construction managers understand what type of construction equipment is most appropriate for each construction task and how to estimate equipment productivity and costs. Success in construction is greatly influenced by the selection of equipment for the tasks to be performed.

The capabilities of construction equipment are described in manufacturers' literature and can be used to estimate equipment productivity. The costs to be considered are the cost of owning, leasing, or renting the equipment and the costs of operating, maintaining, and repairing it. The effectiveness of a contractor's preventive maintenance program will significantly influence equipment operating and repair costs.

1.2   *Equipment Selection Factors*

Most construction operations can be performed by more than one type of equipment. The equipment selected should complete the work in accordance with the project plans and specifications, in the required time frame, and at the least overall cost. The following factors should be considered in selecting equipment for a project:

- *Cost effectiveness.* This means not only selecting the appropriate type of equipment for the task, but also selecting an appropriate-sized machine. This involves comparison of the increased production rates of larger machines with their increased ownership and operating costs. Where possible, contractors should select the size of equipment that minimizes the unit cost (e.g., dollars per cubic yard) of performing the construction task. The soil conditions of the job site may dictate the type of equipment that should be selected. Tracked equipment usually is selected when the surface condition of the job site is soft or wet, because they exert less ground pressure and generally have better traction than wheeled equipment under such conditions. Construction site access or working-area restrictions may also limit the types and sizes of equipment that can be used on a construction site.
- *Versatility.* To control total project costs and minimize equipment transportation costs, equipment should be selected that can perform multiple tasks on a given project site. Using a tractor to excavate for a foundation, backfill the completed foundation, and grade around the newly constructed building is usually more efficient than using a different type of equipment for each task. The project must be analyzed in its entirety to select the most cost-effective set of construction equipment to be used on the project.

1.3   *Organization of This Book*

The purpose of this book is to provide the student with (1) an understanding of the basic issues involved in construction equipment management and (2) an ability to estimate equipment productivity and cost. Concepts are discussed at the beginning of each chapter, followed by example problems illustrating the concepts introduced. A set of problems is provided at the end of most chapters to provide students an opportunity to apply the concepts discussed.

Chapters 2, 3, and 4 are devoted to learning techniques for estimating equipment ownership and operating costs. Chapter 5 introduces students to cost estimating using equipment productivity and cost data. Chapter 6 demonstrates the use of equipment productivity in developing construction schedules. Chapters 7 through 21 are devoted to learning the capabilities of specific types of equipment and methods for estimating productivity and cost data. Chapter 22 concludes the book with a discussion of equipment fleet management issues. A glossary of terms is in Appendix A, common conversion factors are in Appendix B, and interest tables are in Appendix C.

2

Time Value of Money

2.1   Introduction

It is generally acknowledged that money has a time value. One dollar today is worth more than one dollar tomorrow. The reason why the value of money increases with time is because of the **interest rate**, which represents the cost of borrowing the money or the return obtainable by investing it. Because of the cost of money, interest must be considered by contractors when making decisions regarding their equipment. This requires a cash flow analysis, which recognizes that money has a different economic value depending on when it is received or paid.

Contractors continually analyze their equipment fleets to ensure that none of their equipment is losing money for them. Major company decisions include purchasing, leasing, depreciating, repairing, and replacing equipment. These management decisions are based on economic analysis of each alternative course of action. The **time value of money** must be considered in order to make the best decisions.

2.2   Equivalence Concept

The concept of **equivalence** means that payments that differ in magnitude but are made at different time periods may be equivalent to one another. The cash flow factors described in Sections 2.3 and 2.4 can be used to determine the equivalent value of money at a time period different from the one in which the money is paid or received. This involves consideration of time and the interest rate. For example, a contractor might be interested in purchasing a truck in five years and wants to determine how much he or she should invest today to have sufficient funds at the end of the five-year period. Another example might be a contractor who is considering either purchasing or leasing a crane.

Each alternative has differing costs that are incurred at different times. To compare the two, the contractor decides to determine an equivalent cost for each based on its **present worth,** which means determining an equivalent cost at today's value.

To be meaningful, *any economic comparison must be based on equivalent costs at the same point in time.* In other words, comparing a future cost of one alternative with the present worth cost of a second alternative is not valid, and therefore not meaningful.

2.3   Single Payments

Single payments may occur either today or at some time in the future. P is used to indicate a sum paid or received today, and F is used to indicate a future sum. Let's determine the future value of $10 invested at 6% for one year.

$$\$10 \, (1 + 0.06) = \$10.60$$

This can be written symbolically as

$$F = P \, (1 + i)$$

where i is the interest rate.

For n periods, the formula becomes

$$F = P \, (1 + i)^n$$

The term $(1 + i)^n$ is called the **single payment compound amount factor,** which is used to determine the future worth of a present sum of money. The reciprocal, or $1/(1 + i)^n$, is called the **single payment present worth factor** which is used to determine the present worth of a future sum of money. In solving economic analysis problems, students may use either their calculators and the formulas for each factor or a shorthand notation and the interest tables in Appendix C. In this text, we will set up the example problems both ways, but we will use the shorthand notation for problem solution.

The shorthand notation for the single payment compound amount factor is written as $(F/P, i, n)$ which means find a future sum given a present value at i interest for n time periods. The i identifies on which page in Appendix C to look for the value, F/P identifies which column on that page, and n indicates in which row in the column you will find the numerical value for the factor. For example, determine the single payment compound amount factor for 10 years at an interest rate of 5%. Looking on page 340, which contains all the factors for an interest rate of 5%, read down the column under the heading n until you come to 10; then read across to the column under the heading F/P, and read the factor value as 1.629. This means that $1,000 invested today at an effective interest rate of 5% will be worth ($1,000)(1.629) or $1,629 at the end of 10 years.

A similar shorthand notation for the single payment present worth factor would be $(P/F, i, n)$. This means: Find the present worth of a given future sum received or paid at the end of n periods at an effective interest rate of i. Using the same 5% example discussed above, find the present worth compound amount factor for a sum to be paid at the end of 15 years. Again looking on page 340, read down the column under the heading n until you come to 15; then read across to the column under the heading P/F, and read the factor value as 0.481. This means that the present worth value of $1,000 to be paid at the end of 15 years at an interest rate of 5% is ($1,000)(0.481) or $481. Now let's look at two example problems.

Example 2.1

A contractor plans to purchase a pickup truck in 5 years. How much should the contractor invest at 6% interest today to have the $30,000 needed to purchase the truck at the end of the 5 years?

Solution

In this problem, the purchase price is a known future value, and the unknown is the present worth amount. Mathematically, this can be written as

$$P = \frac{F}{(1 + i)^n} = \frac{\$30,000}{(1 + 0.006)^5}$$

Using our shorthand notation, it is written as

$$P = F(P/F, i, n) = (\$30,000)(P/F, 6\%, 5)$$

Note that the unknown is always the numerator in the shorthand notation (P/F), and the known is the denominator. Looking on page 341, we find the factor value to be 0.747. Solving the equation yields the following answer:

$$P = (\$30,000)(0.747) = \$22,410$$

Example 2.2

A contractor is considering the purchase of a new pump that will be used to remove storm runoff from open excavations. The pump will cost $15,000 and have an expected life of 10 years. After 10 years of use, the contractor estimates the pump salvage value will be $4,000. What is the contractor's total cost (on a present worth basis) of owning the pump, if the effective interest rate is 8%?

Solution

In this problem, the purchase price is a known present worth cost and the salvage value is a future receipt. To determine the present worth of the total cost, we subtract the present worth of the salvage value from the initial cost. Mathematically, this is written as

$$P = \$15,000 - \frac{\$4,000}{(1 + 0.08)^{10}}$$

Using our shorthand notation, it is written as

$$P = \$15,000 - [(\$4,000)(P/F, 8\%, 10)]$$

Inserting the factor value from page 343 yields the following:

$$P = \$15,000 - [(\$4,000)(0.463)] = \$15,000 - \$1,852 = \mathbf{\$13,148}$$

2.4   Uniform Series of Payments

In some situations, it is desirable to determine the present worth or future worth of a uniform series of payments or receipts. In other situations, it is necessary to determine a series of equal payments or receipts. To accomplish these analyses, we will introduce A, which is defined as a series of equal payments or receipts that occur *at the end* of each period for n periods. *It is important that students learn this definition and understand that A is not used for payments or receipts made or received at the beginning of each time period.*

The *uniform series compound amount factor* is used to determine the future worth of a series of equal payments or receipts. Mathematically, it is written as $[(1 + i)^n - 1]/i$, and the shorthand notation is $(F/A, i, n)$.

The *uniform series present worth factor* is used to determine the present worth of a series of equal payments or receipts. Mathematically, it is written as $[(1 + i)^n - 1]/[i(1 + i)^n]$, and the shorthand notation is $(P/A, i, n)$.

The *uniform series sinking fund factor* is used to determine a series of equal payments or receipts that is equivalent to a stated or required future sum. Mathematically, it is written as $i/[(1 + i)^n - 1]$, and the shorthand notation is $(A/F, i, n)$.

The *uniform series capital recovery factor* is used to determine a series of equal payments or receipts that is equivalent to a given present worth sum. Mathematically, it is written as $[i(1 + i)^n]/[(1 + i)^n - 1]$, and the shorthand notation is $(A/P, i, n)$. Now let's apply these factors in two example problems.

Example 2.3

A contractor is investing \$5,000 per year in savings certificates at an interest rate of 6% and plans to continue the investment program for 6 years. He is doing this so he will have a down payment for some new construction equipment. What will the value of the contractor's investment be at the end of 6 years?

Solution

In this problem, the annual investment is an annual uniform series, and the unknown is the future worth. Mathematically, this can be written as follows:

$$F = \frac{A[(1 + i)^n - 1]}{i} = \frac{(\$5,000)[(1 + 0.06)^6 - 1]}{0.06}$$

Using our shorthand notation, it is written as

$$F = (\$5,000)(F/A, 6\%, 6)$$

Inserting the factor value from page 341 yields the following:

$$F = (\$5,000)(6.975) = \mathbf{\$34,875}$$

Example 2.4

A contractor has purchased a new truck for $125,000 and plans to use the truck for 6 years. After 6 years of use, the estimated salvage value for the truck will be $30,000. What is the contractor's annual cost (annual uniform series) for the truck at an interest rate of 10%?

Solution

In this problem, the purchase price is given as a present value and the salvage value as a future value. The unknown is a series of equal annual payments. Mathematically, this can be written as

$$A = \frac{(\$125,000)[(0.1)(1 + 0.1)^6]}{[(1 + 0.1)^6 - 1]} - \frac{(\$30,000)(0.01)}{[(1 + 0.1)^6 - 1]}$$

Using our shorthand notation, it is written as

$$A = [(\$125,000)(A/P, 10\%, 6)] - [(\$30,000)(A/F, 10\%, 6)]$$

Inserting the factor values from page 345 yields the following:

$$A = [(\$125,000)(0.230)] - [(\$30,000)(0.130)] = \$28,750 - \$3,900 = \mathbf{\$24,850}$$

2.5   Cash Flow Diagrams

Cash flow diagrams are used to analyze economic alternatives. Although they are not always necessary in simple problems, such diagrams allow the student to better visualize each of the individual sums and uniform series involved in the alternative.

The following conventions are used to standardize cash flow diagrams:

- The horizontal (time) axis is marked off in equal increments, one per interest period, up to the end of the time period under consideration (period of ownership). The interest period may be years, months, days, or any other equal time period.
- *Receipts* are represented by arrows directed up and *payments* are represented by arrows pointing down.
- Two or more receipts or payments in the same period are placed end-to-end, and these may be combined.
- All cash that flows during an interest period is considered to flow at the end of the period. This is known as the **year-end convention.**

These conventions are illustrated in the following example.

Example 2.5

A contractor purchased a small used tractor for $20,000 that she intends to use for landscaping around newly constructed houses. Maintenance costs for the tractor are estimated to be $1,000 per year. The contractor plans to dispose of the tractor after 5 years and realize a salvage value of $7,000. Annual income generated by the tractor is estimated to be $5,000 per year. Draw the cash flow diagram.

Solution

Arrows representing the initial purchase price and the annual maintenance costs will be drawn down in accordance with our convention, since they are payments. The salvage value and the income will be represented by arrows pointing up, because they are receipts. The resulting cash flow diagram is shown below.

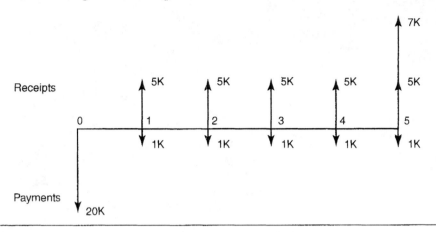

2.6   *Alternative Analysis*

When two or more alternatives are capable of performing the same function, the economically superior alternative will be the one with the least present worth cost. This *present worth method* of alternative comparison should be restricted to evaluating alternatives with equal life spans. Alternatives that accomplish the same function but have unequal lives must be compared using the *annual cost method* of comparison. The annual cost method assumes that each alternative will be replaced by an identical twin at the end of its useful life (infinite renewal).

The first step in comparing economic alternatives is to construct a cash flow diagram for each alternative. Then a common basis (either *P, F,* or *A*) is selected for comparing the alternatives, and an equivalent sum or uniform annual series is determined for each. Using the common basis, the alternatives are compared to select the one that is most favorable. Contractors are usually interested in earning more from their equipment investment than simply the cost of money. They often use a *minimum attractive rate of return* to perform cash flow analysis. The minimum attractive rate of return usually includes the *cost of money* (interest), taxes on the equipment, and equipment insurance costs. It is used as the effective interest rate in cash flow analysis. These concepts are illustrated in the following examples. For the remainder of this chapter, we will use only the shorthand notation in the sample problems.

Example 2.6

A contractor is considering purchasing a used tractor for $180,000 that she could use for 10 years and then sell for an estimated salvage value of $10,000. Annual maintenance and repair costs for the used tractor are estimated to be $15,000 per year. As an alternative, the contractor could lease a similar tractor for $4,000 per month. Should the contractor purchase the used tractor or lease the tractor from an equipment dealer? Annual operating cost are approximately the same for both alternatives. Use a minimum attractive rate of return of 12%.

Solution

Since the rental alternative is known on an annual cost basis, we will compare the alternatives on an annual cost basis. The annual cost for the rental alternative is

$$A = (12 \text{ months})(\$4,000/\text{month}) = \$48,000$$

Following is a cash flow diagram for the purchase alternative:

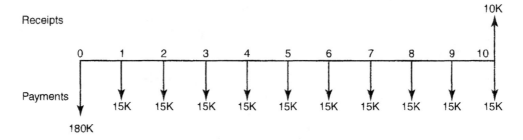

The annual cost can be determined using the following equation:

$$A = [(\$180,000)(A/P, 12\%, 10)] + \$15,000 - [(\$10,000)(A/F, 12\%, 10)]$$

Substituting factor values from Appendix C yields the following:

$$A = [(\$180,000)(0.177)] + \$15,000 - [(\$10,000)(0.057)]$$
$$= \$31,860 + \$15,000 - \$570 = \$46,290$$

The contractor should purchase the used tractor, because it has a lower annual cost.

Example 2.7

A contractor has decided to add a grader to his equipment fleet. He could purchase either a new or a used one. Interest, insurance, and taxes total about 12%, and the contractor anticipates using the grader about 2,000 hours per year. Which of the following alternatives should the contractor select?

a. The new grader costs $120,000 to purchase and is expected to have a useful life of 16,000 hours of operation. Tires cost $5,000 to replace (estimated to occur after every 4,000 hours of use) and major repairs will be needed after 8,000 hours of operation at a cost of $6,000. Fuel, oil, and minor maintenance cost about $15.25 for each hour the grader is used. Estimated salvage value at the end of 16,000 hours of operation is $10,000.

b. The used grader costs $75,000 to purchase and is expected to have a useful life of 8,000 hours of operation. Tires cost $5,000 to replace (estimated to occur after every 4,000 hours of use). Fuel, oil, and minor maintenance cost about $18.25 for each hour the grader is used. Estimated salvage value at the end of 8,000 hours of use is $8,000.

Solution

Following is the cash flow diagram for the new grader alternative. Annual fuel, oil, and minor maintenance cost is (2,000 hr.)($15.25/hr.) or $30,500.

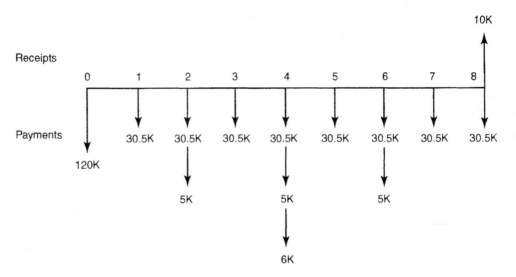

The cash flow diagram for the used grader alternative is shown below. Annual fuel, oil, and minor maintenance cost is (2,000 hr.)($18.25/hr.) or $36,500.

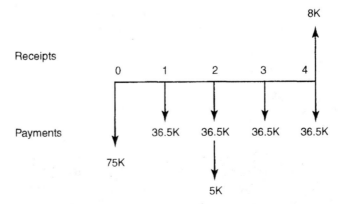

Because the two alternatives have different lives, an annual cost comparison will be used.

The annual cost for the new grader alternative can be determined with the following equation:

$$A = [(\$120,000)(A/P,\ 12\%,\ 8)] + \$30,500$$
$$+ [(\$5,000)(P/F,\ 12\%,\ 2)(A/P,\ 12\%,\ 8)]$$
$$+ [(\$11,000)(P/F,\ 12\%,\ 4)(A/P,\ 12\%,\ 8)]$$
$$+ [(\$5,000)(F/P,\ 12\%,\ 2)(A/F,\ 12\%,\ 8)]$$
$$- [(\$10,000)(A/F,\ 12\%,\ 8)]$$

Note that the single sums that occur within the analysis period must be moved to one end or the other (P or F) prior to applying a cash flow factor to determine an equivalent annual cost.

Substituting the cash flow factors from Appendix C yields the following:

$$A = [(\$120,000)(0.201)] + \$30,500$$
$$+ [(\$5,000)(0.797)(0.201)]$$
$$+ [(\$11,000)(0.636)(0.201)]$$
$$+ [(\$5,000)(1.254)(0.081)]$$
$$- [(\$10,000)(0.081)]$$
$$= \$24,120 + \$30,500 + \$801 + \$1,406 + \$508 - \$810 = \$56,525$$

The annual cost for the used grader alternative can be determined with the following equation:

$$A = [(\$75,000)(A/P,\ 12\%,\ 4)] + \$36,500$$
$$+ [(\$5,000)(P/F,\ 12\%,\ 2)(A/P,\ 12\%,\ 4)]$$
$$- [(\$8,000)(A/F,\ 12\%,\ 4)]$$

Substituting the cash flow factors from Appendix C yields the following:

$$A = [(\$75,000)(0.329)] + \$36,500$$
$$+ [(\$5,000)(0.797)(0.329)]$$
$$- [(\$8,000)(0.209)]$$
$$= \$24,675 + \$36,500 + \$1,311 - \$1,672 = \$60,814$$

The contractor should purchase the new grader because it has the lower annual cost.

2.7   Rate of Return Analysis

Contractors often want to estimate the prospective rate of return on an investment or compare anticipated rates of return for several alternative investments. The **rate of return** is the annual interest rate at which the sum of investment and expenditures equals total income from the investment. Rate of return analysis involves setting receipts equal to expenditures and solving for the interest rate. Sometimes the interest rate can be solved for directly, but in most cases it can be found only through a trial-and-error solution. In these cases, two or more interest rates are assumed, equivalent present worth or annual costs are calculated, and the rate of return is found by interpolation. Both types of problems are illustrated in the following two examples.

Example 2.8

A contractor is considering making a $300,000 investment in used construction equipment. He estimates that his annual maintenance and repair costs for the equipment will be $60,000 and that his annual income from the equipment will be $115,000. He estimates that he can get 8 years of use out of the equipment, but that there will be no salvage value at the end of the 8 years. What would be the contractor's prospective rate of return from this investment?

Solution

Following is a cash flow diagram for the investment:

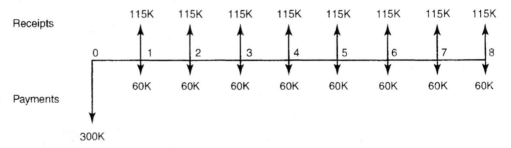

This problem could be solved either on a present worth or an annual cost basis. Let's use the annual cost basis. Setting income equal to expenditures yields the following equation:

$$\$115,000 = \$60,000 + \$300,000 \,(A/P, i, 8)$$

Solving for the uniform series capital recovery factor yields the following:

$$(A/P, i, 8) = \frac{\$115,000 - \$60,000}{\$300,000} = \frac{\$55,000}{\$300,000} = 0.183$$

Now we must find the appropriate interest rate from the interest tables in Appendix C. A/P tells us which column to look at and 8 tells us which row, but we must find i by selecting the appropriate page. Examining the interest tables reveals the following:

$$(A/P, 9\%, 8) = 0.181$$
$$(A/P, 10\%, 8) = 0.187$$

The prospective rate of return can now be found by interpolation.

$$i = 9 + \frac{0.183 - 0.181}{0.187 - 0.181} = 9 + 0.3 = 9.3\%$$

Example 2.9

A contractor is considering the purchase of a new dump truck at a cost of $85,000. Annual maintenance and repair costs are estimated to be $4,000 per year. The truck would be used for 8 years and then sold for an estimated salvage value of $10,000. The contractor estimates that the annual income generated by the truck will be $16,000 per year. What is the prospective rate of return for this investment?

Solution

Following is the cash flow diagram for this investment:

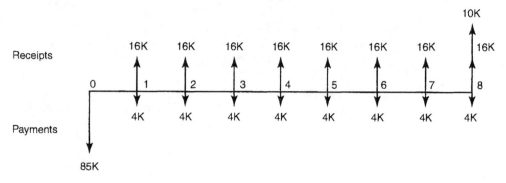

Let's use a present worth analysis and set total costs equal to total receipts to find the prospective rate of return.

$$\$85,000 + [(\$4,000)(P/A, i, 8)] = [(\$16,000)(P/A, i, 8)] + [(\$10,000)(P/F, i, 8)]$$

Simplifying the equation by subtracting ($4,000)(P/A, i, 8) from both sides of the equation yields the following:

$$\$85,000 = [(\$12,000)(P/A, i, 8)] + [(\$10,000)(P/F, i, 8)]$$

Now we must use a trial-and-error method to find the solution.

Let's try an interest rate of 5%.

$$P = [(\$12,000)(P/A, 5\%, 8)] + [(\$10,000)(P/F, 5\%, 8)]$$

Substituting the factor values from Appendix C yields

$$P = [(\$12,000)(6.463)] + [(\$10,000)(0.677)]$$
$$P = \$77,556 + \$6,770 = \$84,326 \text{ (which is less than the \$85,000)}$$

Next, let's try an interest rate of 4%.

$$P = [(\$12,000)(P/A, 4\%, 8)] + [(\$10,000)(P/F, 4\%, 8)]$$

Substituting the factor values from Appendix C yields

$$P = [(\$12,000)(6.733)] + [(\$10,000)(0.731)]$$
$$P = \$80,796 + \$7,310 = \$88,106 \text{ (which is greater than the \$85,000)}$$

Now we can determine the prospective rate of return by interpolation.

$$i = 4 + \frac{\$88,106 - \$85,000}{\$88,106 - \$84,326} = 4 + \frac{\$3,106}{\$3,780} = 4.8\%$$

2.8   Problems

1. A contractor borrowed $250,000 from a bank at an interest rate of 6% to purchase new construction equipment. What annual payment must the contractor make if the loan is to be paid off in 10 years?

2. A grader costs $350,000 to purchase and is expected to have a useful life of 8 years. Annual operating and maintenance costs are estimated to be $35,000 per year, and the salvage value after 8 years of use is estimated to be $50,000. At an interest rate of 9%, what is the present worth equivalent cost to the contractor of owning and operating the grader?

3. Using an interest rate of 12%, find the equivalent uniform annual cost for a piece of construction equipment that has an initial purchase cost of $30,000, an estimated economic life of 8 years, and an estimated salvage value of $10,000. Annual maintenance will amount to $600 per year and periodic overhauls costing $1,000 each will occur at the end of the second, fourth, and sixth years.

4. A company owns a fleet of trucks and operates its own maintenance shop. A certain type of truck, normally used for 5 years, has an initial cost of $45,000 and a salvage value of $5,000. Maintenance costs, which are $3,000 for the first year, increase by $2,000 each year. Assuming interest at 10%, find the equivalent annual cost of owning and maintaining the truck.

5. A contractor is considering the purchase of a new $40,000 truck, which has an estimated useful life of 8 years. He believes that he can sell the used truck for $8,000 at the end of the 8 years. Annual operating costs are estimated to be $2,000 per year. As an alternative, the contractor can purchase a used truck for $20,000 with an estimated useful life of 4 years. Annual operating costs for the used truck are estimated to be $2,800 per year, and the salvage value should be $2,000 at the end of the 4 years. At an interest rate of 8%, which alternative should the contractor select?

6. Is it more economical to replace the engine on a tractor with a new one, or rebore the cylinders of the old engine and thoroughly recondition it? The original cost of the engine 10 years ago was $7,000. To rebore and recondition it now will extend its useful life for an estimated 5 years and will cost $2,800. A new engine will have an initial cost of $6,200 and will have an estimated life of 10 years. It is expected that the annual cost of fuel and lubricants with the reconditioned engine will be about $2,000 and that this cost will be 15% less with the new engine. It is also believed that repairs will be about $250 a year less with the new engine than with the reconditioned one. Assume that neither engine has any realizable value when retired. At an interest rate of 6%, which alternative should be selected?

7. A contractor has purchased a small backhoe for $120,000 that he plans to use in excavating ditches for utilities construction. He plans to use the backhoe for 8 years

and sell the used machine for $40,000. He must replace the tires on the backhoe after each 3,000 hours of use at a cost of $15,000. Annual operating costs are estimated to be $20,000 per year. The contractor estimates that the backhoe will be used about 1,000 hours per year. If the prevailing rate for interest, insurance, taxes, and storage is 12%, what is the hourly owning and operating cost for the backhoe?

8. A used Caterpillar D8K crawler tractor costs $135,000. It will be operated for 5 years, when it will be sold for an estimated value of $65,000. It will cost $80,000 to maintain and operate for the first year. This will increase by $5,000 per year over the life of the machine. If the prevailing rate for interest, insurance, taxes, and storage is 14%, what is the equivalent annual cost of owning and operating the machine?

9. A project has a first cost of $120,000 and an estimated salvage value after 25 years of $20,000. Estimated average annual receipts are $25,900; estimated average annual disbursements are $15,060. Assuming that annual receipts and disbursements will be uniform, compute the prospective rate of return.

10. A contractor has purchased a wheeled loader for $130,000 and expects to use the loader an average of 1,500 hours per year. Tires cost $6,000 to replace (estimated to occur after each 4,500 hours of use), and major repairs will be needed every 6,000 hours at a cost of $5,000. The contractor expects to be able to sell the loader for $10,000 after she has used it for 15,000 operating hours. Fuel, oil, and minor maintenance cost about $19.75 for each hour the loader is used. Interest, insurance, and taxes total about 16%. How much should the contractor charge per hour for use of the loader to recover her costs?

Depreciation Accounting Techniques

3.1   Introduction

Construction equipment loses value with age. This loss in value is called *depreciation*. It occurs because of wear and tear from use, obsolescence, which leads to a decrease in the market value for used equipment. The value of the equipment at the time of purchase is the *purchase price*, and the value at time of disposal or retirement is the *salvage value*.

Contractors generally use the estimated annual loss of value of their equipment to offset income for tax purposes. To accomplish this, they use one of the approved methods of *depreciation accounting* to determine the annual depreciation and a residual book value for their equipment. Depreciation is an artificial expense that spreads the depreciable value of the equipment over the depreciation period, usually several years. The *depreciable value* is the purchase price less the estimated salvage value. The *depreciation period* is the number of years the equipment is owned. The *book value* is the initial cost less the depreciation to the piece of equipment.

For example, if a truck cost $60,000 to purchase and can be resold for $10,000 after 5 years of use, the depreciable value is ($60,000 − $10,000) or $50,000, and the depreciation period is 5 years. Each year, depreciation is calculated and subtracted from the purchase price ($60,000). The book value at the end of each year is the purchase price less the total depreciation to that date. Depreciation is subtracted from the purchase price each year until the book value equals the salvage value. No further depreciation is allowed.

Three depreciation accounting methods are discussed in this chapter that have been approved for use by the United States Internal Revenue Service for tax purposes. Contractors generally select the method that best serves their business interests. Generally, current tax regulations do not allow the cost of an item of equipment to be depreciated in the year of its purchase. In this chapter's example problems, this is called the "zero" year. Only disposable or expendable items can be depreciated entirely during a single year. Examples would be office supplies, fuel, oil, and hand tools.

3.2   Straight-Line Method

The straight-line method of depreciation accounting depreciates the equipment value equally in each of the years the equipment is owned. The *annual depreciation rate* (R) is

$$R = 1/N \qquad (3\text{--}1)$$

where   N is the number of years the equipment is owned

The *annual depreciation amount* (D) can be determined by the following equation:

$$D = R(P - F) \qquad (3\text{--}2)$$

where   P is the purchase price

F is the salvage value at the end of N years

The book value (BV) is the equipment value at the end of each year after the annual depreciation amount has been subtracted. It can be determined by the following equation:

$$BV_m = BV_{m-1} - D_m \qquad (3\text{--}3)$$

where   m is the specific year for which the book value is being determined

The book value at the end of the depreciation period must be the salvage value. Let's now look at an example problem.

Example 3.1

A contractor purchased a tractor at a cost of $135,000 and plans to use it for 5 years, at which time she estimates the salvage value of the tractor will be $65,000. Using the straight-line method of depreciation accounting, what is the book value of the tractor at the end of each of the 5 years?

Solution

The annual depreciation rate can be determined with Equation 3–1 to be

$$R = \frac{1}{5} = 0.2$$

The annual depreciation amount can be determine with Equation 3–2 to be

$$D = R(P - F) = (0.2)(\$135,000 - \$65,000) = \$14,000$$

The book value for each year can be determined with Equation 3–3 to be as follows:

After Year	Book Value
1	$121,000
2	$107,000
3	$93,000
4	$79,000
5	$65,000

Note that the initial book value is the purchase price, and the final book value is the salvage value.

3.3   Sum-of-the-Years Method

In the sum-of-the-years method, the annual depreciation rate is not the same for each year. The annual depreciation rate is

$$R_m = \frac{N - m + 1}{SOY} \qquad (3\text{–}4)$$

where N is the number of years the equipment is owned

m is the specific year in which depreciation is being determined

SOY is the sum of the years which equals
$N + (N - 1) + (N - 2) + (N - 3) + \ldots + 1$

A simpler method for determining the sum of the years is to use the following equation:

$$SOY = \frac{N(N + 1)}{2} \qquad (3\text{–}5)$$

The annual depreciation amount is

$$D_m = R_m(P - F) \qquad (3\text{–}6)$$

Once the annual depreciation amount has been determined, the book value can be determined with Equation 3–3. Now, let's look at an example problem.

Example 3.2

Using the sum-of-the-years method of depreciation accounting, determine the book value of the tractor described in Example 3.1 at the end of each of the 5 years. The contractor purchased the tractor for $135,000 and anticipates a salvage value of $65,000 after 5 years of use.

Solution

The sum of the years is $5 + 4 + 3 + 2 + 1 = 15$, or using Equation 3–5:

$$SOY = \frac{N(N + 1)}{2} = \frac{(5)(6)}{2} = 15$$

The annual depreciation rate can be determined with Equation 3–4, the annual depreciation amount with Equation 3–6, and the book value with Equation 3–3. The results are summarized below.

After Year	Depreciation Rate	Depreciation Amount	Book Value
1	5/15	$23,333	$111,667
2	4/15	$18,667	$93,000
3	3/15	$14,000	$79,000
4	2/15	$9,333	$69,667
5	1/15	$4,667	$65,000

Once again, the initial book value is the purchase price, and the ending book value is the salvage value.

3.4   Declining-Balance Method

In the declining-balance method of depreciation accounting, an annual depreciation rate is applied each year to the remaining book value. The annual depreciation rate is

$$R = X / N \tag{3–7}$$

where X can range from 1.25 to 2 depending upon the degree of acceleration desired

            N is the number of years the equipment is owned

The annual depreciation amount can be determined by multiplying the depreciation rate times the book value at the end of the previous period. Mathematically, this is

$$D_m = (BV_{m-1}) R \tag{3–8}$$

where BV is the book value

            m is the specific year in which the depreciation is being determined

            R is the depreciation rate

Once the annual depreciation amount has been determined, the book value can be determined with Equation 3–3. *Note that the book value cannot be depreciated below the salvage value.* Once the book value is reduced to the salvage value, no further depreciation can be taken. In accelerated depreciation methods, such as the double-declining-balance method, the item of equipment may be fully depreciated during the first few years of ownership, and no further depreciation can be taken during the remaining years the contractor owns the item. Let's look at an example to illustrate.

Example 3.3

For the tractor described in Example 3.1, determine the book value at the end of each year of use using (a) the 1.5 declining-balance method and (b) the double-declining-balance method of depreciation accounting. The contractor purchased the tractor for $135,000 and anticipates a salvage value of $65,000 after 5 years of use.

Solution

a. The depreciation rate in the 1.5 declining-balance method can be determined with Equation 3–7:

$$R = \frac{1.5}{5} = 0.3$$

The annual depreciation amount for each year is determined with Equation 3–8, and the resulting book value is determined with Equation 3–3. The results are summarized below.

After Year	Depreciation Amount	Book Value
1	$40,500	$94,500
2	$28,350	$66,150
3	$1,150	$65,000
4	0	$65,000
5	0	$65,000

Note that the full depreciation amount ($19,845) computed with Equation 3–8 for year 3 could not be taken, because it would reduce the residual book value below the salvage value of $65,000. While the other two methods of depreciation mathematically calculate a book value equal to the salvage value at the end of the depreciation period, the declining-balance method does not. In this method, depreciation ends when the book value is reduced to the salvage value.

b. The depreciation rate in the double-declining-balance method is determined with Equation 3–7 to be

$$R = \frac{2}{5} = 0.4$$

Once again, the annual depreciation amount is determined with Equation 3–8, and the resulting book value is determined with Equation 3–3. The results are summarized below.

After Year	Depreciation Amount	Book Value
1	$54,000	$81,000
2	$16,000	$65,000
3	0	$65,000
4	0	$65,000
5	0	$65,000

Figure 3.1
Depreciation Curves for
Three Methods of Depreciation
Accounting

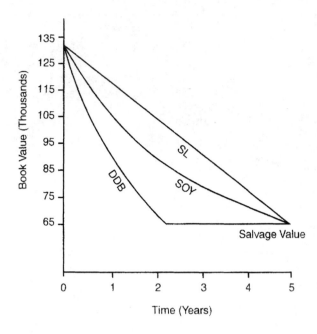

3.5   *Comparison and Uses*

Figure 3.1 shows a graphical comparison of the three methods using the three example problems. Note that the double-declining-balance method (DDB) depreciates equipment at a faster rate than the sum-of-the-years (SOY) or straight-line (SL) methods. This method usually is used by contractors in determining their tax liability, because it allows them to more rapidly depreciate the value of their equipment. This method also comes closest to determining the actual book value, because new equipment loses value more rapidly in the early years of ownership than it does in the later years. Contractors may use one method of depreciation for tax accounting purposes and another for determining rates to charge projects for equipment use.

The straight-line method is usually used to estimate equipment maintenance and repair costs when estimating ownership and operating costs. This concept will be discussed in the next chapter.

3.6   *Problems*

1. A contractor has purchased a tractor for $180,000 and anticipates using it for 9 years. Salvage value of the tractor at the end of the 9 years is estimated to be $27,000. Using the straight-line method of depreciation accounting, determine the book value of the tractor at the end of each of the 9 years.
2. Determine the book value at the end of each of the 9 years for the tractor described in Problem 1 using the sum-of-the-years method of depreciation accounting.

3. Determine the book value at the end of each of the 9 years for the tractor described in Problem 1 using the 1.80 declining-balance method of depreciation accounting.

4. A crane has an initial cost of $150,000 and an estimated useful life of 10 years. The salvage value after 10 years of use is estimated to be $40,000.

   a. What is the book value at the end of the fifth year if you use the straight-line method of depreciation accounting?

   b. What is the book value at the end of the fifth year if you use the sum-of-the-years method of depreciation accounting?

   c. What is the book value at the end of the fifth year if you use the double-declining-balance method of depreciation accounting?

5. A grader has an initial cost of $220,000 and an estimated useful life of 12 years. The salvage value after 12 years of use is estimated to be $25,000.

   a. What is the annual depreciation amount if the straight-line method of depreciation accounting is used?

   b. What is the book value after 10 years if the straight-line method of depreciation accounting is used?

   c. What is the annual depreciation amount in the ninth year if the sum-of-the-years method of depreciation accounting is used?

   d. What is the book value at the end of the sixth year if the sum-of-the-years method of depreciation accounting is used?

   e. What is the annual depreciation amount in the fourth year if the 1.5 declining-balance method of depreciation accounting is used?

   f. What is the book value at the end of the fifth year if the 1.5 declining-balance method of depreciation accounting is used?

6. A loader has an initial cost of $154,000 and an estimated useful life of 8 years. The salvage value after 8 years of use is estimated to be $10,000.

   a. What is the annual depreciation amount if the straight-line method of depreciation accounting is used?

   b. What is the book value after 6 years if the straight-line method of depreciation accounting is used?

   c. What is the annual depreciation amount in the fifth year if the sum-of-the-years method of depreciation accounting is used?

   d. What is the book value at the end of the sixth year if the sum-of-the-years method of depreciation accounting is used?

   e. What is the annual depreciation amount in the fourth year if the double-declining-balance method of depreciation accounting is used?

   f. What is the book value at the end of the fifth year if the double-declining-balance method of depreciation accounting is used?

Ownership and Operating Costs

4.1   *Introduction*

As discussed in Chapter 1, construction equipment must earn sufficient revenue to cover the contractor's investment cost (ownership cost) and operating cost. In estimating total project costs, the cost of equipment ranks second only to that of labor in terms of uncertainty. Thus, equipment costs significantly affect the profitability of any project.

Contractors must be able to estimate both their ownership and operating costs for each piece of equipment, whether owned, rented, or leased. These costs are used to determine rates to charge projects for equipment use and to make decisions regarding disposal, purchase, rental, or lease of equipment. The best source of information to estimate these costs is the contractor's accounting system, which contains historic data regarding equipment costs. If historic data are not available, manufacturers' literature may be the next best source of data.

Equipment ownership costs are incurred by the contractor whether the equipment is used or not. Operating costs are incurred only when the equipment is used. Typical ownership and operating costs are listed below.

Ownership Costs	Operating Costs
Depreciation	Maintenance and repair
Interest	Tires (repair/replacement)
Taxes	Fuel
Insurance	Service (filters, oil, and grease)
Storage	Downtime
License fee	Operator (labor)

Ownership costs generally decline with equipment age, while operating costs tend to increase with age, as illustrated in Figure 4.1. Ownership costs decline because the rate of

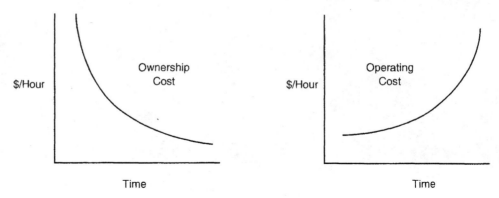

Figure 4.1
Change in Ownership and Operating Costs with Time

depreciation tends to be greatest in the initial ownership period and declines with time. Operating costs increase with equipment age, because repair costs tend to increase with equipment usage.

4.2 Ownership Costs

Ownership costs are best estimated by the *time value of money analysis* techniques discussed in Chapter 2. The contractor will know the purchase price and must estimate the ownership period and the residual salvage value. This will account for depreciation. Interest, taxes, insurance, storage, and license costs are used to establish the minimum attractive rate of return for use in the economic analysis.

Interest is the charge for borrowed money or the return expected from invested money. The interest rate changes with time, requiring contractors to estimate the average effective interest rate over the period of ownership. Equipment *taxes* are the personal property taxes paid to local governments. *Insurance* costs are for general liability insurance to cover damage or injury caused by the equipment and equipment insurance to cover physical damage to the equipment. *Storage* is the cost of protecting the equipment when it is not in use on a project. *License* costs are the fees paid for license plates and any other use permits.

The economic life of construction equipment generally is estimated in terms of hours of use. Table 4.1 provides typical useful life periods for various types of construction equipment. Note that the useful life declines as the operating conditions become more adverse. For example, Table 4.1 shows that the expected useful life of a wheeled loader being used to load loose stockpiled soil (favorable conditions) is about 12,000 operating hours, while the same loader being used to load rock in a dusty quarry (unfavorable conditions) is only 8,000 operating hours. To estimate the number of years of anticipated ownership for an item of construction equipment, it is necessary for the contractor to estimate the number of hours of use per year. Dividing the annual usage

Table 4.1
Estimated Useful Life of Construction Equipment in Total Operating Hours

	Operating Conditions		
Equipment	Favorable	Average	Unfavorable
Crawler tractor	15,000 hr.	12,000 hr.	10,000 hr.
Grader	20,000 hr.	15,000 hr.	12,000 hr.
Excavator	15,000 hr.	12,000 hr.	10,000 hr.
Hauler	25,000 hr.	20,000 hr.	15,000 hr.
Scraper	16,000 hr.	12,000 hr.	10,000 hr.
Tracked loader	10,000 hr.	8,000 hr.	6,000 hr.
Wheeled loader	12,000 hr.	10,000 hr.	8,000 hr.

Data for this table was extracted from *Caterpillar Performance Handbook*, 28th ed.
(Peoria, IL: Caterpillar Inc., 1997), pp. 19-6 to 19-8.

into the expected useful life yields the anticipated ownership period that is needed to determine ownership cost. Let's look at an example problem to determine the annual ownership cost of a crawler tractor.

Example 4.1

A contractor has purchased a crawler tractor for $155,000 and estimates that its annual usage will be about 2,000 hours per year. Salvage value at the end of the tractor's useful life is estimated to be about 12% of the purchase price. The contractor estimates his ownership cost factors to be:

Interest	9%
Taxes	2%
Insurance	2%
Storage	1%
License	None, since the tractor will not operate on the highway

What is the estimated annual ownership cost of the tractor if it is operated under average conditions?

Solution

Looking at Table 4.1, the expected useful life for the tractor under average operating conditions is about 12,000 operating hours. Since the contractor estimates his usage will be 2,000 hours per year, the period of ownership is estimated to be 12,000 hr./2,000 hr. per year or 6 years. The *minimum attractive rate of return* will be the sum of the ownership cost factors or

$$9\% + 2\% + 2\% + 1\% = 14\%$$

Following is the cash flow diagram for the ownership cost of the tractor:

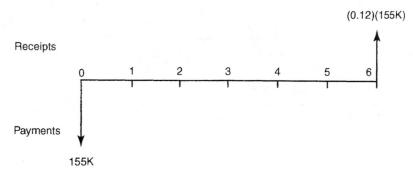

The first step is to determine the present worth of the salvage value, which is

$$P = (0.12)(\$155{,}000)(P/F, 14\%, 6)$$

Substituting the interest factor from Appendix C yields

$$P = (0.12)(\$155{,}000)(0.456) = \$8{,}482$$

Next, we subtract the present worth of the salvage value from the purchase price, which is

$$P = \$155{,}000 - \$8{,}482 = \$146{,}518$$

Now we can convert the resulting present worth to an annual series to determine the annual cost.

$$A = (\$146{,}518)(A/P, 14\%, 6)$$

Substituting the interest factor from Appendix C yields

$$A = (\$146{,}518)(0.257) = \mathbf{\$37{,}655}$$

This means that it costs the contractor $37,655 per year to own the tractor. Since the contractor anticipates using the tractor 2,000 hours per year, he must recover

$$\frac{\$37{,}655/\text{yr.}}{2{,}000\ \text{hr./yr.}} = \$18.83$$

for each hour the tractor is used to cover his ownership costs.

4.3   ***Operating Costs***

The best source of data for estimating operating costs is from historical records. The next best source is to use the cost factors provided by equipment manufacturers for their specific equipment. Operating costs are greatly influenced by the age of the equipment, its state of repair, and the operating conditions. The methods discussed in this section should only be used when neither historical data nor manufacturers' literature are available.

Maintenance and repair costs can be roughly estimated by using a percentage of the annual straight-line depreciation amount. Tire replacement is treated as a separate cost

Table 4.2
Equipment Repair Factors Based on a 10,000-Hour Useful Life
(Factors are a percentage of the hourly straight-line depreciation amount)

Equipment	Operating Conditions		
	Favorable	Average	Unfavorable
Bottom dumps (less tires)	30%	35%	45%
Crawler tractors			
General contracting	40%	60%	80%
Quarrying	50%	85%	115%
Haulers (less tires)	37%	45%	60%
Loaders (less tires)	45%	55%	70%
Scrapers (less tires)	42%	50%	62%

Data for this table was extracted from *Production and Cost Estimating of Material Movement with Earthmoving Equipment* (Hudson, OH: Terex Corporation, 1981), p. 59.

for wheeled equipment, because tires have shorter useful lives than basic machines. Techniques for estimating tire costs are discussed later in this section. Special wear items such as cutting edges, bucket teeth, and ripper and scarifier teeth also are often treated as separate cost items, because they are replaced frequently. The useful lives of these components will vary depending on the frequency of use and operating technique. Table 4.2 provides factors that can be used to estimate hourly maintenance and repair costs.

Since the factors are based on 10,000 operating hours of useful life, they must be adjusted for the anticipated useful life of the equipment being evaluated. This can be done using the following equation:

$$\text{Hourly Repair Cost} = \frac{(RF)(\text{Useful Life in hr.})(HDR)}{10,000 \text{ hr.}} \quad (4\text{--}1)$$

where RF is the equipment repair factor from Table 4.2

HDR is the hourly depreciation rate

As mentioned, *tires* are treated as a separate operating cost because they have a different useful life than the basic item of equipment. The value of the tires is subtracted from the purchase price of the basic item of equipment when determining the ownership cost, and a separate cash flow analysis is performed for the tires. Track replacement cost for track-mounted equipment is included in the maintenance and repair cost computed with Table 4.2. The life of a tire is greatly influenced by such operating variables as tire maintenance, operating speed, haul road conditions, curves, grades, position under the piece of equipment, and frequency of overload. The Goodyear Tire and Rubber Company has developed a tire life estimating system to account for these variables.[1] For the purpose of this book, we will use the data contained in Table 4.3 to estimate tire life.

---

[1]For a description of this system, students should consult *Caterpillar Performance Handbook*, 28th ed. (Peoria, IL: Caterpillar Inc., 1997), p. 19-29.

Table 4.3

Estimated Average Tire Life in Hours of Use

Equipment	Operating Conditions		
	Favorable	*Average*	*Unfavorable*
Bottom dumps	8,000 hr.	5,000 hr.	3,500 hr.
Grader	3,500 hr.	2,300 hr.	1,000 hr.
Hauler	4,000 hr.	3,200 hr.	2,200 hr.
Loader	4,000 hr.	3,200 hr.	1,700 hr.
Scraper			
Single engine	4,000 hr.	3,000 hr.	2,500 hr.
Twin engine	4,000 hr.	3,000 hr.	2,500 hr.
Push-pull	3,600 hr.	2,700 hr.	2,250 hr.

Data for this table was extracted from *Production and Cost Estimating of Material Movement with Earthmoving Equipment* (Hudson, OH: Terex Corporation, 1981), p. 58.

Using the data in Table 4.3 and the tire cost, a contractor can set up a cash flow analysis using the principles discussed in Chapter 2. Tire maintenance and repair cost are estimated at 15% of the hourly straight-line depreciation amount for the tires.[2]

Most construction equipment is driven by internal combustion engines that burn either gasoline (spark ignition) or diesel (compression ignition). The rate of fuel consumption varies with the rated horsepower, the duty cycle of the engine, and the operating conditions. The duty cycle represents the percentage of the time the engine is operating at maximum output, which will vary with type of equipment. This has been considered in the development of the fuel factors shown in Table 4.4 for both gasoline and diesel engines. *Fuel costs* can be estimated using the data shown in Table 4.4, the flywheel horsepower rating of the individual item of equipment, and the cost of a gallon of fuel.

$$\text{Hourly Fuel Cost} = (\text{Flywheel Horsepower})(\text{Fuel Factor})(\text{Fuel Cost}) \qquad (4\text{--}2)$$

Servicing (filter, oil, and grease) costs usually are estimated as a percentage of the hourly fuel cost. Actual servicing costs will vary with the severity of the operating conditions. Equipment operating in dusty conditions requires more frequent servicing than equipment operating where there is little dust. Table 4.5 provides equipment service cost factors for estimating the filter, oil, and grease costs.

Downtime is considered by using an **operating factor** when determining productivity rates. The operating factor is a percentage equal to the actual number of minutes per hour the equipment is working and not idling. Equipment operators do not work continuously, but take breaks, and this must be considered in determining productivity.

The *labor cost* must be estimated using local wage rates and fringe percentages. The effective labor rate should include the hourly wage rate plus the cost of fringe benefits

---

[2]The 15% factor came from *Construction Equipment Ownership and Operating Expense Schedule, Region VII.* (Washington, DC: U.S. Government Printing Office, 1995), pp. 2–9.

Table 4.4

Equipment Fuel Factors in Gallons per Horsepower-Hour

Equipment	Average Conditions		Unfavorable Conditions	
	Gasoline	Diesel	Gasoline	Diesel
Bottom dumps	0.067	0.036	0.088	0.047
Crawler tractors	0.072	0.039	0.094	0.051
Excavators	0.062	0.033	0.081	0.043
Graders	0.062	0.033	0.081	0.043
Haulers	0.041	0.022	0.054	0.029
Scrapers	0.062	0.033	0.081	0.043
Wheeled loaders	0.067	0.036	0.088	0.047

Data for this table was extracted from *Construction Equipment Ownership and Operating Expense Schedule, Region VII* (Washington, DC: U.S. Government Printing Office, 1995), pp. D-2 to D-15.

Table 4.5

Equipment Service Cost Factors
(Factors are a percentage of the hourly fuel cost)

Operating Conditions	Equipment Service Factor
Favorable	20%
Average	33%
Unfavorable	50%

Data for this table was extracted from *Production and Cost Estimating of Material Movement with Earthmoving Equipment* (Hudson, OH: Terex Corporation, 1981), p. 61.

for vacation, retirement, medical insurance, employer's contribution to Social Security, unemployment insurance, and workers' compensation insurance. The fringe benefits often add 20% to 30% to the actual wage rate.

Let's now look at an example problem and see how we can estimate operating costs with the data provided in this section.

Example 4.2

A contractor has purchased a wheeled loader for $114,000 and plans to use it about 2,000 hours per year. At this usage rate, the contractor anticipates disposing of the loader after using it for 6 years and realizing a salvage value of $35,000. Tires for the loader cost $4,000 for a set of four, and the brake horsepower rating of the loader's diesel engine is 105 horsepower. The loader operator will earn $34.00 per hour including fringe benefits, and diesel fuel costs $1.20 per gallon. At a minimum attractive rate of return of 12%, what are the contractor's hourly ownership and operating costs for the loader?

Solution

The first step is to determine the hourly ownership costs without the tires. Since the tires have a different period of ownership than the loader, we will determine the hourly tire cost separately. The purchase price of the loader (less tires) is $114,000 – $4,000, or $110,000. The tires are assumed to have no salvage value, so the full $35,000 salvage value will be attributed to the loader. A cash flow diagram for the loader is shown below.

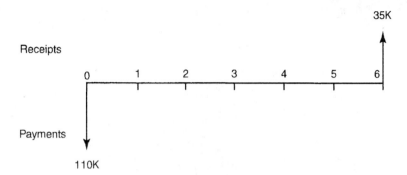

The annual ownership cost can be determined by the following equation:

$$A = [(\$110,000)(A/P, 12\%, 6)] - [(\$35,000)(A/F, 12\%, 6)]$$

Substituting the values for the interest factors from Appendix C yields the following:

$$A = [(\$110,000)(0.243)] - [(\$35,000)(0.123)]$$
$$A = \$26,730 - \$4,305 = \$22,425/\text{yr.}$$

The hourly ownership cost can be determined by dividing the annual ownership cost by the expected number of operating hours per year. This yields the following answer:

$$\text{Hourly Ownership Cost} = \frac{\$22,425 \text{ per yr.}}{2,000 \text{ hr. per yr.}} = \textbf{\$11.21/hr.}$$

Hourly maintenance and repair costs for the loader (less tires) can be estimated by using Table 4.2 and the straight-line hourly depreciation amount. Assuming average operating conditions, Table 4.2 indicates that an equipment repair factor of 55% should be used for the loader based on a 10,000-hour useful life. Since the loader has a useful life of 12,000 hours, we must use Equation 4–1 to determine the hourly repair cost.

The hourly straight-line depreciation amount is

$$D = \frac{\$110,000 - \$35,000}{12,000 \text{ hr.}} = \$6.25 \text{ per operating hour}$$

The hourly repair cost can be determined using Equation 4–1:

$$\text{Repair Cost} = \frac{(0.55)(12,000 \text{ hr.})(\$6.25/\text{hr.})}{10,000 \text{ hr.}} = \$4.13/\text{hr.}$$

Assuming average operating conditions, tire life is estimated at 3,200 hours using Table 4.3. Since the contractor intends to use the loader 2,000 hours per year, the useful life of a set of tires is expected to be

$$\frac{3,200 \text{ hr.}}{2,000 \text{ hr./yr.}} = 1.6 \text{ years}$$

The hourly cost of owning a set of tires can be determined by the following, since tires are assumed to have no salvage value:

$$\text{Hourly Cost} = \frac{(\$4,000)(A/P, \ 12\%, \ 1.6)}{2,000 \text{ hr.}}$$

The numerical value for $(A/P, 12\%, 1.6)$ cannot be determined directly from Appendix C. It must be determined by linear interpolation using the value for one year and the value for two years.

$$(A/P, \ 12\%, \ 1) = 1.120$$

$$(A/P, \ 12\%, \ 2) = 0.592$$

$$(A/P, \ 12\%, \ 1.6) = 1.120 - [(0.6)(1.120 - 0.592)] = 1.120 - 0.317 = 0.803$$

$$\text{Hourly Cost} = \frac{(\$4,000)(0.803)}{2.000 \text{ hr.}} = \$1.61/\text{hr.}$$

The hourly tire maintenance and repair cost is estimated at 15% of the straight-line hourly depreciation amount. The hourly depreciation amount is

$$D = \frac{(\$4,000)}{3,200 \text{ hr.}} = \$1.25 \text{ per operating hour}$$

The hourly tire maintenance and repair cost is $(0.15)(\$1.25/\text{hr.})$ or $0.19 per hour. Total hourly operating cost for tires is $1.61 (replacement cost) + $0.19 (maintenance and repair cost) or $1.80 per hour.

The hourly fuel cost can be determined by using Equation 4–2 and Table 4.4. Again assuming average operating conditions, the fuel factor for the wheeled loader is found to be 0.036 in Table 4.4. Using Equation 4–2, the hourly fuel cost can be determined. The cost of a gallon of diesel fuel is $1.20.

$$\text{Hourly Fuel Cost} = (105 \text{ HP})(0.036 \text{ gal./HP-hr.})(\$1.20/\text{gal.}) = \$4.54/\text{hr.}$$

Filter, oil, and grease hourly cost is estimated by determining an equipment service factor from Table 4.5, which is 0.33 for the wheeled loader assuming average operating conditions. The hourly service cost is

$$\text{Hourly Cost} = (0.33)(\$4.54/\text{hr.}) = \$1.50/\text{hr.}$$

The total hourly operating cost can now be determined.

Maintenance and repair cost	$ 4.13/hr.
Tire cost	1.80/hr.
Fuel cost	4.54/hr.
Filter, oil, and grease cost	1.50/hr.
Operator cost	34.00/hr.
Total hourly operating cost	$45.97/hr

The sum of the hourly ownership and operating costs is the contractor's hourly cost for using the loader on a project.

4.4   Use of Manufacturers' Data

Estimated operating costs (except operator wages) for specific construction equipment usually can be obtained from the equipment manufacturer's technical literature. This data is model specific and generally more accurate than generalized cost data developed using the tables provided in Section 4.3. Ownership costs should still be determined using the cash flow analysis discussed in Section 4.2. Some manufacturers provide aggregate hourly operating data for each model produced; others provide individual estimates of fuel consumption, maintenance costs, and service costs; and other manufacturers only provide equipment data that must be used in conjunction with the cost estimating techniques discussed in Section 4.3.

Forms such as the one illustrated in Figure 4.2 can be used to estimate hourly ownership and operating costs. As indicated on the form, the ownership cost is estimated using a cash flow analysis. Operating cost elements are estimated either from manufacturers' technical literature or the techniques discussed in Section 4.3.

4.5   Cost Accounting

The best source of data for estimating ownership and operating costs is the contractor's historical records. In order to create these records, contractors must implement an accounting system to capture significant elements of equipment cost as they are incurred. In designing an accounting system, it is important to collect only data that is needed for economic forecasting or making management decisions. It costs money to collect and manage data, so it is important to be selective in identifying which data to collect.

Data usually captured for each piece of equipment include date of purchase, purchase price, all maintenance and repair costs, fuel consumption, hours used, and service costs. These data are critical to equipment managers in making decisions regarding replacement, repair, or disposal of equipment. The data also are very important in determining the hourly rates to charge individual projects for the use of the equipment. Some contractors with small fleets of equipment use a manual accounting system to record and manage the data. Others with more equipment to manage use sophisticated automated accounting systems for equipment management.

The purpose of a contractor's equipment cost accounting system is to capture historic data for future estimates and replacement decisions. The cost data can then be used to develop realistic rates to charge individual projects and to estimate equipment costs for future projects. A contractor's equipment fleet should be a profit center earning more revenue than it costs to own, rent, or lease and operate. Initially, rates should be

Hourly Ownership and Operating Cost Estimate

Ownership Cost

1. a. Delivered Price _____
    b. Tire Replacement Cost (if wheeled) _____
    c. Delivered Price Less Tires (a – b) _____
2. Estimated Salvage Value _____
3. Minimum Attractive Rate of Return (MARR)
    a. Interest Rate _____
    b. Insurance Rate _____
    c. Tax Rate _____
    d. License and Storage Rate _____
    e. Total MARR (a + b + c + d) _____
4. Estimated Usage per Year (hours/year) _____
5. Estimated Useful Life (hours) _____
6. Estimated Annual Ownership Cost _____
    [Determine present worth of salvage value. Subtract
    result from delivered cost less tires (if wheeled) or
    from delivered cost (if tracked). Convert the result
    to an equivalent series of equal annual payments.]
7. Estimated Hourly Ownership Cost (6 ÷ 4) _____

Operating Cost

8. Maintenance and Repair Cost _____
9. Tire Cost _____
10. Fuel Cost _____
11. Service (filters, oil, and grease) _____
12. Special Wear Items (cost ÷ life) _____
13. Operator's Hourly Wage (including fringes) _____
14. Estimated Hourly Operating Cost _____
    (sum of lines 8 through 13)

Total Hourly Ownership and Operating Cost (7 + 14) _____

Figure 4.2
Hourly Ownership and Operating Cost Estimating Form

set based on historic cost data or published equipment rates.[3] As additional historic data are collected, the equipment rates should be adjusted to reflect the contractor's actual costs. Because of seasonal variation in equipment usage, equipment rates should be determined on an annual basis. It generally takes more than one year of data to develop a

---

[3]Equipment rates are published for different regions of the United States by the U.S. Army Corps of Engineers in a series of books entitled *Construction Equipment Ownership and Operating Expense Schedule* available at U.S. Government Book Stores. Similar rates are also contained in *Cost Reference Guide for Construction Equipment* published by PRIMEDIA Information, Inc., San Jose, CA.

sense for actual equipment costs. Each year will have anomalies, and it is often difficult to identify trends from the examination of a single year's data. However, contractors usually discover significant information about their actual equipment costs during the first year analysis.

The two primary management tools contractors need from their equipment cost accounting systems are *equipment utilization reports* and *equipment cost reports*. A utilization report indicates hours of usage and rates charged for a specific year. This report thus describes the income generated by the equipment fleet (hours used times equipment rate charged). The equipment cost report contains the ownership and operating cost for each piece of equipment. Comparison of these reports allows contractors to make the following management decisions regarding each piece of equipment:

- Determine actual equipment rates to be used in estimating and costing (charging projects for use)
- Purchase new equipment
- Dispose of underutilized or uneconomic equipment
- Compare financial performance of fleet with industry standards
- Establish criteria for rent or lease versus own

Let's now look at an example problem and determine equipment rates using historical data.

Example 4.3

A contractor purchased a new crawler tractor 3 years ago for $140,000. The tractor has an estimated useful life of 12,000 hours and an estimated salvage value at the end of its useful life of 20% of its purchase price. The contractor wants to determine an equipment rate for the tractor under the following three scenarios:

a. Average usage of 800 hours per year
b. Average usage of 1,000 hours per year
c. Average usage of 1,500 hours per year

Operating costs are $42.00 per hour including a $26.50 per hour labor cost for the tractor operator. The contractor desires a profit of 3% on his equipment fleet and a minimum attractive rate of return of 12% to cover his other costs. What equipment rate should the contractor use for each equipment usage scenario?

Solution

a. With 800 hours of use per year, the contractor will use the tractor for

$$\frac{12,000 \text{ hr.}}{800 \text{ hr./yr.}} \text{ or } 15 \text{ years}$$

The annual ownership costs can be determined by the following equation:

$$A = [(\$140,000)(A/P, 12\%, 15)] - [(0.2)(\$140,000)(A/F, 12\%, 15)]$$

Substituting interest factor values from Appendix C yields

$$A = [(\$140,000)(0.147)] - [(\$28,000)(0.027)] = \$20,580 - \$756 = \$19,824/\text{yr.}$$

The hourly ownership and operating cost is

$$\frac{\$19,824/\text{yr.}}{800 \text{ hr./yr.}} + \$42.00/\text{hr.} = \$24.78/\text{hr.} + \$42.00/\text{hr.} = \$66.78/\text{hr.}$$

Adding 3% profit, the equipment rate is

$$(1.03)(\$66.78/\text{hr.}) = \textbf{\$68.78/hr.}$$

b. With 1,000 hours of use per year, the contractor will use the tractor for

$$\frac{12,000 \text{ hr.}}{1,000 \text{ hr./yr.}} \text{ or } 12 \text{ years}$$

The annual ownership costs can be determined by the following equation:

$$A = [(\$140,000)(A/P, 12\%, 12)] - [(0.2)(\$140,000)(A/F, 12\%, 12)]$$

Substituting interest factor values from Appendix C yields

$$A = [(\$140,000)(0.161)] - [(\$28,000)(0.041)] = \$22,540 - \$1,148 = \$21,392/\text{yr.}$$

The hourly ownership and operating cost is

$$\frac{\$21,392/\text{yr.}}{1,000 \text{ hr./yr.}} + \$42.00/\text{hr.} = \$21.39/\text{hr.} + \$42.00/\text{hr.} = \$63.39/\text{hr.}$$

Adding 3% profit, the equipment rate is

$$(1.03)(\$63.39/\text{hr.}) = \textbf{\$65.29/hr.}$$

c. With 1,500 hours of use per year, the contractor will use the tractor for

$$\frac{\$12,000/\text{yr.}}{1,500 \text{ hr./yr.}} \text{ or } 8 \text{ years}$$

The annual ownership costs can be determined by the following equation:

$$A = [(\$140,000)(A/P, 12\%, 8)] - [(0.2)(\$140,000)(A/F, 12\%, 8)]$$

Substituting interest factor values from Appendix C yields

$$A = [(\$140,000)(0.201)] - [(\$28,000)(0.081)] = \$28,140 - \$2,268 = \$25,872/\text{yr.}$$

The hourly ownership and operating cost is

$$\frac{\$25,872/\text{yr.}}{1,500 \text{ hr./yr.}} + \$42.00/\text{hr.} = \$17.25/\text{hr.} + \$42.00/\text{hr.} = \$59.25/\text{hr.}$$

Adding 3% profit, the equipment rate is

$$(1.03)(\$59.25/\text{hr.}) = \textbf{\$61.03}$$

As can be seen from the following summary, the contractor's equipment cost is greatly affected by the annual usage of the tractor. The higher rates the contractor must charge to projects to recover his costs for underutilized equipment may make the contractor noncompetitive when bidding for new work.

Annual Usage	Equipment Rate
800 hr.	$68.78/hr.
1,000 hr.	$65.29/hr.
1,500 hr.	$61.03/hr.

4.6   *Unit Cost Determination*

Besides being used for equipment fleet management decisions, hourly ownership and operating costs are used in conjunction with equipment productivity estimates to determine unit costs for elements of work. The normal unit of measure used in earthmoving work is cubic yards or cubic meters of material. These volumetric units of measure are used for both excavation and fill operations. The objective is to determine a cost per cubic yard or cubic meter for executing the work. This is usually done considering all the equipment required to perform a specific task. For example, if a contractor was planning to use one wheeled loader and three dump trucks to move 2,000 cubic yards of stockpiled soil, he or she would determine the ownership and operating cost per hour for the four pieces of equipment and the fleet productivity. This would permit the contractor to determine the cost per cubic yard to move the soil and the total cost for moving the soil. The basic equation used to calculate the unit cost for any construction task is

$$\text{Unit Cost} = \frac{\text{Hourly Ownership and Operating Cost}}{\text{Hourly Production Rate}} \qquad (4\text{--}3)$$

Let's look at an example problem and determine the unit cost for a specific construction task.

Example 4.4

The contractor of Example 4.3 plans to use the tractor to excavate for the foundation and basement of a new office building. He has evaluated the site working conditions and estimated the tractor productivity will be about 25 cubic yards per hour. What is the unit cost to excavate the soil in dollars per cubic yard for the three scenarios described in Example 4.3?

Solution

The unit cost can be determined by dividing the equipment hourly rate by the productivity. Thus in, the case of 800 hours of usage per year, the unit cost is

$$\frac{\$68.78/\text{hr.}}{25 \text{ cu. yd./ hr.}} = \textbf{\$2.75/cu. yd}$$

If the tractor is used 1,000 hours per year, the unit cost is

$$\frac{\$65.29/hr.}{25 \text{ cu. yd./hr.}} = \$2.61/\text{cu. yd}$$

If the tractor is used 1,500 hours per year, the unit cost is

$$\frac{\$61.03/hr.}{25 \text{ cu. yd./hr.}} = \$2.44/\text{cu. yd}$$

The contractor will select the appropriate unit cost to develop a cost estimate for the excavation by multiplying the total volume to be excavated by the unit cost.

4.7 Problems

1. A crawler tractor is used about 1,500 hours per year. It cost $150,000 new and has a useful life of 15,000 hours. Estimated salvage value after 15,000 hours of use is $25,000. Minimum attractive rate of return is 10%.
   a. What is the hourly ownership cost for the tractor?
   b. What do you estimate the hourly maintenance and repair cost to be if the tractor is used for general contracting under average operating conditions?
   c. The tractor is powered by a 200-horsepower diesel engine. What do you estimate the hourly fuel cost to be if the tractor is used in unfavorable operating conditions and diesel fuel costs $1.25 per gallon?
   d. What do you estimate the hourly cost for filter, oil, and grease to be for the tractor when used in average operating conditions?
2. A contractor has purchased a single-engine scraper for $280,000 and expects to use it about 1,500 hours per year. The contractor expects to sell the scraper after using it for 12,000 hours for $56,000. Tires for the scraper cost $8,000 for a set of four. The scraper is powered by a 360-horsepower diesel engine. Diesel fuel costs $1.10 per gallon.
   a. What is the hourly ownership cost for the scraper (less tires) at a minimum attractive rate of return of 14%?
   b. What do you estimate the hourly maintenance and repair cost for the scraper (less tires) to be under unfavorable operating conditions?
   c. What do you estimate the hourly tire cost to be under average operating conditions?
   d. What do you estimate the hourly fuel cost to be for the scraper under average operating conditions?
   e. What do you estimate the hourly filter, oil, and grease cost to be for the scraper under unfavorable working conditions?
3. A contractor has purchased a grader for $150,000 and expects to use it about 1,000 hours per year. The contractor plans to use the grader for 12 years and then realize a salvage value of about $27,000. Tires for the grader cost $7,200 for a set of six tires. The useful life of a set of tires is estimated at 3,500 hours. The grader is powered by a 135-horsepower diesel engine, and diesel fuel costs $1.05 per gallon.

a. What is the hourly ownership cost for the grader (less tires) at a minimum attractive rate of return of 9%?

b. The equipment repair factor for the grader is estimated to be about 50% of the hourly straight-line depreciation for the 12 years of ownership. What do you estimate the hourly maintenance and repair cost for the grader (less tires) to be?

c. What do you estimate the hourly tire cost to be for the grader?

d. What do you estimate the hourly fuel cost to be for the grader under unfavorable working conditions?

e. What do you estimate the hourly filter, oil, and grease cost to be for the grader under unfavorable working conditions?

f. What hourly equipment rate should the contractor charge a project for use of the grader if a profit of 2% is desired from the equipment fleet and operator costs for the grader are $28.00 per hour?

4. A contractor has a project to construct a new motel with an underground parking garage. The contractor has evaluated the size of the excavation required for the parking garage and decided to remove the soil using a three-cubic-yard excavator and four dump trucks. The contractor determined the following cost data for the equipment from historical records:

Equipment	Ownership Cost	Operating Cost (Less Labor Cost)	Labor Cost (Operator)
Excavator	$32.00	$90.00	$29.00
Dump truck	$12.00	$48.00	$25.00

After analysis of the working conditions and the haul distance for the trucks, the contractor determined that the productivity of the combined equipment fleet will be about 120 cubic yards per hour. What is the estimated unit cost per cubic yard to excavate for the parking garage and haul the soil away?

5. A contractor has a project that involves the construction of a large fill for a parking lot. After detailed analysis of the task, the contractor selected an equipment fleet of three scrapers, one crawler tractor to push load the scrapers, one grader to spread the fill material and grade the surface, and one compactor to compact the loose fill material dumped by the scrapers. The contractor determined the following cost data from historical records:

Equipment	Ownership Cost	Operating Cost (Less Labor Cost)	Labor Cost (Operator)
Scraper	$20.00	$65.00	$28.00
Crawler tractor	$15.00	$38.00	$28.00
Grader	$10.00	$18.00	$28.00
Compactor	$12.00	$24.00	$26.00

After analysis of the working conditions and the haul distance for the scrapers, the contractor determined that the productivity of the combined equipment fleet will be about 600 cubic yards per hour. What do you estimate the unit cost per cubic yard to construct the fill for the parking lot to be?

Construction Equipment Cost Estimating

5.1   Introduction

To be successful, contractors must be able to predict or estimate the cost of executing specific construction tasks and then control the cost of performing them. The primary costs associated with most *site work* tasks are equipment and labor. Material costs usually are minor for these tasks. As discussed in Chapter 1, the selection of equipment can greatly influence the cost of construction. The unit cost for site work, usually expressed in dollars per cubic yard, is a function of equipment productivity and the equipment hourly ownership and operating costs. We examined the components of ownership and operating costs in Chapter 4, and we will examine productivity in Chapters 8 through 21.

The purpose of this chapter is not to cover all the facets of cost estimating, but to give the reader an understanding of why equipment productivity discussions in this and the following chapters are so important for proper equipment selection and cost management.

Construction cost estimates are based on the quantity of work to be performed and the unit price of the work. Project plans and specifications are used to determine the quantity of work. Unit prices may be determined in several ways, one of which is from contractor's historical cost records. If a contractor uses historical unit cost data, it must be adjusted for inflation and changes in labor and equipment costs to determine unit costs for current projects. If historical cost data are not available, published cost manuals or the methods discussed in Chapter 4 can be used to estimate the costs.

Estimating the cost of site work requires an understanding of the following:

- Site conditions
    Subsurface materials
    Drainage
    Accessibility

- Equipment capabilities
- Haul distances
- Crew and equipment requirements for specific tasks

To understand the project site conditions, a contractor must study the soils report for the project site and investigate the site for drainage and access conditions.

The basic steps in developing a cost estimate are shown in Figure 5.1. First, the plans and specifications are studied carefully to understand the complete scope of work to be performed. Next, the contractor breaks the total scope of work down into individual elements of work called ***work packages***. The work packages are combinations of activities that are used to develop cost estimates and construction schedules and manage project execution. The process of identifying work packages and activities is known as ***work breakdown***. Typical work packages for site work include

- Site clearing
- Foundation excavation

Figure 5.1

Steps in Developing a Cost Estimate for Individual Work Packages

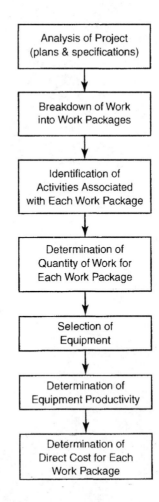

- Utilities excavation
- Utilities installation
- Site grading
- Backfill
- Landscaping
- Parking area construction
- Paving

The individual activities required for each work package are identified next. For example, site clearing might involve the following two activities:

- Vegetation removal
- Topsoil removal and stockpile

Once the work requirements have been determined, specific items of equipment are selected to perform each task. Next, the productivity for each piece of equipment is determined for each set of expected operating conditions.

The last step is costing the individual work packages to build the cost estimate. Quantities of work are calculated and costs estimated using unit cost data. The costs for all work packages are then summed to determine the total **direct cost** for the project, which includes labor, equipment, and material costs. The direct cost is then marked up to cover **indirect costs** such as overhead, profit, taxes, insurance, and bonding. (In this text, we will discuss direct costs only. For a complete discussion of cost estimation techniques, the reader should refer to a cost estimating text.)

5.2   Quantity Take-Off

The term **quantity take-off** refers to measuring the quantity of work to be performed. The contract drawings and specifications are examined to measure the scope for each task. Dimensions are measured or read, and the area or volume of work calculated. Volume measures are used to determine the quantity of work for excavating, hauling, and fill operations; area measures are used for land clearing and paving operations; and linear dimensions are used for utility line construction.

The unit cost for moving earth is a function of both the characteristics of the material to be moved and the distance it is to be moved. The disposal site for spoil material and the borrow site for fill material must be located. The equipment travel distance between these sites will have a significant impact on equipment productivity. Let's now look at an example problem to illustrate quantity take-off techniques.

Example 5.1

A contractor has obtained a set of plans and specifications for the construction of a small two-story office building. Examination of the site drawings indicates that the vegetation and 9 inches of topsoil must be removed from the 180-foot-by-100-foot building site and adjacent parking area. The concrete foundation for the building will be 40 feet wide by 90 feet long by 20 feet deep. Excess material that is not required for backfill around the foundation is to be hauled to a disposal site 1.5 miles from the construction site. The plans also indicate that the 180-foot-by-60-foot parking lot will be paved with 8 inches of asphalt concrete placed on top of 10 inches of well-graded compacted gravel.

Solution

Following is a sketch of the project site:

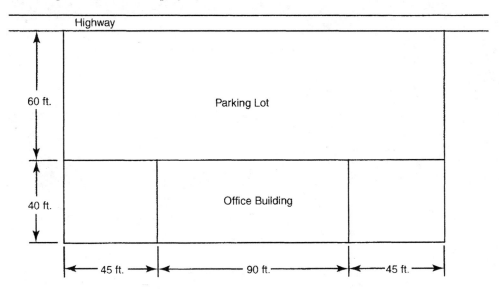

The first step in preparing the quantity take-off is the identification of work packages. For the site work on this project, the following work packages were selected:

- Site clearing
- Foundation excavation
- Foundation backfill
- Parking lot construction
- Parking lot paving

Site clearing will involve two activities: vegetation removal and topsoil removal. The estimated quantity of vegetation to be removed is

$$\frac{(180 \text{ ft.})(100 \text{ ft.})}{9 \text{ sq. ft./sq. yd.}} = \textbf{2,000 sq. yd.}$$

The estimated quantity of topsoil to be removed is

$$\frac{(180 \text{ ft.})(100 \text{ ft.})(9 \text{ in.})}{(27 \text{ cu. ft./cu. yd.})(12 \text{ in./ft.})} = \textbf{500 cu. yd.}$$

Unless the excavation for the foundation is shored, the sides must be excavated to the natural angle of repose for the soil. In this case, we estimate the natural angle of repose to be 1:2, which means 1 foot horizontal for each 2 feet vertical. Two feet will be added to the length and width of the excavation to allow for form construction for the concrete foundation, which will make the bottom of the excavation 42 feet by 92 feet. Because the sides of the excavation are to be sloped at an angle of one foot horizontal for each two feet vertical, 20 feet must be added to the length and width of the top of the excavation, as illustrated in the section shown below. This means the top of the excavation will measure 62 feet by 112 feet.

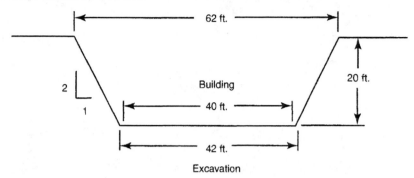

Excavation

The volume of soil to be excavated is therefore the sum of one rectangular prism, the four triangular prisms around the perimeter, and the four corners. The volume of the rectangular prism is (length)(width)(depth), which is

$$\frac{(92 \text{ ft.})(62 \text{ ft.})(20 \text{ ft.})}{27 \text{ cu. ft./cu. yd.}} = 4{,}225.2 \text{ cu. yd.}$$

The volume of a triangular prism is (1/2)(length)(width)(depth). For the four prisms in this problem, the volume is

$$\frac{(2)(1/2)(92 \text{ ft.})(10 \text{ ft.})(20 \text{ ft.})}{27 \text{ cu. ft./cu. yd.}} + \frac{(2)(1/2)(62 \text{ ft.})(10 \text{ ft.})(20 \text{ ft.})}{27 \text{ cu. ft./cu. yd.}}$$

$$= 681.5 \text{ cu. yd.} + 459.3 \text{ cu. yd.} = 1{,}140.8 \text{ cu. yd.}$$

The volume of a corner section is (1/4)(length)(width)(depth). For the four corner sections in this problem, the volume is

$$\frac{(4)(1/4)(10 \text{ ft.})(10 \text{ ft.})(20 \text{ ft.})}{27 \text{ cu. ft./cu. yd.}} = 74.1 \text{ cu. yd.}$$

Therefore, the total volume to be excavated is

$$4{,}225.2 \text{ cu. yd.} + 1{,}140.8 \text{ cu. yd.} + 74.1 \text{ cu. yd.} = 5{,}440.1 \text{ cu. yd.}$$

The total volume to be filled by the concrete foundation is

$$\frac{(60 \text{ ft.})(90 \text{ ft.})(20 \text{ ft.})}{27 \text{ cu. ft./cu. yd.}} = 4{,}000 \text{ cu. yd.}$$

Therefore, the total volume to be backfilled is

$$5{,}440.1 \text{ cu. yd.} - 4{,}000 \text{ cu. yd} = \mathbf{1{,}440.1 \text{ cu. yd.}}$$

When the soil is excavated, it expands; when compacted, it contracts to a density that generally is greater than its natural density before being excavated. The concepts of *swell* and *shrinkage* will be discussed in Chapter 7. For this problem, assume that the soil will lose 20% of its natural, in situ volume when compacted during the backfill operation. To account for this change in volume during compaction, we need to divide the required backfill volume by 80% to determine the required quantity of backfill material. Therefore, (1,440.1 cu. yd)/(0.8) or **1,800.1 cu. yd.** of the excavated soil will be required to backfill around the exterior of the concrete foundation. Thus, the quantity of excess excavated soil that must be taken to the disposal site is

$$5{,}440.1 \text{ cu. yd.} - 1{,}800.1 \text{ cu. yd.} = \textbf{3{,}640 cu. yd.}$$

Parking lot construction will involve two activities: *grading and compaction of the subgrade and placement* and *compaction of gravel*. The estimated quantity of subgrade to be graded and compacted is

$$\frac{(180 \text{ ft.})(60 \text{ ft.})}{9 \text{ sq. ft./sq. yd.}} = \textbf{1{,}200 sq. yd.}$$

The estimated volume of gravel needed to construct the parking lot is

$$\frac{(10 \text{ in.})(180 \text{ ft.})(60 \text{ ft.})}{(12 \text{ in./ft.})(27 \text{ cu. ft./cu yd.})} = \textbf{333.3 cu. yd.}$$

Parking lot paving will involve two activities: *application of prime coat* and *placement and compaction of asphalt*. The estimated quantity of gravel to be primed is:

$$\frac{(180 \text{ ft.})(60 \text{ ft.})}{9 \text{ sq. ft./sq. yd.}} = \textbf{1{,}200 sq. yd.}$$

The volume of asphalt concrete needed to surface the parking lot is

$$\frac{(8 \text{ in.})(180 \text{ ft.})(60 \text{ ft.})}{(12 \text{ in./ft.})(27 \text{ cu. ft./cu yd.})} = \textbf{266.7 cu. yd.}$$

Now that we have completed the quantity take-off for each of the work packages, we can complete the following table to summarize the results:

Work Package	Unit of Measure	Estimated Quantity
Site clearing		
Vegetation removal	sq. yd.	2,000.0
Topsoil removal	cu. yd.	500.0
Foundation excavation		
Excavation and stockpile	cu. yd.	1,800.1
Excavation and disposal	cu. yd.	3,640.0
Foundation backfill	cu. yd.	1,800.1
Parking lot construction		
Grade and compact subgrade	sq. yd.	1,200.0
Place and compact gravel	cu. yd.	333.3
Parking lot paving		
Prime gravel	sq. yd.	1,200.0
Place and compact asphalt	cu. yd.	266.7

5.3   *Equipment Selection*

As discussed in Chapter 1, the selection of equipment to use on a project has a major influence on the efficiency and profitability of the construction operation. The basic criteria that should be used in selecting equipment for specific tasks are

- The capability of the equipment to perform the work
- The capability of the equipment to perform effectively under the working conditions of the job site
- The availability of the equipment, either from the contractor's equipment fleet or from a rental or leasing agency
- The reliability of the equipment and predicted maintenance requirements
- The availability of parts and service support for the equipment
- The capability of the equipment to perform multiple tasks on the project
- Safety features available with the equipment

Selection involves the type and size of equipment and its manufacturer. If the contractor owns a fleet of equipment, the choice might be limited to equipment that is available at the time needed. If the equipment is to be rented or leased, there may be a wider selection from which to choose. Generally, contractors select the set of equipment for a project that minimizes the unit cost (e.g., dollars per cubic yard) of performing the required work. Mobilization and demobilization costs also must be considered, and a set of multifunctional equipment might represent the best choice to minimize mobilization and demobilization costs. For example, a contractor might select a crawler tractor with dozer blade to excavate for a foundation, rough grade the site, and backfill the foundation, rather than select a different piece for each task.

Earthmoving tasks typically involve some combination of excavating, loading, hauling, spreading, compacting, and grading. Excavating can be performed with a tractor with a dozer blade, a loader, an excavator, a front shovel, a clamshell, a dragline, or a scraper. The best choice depends on the work requirements of the project. The tractor can dig and push the excavated material out of the way. The scraper can load itself and haul the material away. Trucks can be loaded and used to haul the excavated material to a dump site. Loading is done with a loader, a front shovel, a clamshell, a dragline, or an excavator. Hauling is done with trucks, haulers, or scrapers. Spreading usually is done by a scraper, tractor, or grader. Compacting is done with one of the many types of compactors manufactured. Grading is done with a grader.

The conditions of the project site and the haul distances often dictate the type of equipment to use. Because of its greater traction, tracked equipment is used where the site is wet. Equipment selection is based on an analysis of the haul distance, underfoot conditions, grades, material type, production rate, and operator skill. Distance is used as the basis for initial equipment selection. The economic haul distances (one way) for different types of mobile construction equipment are shown in Figure 5.2. The cross-hatched portions of the bars represent the most economical haul distances for the indicated systems. This figure can be used for initial selection of the appropriate type of hauling equipment.

Once the type of equipment has been selected, the contractor must select the size to use. The alternatives may be limited by the contractor's equipment fleet or what is avail-

Figure 5.2
Economic Haul Distance for
Mobile Construction Equipment

Courtesy Caterpillar Inc.

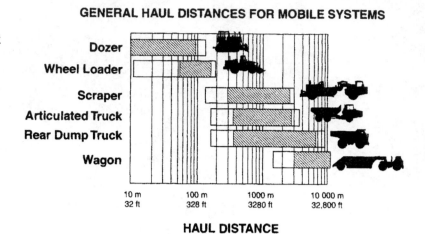

GENERAL HAUL DISTANCES FOR MOBILE SYSTEMS

HAUL DISTANCE

able from a rental or leasing agency. Larger equipment generally has higher productivity than do smaller models, but they also cost more to own or rent and operate. The labor costs generally are the same irrespective of the size of equipment selected, but the rental and other operating costs will increase with larger models. The contractor should attempt to select the size of equipment that will perform the required tasks at the least cost. This involves determining a unit cost for each activity by considering the equipment productivity and the hourly ownership or rental and operating cost.

5.4   *Productivity Estimation*

Estimating the hourly production rate for a piece of equipment or a set of equipment involves first determining the volume of material moved per load cycle and then the number of cycles performed per hour. To determine the volume moved per load cycle, you must know the characteristics of the material and the capacity or capability of the specific piece of equipment. Material characteristics will be discussed in Chapter 7, and the equipment characteristics can be determined from manufacturers' literature.

Cycle time is a function of equipment speed, travel distance, and operational efficiency. Equipment generally is not operated continuously for 60 minutes per hour. *Operational efficiency* is the estimated number of effective working minutes per hour, such as 50 or 45 minutes per hour. The **operating factor** is the operational efficiency divided by 60. It also can be estimated by evaluating the management and job conditions at the project site using Table 5.1. Management conditions include the skill, training, and motivation of the equipment operators; the state of repair of the equipment; and the organization and coordination of the work. Job conditions comprise the surface and weather conditions, including the topography of the project site.

The productivity of an item of equipment can be determined by the following equation:

$$\text{Productivity} = (\text{Load per cycle})(\text{Cycles per hour}) \tag{5--1}$$

Table 5.1
Operating Factors for Earthmoving Operations

Job Conditions	Management Conditions			
	Excellent	Good	Poor	Fair
Excellent	0.84	0.81	0.76	0.70
Good	0.78	0.75	0.71	0.65
Poor	0.72	0.69	0.65	0.60
Fair	0.63	0.61	0.57	0.52

Walker's Building Estimator's Reference Book, 25th ed. (Lisle, IL: Frank R. Walker Company, 1995), p. 2.38.

Table 5.2
Site Work Cost Estimation

Work Package	Estimated Quantity	Unit Cost	Extension
Clearing and grubbing site	1,500 sq. yd.	$12.50/sq. yd.	$18,750
Foundation excavation	3,800 cu. yd.	$4.25/cu. yd.	$16,150
Site grading	600 sq. yd.	$1.40/sq. yd.	$ 840
Foundation backfill	1,100 cu. yd.	$2.10/cu. yd.	$ 2,310

5.5 *Costing Elements of Work*

Cost estimation is based on a unit cost for each work item. The unit cost is determined by the following equation:

$$\text{Unit Cost} = \frac{\text{Hourly Ownership and Operating Cost}}{\text{Hourly Production Rate}} \tag{5-2}$$

The total cost to perform a specific task is simply the product of the quantity of work to be performed and the unit cost, as illustrated in Table 5.2. Let's look at an example problem and determine the total cost for the site work tasks analyzed in Example 5.1.

Example 5.2

The contractor of Example 5.1 has decided to use 2 crawler tractors to clear the vegetation from the project site and to remove and stockpile the topsoil. The contractor estimates the productivity of each tractor to be 30 square yards per hour when clearing vegetation and 250 cubic yards per hour when removing and stockpiling the topsoil. The contractor has decided to use a hydraulic excavator to excavate for the building foundation and load dump trucks with the excavated material. The material needed to backfill the foundation will be stockpiled near the construction site. The excess material will be hauled in dump trucks to the disposal site 1.5 miles away. Two dump trucks will be required to stockpile the backfill material, and 6 dump trucks will be required to remove the excess material. The productivity of the excavator and 2 dump trucks is estimated to be 150 cubic yards per hour, and the productivity of the excavator and 6 dump trucks is estimated to be 125 cubic yards per hour. A wheeled loader and 3 hand-operated plate compactors will be used to backfill the foundation. Productivity of the backfill operation is estimated to be 90 cubic yards per hour. One grader and 1 vibratory compactor will be used to grade and compact the subgrade for the parking lot. Productivity for this operation is estimated to be 400 square yards per hour. The contractor plans to use 3 dump trucks to haul in the gravel for the parking lot, a grader to spread the gravel, and a vibratory compactor to compact the gravel fill. Productivity of this set of equipment is estimated to be 190 cubic yards per hour. The parking lot will be primed with a truck-mounted asphalt distributor with an estimated productivity of 300 square yards per hour. The paving operation will involve 1 asphalt paving machine, 2 compactors, and 6 dump trucks. Productivity of the paving operation is estimated to be 56 cubic yards per hour.

The contractor has determined the following hourly ownership and operating costs (including labor costs) for the equipment that is to be used on this project:

Asphalt compactor	$ 52
Asphalt distributor	205
Asphalt paving machine	282
Crawler tractor	183
Dump truck	49
Grader	130
Hand-operated plate compactor	25
Hydraulic excavator	201
Vibratory compactor	66
Wheeled loader	103

What are the equipment costs for the work packages identified in Example 5.1?

Solution

The first step is to determine unit equipment costs for each work package. The cost of the gravel must be added to the equipment cost to determine the total cost for the construction of the parking lot and the cost of the asphalt needs to be added to the equipment cost to determine the total cost for the paving operation. Using Equation 5.2, the equipment unit cost for each work package can be determined as follows.

Vegetation removal productivity is estimated to be 60 square yards per hour (30 sq. yd./hr. for each tractor). Hourly equipment cost for this activity is ($183)(2) or $366 for 2 tractors.

$$\text{Equipment Unit Cost} = \frac{\$366/\text{hr.}}{60 \text{ sq. yd./hr.}} = \$6.10/\text{sq. yd.}$$

Topsoil removal productivity is estimated to be 500 cubic yards per hour (250 cu. yd./hr. for each tractor). Hourly equipment cost for this activity is $366.

$$\text{Equipment Unit Cost} = \frac{\$366/\text{hr.}}{500 \text{ cu. yd./hr.}} = \$0.73/\text{cu. yd.}$$

Foundation excavation and stockpiling for backfill productivity is estimated to be 150 cubic yards per hour. Hourly equipment cost for this activity is $201 (for excavator) plus $98 (for 2 dump trucks) or $299.

$$\text{Equipment Unit Cost} = \frac{\$299/\text{hr.}}{150 \text{ cu. yd./hr.}} = \$1.99/\text{cu. yd.}$$

Foundation excavation and disposal of excess material productivity is estimated to be 125 cubic yards per hour. Hourly equipment cost for this activity is $201 (for excavator) plus $294 (for 6 dump trucks) or $495.

$$\text{Equipment Unit Cost} = \frac{\$495/\text{hr.}}{125 \text{ cu. yd./hr.}} = \$3.96/\text{cu. yd.}$$

Backfill productivity is estimated to be 90 cubic yards per hour. Hourly equipment cost for this work package is $103 (for loader) plus $75 (for 3 hand-operated compactors) or $178.

$$\text{Equipment Unit Cost} = \frac{\$178/\text{hr.}}{90 \text{ cu. yd./hr.}} = \$1.98/\text{cu. yd.}$$

The productivity of the grading and compaction of the subgrade is estimated to be 400 square yards per hour. Hourly equipment cost for this activity is $130 (for a grader) plus $66 (for a vibratory compactor) or $196.

$$\text{Equipment Unit Cost} = \frac{\$196/\text{hr.}}{400 \text{ sq. yd./hr.}} = \$0.49/\text{sq. yd.}$$

The productivity of the placement and compaction of the gravel is estimated to be 190 cubic yards per hour. Hourly equipment cost for this activity is $147 (for 3 dump trucks) plus $130 (for a grader) plus $66 (for a vibratory compactor) or $343.

$$\text{Equipment Unit Cost} = \frac{\$343/\text{hr.}}{190 \text{ cu. yd./hr.}} = \$1.81/\text{cu. yd.}$$

The productivity of the priming operation is estimated to be 300 square yards per hour. Hourly equipment cost for this activity is $205 (for an asphalt distributor).

$$\text{Equipment Unit Cost} = \frac{\$205/\text{hr.}}{300 \text{ sq. yd./hr.}} = \$0.68/\text{sq. yd.}$$

Parking lot paving productivity is estimated to be 56 cubic yards per hour. Hourly equipment cost for this activity is $282 (for an asphalt paving machine) plus $294 (for 6 dump trucks) plus $104 (for 2 asphalt compactors) or $680.

$$\text{Equipment Unit Cost} = \frac{\$680/\text{hr.}}{56 \text{ cu. yd./hr.}} = \$12.14/\text{cu. yd.}$$

Using the quantities determined in Example 5.1, we can now determine the equipment cost for each activity as shown below.

Work Package	Estimated Quantity	Unit Cost	Extension
Site clearing			
Vegetation removal	2,000.0 sq. yd.	$6.10/sq. yd.	$12,200
Topsoil removal	500.0 cu. yd.	$0.73/cu. yd.	$ 365
Foundation excavation			
Excavation and stockpile	1,800.1 cu. yd.	$1.99/cu. yd.	$ 3,582
Excavation and disposal	3,640.0 cu. yd.	$3.96/cu. yd.	$ 4,414
Foundation backfill	1,800.1 cu. yd.	$1.98/cu. yd.	$ 3,564
Parking lot construction			
Grade and compact subgrade	1,200.0 sq. yd.	$0.49/sq. yd.	$ 588
Place and compact gravel	333.3 cu. yd.	$1.81/cu. yd.	$ 603
Parking lot paving			
Prime gravel	1,200.0 sq. yd.	$0.68/sq. yd.	$ 816
Place and compact asphalt	266.7 cu. yd.	$12.14/cu. yd.	$ 3,238

5.6   *Costing with Cost References*

There are many equipment cost references that can be used to estimate site work costs. We will discuss the following four:

1. *Contractors' Equipment Cost Guide*, published by PRIMEDIA Information, Inc.
2. *Construction Equipment Ownership and Operating Expense Schedule*, published by the United States Army Corps of Engineers
3. *Site Work & Landscape Cost Data*, published by R. S. Means Company, Inc.
4. *Walker's Building Estimator's Reference Book*, published by Frank R. Walker Company

The *Contractors' Equipment Cost Guide* is a comprehensive guide to ownership and operating costs developed by PRIMEDIA Information, Inc., with the assistance of the Associated General Contractors of America (AGC). Cost data are developed based on surveys taken of AGC members throughout the United States. An example of the type of data contained in the *Contractors' Equipment Cost Guide* is shown in Figure 5.3. Operator labor costs are not included in the operating cost and must be added to determine the total operating cost. The monthly rates are determined based on 22 8-hour work days per month. The weekly rates assume a loss of 2 work days per month, the daily rates assume a loss of 4 working hours per week, and the daily rates assume the loss of 1 hour per day. The operating costs shown are for average working conditions. If the working conditions are severe, the operating costs should be increased appropriately to account for a more adverse working environment. The CFC column under hourly ownership expenses is the hourly cost of facilities capital. Let's now look at an example using the data shown in Figure 5.3.

E X C A V A T I N G

CRAWLER MOUNTED HYDRAULIC EXCAVATORS

(Includes standard bucket, unless otherwise noted.)

Cost of Money Rate = 5.875%
Diesel = $.99 per gallon
Gasoline = $1.18 per gallon
Mechanic's Wage = $27.15 (incl. fringe benefits)

Model (Yr.Disc.)	Bucket Capacity	Approximate Base Price $	Economic Hours	Annual Use Hours	Hourly Ownership Expenses		Hourly Repair & Fuel Expenses						Combined Ownership & Repair Expenses			
					Depreciation	CFC	Labor	Parts	Supplies	Tires	Fuel	Lube	$ Monthly	$ Weekly	$ Daily	$ Hourly
DIESEL POWERED																
CATERPILLAR																
231D (1993)	2.000 CY	273,045	9,210	1,420	22.59	7.57	12.83	15.77	3.94	.00	8.71	3.36	13,160	3,290	730	104
231D LC (1993)	1.750 CY	280,925	9,210	1,420	23.24	7.79	12.83	18.22	4.06	.00	8.71	3.36	13,413	3,353	744	106
235 (1986)	1.875 CY	291,170	9,210	1,420	24.09	8.07	12.83	22.20	5.55	.00	8.49	3.28	14,874	3,719	826	118
235B (1988)	1.500 CY	318,570	9,210	1,420	26.38	8.83	12.83	22.92	5.73	.00	9.37	3.62	15,760	3,945	876	125
235C (1992)	2.000 CY	375,895	9,210	1,420	31.11	10.42	12.83	23.33	5.63	.00	10.89	4.20	17,355	4,339	963	138
235D (1994)	2.130 CY	399,475	9,210	1,420	33.05	11.08	12.83	22.07	5.52	.00	10.89	4.20	17,537	4,384	973	139
235D LC (1994)	2.130 CY	405,975	9,210	1,420	33.59	11.28	12.83	22.43	5.61	.00	10.89	4.20	17,743	4,436	985	141
245 (1988)	3.000 CY	501,980	9,210	1,420	41.63	13.92	12.83	38.11	9.03	.00	14.16	5.47	23,417	5,854	1,300	186
245B (1990)	3.125 CY	547,790	9,210	1,420	45.32	16.19	12.83	36.70	9.18	.00	15.88	6.05	24,807	6,202	1,377	197
245B SERIES II (1993)	3.125 CY	582,870	9,210	1,420	48.21	16.15	12.83	33.84	8.41	.00	15.88	6.05	24,811	6,203	1,377	197
245D (1993)	2.820 CY	599,534	9,210	1,420	49.60	16.62	12.83	34.82	8.86	.00	18.77	8.47	25,820	6,405	1,422	203
307	.380 CY	72,307	7,800	1,180	7.35	2.33	8.33	4.71	1.18	.00	1.92	.45	4,272	1,068	237	34
311	.420 CY	97,272	8,300	1,180	9.41	3.12	7.46	8.33	1.56	.00	2.82	.67	5,528	1,382	307	44
312	.420 CY	108,739	7,900	1,180	10.85	3.44	7.98	8.95	1.74	.00	2.99	.71	6,100	1,525	339	48
315	.880 CY	122,578	7,900	1,180	12.46	3.95	7.98	7.98	2.00	.00	3.63	.83	6,818	1,704	378	54
315L	.880 CY	127,401	7,900	1,180	12.95	4.11	7.98	8.29	2.07	.00	3.53	.63	6,996	1,750	389	56
320	1.250 CY	175,760	7,900	1,180	16.95	5.65	7.98	11.44	2.88	.00	4.56	1.76	9,048	2,262	502	72
320L	1.250 CY	182,660	7,900	1,180	17.84	8.08	7.98	11.90	2.98	.00	4.56	1.76	9,310	2,328	517	74
320N	1.250 CY	182,860	7,900	1,180	17.84	7.84	7.98	11.90	2.96	.00	4.56	1.76	9,310	2,328	517	74
322L	1.380 CY	232,060	7,900	1,180	22.38	7.72	7.98	15.10	3.76	.00	5.45	2.10	11,354	2,839	630	90
325 (1994)	1.440 CY	230,590	7,900	1,180	22.24	7.67	7.98	15.98	3.99	.00	5.99	2.31	11,641	2,910	648	92
325L	1.380 CY	257,460	7,900	1,180	24.83	8.57	7.98	16.76	4.19	.00	5.99	2.31	12,431	3,108	690	99
330 (1994)	1.830 CY	273,080	7,900	1,180	28.34	9.09	7.98	16.89	4.72	.00	7.91	3.05	13,724	3,431	762	109
330L	1.750 CY	307,070	9,210	1,420	25.41	8.51	12.83	15.98	3.99	.00	9.67	3.73	14,098	3,525	783	112
350 (1995)	3.500 CY	451,820	9,210	1,420	37.36	12.52	12.83	23.99	6.00	.00	12.46	4.81	19,355	4,839	1,074	154
350L	3.000 CY	481,228	9,210	1,420	39.81	13.34	12.83	25.01	6.25	.00	12.46	4.81	20,154	5,039	1,119	160
375	4.250 CY	775,888	9,210	1,420	84.16	21.51	12.83	40.31	10.08	.00	18.84	7.20	30,756	7,889	1,707	244
375L	4.250 CY	808,288	9,210	1,420	86.71	22.35	12.83	41.90	10.46	.00	18.84	7.20	31,899	7,925	1,759	252

Figure 5.3

Sample Data Page from *Contractors' Equipment Cost Guide*

Printed with permission of PRIMEDIA Information, Inc.

Example 5.3

A contractor has completed reviewing the plans and specifications for the construction of a new office building. The plans call for the construction of an underground parking garage for the building. The contractor plans to use a Caterpillar 350 hydraulic excavator to dig the foundation and load the excavated soil into dump trucks. The contractor has evaluated the site working conditions and estimated the excavator productivity to be about 200 cubic yards per hour. What is the contractor's unit cost for excavating the soil, if the excavator operator earns $26.00 per hour?

Solution

The hourly ownership and operating cost for the Caterpillar 350 hydraulic excavator can be estimated by using Figure 5.3. The last column of the figure shows the hourly ownership and operating cost (not including operator wages) is $154 per hour. Adding the operator's wages increases the hourly cost to $180 ($154 + $26). The direct unit cost can be estimated by using Equation 5–2.

$$\text{Unit Cost} = \frac{\$180.00/\text{hr.}}{200 \text{ cu. yd./hr.}} = \$0.90/\text{cu. yd.}$$

The *Construction Equipment Ownership and Operating Expense Schedule* is published by the United States Army Corps of Engineers in 12 volumes providing cost data for 12 separate regions of the United States. The books are printed by the United States Government Printing Office and can be obtained from a United States Government bookstore. Figures 5.4 and 5.5 show examples of the type data contained in the *Construction Equipment Ownership and Operating Expense Schedule*. Figure 5.4 provides hourly rates for average operating conditions for selected elevating scrapers. Figure 5.5 provides hourly rate elements for both average and severe operating conditions. Operator labor costs are not included and must be added to determine the total hourly operating cost. The abbreviation TEV stands for "total equipment value", which includes the basic price plus sales tax and transportation costs. The abbreviation FCCM stands for "facilities capital cost of money." The abbreviation FOG stands for the hourly cost for "filter, oil and grease." Now, let's look at an example using the data contained in Figures 5.4 and 5.5.

Example 5.4

A contractor needs to haul fill material to a project site that is located 1 mile from the source of the material. The contractor has decided to use 4 John Deere 862B elevating scrapers to excavate the needed soil and haul it to the project site. The contractor estimates the productivity of each scraper to be 80 cubic yards per hour when used under average operating conditions. If the scraper operator earns $24 per hour, what is the estimated equipment unit cost (in dollars per cubic yard) for this task under average operating conditions? under severe operating conditions?

HOURLY EQUIPMENT OWNERSHIP AND OPERATING EXPENSE

ID.NO.	MODEL	EQUIPMENT DESCRIPTION	ENGINE HORSEPOWER - FUEL TYPE: MAIN	ENGINE HORSEPOWER - FUEL TYPE: CARRIER	VALUE (TEV) ($)	TOTAL HOURLY RATES ($/HR): AVERAGE	TOTAL HOURLY RATES ($/HR): STANDBY	ADJUSTABLE ELEMENTS OWNERSHIP: DEPR	ADJUSTABLE ELEMENTS OWNERSHIP: FCCM	FUEL	CWT
S10	**SCRAPERS, ELEVATING**										
0.01	**0 THRU 200 HP**										
		CATERPILLAR, INC.									
S10CA001	613-C	11 CY, 13 TON, POWERSHIFT	175HP D-off		$190,628	46.19	12.42	14.55	5.14	5.70	325
		DRESSER (Formerly INTERNATIONAL / DRESSER)									
S10ID001	412B	11 CY, POWERSHIFT	165HP D-off		$176,810	43.35	11.47	13.39	4.77	5.37	335
		JOHN DEERE									
S10JD001	762B	11 CY, 13.7 TON, POWERSHIFT	180HP D-off		$169,133	42.76	10.89	12.65	4.56	5.86	371
0.02	**OVER 200 HP**										
		CATERPILLAR, INC.									
S10CA002	615-C	16 CY, 19 TON, POWERSHIFT	265HP D-off		$282,712	66.23	18.86	22.96	7.38	8.63	509
S10CA003	623-E	22 CY, 25 TON, POWERSHIFT	365HP D-off		$416,256	96.87	27.69	33.64	10.87	11.88	741
		FIATALLIS NORTH AMERICA INC.									
S10FI002	261B	23 CY, 26.5 TON, POWERSHIFT	330HP D-off		$419,539	95.10	28.09	34.25	10.96	10.74	635
		JOHN DEERE									
S10JD002	862B	16 CY, 20.0 TON, POWERSHIFT	265HP D-off		$241,001	59.23	15.88	19.16	6.30	8.63	482

Figure 5.4
Sample Hourly Equipment Ownership and Operating Cost Data for Average Working Conditions
From *Construction Equipment Ownership and Operating Expense Schedule*

HOURLY RATE ELEMENTS

CAT	ID. No	AVERAGE OPERATING CONDITIONS								SEVERE OPERATING CONDITIONS							
		DEPR	FCCM	FUEL	FOG	TIRE WEAR	TIRE REPAIR	REPAIR	TOTAL RATE	DEPR	FCCM	FUEL	FOG	TIRE WEAR	TIRE REPAIR	REPAIR	TOTAL RATE
R55	*cont.*																
	R55GL003	0.88	0.18	0.00	0.75	0.04	0.01	0.90	2.76								
	R55GL004	1.10	0.22	0.00	0.75	0.04	0.01	1.13	3.25								
	R55GL005	3.67	0.72	2.00	0.49	0.00	0.00	3.74	10.62								
	R55GL006	4.37	0.86	2.00	0.49	0.00	0.00	4.45	12.17								
	R55GL007	1.18	0.23	1.44	0.36	0.00	0.00	1.20	4.41								
	R55GL008	0.27	0.05	0.32	0.08	0.00	0.00	0.28	1.00								
	R55GL009	0.21	0.04	0.64	0.16	0.00	0.00	0.21	1.26								
	R55GL010	0.37	0.07	1.28	0.32	0.00	0.00	0.37	2.41								
	R55GL011	0.37	0.07	1.28	0.32	0.00	0.00	0.38	2.42								
S10																	
	S10CA001	14.55	5.14	5.70	2.35	2.64	0.41	15.40	46.19	18.18	5.27	7.39	3.04	4.40	0.68	20.54	59.50
	S10CA002	22.96	7.38	8.63	2.84	4.03	0.62	19.77	66.23	28.70	7.58	11.19	3.69	6.70	1.04	26.62	85.52
	S10CA003	33.64	10.87	11.88	3.92	6.56	1.01	28.99	96.87	42.04	11.16	15.42	5.08	10.90	1.68	39.03	125.31
	S10FI002	34.25	10.96	10.74	3.54	5.31	0.82	29.48	95.10	42.81	11.25	13.94	4.59	8.81	1.36	39.68	122.44
	S10ID001	13.39	4.77	5.37	2.21	2.95	0.46	14.20	43.35	16.73	4.88	6.97	2.87	4.89	0.76	18.93	56.03
	S10JD001	12.65	4.56	5.86	2.41	3.32	0.51	13.45	42.76	15.81	4.67	7.60	3.13	5.51	0.85	17.94	55.51
	S10JD002	19.16	6.30	8.63	2.84	4.97	0.77	16.56	59.23	23.95	6.46	11.19	3.69	8.26	1.28	22.29	77.12
S15																	
	S15CA001	29.14	9.49	9.58	3.16	6.56	1.01	25.15	84.09	36.42	9.74	12.49	4.12	10.90	1.68	33.86	109.21
	S15CA002	46.58	15.13	13.07	4.31	9.98	1.54	40.18	130.79	58.22	15.53	17.03	5.61	16.58	2.56	54.09	169.62
	S15CA003	60.73	19.67	15.97	5.26	12.29	1.90	52.36	168.18	75.91	20.19	20.81	6.86	20.42	3.15	70.49	217.83
	S15FI001	30.01	9.72	9.58	3.16	6.09	0.94	25.87	85.37	37.51	9.98	12.49	4.12	10.12	1.56	34.83	110.61
	S15TE001	40.08	13.20	13.94	4.59	10.75	1.66	34.65	118.87	50.10	13.55	18.16	5.99	17.86	2.76	46.65	155.07

Figure 5.5

Sample Hourly Rate Elements for Average and Severe Operating Conditions

From *Construction Equipment Ownership and Operating Expense Schedule*

Solution

The hourly ownership and operating cost (less labor) for the scraper for average operating conditions is determined from Figure 5.4 to be $59.23. When labor is added, the total hourly cost is $59.23 + $24.00, or $83.23. The unit cost for each scraper is

$$\frac{\$83.23/hr.}{80 \text{ cu. yd./hr.}} = \$1.04/\text{cu. yd.}$$

The hourly ownership and operating cost (less labor) for severe operating conditions is determined from Figure 5.5 to be $77.12 by using the identification number for the 862B shown in Figure 5.4 (S10JD002). When labor is added, the total hourly cost is $77.12 + $24.00 or $101.12. The scraper productivity under severe operating conditions is estimated by using Table 5.1. We will assume that average operating conditions mean good management conditions and good job conditions and that severe operating conditions mean good management conditions and fair job conditions. Each estimator must make a judgment based on anticipated job and management conditions.

Using our assumption and the appropriate factors from Table 5.1, we can estimate scraper productivity under severe operating conditions as follows:

$$\text{Productivity} = \frac{(80 \text{ cu. yd./hr.})(0.61)}{0.75} = 65 \text{ cu. yd./hr.}$$

The equipment unit cost for each scraper under severe operating conditions is

$$\frac{\$101.12/hr.}{65 \text{ cu. yd./hr.}} = \$1.56/\text{cu. yd.}$$

R. S. Means Company, Inc., annually publishes numerous volumes of cost data that can be used in estimating construction work. The most useful volumes for estimating site work and earthmoving tasks are *Means Heavy Construction Cost Data* and *Means Site Work & Landscape Cost Data*. We will use an extract from the latter volume to demonstrate the use of these publications. The cost data provided in the Means Cost Data books are based on national averages and may require adjustments for local situations. Equipment rental and hourly operating costs (less labor) are shown in Figure 5.6. The crew equipment cost is a daily rate determined by dividing the weekly rate by 5 (number of working days per week) and adding the hourly operating cost times 8 (number of working hours per day). The use of the data is demonstrated the following example.

Example 5.5

A contractor plans to use a 3-cubic-yard wheeled loader to excavate for the foundation of a small office building. She estimates the loader productivity to be 94 cubic yards per hour for the excavation operation. The contractor plans to rent the loader on a weekly basis and pay the operator $23.75 per hour. What is the estimated equipment unit cost for this operation?

016 400 | Equipment Rental

		UNIT	HOURLY OPER. COST	RENT PER DAY	RENT PER WEEK	RENT PER MONTH	CREW EQUIPMENT COST
3000	Roller, tandem, gas, 3 to 5 ton	Ea.	5.90	158	475	1,425	142.20
3050	Diesel, 8 to 12 ton		8.64	267	800	2,400	229.10
3100	Towed type, vibratory, gas 12.5 H.P., 2 ton		3.83	117	350	1,050	100.65
3150	Sheepsfoot, double 60" x 60"		4.50	133	400	1,200	116
3200	Pneumatic tire diesel roller, 12 ton		8.59	267	800	2,400	228.70
3250	21 to 25 ton		16.35	320	960	2,875	322.80
3300	Sheepsfoot roller, self-propelled, 4 wheel, 130 H.P.		20.33	640	1,920	5,750	546.65
3320	300 H.P.		26.16	740	2,225	6,675	654.30
3350	Vibratory steel drum & pneumatic tire, diesel, 18,000 lb.		11.18	415	1,250	3,750	339.45
3400	29,000 lb.		12.30	500	1,500	4,500	398.40
3410	Rotary mower, brush, 60", with tractor		8.28	237	710	2,125	208.25
3450	Scrapers, towed type, 9 to 12 C.Y. capacity		2.90	80	240	720	71.20
3500	12 to 17 C.Y. capacity		5.85	247	740	2,225	194.80
3550	Scrapers, self-propelled, 4 x 4 drive, 2 engine, 14 C.Y. capacity		60.09	1,825	5,445	16,300	1,570
3600	2 engine, 24 C.Y. capacity		71.79	2,150	6,465	19,400	1,867
3650	Self-loading, 11 C.Y. capacity		26.70	735	2,200	6,600	653.60
3700	22 C.Y. capacity		32.71	1,150	3,450	10,400	951.70
3710	Screening plant 110 hp. w / 5' x 10'screen		15.99	415	1,240	3,725	375.90
3720	5' x 16' screen		17.08	480	1,445	4,325	425.65
3850	Shovels, see Cranes division 016-460						
3860	Shovel/backhoe bucket, 1/2 C.Y.	Ea.	.95	73.50	220	660	51.60
3870	3/4 C.Y.		3.40	117	350	1,050	97.20
3880	1 C.Y.		3.65	167	500	1,500	129.20
3890	1-1/2 C.Y.		4.19	200	600	1,800	153.50
3910	3 C.Y.		7.76	365	1,100	3,300	282.10
3950	Stump chipper, 18" deep, 30 H.P.		1.71	242	725	2,175	158.70
4110	Tractor, crawler, with bulldozer, torque converter, diesel 75 H.P.		10.61	335	1,000	3,000	284.90
4150	105 H.P.		14.45	510	1,525	4,575	420.60
4200	140 H.P.		16.78	605	1,810	5,425	496.25
4260	200 H.P.		29.25	1,025	3,100	9,300	854
4310	300 H.P.		38.90	1,325	4,000	12,000	1,111
4360	410 H.P.		46.25	1,575	4,700	14,100	1,310
4380	700 H.P.		93.75	3,525	10,600	31,800	2,870
4400	Loader, crawler, torque conv., diesel, 1-1/2 C.Y., 80 H.P.		12.18	445	1,340	4,025	365.45
4450	1-1/2 to 1-3/4 C.Y., 95 H.P.		14.50	455	1,365	4,100	389
4510	1-3/4 to 2-1/4 C.Y., 130 H.P.		18.50	575	1,725	5,175	493
4530	2-1/2 to 3-1/4 C.Y., 190 H.P.		29.86	965	2,900	8,700	818.90
4560	4-1/2 to 5 C.Y., 275 H.P.		41.71	1,350	4,020	12,100	1,138
4610	Tractor loader, wheel, torque conv., 4 x 4, 1 to 1-1/4 C.Y., 65 H.P.		9.10	267	800	2,400	232.80
4620	1-1/2 to 1-3/4 C.Y., 80 H.P.		11.65	365	1,090	3,275	311.20
4650	1-3/4 to 2 C.Y., 100 H.P.		12.75	375	1,130	3,400	328
4710	2-1/2 to 3-1/2 C.Y., 130 H.P.		18.33	465	1,400	4,200	426.65
4730	3 to 4-1/2 C.Y., 170 H.P.		21.61	735	2,200	6,600	612.90
4760	5-1/4 to 5-3/4 C.Y., 270 H.P.		38.27	965	2,900	8,700	886.15
4810	7 to 8 C.Y., 375 H.P.		57.29	1,275	3,820	11,500	1,222
4870	12-1/2 C.Y., 690 H.P.		114.06	2,225	6,700	20,100	2,252
4880	Wheeled, skid steer, 10 C.F., 30 H.P. gas		4.81	107	320	960	102.50
4890	1 C.Y., 78 H.P., diesel		6.62	330	990	2,975	250.95
4891	Attachments						
4892	Auger	Ea.	.10	80	240	720	48.80
4893	Backhoe		.12	105	315	945	63.95
4894	Broom		.12	100	300	900	60.95
4895	Forks		.04	36.50	110	330	22.30
4896	Grapple		.10	83.50	250	750	50.80
4897	Concrete hammer		.23	177	530	1,600	107.85
4898	Tree spade		.33	108	325	975	67.65
4899	Trencher		.35	257	770	2,300	156.80
4900	Trencher, chain, boom type, gas, operator walking, 12 H.P.		1.91	117	350	1,050	85.30

Figure 5.6

Sample Equipment Rental and Hourly Operating Cost Data from *Means Site Work & Landscape Cost Data*

Solution

The hourly rental and operating cost (less labor) can be determined from Figure 5.6. The weekly rental rate is estimated to be $2,200, and the hourly operating cost is estimated to be $21.61. The total hourly cost is estimated to be

$$\frac{\$2,200/wk.}{(5 \text{ day/wk.}) \times (8 \text{ hr./day}).} + \$21.61/hr. + \$23.75/hr.$$

$$= \$55.00/hr. + \$21.61/hr. + \$23.75/hr. = \$100.36/hr.$$

The equipment unit cost is estimated to be

$$\frac{\$100.36/hr.}{94 \text{ cu. yd./hr.}} = \$1.07/\text{cu. yd.}$$

Walker's Building Estimator's Reference Book is published by Frank R. Walker Company. It contains tabular data that can be used to develop cost estimates for site work tasks. Some of the tables provide estimated direct unit costs for selected site work tasks, while others provide hourly productivity and ownership and operating cost estimates.

5.7   *Costing with Productivity References*

The *Means Cost Data* books discussed in the previous section also contain crew productivity and unit price data that can be used in developing cost estimates for site work tasks. Figures 5.7 and 5.8 show examples of the type of data contained in these volumes. The crew number listed under the crew column in Figure 5.7 refers to the crew description in Figure 5.8. For example, the B-12A crew for a 1-cubic-yard hydraulic backhoe consists of an operator and an oiler. *Total Bare Costs* are the direct costs per unit specified in the *Unit* column. The *Total Including O&P* means total unit cost including overhead and profit. Let's now look at an example using the data contained in Figure 5.7.

Example 5.6

A contractor is planning to use a 3-cubic-yard hydraulic backhoe to excavate for an underground parking garage. What do you estimate the hourly productivity and the labor and equipment unit cost for this excavation task to be?

Solution

Using Figure 5.7, we can estimate the daily productivity for the backhoe to be 1,280 cubic yards. The hourly productivity is estimated to be

$$\frac{1,280 \text{ cu. yd./day}}{8 \text{ hr./day}} = \mathbf{160 \text{ cu. yd./hr.}}$$

The labor and equipment unit cost is estimated to be **$1.99/cu. yd.** from Figure 5.7.

022 | Earthwork

	022 200	Excav./Backfill/Compact.	CREW	DAILY OUTPUT	LABOR-HOURS	UNIT	MAT.	LABOR	EQUIP.	TOTAL	TOTAL INCL O&P
4500	City block within zone of influence, minimum		A-8	25,200	.001	S.F.		.03		.03	.04
4600	Maximum		"	15,100	.002	"		.05		.05	.07
5000	Excavate and load boulders, less than 0.5 C.Y.		B-10T	80	.150	C.Y.		3.69	5.35	9.04	11.55
5020	0.5 C.Y. to 1 C.Y.		B-10U	100	.120			2.95	8.85	11.80	14.30
5200	Excavate and load blasted rock, 3 C.Y. power shovel		B-12T	1,530	.010			.27	.80	1.07	1.29
5400	Haul boulders, 25 Ton off-highway dump, 1 mile round trip		B-34E	330	.024			.52	1.96	2.48	2.94
5420	2 mile round trip			275	.029			.62	2.35	2.97	3.53
5440	3 mile round trip			225	.036			.76	2.87	3.63	4.32
5460	4 mile round trip		▼	200	.040	▼		.85	3.23	4.08	4.86
5600	Bury boulders on site, less than 0.5 C.Y., 300 H.P. dozer										
5620	150' haul		B-10M	310	.039	C.Y.		.95	3.58	4.53	5.40
5640	300' haul			210	.057			1.41	5.30	6.71	7.95
5800	0.5 to 1 C.Y., 300 H.P. dozer, 150' haul			300	.040			.98	3.70	4.68	5.60
5820	300' haul		▼	200	.060	▼		1.48	5.55	7.03	8.40
0010	**EXCAVATING, BULK BANK MEASURE** Common earth piled R022 -240										
0020	For loading onto trucks, add									15%	15%
0050	For mobilization and demobilization, see division 022 274 R022 -250										
0100	For hauling, see division 022-266										
0200	Backhoe, hydraulic, crawler mtd., 1 C.Y. cap. = 75 C.Y./hr.		B-12A	600	.027	C.Y.		.68	.92	1.60	2.04
0250	1-1/2 C.Y. cap. = 100 C.Y./hr.		B-12B	800	.020			.51	.89	1.40	1.76
0260	2 C.Y. cap. = 130 C.Y./hr.		B-12C	1,040	.015			.39	.94	1.33	1.63
0300	3 C.Y. cap. = 160 C.Y./hr.		B-12D	1,280	.013			.32	1.67	1.99	2.31
0310	Wheel mounted, 1/2 C.Y. cap. = 30 C.Y./hr.		B-12E	240	.067			1.69	1.39	3.08	4.12
0360	3/4 C.Y. cap. = 45 C.Y./hr.		B-12F	360	.044			1.13	1.25	2.38	3.10
0500	Clamshell, 1/2 C.Y. cap. = 20 C.Y./hr.		B-12G	160	.100			2.54	2.95	5.49	7.10
0550	1 C.Y. cap. = 35 C.Y./hr.		B-12H	280	.057			1.45	1.98	3.43	4.39
0950	Dragline, 1/2 C.Y. cap. = 30 C.Y./hr.		B-12I	240	.067			1.69	2.03	3.72	4.83
1000	Dragline, 3/4 C.Y. cap. = 35 C.Y./hr.			280	.057			1.45	1.74	3.19	4.14
1001	3/4 C.Y. cap. = 35 C.Y./hr.		▼	280	.057			1.45	1.74	3.19	4.14
1050	1-1/2 C.Y. cap. = 65 C.Y./hr.		B-12P	520	.031			.78	1.52	2.30	2.86
1100	3 C.Y. cap. = 112 C.Y./hr.		B-12V	900	.018			.45	1.13	1.58	1.94
1200	Front end loader, track mtd., 1-1/2 C.Y. cap. = 70 C.Y./hr.		B-10N	560	.021			.53	.65	1.18	1.54
1250	2-1/2 C.Y. cap. = 95 C.Y./hr.		B-10O	760	.016			.39	.65	1.04	1.31
1300	3 C.Y. cap. = 130 C.Y./hr.		B-10P	1,040	.012			.28	.79	1.07	1.31
1350	5 C.Y. cap. = 160 C.Y./hr.		B-10Q	1,620	.007			.18	.70	.88	1.05
1500	Wheel mounted, 3/4 C.Y. cap. = 45 C.Y./hr.		B-10R	360	.033			.82	.65	1.47	1.98
1550	1-1/2 C.Y. cap. = 80 C.Y./hr.		B-10S	640	.019			.46	.49	.95	1.24
1600	2-1/4 C.Y. cap. = 100 C.Y./hr.		B-10T	800	.015			.37	.53	.90	1.16
1601	3 C.Y. cap. = 100 C.Y./hr.		"	1,100	.011			.27	.39	.66	.85
1650	5 C.Y. cap. = 185 C.Y./hr.		B-10U	1,480	.008			.20	.60	.80	.97
1800	Hydraulic excavator, truck mtd. 1/2 C.Y. = 30 C.Y./hr.		B-12J	240	.067			1.69	2.53	4.22	5.35
1850	48 inch bucket, 1 C.Y. = 45 C.Y./hr.		B-12K	360	.044			1.13	2.17	3.30	4.10
3700	Shovel, 1/2 C.Y. capacity = 55 C.Y./hr.		B-12L	440	.036			.92	1.09	2.01	2.61
3750	3/4 C.Y. capacity = 85 C.Y./hr.		B-12M	680	.024			.60	.81	1.41	1.80
3800	1 C.Y. capacity = 120 C.Y./hr.		B-12N	960	.017			.42	.65	1.07	1.36
3850	1-1/2 C.Y. capacity = 160 C.Y./hr.		B-12O	1,280	.013			.32	.70	1.02	1.25
3900	3 C.Y. cap. = 250 C.Y./hr.		B-12T	2,000	.008			.20	.61	.81	.98
4000	For soft soil or sand, deduct									15%	15%
4100	For heavy soil or stiff clay, add									60%	60%
4200	For wet excavation with clamshell or dragline, add									100%	100%
4250	All other equipment, add									50%	50%
4400	Clamshell in sheeting or cofferdam, minimum		B-12H	160	.100			2.54	3.46	6	7.70
4450	Maximum		"	60	.267	▼		6.75	9.20	15.95	20.50
8000	For hauling excavated material, see div. 022-266										

Figure 5.7

Sample Productivity and Unit Cost Data from *Means Site Work & Landscape Cost Data*

Figure 5.8

Sample Crew Data from *Means Site Work & Landscape Cost Data*

From *Means Site Work & Land-scaping 1997*. Copyright R. S. Means Co., Inc., Kingston, MA, 781–585–7880, all rights reserved.

Crews

Crew No.	Bare Costs		Incl. Subs O & P		Cost Per Labor-Hour	
	Hr.	Daily	Hr.	Daily	Bare Costs	Incl. O&P
Crew B-12						
1 Equip. Oper. (crane)	$27.85	$222.80	$42.60	$340.80	$25.35	$38.78
1 Equip. Oper. Oiler	22.85	182.80	34.95	279.60		
16 L.H., Daily Totals		$405.60		$620.40	$25.35	$38.78
Crew B-12A	Hr.	Daily	Hr.	Daily	Bare Costs	Incl. O&P
1 Equip. Oper. (crane)	$27.85	$222.80	$42.60	$340.80	$25.35	$38.78
1 Equip. Oper. Oiler	22.85	182.80	34.95	279.60		
1 Hyd. Excavator, 0.76 m³		549.35		604.30	34.33	37.77
16 L.H., Daily Totals		$954.95		$1224.70	$59.68	$76.55
Crew B-12B	Hr.	Daily	Hr.	Daily	Bare Costs	Incl. O&P
1 Equip. Oper. (crane)	$27.85	$222.80	$42.60	$340.80	$25.35	$38.78
1 Equip. Oper. Oiler	22.85	182.80	34.95	279.60		
1 Hyd. Excavator, 1.15 m³		710.95		782.05	44.43	48.88
16 L.H., Daily Totals		$1116.55		$1402.45	$69.78	$87.66
Crew B-12C	Hr.	Daily	Hr.	Daily	Bare Costs	Incl. O&P
1 Equip. Oper. (crane)	$27.85	$222.80	$42.60	$340.80	$25.35	$38.78
1 Equip. Oper. Oiler	22.85	182.80	34.95	279.60		
1 Hyd. Excavator, 1.53 m³		973.40		1070.70	60.84	66.92
16 L.H., Daily Totals		$1379.00		$1691.15	$86.19	$105.70
Crew B-12D	Hr.	Daily	Hr.	Daily	Bare Costs	Incl. O&P
1 Equip. Oper. (crane)	$27.85	$222.80	$42.60	$340.80	$25.35	$38.78
1 Equip. Oper. Oiler	22.85	182.80	34.95	279.60		
1 Hyd. Excavator, 2.67 m³		2133.00		2346.30	133.31	146.64
16 L.H., Daily Totals		$2538.60		$2966.70	$158.66	$185.42
Crew B-12E	Hr.	Daily	Hr.	Daily	Bare Costs	Incl. O&P
1 Equip. Oper. (crane)	$27.85	$222.80	$42.60	$340.80	$25.35	$38.78
1 Equip. Oper. Oiler	22.85	182.80	34.95	279.60		
1 Hyd. Excavator, 0.38 m³		333.05		366.35	20.82	22.90
16 L.H., Daily Totals		$738.65		$986.75	$46.17	$61.68
Crew B-12F	Hr.	Daily	Hr.	Daily	Bare Costs	Incl. O&P
1 Equip. Oper. (crane)	$27.85	$222.80	$42.60	$340.80	$25.35	$38.78
1 Equip. Oper. Oiler	22.85	182.80	34.95	279.60		
1 Hyd. Excavator, 0.57 m³		451.25		496.40	28.20	31.02
16 L.H., Daily Totals		$856.85		$1116.80	$53.55	$69.80
Crew B-12G	Hr.	Daily	Hr.	Daily	Bare Costs	Incl. O&P
1 Equip. Oper. (crane)	$27.85	$222.80	$42.60	$340.80	$25.35	$38.78
1 Equip. Oper. Oiler	22.85	182.80	34.95	279.60		
1 Power Shovel, 0.38 m³		427.35		470.10		
1 Clamshell Bucket, 0.38 m³		44.40		48.85	29.48	32.43
16 L.H., Daily Totals		$877.35		$1139.35	$54.83	$71.21

5.8   Problems

1. A contractor has been awarded the contract for the construction of a small shopping center. The contractor has decided to use crawler tractors with dozer blades to remove the vegetation and topsoil from the project site, but is unsure which size tractor to use. The productivity of a medium-sized tractor is estimated to be 100 square yards per day, and the productivity for a heavy tractor is estimated to be 190 square yards per day. The average hourly ownership and operating cost (including labor cost) for the medium tractor is $85, and for the heavy tractor is $126.

   a. Which tractor should the contractor select to minimize the direct equipment cost for clearing and grubbing the project site?

    b. Using the tractor selected above, what is the estimated equipment cost for clearing and grubbing the 200-foot-by-270-foot site?

2. The contractor of Problem 1 is now evaluating alternative sizes of hydraulic excavators to select the most economical size to excavate for the foundation for the shopping center. The estimated volume to be excavated is 6,750 cubic yards. Two hydraulic excavators are available; a 1.5-cubic-yard model and a 3-cubic-yard model. The estimated ownership and operating cost (including labor cost) for the 1.5-cubic-yard model is $140 per hour and for the 3-cubic-yard model is $185 per hour. The estimated productivity for the 1.5-cubic-yard model is 90 cubic yards per hour and for the 3-cubic-yard model is estimated to be 144 cubic yards per hour.

    a. Which excavator should the contractor select to minimize the direct equipment cost for the excavation operation?

    b. Using the excavator selected above, what is the estimated equipment cost for the excavation operation?

3. A contractor is considering whether to use a Caterpillar 320L hydraulic excavator or a Caterpillar 330L hydraulic excavator to excavate for the foundation for an apartment complex. The productivity of the 320L is estimated to be 88 cubic yards per hour, and that of the 330L is estimated to be 120 cubic yards per hour.

    a. Which excavator should the contractor select to minimize the unit cost for the excavation operation? Use the cost data contained in Figure 5.3 in making your determination.

    b. What is the estimated equipment cost for the excavating operating, if the operator earns $25 per hour and the volume of material to be removed is 5,260 cubic yards?

4. A contractor plans to use three Caterpillar 623E elevating scrapers to excavate the face of a hill to create a level building site for a small industrial complex. Since the work will be done in January, the working conditions will be considered severe. The productivity of each scraper is estimated to be 87 cubic yards per hour when operated under severe working conditions. Each scraper operator earns $22.50 per hour. Using Figures 5.4 and 5.5, what is the estimated equipment cost for this excavation operation, if the volume of material to be moved is estimated to be 12,750 cubic yards?

5. A residential builder rents a 2.5-cubic-yard tracked (crawler) loader on a monthly basis to excavate basements in a new housing development. The average number of working days per month is 22, and the loader operator earns $23.60 per hour.

    a. Using Figure 5.6, estimate the hourly rental and operating (including labor) cost for the loader. Assume the builder works 8 hours per day.

    b. Using Figure 5.7 and the answer to (a), estimate the equipment unit cost in dollars per cubic yard for basement excavation.

6

Construction Equipment Project Scheduling

6.1 Introduction

To be successful, contractors must be able to estimate the time required to complete a construction project. This is just as important as the ability to estimate the cost for completing the project. Most construction contracts specify a required completion date, and contractors need to ensure that they can complete the project in accordance with the plans and specifications by the specified date. To accomplish this, contractors carefully analyze the plans and specifications, identify the means and methods for executing the various tasks involved, and develop a schedule that depicts the individual tasks, or activities, that must be performed in completing the project.

The purpose of this chapter is not to make the reader an expert in construction scheduling, but to show how equipment selection and fleet productivity are used in developing a construction schedule. We will focus on site work tasks, as we did in our discussion of cost estimating in Chapter 5, with a brief discussion of manual schedule development and analysis. There are many automated software programs on the market today that can be used for schedule development, and the reader should refer to one of the many scheduling textbooks for a discussion of them.

The principal scheduling tools used in construction are bar charts and network diagrams. For simple projects, a bar chart is usually adequate. For more complex projects, a network diagram is usually a better management tool. Both are discussed in this chapter.

6.2 Task Analysis

The first step in developing a construction schedule for a project is the development of a list of all the individual tasks, called *activities*, that are required to complete the project. As discussed at the beginning of Chapter 5, the contractor first divides the entire

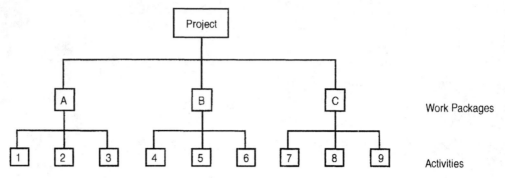

Figure 6.1
Work Breakdown for a Construction Project

project's scope of work into individual work packages, such as site clearing, foundation excavation, or site grading. Each work package is then divided into a set of activities that are required to perform all the work to complete the work package. These activities become the building blocks for the development of the construction schedule. Each activity must have a single duration, or time for completion, and an identifiable beginning and end. This concept of ***work breakdown*** is illustrated in Figure 6.1.

The degree of detail required in the development of the list of activities is up to the contractor. It is a function of the complexity of the project and the level at which the contractor wants to manage the execution of the project. Some work packages may stand alone for scheduling purposes, while others are divided into multiple activities. Let's look at an example problem to illustrate the concept of work breakdown.

Example 6.1

The contractor of Example 5.1 in Chapter 5 has asked you to develop a work breakdown structure for the site work for the two-story office building.

Solution

The first step in work breakdown is the identification of the individual work packages, which was done in Example 5.1. The following work packages were identified for this project:

- Site clearing
- Foundation excavation
- Foundation backfill
- Parking lot construction
- Parking lot paving

Next, individual activities are identified for each work package. The activities involved in site clearing are

- Vegetation removal
- Topsoil removal

The activities involved in foundation excavation are

- Site layout
- Excavation and stockpile
- Excavation and disposal

The activities involved in foundation backfill are hauling, dumping, and compaction of the backfill material. Since they are all concurrent, we will not identify separate activities for this work package.

The activities involved in parking lot construction are

- Grade and compact subgrade
- Place and compact gravel

The activities involved in parking lot paving are

- Prime gravel
- Place and compact asphalt

6.3   Equipment Selection

As discussed in Chapter 5, the selection of equipment to be used to accomplish each task, or activity, has a major influence on the time required to compete the task. Equipment selection criteria are the same as discussed in Section 5.3 of Chapter 5. Equipment selection involves selection of both the type and size to use. Larger equipment generally has greater productivity but costs more to own or rent and operate. The contractor should select the set of equipment that minimizes construction costs, yet meets the time schedule required to complete the project within the time frame specified in the contract.

6.4   Productivity Estimation

Once the equipment to be used for each activity has been selected, the contractor needs to determine the equipment and crew productivity for each activity. Productivity estimates can be determined from the contractor's historical records for equipment that is owned by the contractor, from reference books as discussed in Section 5.7 of Chapter 5, or by the methods that we will discuss in Chapters 8 through 21. The equipment productivity is used in scheduling to determine the *duration*, or time required to complete, for each activity. The amount of work required to complete each activity is determined by the quantity take-off methods discussed in Section 5.2 of Chapter 5. Using the equipment and crew productivity, the activity duration can be determined by the following equation.

$$\text{Activity Duration (days)} = \frac{\text{Quantity of Work}}{(\text{Productivity/hr.})(8 \text{ hr./day})} \qquad (6\text{--}1)$$

Equation 6–1 is based on 8 working hours per day. If the equipment is to be worked on a double-shift basis or a different number of hours per day, the denominator of the equation must be changed appropriately.

6.5   Activity Analysis

There are two major aspects of activity analysis. The first is the determination of the duration for each activity. This can be accomplished using Equation 6–1. The second is to determine the sequence in which the activities must be completed. This involves determining the answers to the following three questions regarding each activity:

- What activities must be completed before this activity can start?
- What activities cannot be started until this activity is completed?
- What activities can be completed concurrently with this activity?

The answers to these questions will be used in the next section to establish the interrelationships between the activities and develop a construction schedule.

6.6   Schedule Development

The simplest form of construction schedule that depicts the interrelationships between the individual activities is a bar chart, which is sometimes referred to as a Gantt chart. This type of scheduling was introduced by Henry Gantt in the early 1900s when he used these charts to analyze industrial production. A bar chart is constructed by determining the durations of all activities and plotting them on a time-scaled axis. The start point for each activity is determined by answering the three questions in Section 6.5 above. Let's look at an example problem to illustrate the development of a bar chart schedule.

Example 6.2

Using the work breakdown structure identified in Example 6.1, develop a bar chart schedule for the site work activities.

Solution

The first step in developing the bar chart schedule is determining the duration for each activity using Equation 6–1. The estimated quantity for each activity was determined in Example 5.1, and the productivity for each activity is given in Example 5.2.

The total quantity of vegetation to be removed is 2,000 square yards, and the activity productivity is estimated to be 60 square yards per hour for the two tractors. With Equation 6–1, the duration of the vegetation removal activity can be estimated to be

$$\frac{2,000 \text{ sq. yd.}}{(60 \text{ sq. yd./hr.})(8 \text{ hr./day})} = 4.2 \text{ days}$$

The total quantity of topsoil to be removed is 500 cubic yards, and the activity productivity is estimated to be 500 cubic yards per hour for the two tractors. The duration of the topsoil removal activity can be similarly estimated to be

$$\frac{500 \text{ cu. yd.}}{(500 \text{ cu. yd./hr.})(8 \text{ hr./day})} = 0.1 \text{ days}$$

The site layout activity was not analyzed in Chapter 5, because it does not involve the use of construction equipment. We will estimate its duration to be **0.5 days.**

The quantity of soil to be excavated and stockpiled is 1,800.1 cubic yards, and the activity productivity is estimated to be 150 cubic yards per hour. With Equation 6–1, the duration of the excavation and stockpile activity can be estimated to be

$$\frac{1,800.1 \text{ cu. yd.}}{(150 \text{ cu. yd./hr.})(8 \text{ hr./day})} = \textbf{1.5 days}$$

The quantity of soil to be excavated and disposed of is 3,640 cubic yards, and the activity productivity is estimated to be 125 cubic yards per hour. The duration for the excavation and disposal activity can be estimated to be

$$\frac{3,640 \text{ cu. yd.}}{(125 \text{ cu. yd./hr.})(8 \text{ hr./day})} = \textbf{3.6 days}$$

The quantity of soil to be backfilled and compacted is 1,800.1 cubic yards, and the activity productivity is estimated to be 90 cubic yards per hour. The duration for foundation backfill can be estimated to be

$$\frac{1,800.1 \text{ cu. yd.}}{(90 \text{ cu. yd./hr.})(8 \text{ hr./day})} = \textbf{2.5 days}$$

The quantity of subgrade to be graded and compacted for the parking lot is 1,200 square yards, and the activity productivity is estimated to be 400 square yards per hour. The duration for the grading and compaction of the subgrade activity can be estimated to be

$$\frac{1,200 \text{ sq. yd.}}{(400 \text{ sq. yd./hr.})(8 \text{ hr./day})} = \textbf{0.4 day}$$

The quantity of gravel needed to construct the parking lot is 333.3 cubic yards, and the activity productivity is estimated to be 190 cubic yards per hour. The duration for the construction of the gravel base for the parking lot can be estimated to be

$$\frac{333.3 \text{ cu. yd.}}{(190 \text{ cu. yd./hr.})(8 \text{ hr./day})} = \textbf{0.2 day}$$

The quantity of gravel to be primed is 1,200 square yards, and the activity productivity is estimated to be 300 square yards per hour. The duration for the application of the prime coat can be estimated to be

$$\frac{1,200 \text{ sq. yd.}}{(300 \text{ sq. yd./hr.})(8 \text{ hr./day})} = \textbf{0.5 day}$$

The quantity of asphalt concrete needed to pave the parking lot is 266.7 cubic yards, and the activity productivity is estimated to be 56 cubic yards per hour. The duration for the paving operation can be estimated to be

$$\frac{266.7 \text{ cu. yd.}}{(56 \text{ cu. yd./hr.})(8 \text{ hr./day})} = \textbf{0.6 day}$$

Once the duration has been determined for each activity, we must determine the sequence in which the activities will be completed. This is accomplished by answering the three questions posed in Section 6.5 for each activity.

Vegetation removal is the first activity to be performed. Once it is completed, the topsoil can be removed and stockpiled. Next, the site is to be laid out. The material to be stockpiled will be excavated first, followed by the material that is to be hauled to the disposal site. Once the excavation for the foundation has been completed, the foundation can be constructed by others. After the foundation is completed, it is backfilled. Parking lot construction can begin as soon as the topsoil has been removed and stockpiled. The sequence of parking lot construction is subgrade grading and compaction, followed by gravel placement and compaction. Next, the gravel is primed, and finally the pavement is placed and compacted.

The following bar chart schedule can now be constructed to depict the timing of the various activities involved in the site work portion of this construction project. To schedule the foundation backfill activity, it is necessary to estimate a duration for the construction of the foundation, which we will estimate to be 9 days.

Activity	Duration	1st Week					2nd Week					3rd Week					4th Week					5th Week				
		1	2	3	4	5	1	2	3	4	5	1	2	3	4	5	1	2	3	4	5	1	2	3	4	5
Vegetation removal	4.2 days	■	■	■	■																					
Topsoil removal	0.1 days					■																				
Site layout	0.5 days					■																				
Excavation and stockpile	1.5 days						■	■																		
Excavation and disposal	3.6 days							■	■	■																
Foundation construction	9.0 days											■	■	■	■	■	■									
Foundation backfill	2.5 days																		■	■						
Grade and compact subgrade	0.4 days					■																				
Place and compact gravel	0.2 days					■																				
Prime gravel	0.5 days					■																				
Place and compact asphalt	0.6 days					■																				

The use of network diagrams as construction schedules was originated in the late 1950s by the DuPont Corporation and the United States Navy. These diagrams depict the sequence and interrelation of all project activities and support numerical analysis to determine project duration. They can be used to determine which activities are *critical* and which have *float*. Critical activities are defined as those activities that determine the time required to complete the project. The chain of critical activities through a network

Figure 6.2
Activity Notation for Network Diagrams

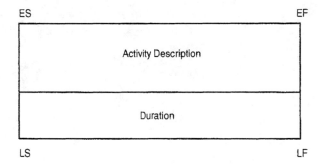

diagram is called the ***critical path***. Activities that are not on the critical path have some float, which means they can be delayed without delaying the overall completion of the project.

In our discussion of network diagrams, we will use the labeling notation shown in Figure 6.2. We will determine the duration for each activity in days. The ***early start*** (ES) is the earliest time that the activity can be started, and the ***early finish*** (EF) is the earliest time the activity can be completed. The difference between the early finish and the early start is the activity duration. The ***late start*** (LS) is the latest time that the activity can be started without affecting the overall completion of the project, and the ***late finish*** (LF) is the latest time the activity can be completed without affecting the overall completion of the project. The difference between the late start and the early start is known at the ***activity float***. The calculation and use of these times will be illustrated in Example 6.3.

Example 6.3

A contractor has carefully reviewed the plans and specifications for the construction of a small warehouse, identified the following activities during her work breakdown analysis, and estimated the duration for each activity:

Activity	Duration
Clear and grade site	5 days
Construct slab foundation	8 days
Frame building	21 days
Install roof	7 days
Install exterior finish	4 days
Finish interior	35 days
Construct sidewalk	5 days
Construct parking area	4 days

Construct a network diagram schedule for the project, determine the earliest date the project will be completed, and determine the early start and late start for each activity.

Solution

The first step in developing the schedule is to answer the questions posed in Section 6.5 for each activity. The contractor has determined the following construction logic for the project: The site clearing and grading must be completed before the foundation construction can begin. The foundation must be completed before framing and sidewalk construction can start. Once the framing is completed, both the exterior finish and the roof can begin. Both the exterior finish and the roof must be completed before the interior can be finished. The sidewalk must be completed before the parking area is constructed. The following network diagram now can be constructed for this project using the notation introduced in Figure 6.2. This diagram is a graphical representation of the construction logic described above.

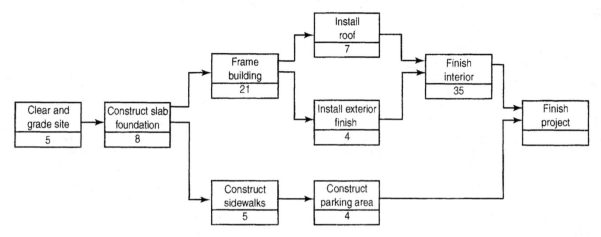

Once the basic schedule has been developed, we can determine the early start (ES) and early finish (EF) for each activity. Starting the project at time = 0, we can determine the early finish for *clear and grade site* to be day 5 because

$$EF = ES + \text{duration}$$

The finish for *clear and grade site* now becomes the early start for *construct slab foundation*. The early finish for this activity becomes the early start for the two following activities: *frame building* and *construct sidewalks*. When multiple activities precede an activity, such as *finish interior*, the early start for the activity is the latest early finish of all preceding activities. This is because all preceding activities must be completed before the activity can begin. The early finish for the last activity in the schedule is the duration for the entire project.

Once the project duration has been determined, the latest start (LS) and latest finish (LF) can be determined for each activity. The latest finish for an activity is the latest start for all succeeding activities. Where there is more than one succeeding activity, the latest finish is the earliest latest finish among the succeeding activities. The latest start for an activity can be determined by the following relationship:

$$LS = LF - \text{duration}$$

Now we can determine the early start, early finish, late start, and late finish for all the activities in our schedule, as shown on the following page.

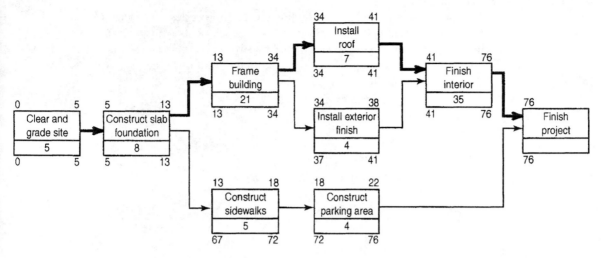

The chain of activities that determine the project duration is known as the *critical path*. This path is indicated with bold lines in the schedule above. Each activity on the critical path has a late start date that is equal to the early start date. Activities that are not on the critical path have *float*, which means that they can be delayed without delaying the overall project. The float for any activity can be determined by the following equation:

$$\text{float} = \text{LS} - \text{ES}$$

6.7   Problems

1. A contractor has a contract for the construction of a service station for a major oil company. The contractor has completed the work breakdown analysis for the project, identified the following project activities, and estimated the duration for each identified activity. Construct a bar chart schedule for the project.

Activity	Duration
Clear and grade site	4 days
Excavate for storage tanks	3 days
Install underground tanks	2 days
Excavate for building foundation	3 days
Construct building foundation	6 days
Backfill foundation and tanks	2 days
Frame building	9 days
Install roof	5 days
Finish building exterior	3 days
Finish building interior	10 days
Install gasoline dispensing equipment	4 days
Site cleanup	1 day

2. Construct a network diagram schedule for the project described in Problem 1.
3. You have been given the task of developing a schedule for the construction of a small industrial project. You have completed the work breakdown analysis, identified the following project activities, and estimated the duration for each activity. Construct a bar chart schedule for the project.

Activity	Duration
Clear and grade site	6 days
Excavate for utilities	3 days
Excavate for building foundation	5 days
Install underground utilities	5 days
Backfill utilities	2 days
Construct building foundation	10 days
Backfill foundation	4 days
Frame building	15 days
Install roof	6 days
Finish building exterior	5 days
Finish building interior	18 days
Install mechanical equipment	9 days
Install perimeter fence	5 days
Construct parking area	6 days
Site cleanup	1 day

4. Construct a network diagram schedule for the project described in Problem 3. Determine the early start and late start for each activity.

Fundamentals of Earthmoving

7.1   Introduction

Earthmoving is the process of moving soil or rock from one location to another, and in some cases, processing it to meet contract specification requirements. Earthmoving construction tasks include excavating, loading, hauling, spreading, compacting, and grading. To determine equipment productivity for a specific task, you must understand both the physical characteristics of the material to be moved and the performance characteristics of the equipment to be used. The material characteristics are discussed in this chapter, and performance characteristics of equipment used in earthmoving will be discussed in Chapters 8 through 16.

The sequence of earthmoving tasks involved in site work include

- Clearing and grubbing, which means the removal of vegetation
- Removal of topsoil, which contains organic material and is unsuitable for construction use
- Excavation for utilities and building foundation
- Removal of excess excavated material not needed for backfill
- Backfill of utility trenches and around foundation, and compaction of fill material
- Grading of site to meet contract requirements
- Spreading and compacting soil in areas to be paved
- Spreading topsoil and landscaping

As discussed in Chapters 4 and 5, equipment selection and productivity estimation are essential to our ability to estimate the cost of site work activities. Before studying specific types of equipment, we will first examine the earthmoving principles that are used to determine equipment productivity. In this chapter, we will discuss some of the primary properties of soil and the effects of soil type and job site conditions on equipment performance.

7.2   *Soil Properties*

Soil properties have a direct effect on equipment selection and productivity. Soils are classified as gravel, sand, silt, clay, organic, or some combination thereof. To obtain the desired properties for construction, soils are often blended. For a detailed discussion of soil properties, refer to a textbook on geotechnical engineering.[1] This book discusses only those properties that affect equipment productivity.

Soil has three basic components: solids, water, and air, as illustrated in Figure 7.1. The air component occupies volume but contributes no weight to the soil mass. Thus the weight of the soil is composed of the weight of the solids and the weight of the water.

The soil properties of interest in earthmoving operations are type of soil and its density and moisture content. The soil type, such as sand, clay, or gravel, affects equipment working conditions. Soil density is expressed in pounds per cubic foot, pounds per cubic yard, or kilograms per cubic meter. It affects equipment productivity, because the equipment carrying capacities are limited by both volume and weight constraints. The **moisture content** is a percentage representing the weight of water in a soil mass divided by the weight of the solids. It is calculated by the following equation:

$$\text{Moisture Content (\%)} = \frac{(\text{Wet Unit Weight} - \text{Dry Unit Weight})(100\%)}{\text{Dry Unit Weight}} \qquad (7\text{--}1)$$

The moisture content of the soil will be of great interest when we discuss compaction in Chapter 15. Let's look at an example problem involving moisture content.

Figure 7.1

Primary Soil Components

From W. L. Schroeder and S. E. Dickenson, *Soils in Construction*, 4/e, ©1996. Reprinted by permission of Prentice-Hall, Inc., Upper Saddle River, NJ.

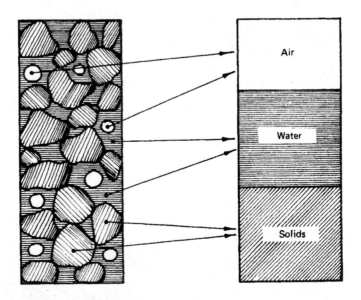

---

[1]*Soils in Construction* by W. L. Schroeder and S. E. Dickenson (Englewood Cliffs, NJ: Prentice-Hall, 1996), and *Soil Mechanics in Engineering Practice*, 3rd ed., by Karl Terzaghi, Ralph B. Peck, and Gholamreza Mesri (New York: John Wiley & Sons, 1996), are good references.

Example 7.1

A contractor is planning to haul in soil to construct a parking lot for a shopping center she is constructing. Density tests taken on the soil in its natural state (wet) indicate a unit weight of 101 pounds per cubic foot. The contractor heated a soil sample in an oven and determined the dry unit weight to be 96 pounds per cubic foot.

a. What is the moisture content of the soil?
b. To minimize the amount of compaction required to achieve the design density for the parking lot, the contractor wants to increase the moisture content to 10%. How many gallons of water should she add to each cubic yard of soil to increase the moisture content to 10%?

Solution

a. Using Equation 7–1

$$\text{Moisture Content} = \frac{(101 \text{ lb./cu. ft.} - 96 \text{ lb./cu. ft.})(100\%)}{96 \text{ lb./cu. ft.}} = \textbf{5.2\%}$$

b. The weight of water that must be added to each cubic foot of soil to increase the moisture content from 5.2% to 10% can be determined as follows:

$$\text{Weight of Additional Water} = \frac{(10\% - 5.2\%)(96 \text{ lb./cu. ft.})}{100\%} = 4.6 \text{ lb./cu. ft.}$$

Since one gallon of water weighs 8.34 pounds, we can determine the volume of additional water needed per cubic yard of soil as follows·

$$\text{Volume of Additonal Water} = \frac{(4.6 \text{ lb./cu. ft.})(27 \text{ cu. ft./cu. yd.})}{8.34 \text{ lb./gal.}} = \textbf{14.9 gal./cu. yd.}$$

7.3   Swell and Shrinkage

When soil is loosened and excavated, it breaks up into different-sized particles, creating air pockets or voids that reduce its density. This increase in volume or reduction in density is known as *swell.* The density of soil in its natural state or in situ is known as its *bank* (or "in-place") density. When excavated, the density of the soil decreases and is referred to as its *loose* density. To convert bank density to loose density, we need to determine the *percent swell* of the soil, which is defined as

$$\text{Percent Swell} = \frac{(V_L - V_B)(100\%)}{V_B} \tag{7--2}$$

where V_L is the loose volume
V_B is the bank volume

Table 7.1

Representative Material Properties

Material	Loose Density		Bank Density		Percent Swell
	lb./cu. yd.	*kg./cu. m.*	*lb./cu. yd.*	*kg./cu. m.*	
Clay, dry	2,500	1,480	3,100	1,840	24%
Clay, wet	2,800	1,660	3,500	2,080	25%
Clay & gravel, dry	2,400	1,420	2,800	1,660	17%
Clay & gravel, wet	2,600	1,540	3,100	1,840	19%
Earth, dry	2,550	1,510	3,200	1,900	25%
Earth, wet	2,700	1,600	3,400	2,020	26%
Gravel, dry	2,850	1,690	3,200	1,900	12%
Gravel, wet	3,400	2,020	3,800	2,260	12%
Limestone	2,600	1,540	4,400	2,610	69%
Loam	2,100	1,250	2,600	1,540	24%
Sand, dry	2,400	1,420	2,700	1,600	13%
Sand, wet	3,100	1,840	3,500	2,080	13%
Sandstone	2,550	1,510	4,250	2,520	67%
Shale	2,100	1,250	2,800	1,660	33%

Data for this table was extracted from *Caterpillar Performance Handbook*, 28th ed.
(Peoria, IL: Caterpillar Inc., 1997), p. 26-4.

Since density is weight per unit volume, we can rewrite Equation 7–2 in terms of density as

$$\text{Percent Swell} = \frac{(D_B - D_L)(100\%)}{D_L} \qquad (7\text{–}3)$$

where D_B is the bank density

D_L is the loose density

Bank and loose densities for typical soils are shown in Table 7.1.

Solving Equation 7–2 for V_B yields the following equation, which will be useful in converting loose volume to bank volume:

$$V_B = \frac{(V_L)(100\%)}{100\% + \text{Percent Swell}} \qquad (7\text{–}4)$$

When soil is compacted, some of the air is forced out, which reduces the soil void spaces and thus increases the soil density. The resulting compacted density usually is greater than the in situ or natural bank density. This decrease in volume (increase in density) is called **shrinkage.** To convert bank density to compacted density, we need to determine the percent shrinkage of the soil, which is defined as

$$\text{Percent Shrinkage} = \frac{(V_B - V_C)(100\%)}{V_B} \qquad (7\text{–}5)$$

where V_C is the compacted volume

          V_B is the bank volume

We can rewrite Equation 7–5 in terms of density as

$$\text{Percent Shrinkage} = \frac{(D_C - D_B)(100\%)}{D_C} \tag{7–6}$$

where D_B is the bank density

          D_C is the compacted density

The percent shrinkage that will occur on a project is a function of both the soil type and the amount of compaction applied to the soil. Because the compactive effort varies, a table similar to Table 7.1 cannot be developed providing percent shrinkage for each soil type. Compacted densities normally are determined in a laboratory or from on-site measurement. As a rule of thumb, you can expect sandy soils to shrink between 10% and 15%, clay soils to shrink between 15% and 25%, and soil with high organic content to shrink about 40%.[2]

Solving Equation 7–5 for V_B yields the following equation that will be useful in converting compacted volume to bank volume:

$$V_B = \frac{(V_C)(100\%)}{100\% - \text{Percent Shrinkage}} \tag{7–7}$$

Combining Equations 7–4 and 7–7 yields the following useful relationship between loose volume and compacted volume:

$$V_L = \frac{(V_C)(100\% + \text{Percent Swell})}{100\% - \text{Percent Shrinkage}} \tag{7–8}$$

Soil volume changes due to excavation and compaction are illustrated in Figure 7.2. Bank volume is used when determining the volume of material to be excavated. This is the unit measure for performing the quantity takeoff from construction drawings. Loose volume is used to describe the volume capacity of excavating and hauling equipment. Compacted volume is used to determine the volume of any earth structure such as a dam or fill. It represents the volume after the required compactive effort has been applied. Students must become familiar with converting a volume from bank to loose, and from loose or bank to compacted. To clearly define which unit of measure is being used, the following notation convention will be used in this book:

Bank volume	BCY for bank (or in-place) cubic yards
Loose volume	LCY for loose cubic yards
Compacted volume	CCY for compacted cubic yards

Now let's look an example problem involving swell and shrinkage.

---

[2]"Construction Equipment's Earthmoving Encyclopedia," in *Construction Equipment* (July 1984): 36.

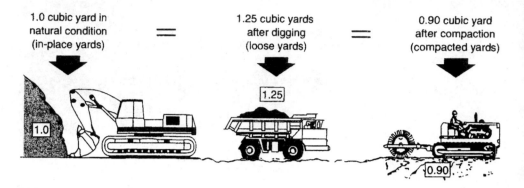

Figure 7.2

Soil Volume Change During Excavation and Compaction

S. W. Nunnally, *Construction Methods and Management*, 4/e, ©1998. Reprinted by permission of Prentice-Hall, Inc., Upper Saddle River, NJ.

Example 7.2

A contractor has a contract for the construction of a new school. One of the project tasks is the construction of a compacted fill that will be used as a parking lot for the school. Inspection of the project plans indicates that 10,000 compacted cubic yards are required for the fill. The contractor has selected a source for the fill material and determined the bank density to be 2,800 pounds per cubic yard, the loose density to be 2,240 pounds per cubic yard, and the compacted density to be 3,415 pounds per cubic yard. He plans to excavate the fill material with a wheeled loader and load dump trucks that will haul the soil to the construction site.

a. What is the percent swell for the fill material?
b. What is the percent shrinkage for the fill material?
c. How many loose cubic yards must the contractor haul in the dump trucks?
d. How many bank cubic yards must the contractor excavate with the loader?

Solution

a. Using Equation 7–3

$$\text{Percent Swell} = \frac{[(2{,}800 \text{ lb./cu. yd.}) - (2{,}240 \text{ lb./cu. yd.})](100\%)}{2{,}240 \text{ lb./cu. yd.}} = \mathbf{25\%}$$

b. Using Equation 7–6

$$\text{Percent Shrinkage} = \frac{[(3{,}415 \text{ lb./cu. yd.}) - (2{,}800 \text{ lb./cu. yd.})](100\%)}{3{,}415 \text{ lb./cu. yd.}} = \mathbf{18\%}$$

c. Using Equation 7–8

$$V_L = \frac{(10{,}000 \text{ CCY})(100\% + 25\%)}{(100\% - 18\%)} = \frac{(10{,}000 \text{ CCY})(125\%)}{82\%} = \mathbf{15{,}244 \text{ LCY}}$$

d. Using Equation 7–7

$$V_B = \frac{(10{,}000 \text{ CCY})(100\%)}{(100\% - 18\%)} = \frac{(10{,}000 \text{ CCY})(100\%)}{82\%} = \textbf{12{,}195 BCY}$$

7.4 Rolling Resistance

Rolling resistance is the resistance of the equipment operating surface to the forward or reverse movement of a piece of wheeled equipment. *It does not apply to tracked equipment*, because the idler, rollers, and sprocket always run on steel track rails. It results from internal friction of the wheel bearings, tire flexing, and penetration of the operating surface due to the pressure of the tires. Penetration is not necessary if the operating surface deflects under load. Rolling resistance is expressed in pounds of resistance per ton of gross weight. It varies with the size, air pressure, and tread of the tires and the condition of the operating surface.

Experience has shown that the minimum rolling resistance (no penetration of the operating surface) is about 40 pounds per ton of gross weight on the tires (30 pounds per ton for radial or dual tires). Additional rolling resistance due to tire penetration is about 30 pounds per ton of gross weight on the tires per inch of penetration.[3] Thus, the rolling resistance for a given operating surface may be estimated by the following equation:

$$\text{Rolling Resistance (lb./ton)} = 40 \text{ lb./ton}^4$$
$$+ [(30 \text{ lb./ton per in.})(\text{in. of tire penetration})] \quad (7\text{--}9)$$

Resistance due to internal friction has been considered by manufacturers in the development of tracked equipment performance charts. Rolling resistance must be considered, however, if a tracked piece of equipment is used to tow a wheeled vehicle. The resisting force due to rolling resistance will be the rolling resistance times the weight of the trailer.

It is not possible to predetermine the rolling resistance of a given operating surface without measuring tire penetration. Table 7.2 provides representative values that can be used for estimating purposes if tire penetration is not known.

The resisting force caused by the rolling resistance (F_{RR}) that acts against the forward or reverse movement of the equipment can be found by the following equation:

$$F_{RR} \text{ (lb.)} = [\text{Rolling Resistance (lb./ton)}][\text{Total Weight (ton)}] \quad (7\text{--}10)$$

7.5 Grade Resistance

Grade resistance is the force due to gravity that a piece of equipment must overcome when moving up a grade. When a vehicle moves down a grade, the force of gravity that assists vehicle movement is called *grade assistance*. Grades are usually described in

---

[3]*Caterpillar Performance Handbook*, 28th ed. (Peoria, IL: Caterpillar Inc., 1997), p. 21-5.
[4]Use 30 lb./ton for radial or dual tires.

Table 7.2

Representative Rolling Resistances for Various Types of Operating Surfaces

Type Operating Surface	Rolling Resistance
Asphalt or Concrete	40 lb./ton
Dirt Surface: Smooth, hard, dry; well-maintained; free of loose material	50 lb./ton
Dirt Surface: Dry, but not firmly packed; some loose material	70 lb./ton
Dirt Surface: Soft; poorly maintained	120 lb./ton
Dirt Surface: Deeply rutted	300 lb./ton
Sand or Gravel: Packed	60 lb./ton
Sand or Gravel: Loose	200 lb./ton

Data for this table was developed from *Production and Cost Estimating of Material Movement with Earthmoving Equipment* (Hudson, OH: Terex Corporation, 1981), p. 18.

terms of percent slope, which is equal to the change in elevation divided by the horizontal distance times 100. For example, a slope that rises 5 feet per 100 feet would be a 5% slope.

Grade resistance (or grade assistance) is equal to 20 pounds per ton of gross weight on the tires or tracks per percent slope. *Note that grade resistance affects both wheeled and tracked equipment.* Grade resistance can thus be calculated as follows:

$$\text{Grade Resistance (lb./ton)} = (20 \text{ lb./ton per \% slope})(\% \text{ slope}) \qquad (7\text{--}11)$$

The resisting force caused by the grade resistance (F_{GR}) that acts against the forward or reverse movement of the item of equipment can be found using the following equation:

$$F_{GR} \text{ (lb.)} = [\text{Grade Resistance (lb./ton)}][\text{Total Weight (ton)}] \qquad (7\text{--}12)$$

7.6   *Total Resistance*

The ***total resisting force*** (F_R) acting against the forward or reverse movement of an item of equipment is the sum of the force due to rolling resistance and the force due to grade resistance.

$$F_R \text{ (lb.)} = F_{RR} \text{ (lb.)} + F_{GR} \text{ (lb.)} \qquad (7\text{--}13)$$

Sometimes the total resisting force is expressed in percentage terms and called the ***effective grade***. The effective grade can be used with some manufacturers' equipment performance charts to determine equipment speed. The effective grade can be determined by the following equation:

$$\text{Effective Grade (\%)} = \text{Actual Grade (\%)} + \frac{\text{Rolling Resistance (lb./ton)}}{20 \text{ lb./ton per \% slope}} \qquad (7\text{--}14)$$

Now let's look at an example problem involving both rolling resistance and grade resistance. *A piece of construction equipment must generate enough force to overcome the total resisting force if it is to move and perform the desired task.*

Example 7.3

A contractor plans to use Caterpillar 623F elevating scrapers to construct a 3-foot compacted fill that will support the concrete slab foundations for a warehouse complex. The empty weight of the scrapers is 38.5 tons, and the contractor has not equipped the four-wheeled scrapers with radial tires. The 2-mile haul road between the borrow site and the construction site has an average uphill grade of 4% when traveling from the borrow site to the construction site. When fully loaded, the scrapers will carry 21.5 tons (loose volume) of fill material. The contractor inspected the haul road, watching a loaded scraper pass, and estimated that the average tire penetration was about 1.5 inches.

a. What do you estimate the rolling resistance force to be against a fully loaded scraper?
b. What do you estimate the grade resistance force to be against a fully loaded scraper?
c. What do you estimate the total resisting forces to be against the scraper on its return trip from the construction site to the borrow site?

Solution

a. Using Equation 7–9

$$\text{Rolling Resistance} = 40 \text{ lb./ton} + [(30 \text{ lb./ton per in.})(1.5 \text{ in.})] = 85 \text{ lb./ton}$$

Using Equation 7–10

$$F_{RR} = (85 \text{ lb./ton})(38.5 \text{ ton} + 21.5 \text{ ton}) = \textbf{5,100 lb.}$$

b. Using Equation 7-11

$$\text{Grade Resistance} = (20 \text{ lb./ton per \% slope})(4\%) = 80 \text{ lb./ton}$$

Using Equation 7–12

$$F_{GR} = (80 \text{ lb./ton})(38.5 \text{ ton} + 21.5 \text{ ton}) = \textbf{4,800 lb.}$$

c. Using Equation 7–10

$$F_{RR} = (85 \text{ lb./ton})(38.5 \text{ ton}) = 3,273 \text{ lb.}$$

Using Equation 7-12

$$F_{GR} = (80 \text{ lb./ton})(38.5 \text{ ton}) = 3,080 \text{ lb.}$$

Using Equation 7–13

$$F_R = 3,273 \text{ lb.} - 3,080 \text{ lb.} = \textbf{193 lb.}$$

Note that a negative grade resistance (grade assistance) is used because the haul road slopes down at a 4% grade when traveling from the construction site to the borrow site.

7.7   Drawbar Pull

The power available to move a crawler tractor and its load is called ***drawbar pull***. The tractor applies force to the ground through its tracks when working. Drawbar pull (usually expressed in pounds) is the power available at the rear hitch of the tractor (called the

Figure 7.3

Performance Chart for Caterpillar D6R Crawler Tractor

Courtesy Caterpillar Inc.

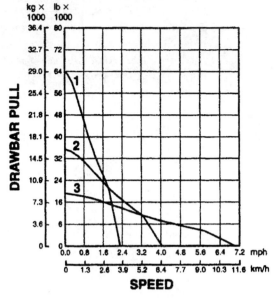

**D6R Standard
Steering Clutches & Brakes (FTC)**

KEY

1 — 1st Gear
2 — 2nd Gear
3 — 3rd Gear

drawbar) when operated under standard conditions. Manufacturers provide performance charts for their tractors that show the available drawbar pull at various speeds and gears. These charts are used to determine cycle times for crawler tractors, which is a key component in productivity estimation. An example of a manufacturer's performance chart is shown in Figure 7.3. *In order to move a load, a crawler tractor must generate more drawbar pull than the total resisting force acting against it.*

7.8 Rimpull

The power available to move a wheeled piece of equipment and its load is called **rimpull.** It is the term that is used to describe the pushing force exerted by the tires against the operating surface (ground). Rimpull (expressed in pounds) is the power available at the rims of the driving wheels under standard operating conditions. Manufacturers provide performance charts for their wheeled equipment that show available rimpull at various speeds and gears. These charts are used to determine travel speeds (and ultimately cycle time) for wheeled equipment. An example of a manufacturer's performance chart is shown in Figure 7.4.

621F Rimpull-Speed-Gradeability
● 33.25-29 Tires | **Wheel Tractor-Scrapers**

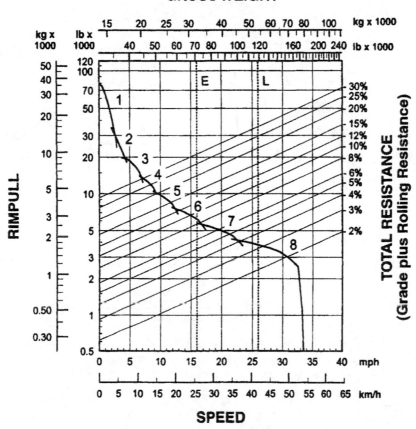

KEY

1 — 1st Gear Torque Converter Drive
2 — 2nd Gear Torque Converter Drive
3 — 3rd Gear Direct Drive
4 — 4th Gear Direct Drive
5 — 5th Gear Direct Drive
6 — 6th Gear Direct Drive
7 — 7th Gear Direct Drive
8 — 8th Gear Direct Drive

KEY

E — Empty 32 070 kg (70,700 lb)
L — Loaded 53 843 kg (118,700 lb)

Figure 7.4
Performance Chart for Caterpillar 621F Wheeled Scraper
Courtesy Caterpillar Inc.

If manufacturers' performance charts are not available for a specific item of equipment, the available rimpull for a specific speed can be estimated by using the following equation:[5]

$$\text{Available Rimpull (lb.)} = \frac{(375)(IIP)(\text{Gear Train Efficiency})}{\text{Speed (mph)}} \qquad (7\text{--}15)$$

where   *IIP* is the engine horsepower

The gear train efficiency is a function of the gear ratios between the engine and the driving wheels. It ranges from 0.70 to 0.85 for most construction equipment.

In order to move a load, wheeled equipment must generate rimpull that is greater than the total resisting forces (sum of the grade resistance force and the rolling resistance force) *acting against it.*

7.9   *Effects of Altitude*

The available drawbar pull or rimpull determined from a manufacturer's performance chart or calculated using Equation 7–15 is for standard conditions, which generally means sea level. At higher altitudes internal combustion engines lose power because of the decreased density of the air, which affects the fuel-to-air ratio in the combustion chamber of the engine, and the available drawbar pull or rimpull will be less. To determine the effect of altitude on engine performance, it is necessary to calculate a ***derating factor.*** This factor will be used to correct the value determined from a manufacturer's performance chart or calculated with Equation 7–15 when estimating equipment performance at higher altitudes. Some manufacturers publish derating factors for their equipment at various altitudes. If such charts are not available, the following rules of thumb can be used to determine a derating factor:[6]

- For four-cycle naturally respirated engines: engine performance is about the same up to 1,000 feet and then decreases about 3% for each 1,000 feet above 1,000 feet.
- For two-cycle naturally respirated engines: engine performance decreases about 1.5% for each 1,000 feet above sea level up to 6,000 feet, and 3% for each 1,000 feet above 6,000 feet.
- For turbocharged engines, there is generally no loss in power up to about 10,000 feet. Derating factors for altitudes above 10,000 feet are quite variable and should come from the manufacturer.

Therefore, for a four-cycle naturally respired engine, the derating factor, which is a measure of power loss due to altitude, can be estimated by the following equation:

$$\text{Derating Factor} = \frac{(0.03)[\text{altitude (ft.)} - 1,000\ (\text{ft.})]}{1,000\ (\text{ft.})} \qquad (7\text{--}16)$$

---

[5]*Factors in Earthmoving* (Moline, IL: Deere & Co., 1989), p. 9.

[6]*Production and Cost Estimating of Material Movement with Earthmoving Equipment* (Hudson, OH: Terex Corporation, 1981), pp. 21–22.

7.10   Traction

The available drawbar pull or rimpull determined from a manufacturer's performance chart or Equation 7–15 and corrected for altitude assumes that adequate traction exists and that the tracks or wheels do not slip. The amount of traction that is available is a function of the type of soil over which the equipment is operating and the weight on the driving wheels or the tracks. The degree of traction between the tire or track and the ground is called the *coefficient of traction*, which is defined as a factor that is multiplied by the total load on a driving wheel or track to determine the maximum possible tractive force that can be applied to the operating surface just before slipping occurs. *The maximum usable drawbar pull or rimpull that can be generated by a piece of equipment is therefore limited by the coefficient of traction* and can be determined by the following equation:

Maximum Usable Tractive Force (drawbar pull or rimpull) (lb.)
= (Coefficient of Traction)[Weight (lb.) on Driving Wheels or Tracks]   (7–17)

Drawbar pull or rimpull generated in excess of that determined by Equation 7–17 will simply cause the wheels or tracks to spin. Typical coefficients of traction for common operating surfaces are provided in Table 7–3.

7.11   Equipment Performance

The productivity of earthmoving equipment is determined by the volume of material carried per load and the number of loads carried (or cycles) per hour. The volume carried is a function of the material characteristics (swell and density) and the equipment capacity. The cycle time is a function of *fixed time* (load and unload time) and *variable*

Table 7.3
Typical Coefficients of Traction

Type of Surface	Rubber Tires	Crawler Tracks
Concrete	0.90	0.45
Clay loam, dry	0.55	0.90
Clay loam, wet	0.45	0.70
Rutted clay loam	0.40	0.70
Sand, dry	0.20	0.30
Sand, wet	0.40	0.50
Quarry pit	0.65	0.55
Gravel road, loose·	0.36	0.50
Firm earth	0.55	0.90
Loose earth	0.45	0.60
Packed snow	0.20	0.27
Ice	0.12	0.12

Caterpillar Performance Handbook, 28th ed. (Peoria, IL: Caterpillar Inc., 1997), p. 26-2.

time (travel time). Travel time is a function of the equipment speed, which is a function of the total resisting forces and available traction. Let's look at two example problems to illustrate these principles.

Example 7.4

A contractor is planning to use a Caterpillar D6R crawler tractor (manufacturer's performance data is shown in Figure 7.3) to clear and grub a construction site. The tractor is powered with a six-cylinder turbocharged diesel engine and weighs 39,800 pounds. The ground conditions are very muddy with an estimated coefficient of traction of 0.6. The construction site is located at an elevation of 4,000 feet. What is the maximum speed that the tractor can clear and grub when operating in second gear up an 8% slope?

Solution

The first step is to determine the maximum usable drawbar pull that can be developed by the tractor before the tracks start to spin. Using Equation 7–17

$$\text{Maximum Usable Drawbar Pull} = (0.6)(39,800 \text{ lb.}) = 23,880 \text{ lb.}$$

Next, we need to determine the total resisting force, which in the case of a crawler tractor is only grade resistance. Using Equations 7–11 and 7–12,

$$F_{GR} + \frac{(20 \text{ lb./ton per \% slope})(8\%)(39,800 \text{ lb.})}{2,000 \text{ lb./ton}} = 3,184 \text{ lb.}$$

Since the drawbar pull required to overcome the total resisting force is less than the maximum usable drawbar pull determined from the coefficient of traction, the tractor can perform the job.

The tractor is powered with a turbocharged engine, so no derating factor is required below 10,000 feet of elevation. Therefore, the maximum speed can be read directly from Figure 7.3 by finding the minimum drawbar pull required (3,184 lb.) on the left axis, reading across to intersect the second-gear performance line, and reading down to determine the maximum speed, which in this case is **3.8 miles per hour in second gear.**

Example 7.5

A contractor is planning to use 16-cubic-yard dump trucks to haul away excess material generated by the excavation of a large foundation. The trucks are powered with 180-horsepower, four-cycle naturally respirated engines, and the gear train efficiency is estimated to be 0.75. The project site is at an elevation of 2,000 feet. The gross weight of a fully loaded truck is 35 tons, and 65% of the loaded weight is carried by the rear driving wheels. The haul road to be used by the trucks slopes up at a 3% grade, tire penetration is estimated at 1 inch, and the coefficient of traction is estimated to be 0.55. The trucks are not equipped with radial tires, and manufacturer's performance data contains the following information:

Gear	Speed
1	2 mph
2	7 mph
3	12 mph
4	20 mph

What is the maximum speed that a fully loaded dump truck can traverse the 3% grade?

Solution

The first step is to determine the maximum usable rimpull that can be developed by the trucks before the wheels spin. Using Equation 7–17

$$\text{Maximum Usable Rimpull} = (0.55)(0.65)(35 \text{ ton})(2{,}000 \text{ lb./ton}) = 25{,}025 \text{ lb.}$$

Note that only 65% of the gross weight is carried by the driving wheels.
Next we need to determine the total resisting forces. Using Equation 7–9

$$\text{Rolling Resistance} = 40 \text{ lb./ton} + [(30 \text{ lb./ton per in.})(1 \text{ in.})] = 70 \text{ lb./ton}$$

Using Equation 7–10

$$F_{RR} = (70 \text{ lb./ton})(35 \text{ ton}) = 2{,}450 \text{ lb.}$$

Using Equations 7–11 and 7–12

$$F_{GR} = (20 \text{ lb./ton per } \% \text{ slope})(3\%)(35 \text{ ton}) = 2{,}100 \text{ lb.}$$

Using Equation 7–13

$$F_R = 2{,}450 \text{ lb.} + 2{,}100 \text{ lb.} = 4{,}550 \text{ lb.}$$

Since the rimpull required to overcome the total resisting force is less than the maximum usable rimpull determined with the coefficient of traction, the trucks can perform the hauling task.

Now we need to determine the available rimpull developed by the truck in each of the gears. Since we have no manufacturer's performance chart, we must use Equation 7–15 to estimate the available rimpull. Let's start with fourth gear. Using Equation 7–15

$$\text{Available Rimpull} = \frac{(375)(180 \text{ HP})(0.75)}{20 \text{ mph}} = 2{,}531 \text{ lb.}$$

Equation 7–15 estimates available rimpull under standard conditions, and we must determine a derating factor, since the project site is at 2,000 feet. Using Equation 7–16

$$\text{Derating Factor} = \frac{(0.03)(2{,}000 \text{ ft.} - 1{,}000 \text{ ft.})}{1{,}000 \text{ ft.}} = 0.03$$

Since the truck engines lose 3% of their sea level performance at 2,000 feet, the available rimpull in fourth gear at 2,000 feet is

$$2532 - (3,531 \text{ lb.})(1 - 0.03) = (3,531 \text{ lb.})(0.97) = 2,455 \text{ lb.}$$

Since the available rimpull in fourth gear is less than that required to overcome the total resisting force, the trucks cannot perform the hauling task in fourth gear. Let's look at third gear. Using Equation 7–15

$$\text{Available Rimpull} = \frac{(375)(180 \text{ HP})(0.75)}{12 \text{ mph}} = 4,219 \text{ lb.}$$

Adjusting for the 2,000 feet elevation, the available rimpull is

$$(4,219 \text{ lb.})(0.97) = 4,092 \text{ lb.}$$

Since the available rimpull in third gear is less than that required to overcome the total resisting force, the trucks cannot perform the hauling task in third gear. Let's look at second gear. Using Equation 7–15

$$\text{Available Rimpull} = \frac{(375)(180 \text{ HP})(0.75)}{7 \text{ mph}} = 7,232 \text{ lb.}$$

Adjusting for the 2,000 feet elevation, the available rimpull is

$$(7,232 \text{ lb.})(0.97) = 7,015 \text{ lb.}$$

Since the available rimpull in second gear is greater than the total resisting force, the trucks can perform the hauling task in second gear at a maximum speed of **7 miles per hour.**

7.12   Problems

1. A contractor is excavating fill material from a borrow site to be used to construct a compacted fill foundation for a parking garage. She has determined that 5,000 compacted cubic yards of soil are required to complete the structural fill. The in situ density of the fill material is 110 pounds per cubic foot, the loose density is 88 pounds per cubic foot, and the compacted density is 125 pounds per cubic foot.
   a. What is the percent swell for the fill material?
   b. What is the percent shrinkage for the fill material?
   c. How many loose cubic yards must be hauled in trucks from the borrow site to construct the fill?
   d. How many bank cubic yards must be excavated and loaded on the trucks to construct the fill?

2. A contractor is planning to haul in fill material to backfill around the foundation of a large commercial building. Tests on the fill material indicate a bank wet unit weight of 98 pounds per cubic foot, a bank dry unit weight of 95 pounds per cubic foot, and a swell of 18%. When compacted to the desired density, the wet soil weighs 111 pounds per cubic foot. Proctor tests indicate that the optimum moisture content for

compacting the soil is about 8%. The total volume of the required backfill is 10,000 compacted cubic yards.

   a. How many bank cubic yards of soil must be excavated and hauled to the project site to construct the backfill?

   b. How many gallons of water should be added to each loose cubic yard of soil delivered to the project site to increase the soil moisture content to 8%?

3. A contractor is planning to use a Caterpillar 5080 excavator to remove the soil for the construction of the foundation for a new hotel. He has determined from the project plans that 3,000 bank cubic yards must be excavated and that 817 compacted cubic yards will be required to backfill the completed foundation. The contractor plans to stockpile the soil needed for backfill on site and haul the excess soil off site using Caterpillar 769C trucks that have a heaped capacity of 30 loose cubic yards. The contractor had the soil tested and determined that the bank density is 2,800 pounds per cubic yard, the loose density is 2,295 pounds per cubic yard, and the compacted density is 3,256 pounds per cubic yard.

   a. What is the percent swell for the soil?

   b. What is the percent shrinkage for the soil after being compacted?

   c. How many bank cubic yards should be stockpiled to be used for the backfill operation?

   d. How many truck loads of excess material should be hauled off site if the trucks are fully loaded to their heaped capacity?

   e. The haul road to be used by the trucks has a 6% average uphill grade. The tire penetration is estimated to be 2.5 inches, and the trucks are not equipped with radial tires. The empty weight of the truck is 68,750 pounds. What is the total resisting force the truck must overcome when traversing the haul road fully loaded?

   f. What is the maximum usable tractive force that can be generated by the truck when operating fully loaded on the haul road if the coefficient of traction is estimated to be 0.5 and 67% of the loaded weight is carried by the rear driving wheels?

4. A wheeled scraper is being used to excavate the side of a hill to construct a level site for the construction of an office building. The scraper weighs 150,000 pounds loaded and 90,000 pounds empty and is equipped with radial tires. The weight distribution is as follows:

Loaded	Empty
60% rear tires	40% rear tires
40% front tires	60% front tires

Only the front tires are powered, and the coefficient of traction for the haul road is 0.3.

   a. What is the total resisting force when the scraper is operated empty up a 3% slope over a road surface with a tire penetration estimated to be 2 inches?

   b. What is the total resisting force when the scraper is operated fully loaded up a 5% slope over a road with a tire penetration estimated to be 0.5 inch?

   c. What is the maximum usable tractive force that can be generated by the scraper when operated empty?

5. A crawler tractor (powered with a four-cycle, naturally respirated engine) is being used to excavate for the foundation of a new four-story office building. The construction site is very muddy (the coefficient of traction is estimated to be 0.7). You determined the following information from the manufacturer's data:

Gear	Drawbar Pull	
1	27,530 lb.	Flywheel Horsepower = 165 HP
2	20,960 lb.	Operating Weight = 39,000 lb.
3	15,740 lb.	

The site is located at an elevation of about 4,000 feet. A ramp at a 6% slope will be used to remove spoil from the excavation.
   a. What is the total resisting force?
   b. What is the maximum tractive force that can be applied without the tracks slipping?
   c. What is the maximum drawbar pull available to move a load when pushing spoil up the 6% ramp in first gear?

6. A contractor owns a Caterpillar D6R crawler tractor and plans to use it to clear and grub a project site and then to excavate for the basements of condominiums to be built on the site. The tractor is powered with a six-cylinder turbocharged diesel engine and weighs 40,000 pounds. A manufacturer's performance chart for the D6R tractor is shown in Figure 7.3. The project site is at an elevation of 4,000 feet, and the coefficient of traction for the soil conditions is estimated to be 0.7.
   a. What is the maximum usable drawbar pull that the tractor can develop before the tracks begin to slip?
   b. What is the maximum speed the tractor can clear and grub up a 10% slope while operating in second gear?
   c. What is the maximum speed the tractor can push the excavated soil up a 15% ramp out of the basement area while operating in first gear?

7. A fully loaded wheeled scraper must travel up a 3% slope on an unmaintained haul road (rolling resistance is estimated to be 200 pounds per ton and the coefficient of traction is estimated to be 0.45). The construction site is located at an elevation of 5,000 feet. You obtain the following information from the manufacturer's data:

Engine: four-cycle, naturally respirated

Gear	Speed	
1	3.4 mph	Flywheel Horsepower = 450 HP
2	4.8 mph	Empty Weight = 97,000 lb.
3	6.0 mph	
4	9.0 mph	Loaded Weight = 172,000 lb.

Only the front tires are powered, and you determine the following weight distribution from the manufacturer's data:

Loaded	Empty
50% rear tires	37% rear tires
50% front tires	63% front tires

a. What is the total resisting force?

b. What is the maximum available rimpull in each gear, if the gear train efficiency is 80%?

c. What is the maximum speed the scraper can operate at on the haul road when loaded?

d. What would be the maximum speed, if the haul road were properly maintained with a rolling resistance of 50 pounds per ton?

Tractors

8.1   Introduction

A tractor is a self-propelled machine that is used to pull a load or attachment or push a load with a front-mounted blade. Tractors are either mounted on tracks, often referred to as *crawler tractors*, or on wheels. A typical crawler tractor is illustrated in Figure 8.1, and a typical wheeled tractor is illustrated in Figure 8.2. Tractors with front-mounted

Figure 8.1
A Crawler Tractor at Work on a
Construction Project
Courtesy Caterpillar Inc.

Figure 8.2
Wheeled Tractor
Courtesy Caterpillar Inc.

blades often are referred to as *dozers* or *bulldozers*. Tractors are very versatile equipment that are used to perform many earthmoving tasks. Crawler tractors generally require some form of truck transportation when being moved from one project site to another, while wheeled tractors usually can be driven from one project site to another.

8.2   *Types and Uses of Tractors*

Crawler tractors are operated at slow speeds (6 to 7 miles per hour), but possess good flotation (low ground pressure) and traction. Wheeled tractors can be operated at higher speeds (up to 30 miles per hour), but exert more ground pressure and generally have lower coefficients of traction. Wheeled tractors are used where mobility and speed are required and the ground conditions are firm. Crawler tractors perform best at speeds up to 3 miles per hour, while wheeled tractors are designed to work best at speeds between 3 and 5 miles per hour. As shown in Figure 5.2, tractors generally are not cost effective if the material is to be moved more than 100 yards. Performance characteristics for a typical tracked tractor are shown in Figure 8.3 and for a typical wheeled tractor are shown in Figure 8.4. As was discussed in Chapter 7, both rolling resistance and grade resistance must be considered in determining rimpull requirements for a wheeled tractor, while only grade resistance is considered in determining drawbar pull requirements for a tracked tractor.

Tractors are multifunctional pieces of equipment that may be used for any of the following operations:

- Backfilling trenches
- Clearing and grubbing
- Creating stockpiles

Figure 8.3

Performance Chart for Caterpillar
D7G Tracked Tractor

Courtesy Caterpillar Inc.

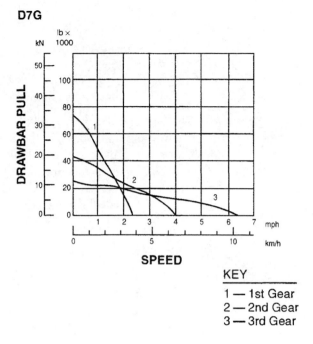

D7G

KEY
1 — 1st Gear
2 — 2nd Gear
3 — 3rd Gear

Figure 8.4

Performance Chart for Caterpillar
814F Wheeled Tractor

Courtesy Caterpillar Inc.

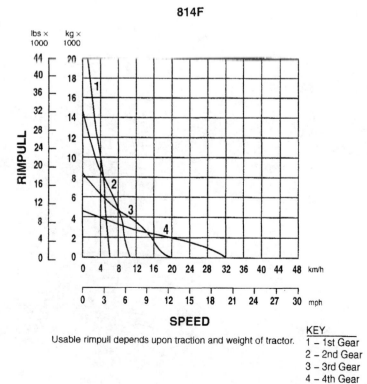

814F

Usable rimpull depends upon traction and weight of tractor.

KEY
1 – 1st Gear
2 – 2nd Gear
3 – 3rd Gear
4 – 4th Gear

- Excavating
- Push loading scrapers
- Ripping compacted soil
- Shaping slopes
- Spreading materials
- Towing compaction equipment

The type and size of tractor to be selected for a given task is greatly influenced by the site working conditions and the scope of the work to be performed. The maximum push or pull that can be exerted is limited by the weight of the tractor and the coefficient of traction. Larger tractors are more productive than are smaller ones, but they cost more per hour to own or rent and operate. The objective is to select the type and size tractor that can accomplish the required tasks in the desired time at the least cost.

8.3   *Tractor Attachments*

There are a number of types of blades that are used on tractors. The four most commonly used are illustrated in Figure 8.5. The straight blade is supported at each end by push arms. It can be tilted by lowering one end to dig a V-ditch in the ground. The straight blade is a heavy-duty blade used for excavating and clearing and grubbing. Angle blades generally are wider than straight blades and can be angled to the right or left. They are used for side casting, such as backfilling a trench. The universal blade is curved over its entire length, reducing the amount of spillage around the ends of the blade. It provides greater load-carrying capacity. Cushion blades are reinforced in the center and are used to push load scrapers.

Figure 8.5
Common Types of Tractor Blades

S. W. Nunnally, *Construction Methods and Management*, 4/e, ©1998. Reprinted by permission of Prentice-Hall, Inc., Upper Saddle River, NJ.

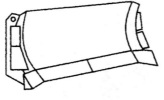

Straight blade

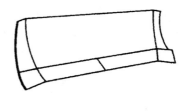

Angle blade

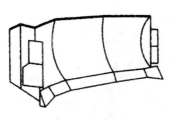

Universal blade

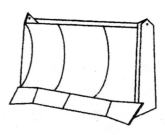

Cushion blade

Figure 8.6
Tractor-Mounted Hydraulically
Operated Ripper

Courtesy John Deere

A ripper may be mounted on the rear of a crawler tractor, as shown in Figure 8.6, to be used to loosen compacted soil or rip weak and weathered rock. A ripper is a plowlike attachment that is forced into the ground and pulled forward, breaking the soil. Rippers often are used to loosen the soil to make it easier for scrapers to excavate and load the material. Ripping is a slow operation, with tractors traveling at speeds under 1 mile per hour.

8.4   *Production Estimation*

A tractor moves earth by lowering the blade and cutting until a full load of soil is obtained in front of the blade. The tractor then pushes the load across the ground to the desired location. Tractor productivity depends on the following factors:

- Size and configuration of the blade
- Size of the tractor
- Distance the material is to be moved
- Type and condition of material to be moved
- Working conditions (rolling resistance, grade resistance, coefficient of traction, and elevation)

Tractor productivity is estimated by

- Estimating the volume of earth that can be moved by the tractor during each operating cycle
- Estimating the number of operating cycles that can be completed during an operating hour

The volume of earth that can be moved per operating cycle varies depending on the type of soil to be moved, as illustrated in Figure 8.7.

Figure 8.7
Configuration of Tractor Blade
Load for Different Soil Types
Courtesy TEREX Americas

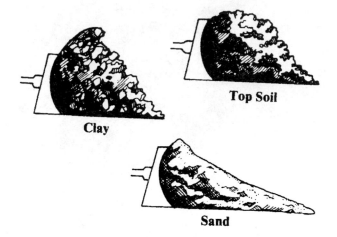

Clay

Top Soil

Sand

Therefore, as shown in Figure 8.8, measurements should be taken to estimate the blade load. Using these measurements, the volume of earth that can be moved during each operating cycle can be estimated by the following equation:

$$V = (0.375)(W)(H)(L) \tag{8–1}$$

where $W = 0.5(W_1 + W_2)$

           $H = 0.5(H_1 + H_2)$

           W_1 and W_2 are load width measurements as shown in Figure 8.8

           H_1 and H_2 are load height measurements as shown in Figure 8.8

           L is the length of the load (width of the blade)

Figure 8.8
Tractor Blade Load Measurements
Courtesy TEREX Americas

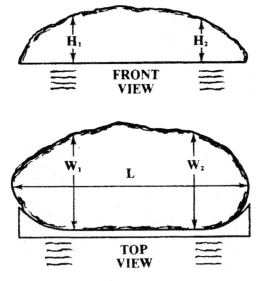

H_1 H_2

**FRONT
VIEW**

W_1 **L** W_2

**TOP
VIEW**

The time required for a tractor to complete one operating cycle, also known as the *cycle time*, can be estimated by the following equation:

$$CT = FT + HT + RT \tag{8–2}$$

where FT is the fixed time to maneuver, shift gears, start loading, and dump

 HT is the haul time

 RT is the return time

The fixed time (FT) should be assumed to be 0.05 minutes for a tractor with a power shift transmission and 0.10 minutes for a tractor with a direct drive transmission.[1] The haul time and the travel time are determined by dividing the haul distance by the tractor speed.

Tractor productivity can now be estimated by the following equation:

$$\text{Productivity} = \frac{(\text{Load Volume})(\text{Operational Efficiency})}{\text{Cycle Time}} \tag{8–3}$$

The operational efficiency is determined either by estimating the number of working minutes per hour or by using the management factors contained in Table 5.1. Now, let's look at an example problem to illustrate the use of these equations.

Example 8.1

A contractor is planning to use a Caterpillar D7G crawler tractor with power shift transmission to excavate 1,500 bank cubic yards for the foundation of a large house. The swell of the excavated material is estimated to be 25%. The tractor must push the excavated material up a 12% slope where it will be stockpiled for later removal. The contractor has measured the pile of excavated material in front of the tractor's universal blade just before spillage occurs and has determined the pile length to be 12.6 feet, the pile width to be 8.1 feet, and the pile height to be 4 feet. The tractor weighs 44,400 pounds, and the coefficient of traction is estimated to be 0.7. The average haul distance is estimated to be 300 feet. What is the estimated productivity of the tractor if the contractor plans to average 50 minutes of operation per hour? Performance characteristics of the tractor are shown in Figure 8.3.

Solution

The first step is to determine the volume of material that can be moved during one operating cycle by using Equation 8.1.

$$V = \frac{(0.375)(8.1 \text{ ft.})(4 \text{ ft.})(12.6 \text{ ft.})}{27 \text{ cu. ft./cu. yd.}} = 5.7 \text{ LCY}$$

---

[1]James J. O'Brien, John A. Havers, and Frank W. Stubbs, Jr., eds., *Standard Handbook of Heavy Construction,* 3rd ed. (New York: McGraw-Hill, 1996), p. B3-17.

Next, we must convert the volume to bank cubic yards by using the percent swell.

$$V = \frac{5.7 \text{ LCY}}{(1 + 0.25)(\text{LCY/BCY})} = 4.6 \text{ BCY}$$

The next step is to determine the cycle time for the tractor. The fixed time will be 0.05 minute, because the tractor has a power shift transmission. The variable time is a function of the travel distance and the tractor speed.

As discussed in Chapter 7, the only resisting force acting against the crawler tractor is grade resistance which can be estimated by Equations 7–11 and 7–12. The total resisting force that must be considered for wheeled tractors is the sum of the resistance due to rolling resistance and that due to grade resistance.

$$F_R = (20 \text{ lb./ton per \% slope})(12\%)(22.2 \text{ ton}) = 5,328 \text{ lb.}$$

Next, we must check to ensure there is adequate traction for the tractor by using Equation 7–17.

$$\text{Maximum Usable Drawbar Pull} = (0.7)(44,400 \text{ lb.}) = 31,080 \text{ lb.}$$

Clearly, the tracks will not slip at the maximum speed that will be determined from Figure 8.3 because the required drawbar pull of 5,328 pounds is less than the maximum usable drawbar pull of 31,080 pounds.

The tractor will be operated in first gear when digging and pushing the load to the stockpile. Examination of Figure 8.3 indicates that the maximum speed in first gear that will provide 5,328 pounds of drawbar pull is 2.1 miles per hour. The tractor will be operated in second gear when backing from the stockpile to the excavation area. Examination of Figure 8.3 indicates that the maximum speed in second gear is 4.0 miles per hour. Minimal drawbar pull is required because there is no resisting force due to the downhill 12% grade. Now the cycle time can be determined with Equation 8–2.

$$CT = 0.05 \text{ min.} + \frac{300 \text{ ft.}}{(2.1 \text{ mi./hr.})(88 \text{ ft./min. per mi./hr.})}$$

$$+ \frac{300 \text{ ft.}}{(4 \text{ mi./hr.})(88 \text{ ft./min. per mi./hr.})}$$

$$= 0.05 \text{ min.} + 1.62 \text{ min.} + 0.85 \text{ min.} = 2.52 \text{ min.}$$

Now we can estimate the tractor productivity with Equation 8–3.

$$\text{Productivity} = \frac{(4.6 \text{ BCY})(50 \text{ min./hr.})}{2.52 \text{ min.}} = \textbf{91.3 BCY/hr.}$$

Crawler tractors often are used to clear and grub a project site to remove existing vegetation and topsoil. Tractor productivity depends on the size of the tractor being used and the size of the vegetation that is to be removed. Table 8.1 can be used to estimate tractor productivity for clearing and grubbing operations.

Table 8.1
Crawler Tractor Clearing and Grubbing Hourly Production Rates
Based on an Operating Factor of 83%

Description of Work	50-HP Tractor	65-HP Tractor	75-HP Tractor	105-HP Tractor	200-HP Tractor
Simple clearing, vegetation, light brush, tree saplings	900 to 1,000 sq. ft.	1,000 to 1,100 sq. ft.	1,150 to 1,250 sq. ft.	1,250 to 1,350 sq. ft.	1,450 to 1,550 sq. ft.
Moderately difficult clearing, thick brush and tree saplings; add extra for trees	300 to 350 sq. ft.	350 to 400 sq. ft.	400 to 450 sq. ft.	600 to 650 sq. ft.	700 to 750 sq. ft.
Strip topsoil and stockpile	15 to 20 cu. yd.	17 to 22 cu. yd.	20 to 25 cu. yd.	22 to 27 cu. yd.	27 to 32 cu. yd.

Data for this table was extracted from *Walker's Building Estimator's Reference Book,* 25th ed.
(Lisle, IL: Frank R. Walker Co., 1995), p. 2.58.

8.5   Cost Analysis

To estimate the cost of performing a construction task with a tractor, it is first necessary to estimate the hourly ownership and operating costs using either the techniques
discussed in Chapter 4, the cost references discussed in Chapter 5, or historical cost
data. These costs can be used in conjunction with the tractor productivity estimated
with Equation 8–3 to estimate the unit cost for the construction task. Multiplying the
unit cost by the total quantity of work to be performed provides an estimate of the total
cost for performing the construction task. Dividing the total quantity of work by the
tractor productivity estimated with Equation 8–3 provides an estimate of the time required to perform the task. Now, let's look at two example problems to illustrate these
concepts.

Example 8.2

The contractor of Example 8.1 estimates the hourly ownership cost for the Caterpillar
D7G to be $22, the hourly operating cost (less labor) to be $39, and the tractor operator's
wages to be $24 per hour.

a. What is the estimated unit cost for excavating the foundation in dollars per bank
cubic yard?
b. What is the total estimated cost for excavating the foundation?
c. What is the estimated duration of the excavating operation?

Solution

a. The total hourly ownership and operating cost for the tractor is estimated to be

$$\$22/hr. + \$39/hr. + \$24/hr. = \$85/hr.$$

The tractor productivity was estimated in Example 8.1 to be 91.3 bank cubic yards per hour. The unit cost is estimated to be

$$\frac{\$85/hr.}{91.3 \text{ BCY/hr.}} = \$0.93/\textbf{BCY}$$

b. The total volume of material to be excavated was stated in Example 8.1 to be 1,500 bank cubic yards. The total equipment cost is estimated to be

$$(1,500 \text{ BCY})(\$0.93 \text{ per BCY}) = \$1,395$$

c. The estimated duration for the excavating operation is

$$\frac{1,500 \text{ BCY}}{91.3 \text{ BCY/hr.}} = 16.4 \text{ hr.}$$

Example 8.3

A contractor is planning to use a 75-horsepower crawler tractor to clear and grub a project site for the construction of a small industrial plant. The contractor estimates the hourly ownership cost for the tractor to be $16, the hourly operating cost (less labor) to be $24, and the hourly labor cost for the tractor operator to be $28. The contractor estimates the clearing and grubbing operation to be moderately difficult.

a. What is the estimated unit cost for the clearing and grubbing operation?
b. The area to be cleared measures 600 feet by 350 feet. What is the estimated cost for the clearing and grubbing operation?
c. What is the estimated duration for the clearing and grubbing operation?

Solution

a. The total hourly ownership and operating cost for the tractor is estimated to be

$$\$16/hr. + \$24/hr. + \$28/hr. = \$68/hr.$$

The productivity of the tractor is estimated from Table 8.1 to be 425 square feet per hour. The middle of the range for a 75-horsepower tractor working under moderately difficult conditions was selected, since there was no basis for taking the low or high estimates. The unit cost is estimated to be

$$\frac{\$68/hr.}{425 \text{ sq. ft./hr.}} = \$0.16/\textbf{sq. ft.}$$

b. The total cost for the clearing and grubbing operation is estimated to be

$$(600 \text{ ft.})(350 \text{ ft.})(\$0.16/\text{sq. ft.}) = \$33,600$$

c. The duration for the clearing and grubbing operation is estimated to be

$$\frac{(600 \text{ ft.})(350 \text{ ft.})}{(425 \text{ sq. ft./hr.})(8 \text{ hr./day})} = 61.8 \text{ days}$$

The contractor may find this duration to be too long and decide to use more than one tractor on the job to complete the task more quickly. Using 3 tractors will allow the contractor to complete the clearing and grubbing operation in

$$\frac{61.8}{3} = 20.6 \text{ days}$$

but the total cost will remain the same.

8.6   Problems

1. Estimate the production rate in loose cubic yards per hour of a crawler tractor that is being used to move sandy dry soil 200 feet horizontally in a 50-minute working hour. The 170-horsepower direct-drive tractor has a straight blade 11 feet long and 3.3 feet high. The average width of the base of the soil pile in front of the blade has been measured to be about 5 feet. Assume that the tractor travels in first gear forward at 1.7 miles per hour and returns in second reverse gear at 2.7 miles per hour.

2. A contractor is planning to use 2 Caterpillar D7G crawler tractors to excavate for the basement and foundation for a parking garage. The capacity of each tractor's blade is estimated to be 5.5 loose cubic yards, and the average haul distance is estimated to be 150 feet (one way) up a 15% slope. The tractors have direct-drive engines and weigh 45,200 pounds, and the coefficient of traction is estimated to be 0.6. The tractors will excavate and push the excavated material in first gear and back up in second gear. What is the estimated productivity of the tractors, if the contractor plans to average 45 minutes of operation per hour? Performance characteristics of the tractors are shown in Figure 8.3.

3. A contractor is planning to use a Caterpillar 814F wheeled tractor with a straight blade to backfill the foundation for an apartment complex. The tractor has all-wheel drive and a power shift engine. The capacity of the blade is estimated to be 3.8 loose cubic yards. The average haul distance (one way) for the tractor is estimated to be 700 feet up an average 2% slope. The tractor weighs 41,000 pounds, the coefficient of traction is estimated to be 0.5, and the rolling resistance is estimated to be 80 pounds per ton. Performance characteristics for the tractor are shown in Figure 8.4.

   a. What is the estimated productivity of the wheeled tractor if the contractor plans to average 45 minutes of operation per hour? Assume the tractor will push in first gear and then back in second gear to get another load.

   b. What is the estimated unit cost for the backfill operation if the hourly ownership cost is $31, the hourly operating cost (less labor) is $42, and the tractor operator earns $22 per hour?

4. A contractor used a 3-cubic-yard hydraulic excavator to dig a hole for the foundation for an office building and stockpile the excavated material. The building foundation

and the first floor have been constructed, and the contractor is planning to use a John Deere 750B crawler tractor to backfill the foundation with material from the loose stockpile. The average haul distance (one way) for the tractor is estimated to be about 350 feet, and the backfill volume is estimated to be 900 compacted cubic yards. The site is fairly level. Soil tests on the backfill material indicate a swell of 25% and a shrinkage of 18% when compacted to the design density. The blade capacity is estimated to be 70 loose cubic feet. The operating weight of the tractor with a straight blade is 31,105 pounds. Assume a fixed time of 0.05 minutes and that the operator will push in first gear at a speed of 1.5 miles per hour and back up in second gear at a speed of 2 miles per hour. Operational efficiency is estimated at 50 minutes per hour. Ownership and operating costs (less labor) are estimated to be $42.00, and the operator earns $21.50 per hour, including fringe benefits.

  a. What is the estimated productivity of the tractor in compacted cubic yards per hour?
  b. What is the estimated unit cost of the backfill operation in dollars per compacted cubic yard?
  c. How many 8-hour days will it take the contractor to complete the backfill operation?
5. A contractor is planning to use a 200-horsepower crawler tractor to strip topsoil from a construction site and stockpile it for later use in site landscaping. Ten inches of topsoil are to be removed from an area that measures 150 feet by 250 feet. The hourly ownership and operating costs (less labor) are estimated to be $80, and the operator will earn $25 per hour. Operational efficiency is estimated to be 50 minutes per hour.
  a. What is the estimated cost for stripping and stockpiling the topsoil?
  b. How many 8-hour days will it take the contractor to complete the topsoil removal operation?

9

Loaders

9.1 Introduction

A loader is a self-propelled machine with a bucket mounted on the front end. As with tractors, loaders are mounted either on tracks or on wheels. They are used to dig soil or other material, carry it, and dump it into trucks, stockpiles, or containers. A typical tracked loader is illustrated in Figure 9.1. Wheeled loaders may have either a straight

Figure 9.1
A Tracked Loader
Courtesy Caterpillar Inc.

Figure 9.2
An Articulated Wheeled Loader
Loading a Dump Truck

Courtesy Caterpillar Inc.

frame or an articulated frame with a pivot point between the front and rear axle. Articulated loaders can turn in a shorter radius than can straight-frame loaders of the same size. An articulated wheeled loader is illustrated in Figure 9.2. The straight-frame loader costs less to purchase and maintain per hour, but the productivity of the articulated loader is greater for truck-loading operations, because of its shorter turning radius. As with tractors, tracked loaders have better traction than do wheeled loaders, but they have slower travel speeds and generally require truck transportation to move them from one project site to another.

9.2   *Types and Uses of Loaders*

Crawler loaders have the advantage of good flotation and traction when ground conditions are soft or uneven. They also operate over sharp objects that would penetrate the rubber tires of a wheeled loader. Wheeled loaders are used when mobility and speed are required and ground conditions are firm. Crawler loaders provide greater traction when digging into hard soil faces or excavating well-compacted soil. Construction tasks performed by loaders are

- Excavating
- Loading trucks or conveyors
- Stockpiling
- Backfilling foundations and utility lines
- Hauling (generally distances less than 500 feet)

Loaders are rated in terms of bucket capacity and operating load. Bucket capacity is provided by the equipment manufacturer in loose cubic yards or loose cubic meters in terms of *heaped capacity* and *struck capacity*. Heaped capacity is the maximum ca-

Figure 9.3
Struck and Heaped Bucket
Capacity
Courtesy Caterpillar Inc.

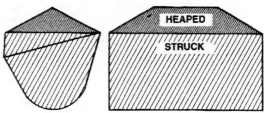

SAE BUCKET RATING

pacity of the bucket, while struck capacity is when the bucket is filled level with the top, as shown in Figure 9.3. Loader buckets generally are equipped with both bolt-on cutting edges and teeth as illustrated in Figure 9.4. The teeth aid in digging and the cutting edges save wear on the bucket, as they are replaced when worn.

The operating load for a loader is the maximum load (weight) the loader can safely carry. Industry standards limit the maximum safe load to

- 50% of the static tipping load for wheeled loaders
- 35% of the static tipping load for crawler loaders

The static tipping load is the minimum weight placed in the loader bucket that causes the front rollers of a crawler loader to clear the tracks or the rear wheels of a wheeled loader to clear the ground.[1] *Loader capacity, therefore, is limited by both a volume and*

Figure 9.4
Typical Loader Bucket
Courtesy Caterpillar Inc.

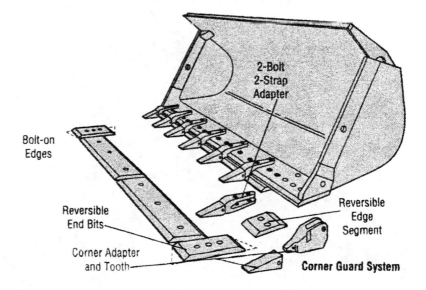

[1]According to the *1996 SAE Handbook*, Vol. 3 (Warrendale, PA: Society of Automotive Engineers, 1996), pp. 40.70 and 40.106.

a weight constraint. Volume generally governs, but the weight criteria may govern when loading dense material.

9.3   *Production Estimation*

Loader productivity usually is expressed in cubic yards per hour and is influenced by the following factors:

- Type of material being loaded
- Bucket capacity
- Maneuver area for loader operation
- Cycle time of loader
- Operational efficiency

Loader productivity is estimated by

- Estimating the volume of material that can be moved by the loader during each operating cycle
- Estimating the number of operating cycles that can be completed during an operating hour

The volume of material that can be moved per operating cycle depends on the bucket capacity and the static tipping load of the loader. The static tipping load determines the maximum weight that can be lifted, and the rated bucket volume determines the maximum volume that can be lifted. Various materials bulk in a loader bucket differently when loaded to its heaped capacity. To account for this variation, a *fill factor* is used to estimate the heaped capacity of the bucket. Bucket fill factors for loaders are shown in Table 9-1. Let's now look at an example.

Table 9.1
Loader Bucket Fill Factors

Material	Fill Factor
Mixed or uniform granular	0.95–1.00
Medium, coarse stone	0.85–0.90
Well-blasted rock	0.80–0.95
Average-blasted rock	0.75–0.90
Poorly blasted rock	0.60–0.75
Rock dirt mixtures	1.00–1.20
Moist loam	1.00–1.10
Cemented materials	0.85–0.95

Data for this table was extracted from *Caterpillar Performance Handbook*, 28th ed. (Peoria, IL: Caterpillar Inc., 1997), p. 12-87.

Example 9.1

A contractor has a wheeled loader with a 2.75-cubic-yard bucket. The static tipping load for the loader is 15,600 pounds.

a. What is the maximum load the loader can carry per cycle when loaded with moist loam weighing 2,000 pounds per loose cubic yard?
b. What is the maximum load the loader can carry per cycle when loaded with wet gravel weighing 3,400 pounds per loose cubic yard?

Solution

a. The maximum weight the loader can carry is 50% of the static tipping load, which is

$$(0.5)(15,600 \text{ lb.}) = 7,800 \text{ lb.}$$

The fill factor for the moist loam can be estimated from Table 9.1. Any factor within the range can be selected, *but the average value should be selected unless you have a basis for selecting a different value.* Using the average value, the fill factor for moist loam is determined to be 1.05. The heaped capacity of the bucket is

$$(2.75 \text{ LCY})(1.05) = 2.9 \text{ LCY}$$

Now, we must check to ensure we are not exceeding the weight constraint. The load weight can be estimated by multiplying the density by the volume, which is

$$\text{Load Weight} = (2.9 \text{ LCY})(2,000 \text{ lb./LCY}) = 5,800 \text{ lb.}$$

Since the load weight (5,800 lb.) is less than the maximum allowable weight (7,800 lb.), the maximum volume the loader can carry per cycle is **2.9 loose cubic yards.**
b. We can use Table 9.1 to estimate the fill factor for the wet gravel to be 0.87 by using the average value for medium, coarse stone. The heaped capacity of the bucket is

$$(2.75 \text{ LCY})(0.87) = 2.4 \text{ LCY}$$

Now, we must check to ensure we are not exceeding the weight constraint. The load weight can be estimated by multiplying the density by the volume, which is

$$\text{Load Weight} = (2.4 \text{ LCY})(3,400 \text{ lb./LCY}) = 8,160 \text{ lb.}$$

Since the load weight (8,160 lb.) exceeds the maximum allowable weight (7,800 lb.), the load volume must be reduced to

$$\text{Load Volume} = \frac{7,800 \text{ lb.}}{3,400 \text{ lb./LCY.}} = 2.3 \text{ LCY}$$

The cycle time for the loader can be estimated by the following equation:

$$CT = FT + VT \tag{9-1}$$

where FT is the fixed time to load the bucket, to shift gears, and to turn and dump the load

          VT is the variable or travel time

The fixed time should be estimated[2]

- Between 0.25 and 0.35 minutes for a crawler loader
- Between 0.45 and 0.60 minutes for an articulated wheeled loader
- Between 0.55 and 0.75 minutes for a straight-frame wheeled loader

The travel time is a function of the travel distance and the average travel speed. Loader productivity can now be estimated using the following equation:

$$\text{Productivity} = \frac{(\text{Bucket Capacity})(\text{Operational Efficiency})}{\text{Cycle Time}} \qquad (9\text{–}2)$$

Now, let's look at an example to illustrate the use of these equations.

Example 9.2

A contractor is planning to use a John Deere 555G crawler loader to excavate for the foundation for a small building. The loader bucket has a rated heaped capacity of 1.5 cubic yards. The static tipping load for the loader is 14,400 pounds. The contractor intends to use the loader to excavate for the foundation and stockpile the excavated material for backfill and landscaping. The average haul distance for the loader is estimated to be 100 feet one way, the average speed when moving loaded is estimated to be 1.6 miles per hour, and the average speed when moving empty is estimated to be 2.4 miles per hour. The material to be excavated is moist loam weighing 2,200 pounds per loose cubic yard. What is the estimated productivity of the loader, if the contractor plans to operate 50 minutes per hour?

Solution

The first step is to determine the maximum load the loader can carry per cycle. The fill factor for moist loam is estimated from Table 9.1 to be 1.05. The adjusted heaped capacity of the loader is

$$(1.5 \text{ LCY})(1.05) = 1.58 \text{ LCY}$$

The load weight is

$$(1.58 \text{ LCY})(2,200 \text{ lb./LCY}) = 3,476 \text{ lb.}$$

The maximum load the loader can carry is 35% of the static tipping load, or

$$(0.35)(14,400 \text{ lb.}) = 5,040 \text{ lb.}$$

Since the load weight (3,476 lb.) is less than the maximum allowed (5,040 lb.), the load volume will be 1.58 loose cubic yards.

---

[2]*Caterpillar Performance Handbook*, 28th ed. (Peoria, IL: Caterpillar Inc., 1997), pp. 12-33 and 12-85.

Next, we must estimate the cycle time for the loader. The fixed time is estimated to be 0.3 minutes by selecting the average from the range provided for a crawler loader. The variable time is estimated by dividing the travel distance by the average speed.

$$VT = \frac{100 \text{ ft.}}{(1.6 \text{ mi./hr.})(88 \text{ ft./min. per mi./hr.})} + \frac{100 \text{ ft.}}{(2.4 \text{ mi./hr.})(88 \text{ ft./min. per mi./hr.})}$$

$$= 0.71 \text{ min.} + 0.47 \text{ min.} = 1.18 \text{ min.}$$

With Equation 9–1 the cycle time can now be estimated:

$$CT = 0.3 \text{ min.} + 1.18 \text{ min.} = 1.48 \text{ min.}$$

With Equation 9–2 the loader productivity can now be estimated:

$$\text{Productivity} = \frac{(1.58 \text{ LCY})(50 \text{ min./hr.})}{1.48 \text{ min.}} = 53 \text{ LCY/hr.}$$

9.4   Cost and Time Analysis

To estimate the cost of performing a construction task with a loader, it is first necessary to estimate the hourly ownership and operating costs using the techniques discussed in Chapter 4, the cost references discussed in Chapter 5, or historical cost data. These costs can be used in conjunction with the productivity estimated with Equation 9–2 to estimate the unit cost for using a loader to perform the task. Multiplying the unit cost by the total quantity of work to be performed yields an estimate of the total cost for the task. This information is needed by the contractor to develop a cost estimate for the entire project. Dividing the total volume of work to be performed by the loader productivity provides an estimate of the time required to perform the task. This information is needed by the contractor to develop a construction schedule. Let's now look at an example.

Example 9.3

The contractor of Example 9.2 estimates the hourly ownership cost for the John Deere 555G to be $6.50, the hourly operating cost to be $18.00, and the operator's hourly wages to be $26.00. The project plans indicate the required excavation to measure 6 feet by 40 feet by 45 feet.

a. What is the estimated unit cost for excavating for the foundation in dollars per bank cubic yard? The swell for the soil is estimated to be 15%.
b. What is the total estimated cost for excavating for the foundation?
c. How long do you estimate it will take the loader to complete the excavation?

Solution

a. The total hourly ownership and operating cost for the loader is estimated to be

$$\$6.50/\text{hr.} + \$18.00/\text{hr.} + \$26.00/\text{hr.} = \$50.50/\text{hr.}$$

The loader productivity was determined in Example 9.2 to be 53 loose cubic yards (LCY) per hour, which we need to convert to bank cubic yards (BCY) per hour using the percent swell:

$$\frac{53 \text{ LCY/hr.}}{1.15 \text{ LCY/BCY}} = 46 \text{ BCY/hr.}$$

The estimated unit cost is

$$\frac{\$50.50 \text{ per hr.}}{46 \text{ BCY/hr.}} = \mathbf{\$1.10/BCY}$$

b. The total volume to be excavated is

$$\frac{(6 \text{ ft.})(40 \text{ ft.})(45 \text{ ft.})}{27 \text{ cu. ft./cu. yd.}} = 400 \text{ BCY}$$

Using the unit cost from (a), we estimate the total cost to be

$$(400 \text{ BCY})(\$1.10 \text{ per BCY}) = \mathbf{\$440.00}$$

c. The estimated time required to complete the excavation is

$$\frac{400 \text{ BCY}}{46 \text{ BCY/hr.}} = \mathbf{8.7 \text{ hr.}}$$

9.5   *Problems*

1. A contractor is using a Case 855E crawler loader to backfill a building foundation. The loader is equipped with a bucket that has a rated heaped capacity of 1.4 cubic yards. The static tipping load for the loader is 11,570 pounds. The soil being used for the backfill is a rock-dirt mixture weighing 2,950 pounds per loose cubic yard. The average travel distance for the loader is 125 feet one way. The average loader speed when loaded is estimated to be 1.5 miles per hour and when empty 2.2 miles per hour. What is the estimated productivity of the loader in loose cubic yards per hour, if the contractor plans an operational efficiency of 45 minutes per hour?

2. A straight-frame wheeled loader with a 2.7-cubic-yard bucket (rated heaped capacity) is excavating a basement 30 feet by 65 feet with an average depth of 10 feet. The material is moist loam weighing 2,800 pounds per bank cubic yard with a swell of 25%. The soil is to be stockpiled an average of 175 feet away from the middle of the basement. The static tipping load for the loader is 19,500 pounds. It is estimated that the average travel speed is 1.7 miles per hour. Using a 50-minute working hour, estimate the total time required for the loader to complete the excavation.

3. A 5.25-cubic-yard (rated heaped capacity) articulated wheeled loader is loading mixed moist aggregate into dump trucks from a stockpile. Assume the loader has an average haul distance of 20 feet (one way), operates at an average speed of 2.8 miles per hour, and works 50 minutes per hour. The static tipping load for the loader is 33,700 pounds. The aggregate weighs 3,000 pounds per loose cubic yard. If the average

hourly ownership and operating cost (including labor cost) is $118 per hour, what is the estimated cost per loose cubic yard to load the trucks? Assume that the loader does not wait for trucks to arrive at the loading site or to be spotted for loading.

4. A contractor is developing a list of equipment needed for a construction project. He has decided to use dump trucks to haul fill material (rock-dirt mixture) from a borrow source that is 10 miles from the construction site. He has selected a bulldozer to rip and stockpile the borrow material, but needs to select a loader to load the dump trucks. The contractor estimates the cycle time for the loading operation to be 0.8 minutes and wants to load 400 loose cubic yards per hour. What is the smallest size loader he should select, if he plans to operate the loader 50 minutes per hour? Ignore the static tipping load check. Once the contractor selects the specific model loader to use, he will need to make the static tipping load check.

5. A contractor needs to load 12-cubic-yard dump trucks with fill material that is needed for foundation backfill on a construction project. The average travel distance is estimated to be 35 feet one way. The fill material is a soil and gravel mixture weighing 2,900 pounds per bank cubic yard with a swell of 20%. The contractor plans to rent a loader and has the following choices:

   a. A 2.5-cubic-yard (rated heaped capacity) straight-frame wheeled loader renting for $750 per day with an hourly operating cost estimated to be $24.50. The static tipping load for the loader is 16,800 pounds. The average travel speed is estimated to be 2.2 miles per hour.

   b. A 3.5-cubic-yard (rated heaped capacity) articulated wheeled loader renting for $1,100 per day with an hourly operating cost estimated to be $29.60. The static tipping load for the loader is 23,400 pounds. The average travel speed is estimated to be 2.5 miles per hour.

   Which loader should the contractor rent to minimize the loading cost per bank cubic yard? Wages for the operator would be the same for either loader. The contractor plans to operate 50 minutes per hour and 8 hours per day.

6. A contractor is planning to use a crawler loader to excavate basements for a large multifamily residential project. The loader is equipped with a bucket that has a rated heaped capacity of 3.75 cubic yards. The material to be excavated is moist loam weighing 2,600 pounds per bank cubic yard with a swell of 25%. The static tipping load for the loader is 30,500 pounds. The average haul distance is estimated to be 200 feet one way, the average loader speed is estimated to be 1.9 miles per hour when loaded, and the average loader speed is estimated to be 3.0 miles per hour when empty. The average hourly ownership and operating cost for the loader is estimated to be $75.43, and the hourly labor cost is the operator's hourly wage of $24.30 plus 20% for fringes. What is the estimated cost per bank cubic yard to excavate basements for an operating efficiency of 50 minutes per hour?

10

Scrapers

10.1 Introduction

A scraper is basically a large bowl with a cutting edge front that is attached to a pulling machine as illustrated in Figures 10.1 and 10.2. It is used to scrape the surface by lowering the cutting edge into the soil and moving forward to fill the bowl. Once the bowl is loaded, its front apron is lowered, sealing the material in the bowl. The bowl is raised and the scraper transports the loaded material to the dump site. To unload, the bowl is lowered just above the ground, the front apron raised slightly, and the ejector (rear of the bowl) moved forward, forcing the material out of the bowl. Scrapers thus are capable of excavating, loading, hauling, and dumping.

While tractors and loaders are efficient for moving material for short distances (up to 300 feet for tractors and 500 feet for loaders), scrapers generally are the most efficient means of moving material for distances from 500 feet up to about 1.5 miles. For longer-haul distances, trucks are usually the most economic means of moving material. Skilled scraper operators can cut a grade to within 0.1 foot and can spread fill with the same degree of accuracy.

10.2 Types and Uses of Scrapers

There are four types of scrapers manufactured:

- Single-engine
- Twin-engine
- Push-pull
- Elevating

Figure 10.1
Single-Engine Scraper
Courtesy Caterpillar Inc.

Figure 10.2
Components of a Scraper Bowl
Reprinted with Permission SAE J741
©1993 Society of Automotive
Engineers, Inc.

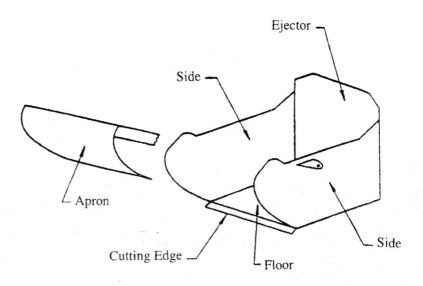

Figure 10.3
Twin-Engine Scraper
Courtesy Caterpillar Inc.

A single-engine scraper is illustrated in Figure 10.1. All the power to drive the scraper is provided by a single engine mounted in the front. A twin-engine scraper is illustrated in Figure 10.3. A second engine is mounted in the rear to help with loading, to provide added power to travel on steep haul roads, and to provide higher hauling speeds. Twin-engine scrapers generally cost 25% to 30% more than the same size single-engine scrapers and typically are used by contractors for specialized work. Both single-engine and twin-engine scrapers require pusher tractors to load to rated capacity, as illustrated in Figure 10.4.

Push-pull scrapers are twin-engine scrapers that have a push block mounted on the rear and a bail mounted on the front. They operate in pairs, as illustrated in Figure 10.5,

Figure 10.4
Scraper Being Push Loaded with Crawler Tractor
Courtesy TEREX Americas

Figure 10.5
Push-Pull Scrapers Loading
Courtesy Caterpillar Inc.

to assist each other in loading, eliminating the need for a push tractor. The trailing scraper pushes the lead scraper while it loads. Then the lead scraper pulls the trailing scraper while it loads. When both are loaded, they disconnect and travel independently to the dump site.

An elevating scraper is illustrated in Figure 10.6. It has power-turned paddles mounted on a continuous chain in front of the bowl as shown in Figure 10.7. These paddles dig into the soil and throw the material into the bowl. This self-loading feature eliminates the need to use a pusher tractor. The disadvantage of elevating scrapers is the dead weight of the elevating mechanism during the haul cycle and the additional cost.

Figure 10.6
Elevating Scraper
Courtesy John Deere

Figure 10.7
Scraper Elevator
Courtesy John Deere

Elevating scrapers may weigh 9,000 to 11,000 pounds more than conventional scrapers with the same payload capacity. They are economical for low-volume work such as utility work or small jobs where the productivity of one unit is all that is needed. Elevating scrapers dump the material by retracting the floor of the bowl rather than lifting an apron in front of the bowl.

Contractors use scrapers to perform the following tasks:

- Topsoil removal
- Contour grading
- Drainage ditch cutting
- Mass excavation
- Fill construction

The most economical scraper to use for an operation depends on (1) the characteristics of the material to be removed; (2) length of the haul road; (3) haul road conditions, such as grade and rolling resistance; and (4) pusher requirements. Elevating scrapers should be considered if the haul distances are short and haul road conditions are good. If the material to be removed contains rocks that are too large to load by the elevator, conventional scrapers should be used. If the haul road has high rolling resistance or steep grades, twin-engine scrapers should be considered. Otherwise, single-engine scrapers usually are the most economical to use.

Scrapers are rated in terms of bowl rated capacity (volume) and rated load (weight). Bowl capacity is provided in loose cubic yards or loose cubic meters in terms of **struck capacity** and **heaped capacity**. The bowl is at struck capacity when it is filled level with the sides of the bowl, and it is at heaped capacity when the material in the bowl is piled above the top of the bowl in the center and tapered down to the top edge of the bowl. *Scraper capacity, therefore, is limited by both a volume and a weight constraint.* Volume usually governs, but the weight criteria may govern when hauling dense material.

10.3. Production Estimation

Scraper productivity depends on the following:

- Volume of scraper bowl
- Rated maximum load (weight)
- Available horsepower
- Nature of material being loaded
- Length, profile, and surface condition of haul road
- Operational efficiency

Scraper productivity is estimated by

- Estimating the volume that can be moved during each operating cycle
- Estimating the number of operating cycles that can be completed during an operating hour

The volume that can be moved during each operating cycle depends on the rated capacity and the load weight. The more severe constraint will govern. Manufacturers' technical literature provides a rated heaped volume, rated struck volume, and a rated load. Since volume generally governs, the first step is to determine the weight of the heaped load using the density of the material to be moved. If the resulting weight is less than the rated load, the scraper can safely carry the full heaped volume. If the weight exceeds the rated load, the maximum volume is determined by dividing the rated load by the material density. This is illustrated in Example 10.1.

Example 10.1

A contractor has a John Deere 862B elevating scraper. The rated heaped volume is 17 cubic yards, and the rated load is 40,800 pounds.

a. What is the maximum load the scraper can carry per cycle when loaded with dry clay weighing 2,700 pounds per bank cubic yard? The swell for the clay is estimated to be 30%.
b. What is the maximum load the scraper can carry per cycle when loaded with wet earth weighing 3,000 pounds per bank cubic yard? The swell for the wet earth is estimated to be 20%.

Solution

a. The weight of 17 loose cubic yards of the dry clay is

$$\frac{(17\ LCY)(2{,}700\ lb./BCY)}{1.3\ LCY/BCY} = 35{,}308\ lb.$$

Since the load weight (35,308 lb.) is less than the rated load (40,800 lb.), the scraper can be loaded to its full heaped capacity of **17 loose cubic yards.**

b. The weight of 17 loose cubic yards of wet earth is

$$\frac{(17\ LCY)(3{,}000\ lb./BCY)}{1.2\ LCY/BCY} = 42{,}500\ lb.$$

Since the load weight (42,500 lb.) exceeds the rated load (40,800 lb.), the scraper cannot safely be loaded to its heaped capacity. The maximum load volume is

$$\frac{(40{,}800\ lb.)(1.2\ LCY/BCY)}{3{,}000\ lb./BCY} = \mathbf{16.3\ LCY}$$

The cycle time for a scraper can be estimated by the following equation:

$$CT = FT + VT \tag{10-1}$$

where FT is the fixed time to load the scraper, dump the load, turn, and spot the scraper for the next cut

VT is the variable or travel time

The fixed time can be estimated from Table 10.1. The variable time depends on the travel distance and the travel speed. The travel speed depends on (1) the grade and rolling resistance of the haul road, (2) the elevation of the project site, and (3) the performance characteristics of the scraper. The performance of an engine is affected by altitude, as discussed in Section 7.9 of Chapter 7; manufacturers' performance data may need modification with an appropriate derating factor. Usable rimpull also may be limited by the coefficient of traction for the haul road surface. These concepts are illustrated in Example 10.2.

The scraper will not operate at its maximum speed for the entire time. It will be accelerating and decelerating during some of its travel time. To account for these lower speeds, the average travel speed is estimated by multiplying the maximum speed with a speed factor, as shown below.

$$\text{Average Speed} = (\text{Maximum Speed})(\text{Speed Factor}) \tag{10-2}$$

Appropriate speed factors are shown in Table 10.2. Speed factors for segment lengths not shown can be estimated by linear interpolation. The travel time can be estimated by dividing the travel distance by the average speed for that segment of the haul road. The total travel time is equal to the sum of the travel times for all haul road segments. Once

Table 10.1
Fixed Times for Scrapers

Job Conditions	Scraper Loading Times (in minutes)			
	Push-Loaded Single-Engine	*Push-Loaded Twin-Engine*	*Push-Pull*	*Self-Loading Elevator*
Favorable	0.5	0.4	0.7	0.8
Average	0.7	0.6	1.0	1.1
Unfavorable	1.0	0.9	1.4	1.5

Job Conditions	Scraper Spot and Delay Times (in minutes)			
	Push-Loaded Single-Engine	*Push-Loaded Twin-Engine*	*Push-Pull*	*Self-Loading Elevator*
Favorable	0.2	0.1	Negligible	Negligible
Average	0.3	0.2	0.1	Negligible
Unfavorable	0.5	0.5	0.3	0.2

Job Conditions	Scraper Turning and Dumping Times (in minutes)		
	Push-Loaded Single-Engine	*Push-Loaded Twin-Engine*	*Self-Loading Elevator*
Favorable	0.3	0.3	0.3
Average	0.5	0.5	0.5
Unfavorable	1.0	0.9	0.8

Data for this table was extracted from *Production and Cost Estimating of Material Movement with Earthmoving Equipment* (Hudson, OH: Terex Corporation, 1981), pp. 32 and 33.

the cycle time is estimated, the productivity of the scraper can be estimated by the following equation:

$$\text{Productivity} = \frac{(\text{Rated Capacity})(\text{Operational Efficiency})}{\text{Cycle Time}} \tag{10–3}$$

Now, let's look at an example to illustrate the use of these equations.

Example 10.2

A contractor is planning to use a Caterpillar 615C Series II elevating scraper to grade a building site for a small medical clinic that is located at an elevation of 3,000 feet. The scraper is powered with a four-cycle, 265-horsepower naturally respirated engine. The material to be removed is dry common earth weighing 2,750 pounds per bank cubic yard with a swell estimated to be 20%. The excavated material will be moved over a 2,000-foot haul road for disposal. The haul road has an uphill grade of 2% when traveling from

Table 10.2
Speed Factors for Scrapers

Length of Segment	Starting from Standstill or Coming to a Stop*	Maximum Speed Compared to Previous Segment	
		Increasing	Decreasing
100 ft.	0.45	0.65	1.75
150 ft.	0.55	0.73	1.62
200 ft.	0.62	0.76	1.51
300 ft.	0.68	0.80	1.39
400 ft.	0.74	0.83	1.33
500 ft.	0.77	0.85	1.28
700 ft.	0.83	0.87	1.23
1,000 ft.	0.86	0.89	1.19
2,000 ft.	0.92	0.93	1.12
3,000 ft.	0.94	0.95	1.07
4,000 ft.	0.95	0.96	1.05
5,000 ft.	0.96	0.97	1.04

*If the scraper stops at both ends of a segment, divide the segment into two parts and determine
a speed factor for each part.

David A. Day and Neal B. H. Benjamin, *Construction Equipment Guide*, 2d ed. (New York: John Wiley
& Sons, 1991), p. 172. Reprinted by permission of John Wiley & Sons, Inc.

the construction site to the dump area. The rolling resistance of the haul road is estimated to be 60 pounds per ton, and the coefficient of traction is estimated to be 0.5. The contractor obtained the following information from the manufacturer's literature for the 615C Series II elevating scraper:

Weight Distribution

Rated heaped capacity: 17 cubic yards

Empty
Drive axle: 66%
Rear axle: 34%

Empty weight: 56,450 pounds

Maximum load: 40,800 pounds

Loaded
Drive axle: 51%
Rear axle: 49%

A performance chart for the scraper is shown in Figure 10.8. What is the estimated productivity of the scraper in bank cubic yards per hour if the contractor operates 45 minutes per hour?

Solution

The first step is to determine the maximum load the scraper safely can carry without exceeding the load weight constraint. The heaped capacity in bank cubic yards is

$$\frac{17 \text{ BCY}}{1.2 \text{ LCY/BCY}} = 14.2 \text{ BCY}$$

Figure 10.8

Performance Chart for Caterpillar 615C Series II Elevating Scraper

Courtesy Caterpillar Inc.

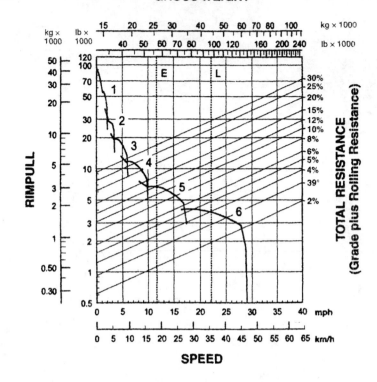

Wheel Tractor-Scrapers | 615C Series II Rimpull-Speed-Gradeability
● 29.5R25 Tires

GROSS WEIGHT

SPEED

KEY

1– 1st Gear Direct Drive
2– 2nd Gear Direct Drive
3– 3rd Gear Direct Drive
4– 4th Gear Direct Drive
5– 5th Gear Direct Drive
6– 6th Gear Direct Drive

KEY

E – Empty 25 605 kg (56,450 lb)
L – Loaded 44 113 kg (97,250 lb)

The weight of the load when filled to heaped capacity is

$$(14.2\ \text{BCY})(2{,}750\ \text{lb./BCY}) = 39{,}050\ \text{lb.}$$

which is less than the maximum rated load of 40,800 pounds. Therefore, the scraper can safely carry 17 loose cubic yards or 14.2 bank cubic yards.

Next, we need to estimate the cycle time for the scraper. We can estimate the fixed time from Table 10.1. The job conditions are assumed to be average, which provides a loading time of 1.1 minutes, negligible spotting and delay time, and a turning and dump time of 0.5 minutes, for a total fixed time of 1.6 minutes. To determine the variable time, we must estimate the maximum speed the scraper can traverse the haul road. We must also determine the maximum rimpull that can be generated without the wheels spinning. This involves multiplying the coefficient of traction by the weight on the driving axle. The maximum rimpull that can be generated when the scraper is empty is

$$(0.5)(0.66)(56,450 \text{ lb.}) = 18,628 \text{ lb.}$$

The maximum rimpull that can be generated when the scraper is loaded is

$$(0.5)(0.51)(56,450 \text{ lb.} + 39,050 \text{ lb.}) = 24,352 \text{ lb.}$$

The total weight when fully loaded is 95,500 lb. (56,450 lb. + 39,050 lb.) or 47.8 tons. The total resisting force on the haul road when traveling loaded is

$$F_R = [(60 \text{ lb./ton})(47.8 \text{ tons})] + [(2\%)(20 \text{ lb./ton per } \% \text{ slope})(47.8 \text{ tons})]$$
$$= 2,868 \text{ lb.} + 1,912 \text{ lb.} = 4,780 \text{ lb.}$$

Since the required rimpull (4,780 lb.) is less than the maximum (24,352 lb.) that can be generated, we will have no problem with traction.

Since we are operating at an altitude of 3,000 feet, we must calculate a derating factor before determining the scraper speed when loaded. The derating factor can be determined with Equation 7–16 to be

$$\text{Derating factor} = \frac{(0.03)(3,000 \text{ ft.} - 1,000 \text{ ft.})}{1,000 \text{ ft.}} = 0.06$$

which means that the scraper can generate only 94% of the rimpull at the speeds indicated in Figure 10.8. To use the performance chart, we must divide the required rimpull by 0.94 which is

$$\frac{4,780 \text{ lb.}}{0.94} = 5,085 \text{ lb.}$$

We can now read the maximum speed the scraper can traverse the haul road when loaded from Figure 10.8 to be 16 miles per hour. Since the scraper will be accelerating from a slow loading speed and decelerating to unload at the dump site, we will use the appropriate speed factor for starting from standstill or coming to a stop. Table 10.2 was developed assuming a stop at only one end of the travel segment. Since the scraper will stop at both ends, we will divide the haul road in half and determine a speed factor for 1,000 feet, which we can read from Table 10.2 to be 0.86. The average speed can now be estimated to be

$$(0.86)(16 \text{ mph}) = 13.8 \text{ mph}$$

The total resisting forces acting against the scraper when returning to the construction site empty is

$$F_R = [(60 \text{ lb./ton})(28.2 \text{ tons})] - [(2\%)(20 \text{ lb./ton per } \% \text{ slope})(28.2 \text{ tons})]$$
$$= 1,692 \text{ lb.} - 1,128 \text{ lb.} = 564 \text{ lb.}$$

Once again, we must divide by 0.94 to read the speed from Figure 10.8.

$$\frac{564 \text{ lb.}}{0.94} = 600 \text{ lb.}$$

We can now estimate the maximum speed that the scraper can traverse the haul road when empty from Figure 10.8 to be 29 miles per hour. Since the scraper will be accelerating from a slow dump speed and decelerating to a near stop to start loading, we again will use the appropriate speed factor from Table 10.2 for starting from a standstill or coming to a stop and 1,000 feet, which is 0.86. The average speed can now be estimated to be

$$(0.86)(29 \text{ mph}) = 24.9 \text{ mph}$$

Now we can complete the following table to determine the variable time:

Distance	Average Speed	Time
2,000 ft. (loaded)	13.8 mph	1.65 min.
2,000 ft. (empty)	24.9 mph	0.91 min.

The travel time is determined by dividing the travel distance by the average speed. The total variable time is determined by summing the times in the above table, or 2.53 minutes. The total cycle time for the scraper is

$$CT = FT + VT = 1.6 \text{ min.} + 2.536 \text{ min.} = 4.16 \text{ min.}$$

With Equation 10–3, the productivity can now be estimated to be

$$\text{Productivity} = \frac{(14.2 \text{ BCY})(45 \text{ min./hr.})}{4.16 \text{ min.}} = \textbf{153.6 BCY/hr.}$$

10.4   *Push Loading Scrapers*

Scrapers require assistance in loading to fill to rated capacity unless they are elevating. Push-pull scrapers work in tandem to assist each other, while other nonelevating scrapers require pushers. Crawler tractors usually are used for pushers because they have better traction than wheeled tractors. The three basic methods for push loading scrapers are illustrated in Figure 10.9. When excavating hard material, ripper-mounted crawler tractors often are used to loosen the soil with their rippers before the scrapers make their cuts. This reduces the loading time for the scrapers, which results in increased scraper productivity.

When scrapers are push loaded, the material in the bowl tends to be compacted to a higher density than its natural loose density. This compaction is due to the pressure of forcing the material into the bowl. Field tests indicate that the resulting density is approximately 10% greater than in an uncompacted loose state. Therefore, the density of the material in the scraper bowl can be determined by the following equation:

$$\text{Density in Scraper Bowl} = \frac{(110\%)(\text{Bank Density})}{100\% + \text{Percent Swell}} \qquad (10–4)$$

To determine the number of scrapers that a pusher can load, we must first determine the pusher cycle time. The cycle time includes the time required to contact the scraper, push it while it leads, boost it out of the cut, and maneuver to contact the next scraper. Where actual job data does not exist, the following equation can be used to estimate the pusher cycle time:[1]

$$CT_p = 1.4 \, L_S + 0.25 \text{ min.} \qquad (10–5)$$

---

[1] *Caterpillar Performance Handbook*, 28th ed., (Peoria, IL: Caterpillar, Inc., 1997), p. 21-12.

Figure 10.9

Methods of Push Loading
Scrapers

S. W. Nunnally, *Construction
Methods and Management*, 4/e,
©1998. Reprinted by permission of
Prentice-Hall, Inc., Upper Saddle
River, NJ.

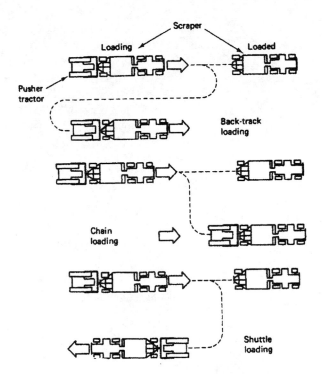

where L_S is the scraper load time in minutes

Boost time (time assisting scraper out of cut) is estimated to be 0.10 minutes

Return time is estimated to be 40% of load time

Maneuver time is estimated to be 0.15 minutes

The number of scrapers that a pusher can load can be determined by the following equation:

$$N_S = \frac{CT_S}{CT_P} \qquad (10\text{--}6)$$

where CT_S is the cycle time for the scrapers

CT_P is the cycle time for the pusher

Scraper operations typically are planned so that scrapers do not have to wait to be push loaded, since idle time for the pusher generally costs less than that for a scraper. An economic analysis often is required to determine the most economic mix of pushers and scrapers. Let's now look at an example problem to estimate the productivity for push-loaded scrapers.

Example 10.3

A contractor is planning to use Caterpillar 631E Series II single-engine scrapers to excavate the side of a large hill to construct a level building site for a school. The soil to be removed is a sandy clay weighing 2,700 pounds per bank cubic yard, and the swell is estimated to be 18%. The scraper is powered with a 450-horsepower turbocharged diesel engine. The haul road to be used by the scrapers is 4,000 feet (one way) with an uphill grade of 3% when traveling from the cut area to the dump area. The rolling resistance of the haul road is estimated to be 85 pounds per ton, and the coefficient of traction is estimated to be 0.4. To load the scrapers to their rated heaped capacity, the contractor plans to use a Caterpillar D8N crawler tractor to push load them. The project site is located at an elevation of 3,000 feet. The contractor obtained the following information from the manufacturer's literature for the 631C Series II scraper:

Weight Distribution

Rated heaped capacity: 31 cubic yards

Empty weight: 96,880 pounds

Maximum load: 75,000 pounds

Empty
Drive axle: 67%
Rear axle: 33%

Loaded
Drive axle: 53%
Rear axle: 47%

A performance chart for the scraper is shown in Figure 10.10.

a. What is the estimated productivity of one scraper in bank cubic yards per hour if the contractor operates 50 minutes per hour and the scraper does not wait in the cut for a pusher?
b. How many scrapers can one pusher load?

Solution

a. The first step is to determine the maximum load the scraper can safely carry without exceeding the load weight constraint. Using Equation 10–4, we can determine the density of the push-loaded material to be

$$\frac{(110\%)(2,700 \text{ lb./BCY})}{118\%} = 2,517 \text{ lb./cu. yd.}$$

The weight of the load when filled to heaped capacity is

$$(31 \text{ cu. yd.})(2,517 \text{ lb./cu. yd.}) = 78,027 \text{ lb.}$$

which is greater than the maximum rated load of 75,000 pounds. Therefore, the scraper can only carry

$$\frac{75,000 \text{ lb}}{2,517 \text{ lb./cu. yd.}} = 29.8 \text{ cu. yd.}$$

or

$$\frac{75,000 \text{ lb.}}{2,700 \text{ lb./BCY}} = 27.8 \text{ BCY}$$

Next, we need to estimate the cycle time for the scraper. We can estimate the fixed time from Table 10.1. The job conditions are assumed to be average, which provides a loading time of 0.7 minutes, a spotting and delay time of 0.3 minutes, and a turning

Figure 10.10
Performance Chart for Caterpillar
631E Series II Scraper

Courtesy Caterpillar Inc.

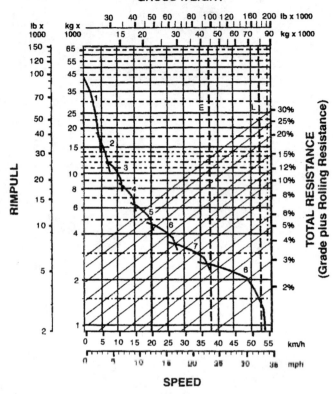

631E Series II Rimpull-Speed-Gradeability
• 37.25-35 Tires

Wheel Tractor-Scrapers

KEY

1– 1st Gear Torque Converter Drive
2– 2nd Gear Torque Converter Drive
3– 3rd Gear Direct Drive
4– 4th Gear Direct Drive
5– 5th Gear Direct Drive
6– 6th Gear Direct Drive
7– 7th Gear Direct Drive
8– 8th Gear Direct Drive

KEY

E – Empty 43 945 kg (96,880 lb)
L – Loaded 77 965 kg (171,880 lb)

and dump time of 0.5 minutes, for a total fixed time of 1.5 minutes. To determine the variable time, we must determine the maximum speed the scraper can traverse the haul road. We must also determine the maximum rimpull that can be generated without the wheels spinning. This involves multiplying the coefficient of traction by the weight on the driving axle. The maximum rimpull that can be generated when the scraper is empty is

$$(0.4)(0.67)(96,880 \text{ lb.}) = 25,964 \text{ lb.}$$

The maximum rimpull that can be generated when the scraper is loaded is

$$(0.4)(0.53)(96,880 \text{ lb.} + 75,000 \text{ lb.}) = 36,439 \text{ lb.}$$

The total weight when fully loaded is 171,880 lb. (96,880 lb. + 75,000 lb.) or 85.9 tons. The total resisting force on the haul road when traveling loaded is

$$F_R = [(85 \text{ lb./ton})(85.9 \text{ tons})] + [(3\%)(20 \text{ lb./ton per \% slope })(85.9 \text{ tons})]$$
$$= 7,302 \text{ lb.} + 5,154 \text{ lb.} = 12,456 \text{ lb.}$$

Since the required rimpull (12,456 lb.) is less than the maximum (36,439 lb.) that can be generated, we will have no problems with traction.

The scraper has a turbocharged engine, and there is no need to determine a derating factor for altitudes less than 10,000 feet. Since the project is at 3,000 feet, we can read the maximum speed directly from Figure 10.10 to be 10 miles per hour. Since the scraper will be accelerating from a slow loading speed and decelerating to unload at the dump site, we will use the appropriate speed factor for starting from standstill or coming to a stop. Because we are stopping at both ends of the haul road, we will divide the travel distance in half to determine the appropriate speed factor from Table 10.2. Using a distance of 2,000 feet, we read the appropriate speed factor to be 0.92. The average speed can now be estimated to be

$$(0.92)(10 \text{ mph}) = 9.2 \text{ mph}$$

The total resisting forces acting against the scraper when returning to the construction site empty are

$$F_R = [(85 \text{ lb./ton})(48.4 \text{ tons})] - [(3\%)(20 \text{ lb./ton per \% slope })(48.4 \text{ tons})]$$
$$= 4,114 \text{ lb.} - 2,904 \text{ lb.} = 1,210 \text{ lb.}$$

On Figure 10.10 we can read the maximum speed the scraper can traverse the haul road when empty to be 33 miles per hour. Since the scraper will be accelerating from a slow dump speed and decelerating to a near stop to start loading, we again will use the appropriate speed factor from Table 10.2 for starting from a standstill or coming to a stop and 2,000 feet, which is 0.92. The average speed can now be estimated to be

$$(0.92)(33 \text{ mph}) = 30.3 \text{ mph}$$

Now we can complete the following table to determine the variable time:

Distance	Average Speed	Time
4,000 feet (loaded)	9.2 mph	4.9 min.
4,000 feet (empty)	30.3 mph	1.5 min.

The travel time is determined by dividing the travel distance by the average speed. The total variable time is determined by summing the times in the above table: 6.4 minutes. The total cycle time for the scraper is

$$CT_S = FT + VT = 1.5 \text{ min.} + 6.4 \text{ min.} = 7.9 \text{ minutes}$$

With Equation 10–3, the productivity can now be estimated to be

$$\text{Productivity} = \frac{(27.8 \text{ BCY})(50 \text{ min./hr.})}{7.9 \text{ min.}} = 176 \text{ BCY/hr.}$$

b. The pusher cycle time can be estimated with Equation 10–5:

$$CT_P = [(1.4)(0.7 \text{ min.})] + 0.25 \text{ min.} = 1.2 \text{ min.}$$

The scraper loading time can be read from Table 10.1. The number of scrapers that one pusher can load is determined with Equation 10–6:

$$N_S = \frac{7.9 \text{ min.}}{1.2 \text{ min.}} = 6.6 \text{ scrapers}$$

This means that one pusher can load **6 scrapers** if the scrapers are not to wait in the cut area for a pusher.

10.5 Cost and Time Analysis

To estimate the cost of performing a construction task with scrapers, it is first necessary to estimate the hourly ownership and operating cost for the scrapers and pusher, if used, with the techniques discussed in Chapter 4, the cost references discussed in Chapter 5, or historical cost data. These costs can be used in conjunction with the overall productivity of the set of equipment involved to estimate the unit cost of performing the task. This information will be needed by a contractor in developing a cost estimate for the project. Dividing the total volume of work to be performed by the overall productivity of the set of equipment provides an estimate of the time required to complete the task. This information is required by the contractor in developing a construction schedule. Let's now look at an example.

Example 10.4

The contractor of Example 10.3 estimates the hourly cost data for the Caterpillar 631E Series II scraper and the D8N pusher to be as follows:

Equipment	Hourly Ownership Cost	Hourly Operating Cost	Effective Hourly Operator Cost
631E Scraper	$46.50	$84.30	$24.00
D8N Tractor	$21.50	$51.00	$20.00

The estimated volume of material to be removed is 80,000 bank cubic yards.

a. What is the estimated unit cost for excavating the side of the hill if the contractor uses 6 scrapers and 1 pusher?

b. What is the estimated unit cost for excavating the side of the hill if the contractor uses 7 scrapers and 1 pusher?

c. How long do you estimate it will take to complete the excavation using 6 or 7 scrapers, whichever is more economical? Assume the contractor plans to work 8 hours per day.

Solution

a. The total hourly cost for 1 scraper is

$$\$46.50/\text{hr.} + \$84.30/\text{hr.} + \$24.00/\text{hr.} = \$154.80/\text{hr.}$$

The total hourly cost for the pusher is

$$\$21.50/\text{hr.} + \$51.00/\text{hr.} + \$20.00/\text{hr.} = \$92.50/\text{hr.}$$

Since one pusher can load 6.6 scrapers (determined in Example 10.3), the pusher will have some idle time when working with a fleet of 6 scrapers. Therefore, the productivity of the fleet will be determined by the productivity of the scrapers, which is

$$(6)(176 \text{ BCY/hr.}) = 1{,}056 \text{ BCY/hr.}$$

The total hourly cost for the fleet is

$$[(6)(\$154.80/\text{hr.})] + \$92.50/\text{hr.} = \$1{,}021.30/\text{hr.}$$

The estimated unit cost is

$$\frac{\$1{,}021.30 \text{ per hr.}}{1{,}056 \text{ BCY/hr.}} = \textbf{\$0.97/BCY}$$

b. With 7 scrapers, the productivity of the pusher will govern, because the scrapers will sit idle in the cut area for short periods of time waiting for a pusher. The productivity of the pusher can be estimated by the following equation:

$$\text{Productivity} = \frac{(\text{Scraper Capacity})(\text{Operational Efficiency})}{\text{Pusher Cycle Time}}$$

$$= \frac{(27.8 \text{ BCY})(50 \text{ min./hr.})}{1.2 \text{ min.}} = 1{,}158 \text{ BCY/hr.}$$

The total hourly cost for the fleet is

$$[(7)(\$154.80/\text{hr.})] + \$92.50/\text{hr.} = \$1{,}176.10/\text{hr.}$$

The estimated unit cost is

$$\frac{\$1{,}761.10/\text{hr.}}{1{,}158 \text{ BCY/hr.}} = \textbf{\$1.02/BCY}$$

c. Since the 6-scraper fleet is the more economical, the estimated time to complete the excavation is

$$\frac{80{,}000 \text{ BCY}}{(1{,}056 \text{ BCY/hr.})(8 \text{ hr./day})} = \textbf{9.5 days}$$

10.6   *Problems*

1. A contractor has just been awarded a contract to construct a parking lot for a small shopping center. The soil conditions are very poor, and the designer has decided to bridge over the poor material with a structural fill 3 feet deep. The total estimated volume of material required is 14,000 compacted cubic yards. The fill material is a sandy clay weighing 2,600 pounds per bank cubic yard. The swell for the fill material is estimated to be 25%, and the shrinkage at the design density is estimated to be 15%. The contractor has selected a borrow source that is a half mile from the construction site. The contractor plans to maintain the haul road with a grader, and the resulting rolling resistance is estimated to be 55 pounds per ton. The coefficient of traction is estimated to be 0.6. The haul road has an uphill grade of 2% when traveling from the construction site to the borrow site. Job conditions are considered to be favorable. The contractor plans to use Caterpillar 615C Series II elevating scrapers to construct the fill. Performance characteristics of the 615C Series II scraper are provided in Example 10.2 and Figure 10.8. How many scrapers should the contractor use to complete the fill in 5 days, if he works 50 minutes per hour and 9 hours per day?

2. A contractor is planning to use 3 Caterpillar 631E Series II single-engine wheeled scrapers to construct a 2-foot compacted fill that is needed to build a parking lot adjacent to a new hospital. Site plans for the project show the compacted fill to measure 400 feet by 350 feet. The contractor has identified a suitable borrow site for the fill material that is located 1.5 miles from the project site. The haul road generally has a 3% uphill grade when traveling from the borrow site to the fill site. Soil tests on the fill material indicate a bank unit weight of 100 pounds per cubic foot. The swell for the soil has been determined to be 15%, and the shrinkage when compacted to the design density has been determined to be 9%. The contractor plans to use a Caterpillar D8N crawler tractor to push load the scrapers to their rated heaped or weight capacity, whichever governs. The rolling resistance of the haul road is estimated to be 75 pounds per ton, and the coefficient of traction is estimated to be 0.6. Job conditions are considered average. How long will it take the contractor (in days) to complete the fill, if he operates his equipment 50 minutes per hour and 8 hours per day? Assume scraper productivity determines the productivity of the entire task. Performance characteristics of the 631E Series II scraper are provided in Example 10.3 and Figure 10.10.

3. A contractor is planning to use Caterpillar 631E Series II single-engine scrapers to move 90,000 bank cubic yards of soil weighing 2,850 pounds per bank cubic yard. The swell for the soil has been determined to be 23%. To load the scrapers to their rated heaped capacity, the contractor plans to use Komatsu 68 E-1 crawler tractors. The 3,000-foot haul road from the borrow site to the fill area is fairly well maintained with a rolling resistance estimated to be 90 pounds per ton. The coefficient of traction is estimated to be 0.5. The haul road generally slopes down at a 1% slope when traveling from the borrow site to the fill area. Ownership and operating cost for each scraper is about $125.90 per hour and for the pusher tractor is about $58.90. A scraper operator earns $19.60 per hour plus 35% for fringes, and a tractor

operator earns $17.60 per hour plus 35% for fringes. Job efficiency is estimated to be 45 minutes per hour, and job conditions are considered average. Performance characteristics of the 631E Series II scraper are provided in Example 10.3 and Figure 10.10.

a. How many scrapers should the contractor plan to use on this job, if he wants to minimize idle time for the pusher tractor?

b. How long (in days) will it take to complete the fill operation, if the contractor uses 5 scrapers and 1 pusher tractor and works 8 hours per day?

c. What is the estimated cost per bank cubic yard for this operation, if the contractor uses 5 scrapers and 1 pusher tractor?

4. A contractor is using Caterpillar 631E Series II single-engine scrapers to move 125,000 bank cubic yards of sandy loam weighing 2,700 pounds per bank cubic yard 3,000 feet to a fill area to be compacted in 6-inch lifts. The swell for the soil has been determined to be 25%. The contractor needs to complete the fill in 6 weeks. The haul road slopes upward at 2% when traveling from the borrow site. If the haul road is not kept graded, the rolling resistance is estimated to be 200 pounds per ton, and the coefficient of traction is estimated to be 0.4. If the haul road is kept graded, the rolling resistance is estimated to be 60 pounds per ton, and the coefficient of traction is estimated to be 0.6. If the scrapers self-load, the fixed time is estimated to be 2.3 minutes to fill the bowl to 85% of the rated heaped capacity. If a pusher tractor is used, the bowl can be filled to its rated heaped capacity. Assume the contractor plans to operate the equipment 50 minutes per hour and 40 hours per week. Job conditions are considered favorable. Performance characteristics of the 631E scraper are provided in Example 10.3 and Figure 10.10.

a. How many scrapers are needed if no pusher tractor is used and the haul road is not maintained?

b. How many scrapers are needed if pusher tractors are used and the haul road is not maintained?

c. How many scrapers are needed if pusher tractors are used and the haul road is maintained?

5. A contractor has a fleet of 7 Caterpillar 631E Series II single-engine scrapers that he plans to use to construct a 100,000 compacted cubic yards fill. Soil tests indicate that the fill material is well-graded sandy clay weighing 2,850 pounds per bank cubic yard with a swell of 35% and a shrinkage of 20% when compacted to the design density. The contractor must transport the fill over a mile-long haul road that has an average uphill slope of 3% when traveling from the borrow site. The rolling resistance of the haul road is estimated to be 90 pounds per ton, and the coefficient of traction is estimated to be 0.4. Road conditions limit the maximum speed to 28 miles per hour. Job conditions are considered unfavorable. The contractor has one Caterpillar D8N crawler tractor that he plans to use to push load the scrapers to 95% of their rated heaped capacity. Ownership and operating cost for each scraper is about $135.75 per hour and for the crawler tractor about $75.40 per hour. The scraper operator's wage is $18.57 per hour and the tractor operator's wage is $16.35 per hour. A fringe of 30% must be added to both to cover insurance, workmen's compensation, etc. Job efficiency is estimated to be 45 minutes per hour. Perfor-

mance characteristics of the 631E Series II scraper are provided in Example 10.3 and Figure 10.10.

a. How many compacted cubic yards of fill can be excavated, hauled, and spread per hour?

b. Is productivity determined by the number of scrapers or the number of pushers?

c. What is the unit cost per compacted cubic yard to excavate, haul, and spread the fill material?

Excavators, Draglines, and Clamshells

11.1   Introduction

In this chapter, we will examine power digging equipment which includes hydraulically operated excavators and cable-operated draglines and clamshells. Two types of hydraulic excavators are manufactured: a *front shovel* with a bucket mounted so the opening faces away from the operator of the machine, and a *backhoe* with a bucket mounted so the opening faces toward the operator. Hitachi produces hydraulic excavators that can be equipped with either a shovel or a backhoe attachment. Draglines and clamshells essentially are cranes with digging attachments mounted on them. Most excavators, draglines, and clamshells are mounted on tracks, but smaller models may be mounted on wheels. Track-mounted equipment is designed for use on rough or loose surfaces or where bearing pressure is of concern. The tracks distribute the weight of the equipment over a larger area than wheels do, significantly reducing the pressure on the working surface. Wheeled versions are manufactured in two types: some are self-propelled with a single engine, while others are mounted on a truck chassis with two engines, one in the truck to move the piece of equipment from one work site to another, and a second engine in a revolving cab that powers the excavator, dragline, or clamshell.

11.2   Hydraulic Front Shovel Excavators

A front shovel was one of the earliest types of construction equipment manufactured. Early models were cable-operated, powered with steam engines, and used to load railroad cars or horse-drawn wagons. Modern front shovels are hydraulically operated, as illustrated in Figure 11.1. They primarily are used for excavating earth, rock, or mixed soil and rock from an embankment that will stand naturally with a fairly vertical face. A

Figure 11.1
Front Shovel Loading a Dump Truck
Courtesy Caterpillar, Inc.

shovel has greater capability for digging hard, compacted soil than does a loader. The loader usually requires a tractor with a blade to loosen the well-compacted soil and create stockpiles that the loader can excavate. The shovel operating cycle consists of loading the bucket by digging, swinging to the dump site, dumping, and swinging back for another load. Because the shovel does not move its undercarriage when loading, it can load trucks in a more confined working space than that required by loaders, which must maneuver during the loading cycle.

The major components of a front shovel are identified in Figure 11.2. The shovel is used to dig above its working platform. The shovel bucket is forced into the material to be excavated at the bottom of the embankment and moved upward in a circular arc. The shovel loads the bucket with a combination of crowding and breakout force, as illustrated in Figure 11.3. After the bucket has been loaded, it is rotated upward to reduce spillage during the swing. Two types of shovel buckets are manufactured: front dumping and bottom dumping. Bottom dumping buckets are more versatile and produce less spillage than front dumping ones, but are heavier and carry slightly less material than front dumping buckets. Once the digging cycle is complete, the shovel is rotated through an *angle of swing* to dump. When the bucket is emptied, the shovel swings back to the digging face for another load.

Figure 11.2

Components of a Front Shovel

S.W. Nunnally, *Construction Methods and Management*, 4/e © 1998. Reprinted by permission of Prentice-Hall, Inc., Upper Saddle River, NJ.

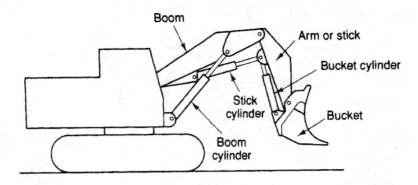

Figure 11.3

Digging Action of Front Shovel

S.W. Nunnally, *Construction Methods and Management*, 4/e © 1998. Reprinted by permission of Prentice-Hall, Inc., Upper Saddle River, NJ.

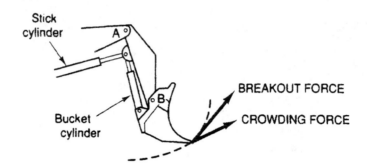

The height of the face being excavated influences the productivity of a front shovel. The *optimum depth* is the depth that will allow the shovel to fill the bucket completely with one vertical pass through the face without undue crowding. If the face is too high, material will spill onto the working surface. If the cut is too shallow, the shovel will have to make more than one pass to get a full bucket. The optimum digging depth for most shovels is between 40% and 50% of the shovel's maximum digging depth. The maximum digging depth can be determined from manufacturer's literature.

Shovel productivity is a function of the following:

- Type of material being excavated
- Depth of cut
- Angle of swing (position of haul unit)
- Size of shovel bucket
- Skill of operator
- Operating conditions

There are two methods for estimating shovel productivity. The first is to use Table 11.1 to estimate the ideal productivity for the shovel *when excavating at the optimum depth and swinging 90° between digging and dumping*. The other is to use Equation 11–1 to estimate ideal productivity. Once the ideal productivity has been estimated, it must be adjusted for actual operating conditions. Tables 11.2 and 11.3 are used to make these adjustments. Both techniques are illustrated in Example 11.1.

Table 11.1
Ideal Shovel Productivity in Bank Cubic Yards per Hour

Bucket Capacity	½ cu. yd.	¾ cu. yd.	1 cu. yd.	1¼ cu. yd.	1½ cu. yd.	1¾ cu. yd.	2 cu. yd.	2½ cu. yd.
Material								
Moist loam	115	165	205	250	285	320	355	405
Sand and gravel	110	155	200	230	270	300	330	390
Common earth	95	135	175	210	240	270	300	350
Tough clay	75	110	145	180	210	235	265	310
Well-blasted rock	60	95	125	155	180	205	230	275
Earth-rock mixture	50	80	105	130	155	180	200	245
Wet clay	40	70	95	120	145	165	185	230
Poorly blasted rock	25	50	75	95	115	140	160	195

Robert L. Peurifoy and William B. Ledbetter, *Construction Planning and Methods,* 4th ed.
(New York: McGraw-Hill, 1985), p. 203.

Table 11.1 provides estimates of ideal shovel productivity for the types of materials and bucket sizes shown when excavating at the optimal depth and swinging 90° between digging and dumping. Estimated ideal productivity is in bank cubic yards per hour.

An alternative method for estimating the ideal shovel productivity is to use the following equation:

$$\text{Ideal Productivity} = \frac{(\text{Bucket Capacity})(\text{Fill Factor})}{\text{Ideal Cycle Time}} \qquad (11–1)$$

Shovel buckets are rated in terms of heaped capacity. Fill factors are used to account for the different bulking properties of the types of material being excavated. Fill factors for various types of materials are shown in Table 11.2.

Analysis of manufacturers' technical literature indicates that the average ideal cycle time for shovels with bottom-dump buckets is between 20 and 28 seconds, and that the average cycle time for shovels with front-dump buckets is between 22 and 32 seconds.

Table 11.2
Front Shovel Bucket Fill Factors

Material	Fill Factor
Bank clay; earth	1.00–1.10
Rock-earth mixtures	1.05–1.15
Poorly blasted rock	0.85–1.00
Well-blasted rock	1.00–1.10
Shale; sandstone	0.85–1.10

Data for this table was extracted from
Catepillar Performance Handbook, 28th ed.
(Peoria, IL: Caterpillar Inc., 1997), p. 4-172.

Table 11.3

Shovel Productivity Correction Factor for Depth of Cut and Angle of Swing

Percent of Optimum Depth	Angle of Swing						
	45°	*60°*	*75°*	*90°*	*120°*	*150°*	*180°*
40%	0.93	0.89	0.85	0.80	0.72	0.65	0.59
60%	1.10	1.03	0.96	0.91	0.81	0.73	0.66
80%	1.22	1.12	1.04	0.98	0.86	0.77	0.69
100%	1.26	1.16	1.07	1.00	0.88	0.79	0.71
120%	1.20	1.11	1.03	0.97	0.86	0.77	0.70
140%	1.12	1.04	0.97	0.91	0.81	0.73	0.66
160%	1.03	0.96	0.90	0.85	0.75	0.67	0.62

Robert L. Peurifoy and William B. Ledbetter, *Construction Planning and Methods*, 4th ed. (New York: McGraw-Hill, 1985), p. 203.

Shovels with bucket capacities of 5 to 10 cubic yards typically have cycle times near the middle of the indicated ranges, those with bucket capacities less than 5 cubic yards typically have ideal cycle times near the low end of the indicated ranges, and those with bucket capacities greater than 10 cubic yards typically have ideal cycle times near the high end of the indicated ranges.

Once the ideal productivity has been estimated for the shovel, *we must correct for the actual digging depth and the actual angle of swing*. The appropriate correction factor can be determined from Table 11.3.

Next, we need to determine a correction factor for the operational efficiency of the shovel operation, which accounts for the job site conditions, operator skill, and management conditions. There are two methods that can be used to determine the operational efficiency. One is to estimate the number of minutes the machine will be operated per hour. The other is to estimate the operating factor from Table 11.4.

The actual shovel productivity is estimated by multiplying the ideal productivity estimated from Table 11.1 or Equation 11-1 by the appropriate correction factor from Table 11.3 and the operating factor. Let's look at an example to illustrate these concepts.

Table 11.4

Operating Factors for Excavating Operations

Job Conditions	Management Conditions			
	Excellent	*Good*	*Poor*	*Fair*
Excellent	0.84	0.81	0.76	0.70
Good	0.78	0.75	0.71	0.65
Poor	0.72	0.69	0.65	0.60
Fair	0.63	0.61	0.57	0.52

Example 11.1

A contractor has a project to construct an apartment complex and must construct a 3-foot compacted fill that will be used to support a parking garage. She has located a suitable borrow site about 3 miles from the construction site and has decided to use 10-cubic-yard dump trucks to haul the needed fill. She plans to load the dump trucks with a 2-cubic-yard front shovel that has a bottom dumping bucket. The material to be loaded is tough, dry clay with a swell of 35%. The height of the cut at the borrow site is about 11.8 feet, and the angle of swing for the shovel will be 150°.

a. Estimate the ideal productivity using both Equation 11–1 and Table 11.1.
b. Estimate the actual shovel productivity if both the job conditions and the management conditions are considered good. The optimum digging depth for the shovel is 9.8 feet.

Solution

a. The ideal productivity can be read directly from Table 11.1 to be 265 bank cubic yards per hour by selecting the productivity of a 2-cubic-yard bucket for tough clay. To estimate the ideal productivity with Equation 11–1, we must first estimate the fill factor and the ideal cycle time. The fill factor can be estimated from Table 11.2 to be 1.05 by taking the average value for bank clay. We will estimate the ideal cycle time to be 21 seconds by selecting a value near the low end of the range suggested. Now we can estimate the ideal productivity with Equation 11–1 to be

$$\frac{(2 \text{ LCY})(1.05)(3600 \text{ sec./hr.})}{(21 \text{ sec.})(1.35 \text{ LCY/BCY})} = \textbf{267 BCY/hr.}$$

b. The percent of optimum depth for this excavating operation is

$$\frac{(11.8 \text{ ft.})(100\%)}{9.8 \text{ ft.}} = 120\%$$

Using the percent of optimum depth (120%) and angle of swing (150°), we can find the appropriate correction factor from Table 11.3 to be 0.77. The appropriate operating factor for good job and management conditions can be determined from Table 11.4 to be 0.75. We can now estimate the actual productivity by using either estimate of ideal productivity. We will use the more conservative value obtained from Table 11.1. Actual productivity is estimated to be

$$(265 \text{ BCY/hr.})(0.77)(0.75) = \textbf{153 BCY/hr.}$$

11.3   Hydraulic Backhoe Excavators

Backhoe excavators are machines with buckets mounted on the end of a boom with the bucket opening facing the machine operator. They are used primarily to excavate below the surface on which they are sitting, as illustrated in Figure 11.4. The major components

Figure 11.4
Hydraulic Backhoe Excavator
Courtesy John Deere

of backhoe excavators are shown in Figure 11.5. Backhoes excavate by rotating the bucket so the cutting teeth face the ground, pushing the bucket down and pulling it toward the operator, rotating the bucket upward when filled, raising the bucket, swinging to dump, dumping the loaded material, and swinging back to the digging position.

Backhoes are used extensively for mass excavations and trench excavations. In utility work, a backhoe can be used both for trench excavation and handling the pipe, as illustrated in Figure 11.6, eliminating the need for a second piece of equipment. The rated lifting capacity for a backhoe, which can be determined from the manufacturer's literature, is different for each machine and varies with the distance between the load and the center of gravity of the machine (known as the *load radius*). Rated lifting ca-

Figure 11.5
Components of a Hydraulic
Backhoe Excavator

S.W. Nunnally, *Construction
Methods and Management*, 4/e
© 1998. Reprinted by permission of
Prentice-Hall, Inc., Upper Saddle
River, NJ.

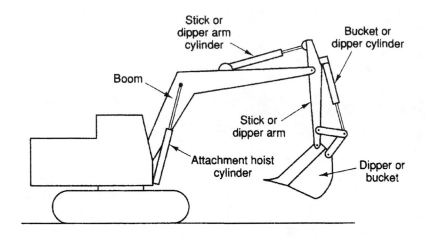

Figure 11.6
Utility Construction with a Backhoe

Courtesy John Deere

Figure 11.7
Small Wheeled Backhoe
Courtesy John Deere

pacity is limited to 75% of the load that would cause the machine to tip on firm, level ground and 87% of the hydraulic capacity of the machine.[1] Backhoe attachments are often mounted on the rear of wheeled tractors, as illustrated in Figure 11.7, for light excavation work on construction projects.

The maximum digging depth for backhoe excavators typically ranges from 12 to 35 feet. Very large backhoes manufactured for mass excavation work can excavate to depths up to 60 feet. The optimal digging depth for a backhoe is between 30% and 60% of its maximum digging depth. There is a wide variety of buckets manufactured, and contractors generally select bucket sizes to match job site requirements. Narrow buckets are used for trench work, while the large wide buckets are used for mass excavation. Material excavated by a backhoe excavator is either stockpiled near the excavation site or loaded into trucks.

---

[1]*1996 SAE Handbook*, Vol. 3 (Warrendale, PA: Society of Automotive Engineers, Inc., 1996), p. 40.382.

Backhoe productivity in terms of volume of material excavated per hour can be estimated using Equation 11–2:

$$\text{Productivity} = \frac{(\text{Bucket Capacity})(\text{Fill Factor})(\text{Operational Efficiency})}{\text{Cycle Time}} \quad (11\text{–}2)$$

Fill factors for backhoe buckets can be estimated from Table 11.5, and cycle times can be estimated from Table 11.6. Operational efficiency is based on the number of minutes spent working per hour. Let's look now at an example that illustrates the use of Equation 11–2.

Example 11.2

A contractor has a project to construct a large office building with an underground parking garage. He has decide to use a Link-Belt 4300 tracked hydraulic backhoe excavator to excavate for the parking garage and load the excavated material into 10-cubic-yard dump trucks. The maximum digging depth of the excavator is 24 feet, and it is equipped with a 2.5-cubic-yard bucket. The material to be excavated is a tough clay, and job conditions are considered to be average. The contractor plans to work an average of 50 minutes per hour. What is the estimated productivity in bank cubic yards per hour if the swell of the excavated material is 35%?

Solution

The fill factor for this operation can be estimated from Table 11.5 by taking the average value for tough clay, which is 0.85. The cycle time for the excavator can be estimated from Table 11.6 by selecting the value under the "2–3 cu. yd." column for average job conditions, which is 22 seconds. The operational efficiency is estimated to be 50 minutes per hour. Now we can estimate the productivity with Equation 11–2 to be

$$\frac{(2.5\ \text{LCY})(0.85)(50\ \text{min./hr.})(60\ \text{sec./min.})}{(22\ \text{sec.})(1.35\ \text{LCY/BCY})} = \textbf{214 BCY/hr.}$$

Table 11.5
Backhoe Bucket Fill Factors

Material	Fill Factor
Moist loam or sandy clay	1.00–1.10
Sand and gravel	0.95–1.10
Hard, tough clay	0.80–0.90
Well-blasted rock	0.60–0.75
Poorly blasted rock	0.40–0.50

Data for this table was extracted from *Caterpillar Performance Handbook*, 28th ed. (Peoria, IL: Caterpillar Inc., 1997), p. 4-108.

Table 11.6
Average Cycle Times for Hydraulic Backhoes

Job Conditions*	Backhoe Bucket Size				
	Less than 1 cu. yd.	1–2 cu. yd.	2–3 cu. yd.	3–4 cu. yd.	Over 4 cu. yd.
Excellent	13 sec.	15 sec.	16 sec.	16 sec.	17 sec.
Above Average	15 sec.	17 sec.	18 sec.	20 sec.	20 sec.
Average	17 sec.	20 sec.	22 sec.	25 sec.	26 sec.
Below Average	19 sec.	23 sec.	24 sec.	30 sec.	32 sec.
Severe	21 sec.	25 sec.	27 sec.	37 sec.	38 sec.

*Excellent conditions are characterized as easy digging (unpacked earth, sand, ditch cleaning, etc.); digging to less than 40% of the machine's maximum digging depth; swing angles less than 30°; dump into spoil pile; no obstructions.

Above average conditions are characterized as medium digging (packed earth, dry clay; soil with less than 25% rock content); depth to 50% of the machine's maximum digging depth; swing angles less than 60°; large dump target; few obstructions.

Average conditions are characterized as medium to hard digging (hard-packed soil with up to 50% rock content); depth to 70% of the machine's maximum digging depth; swing angle up to 90°; loading trucks spotted close to excavator.

Below average conditions are characterized as hard digging (shot rock, tough soil with up to 75% rock content); depth to 90% of the machine's maximum digging depth; swing angle up to 120°; shored trench; small dump target.

Severe conditions are characterized as tough digging (sandstone, shale, limestone, hard frost); depth over 90% of the machine's maximum digging depth, swing angle over 120°; small dump target requiring maximum reach.

Data for this table was extracted from *Caterpillar Performance Handbook*, 28th ed. (Peoria, IL: Caterpillar Inc., 1997), p. 4-143.

As previously discussed, backhoes often are used to excavate trenches for utility work. Contractors generally want to estimate excavation productivity for such operations in terms of linear feet of trench per hour. This can be estimated by the following equation:

$$\text{Productivity} = \frac{(\text{Bucket Capacity})(\text{Fill Factor})(\text{Operational Efficiency})}{(\text{Cycle Time})(\text{Cross-Sectional Area of Trench})} \quad (11\text{–}3)$$

Note that the bucket capacity typically is given in loose cubic yards, and the cross-sectional area is in bank square feet. Since the desired answer usually is bank feet per hour, the bucket capacity must be converted to bank cubic yards by using the percent swell. If the backhoe is used to lift pipe into the excavated trench, the operational efficiency must be adjusted to consider only that portion of time the excavator is actually digging the trench. Use of this equation is illustrated in the following example.

Example 11.3

A contractor has a requirement to install 750 feet of new water line as a part of her project. She plans to use a Hitachi EX 200-V hydraulic backhoe to excavate the trench for the water line and to place the pipe in the open trench. The maximum digging depth of the backhoe is 19 feet, and the bucket capacity is 1.2 cubic yards. The soil to be excavated is sandy clay, which will be stockpiled adjacent to the open trench. The trench to be excavated is to be 7 feet deep and 45 inches wide. Because of the time required to place the pipe, the contractor estimates that actual digging time will average 30 minutes per hour. Job site conditions are considered average. Swell for the excavated material is estimated to be 20%. What is the estimated productivity of the excavator in linear feet of trench per hour?

Solution

The fill factor for this operation can be estimated from Table 11.5 by taking the average value for sandy clay, which is 1.05.

The cycle time for the excavator can be estimated from Table 11.6 by selecting the value under the "1–2 cu. yd." column for average job conditions, which is 20 seconds. The operational efficiency is estimated to be 30 minutes per hour. The cross-sectional area in square feet is

$$\frac{(7 \text{ ft.})(45 \text{ in.})}{12 \text{ in./ft.}} = 26.2 \text{ sq. ft.}$$

Now we can estimate the productivity with Equation 11–3 to be

$$\frac{(1.2 \text{ LCY})(1.05)(30 \text{ min./hr.})(60 \text{ sec./min.})(27 \text{ cu. ft./cu. yd.})}{(20 \text{ sec.})(1.35 \text{ LCY/BCY})(26.2 \text{ sq. ft.})} = \textbf{86.6 ft./hr.}$$

11.4   *Draglines*

A dragline essentially is a crane with a large bucket that is dragged through the surface of the soil scooping up a bucketful of material, as illustrated in Figure 11.8. The major components of a dragline are identified in Figure 11.9. Draglines are used to excavate below the surface upon which they are resting, much like backhoes. The bucket is filled by dropping it into the material to be excavated and dragging it with teeth pointed down toward the base of the machine with the drag cable. Once the bucket is filled, it is lifted with both the drag and hoist cables to the desired height. Tension must be maintained on the hoist cable to keep the open end of the bucket oriented upward to retain the load in the bucket. The operator then swings the machine to the unload site and releases the tension on the drag cable. Gravity then causes the bucket to empty. Once the bucket is empty, the operator swings the machine back to the digging position for the next load. The basic components of a dragline bucket are illustrated in Figure 11.10.

Draglines are used to load hauling units, such as trucks, or create stockpiles. The maximum bucket size that can be used safely on a dragline depends on the size of the engine, the boom length, the size of the counterweight, the bucket weight, and the weight of the material being excavated. The dragline capacity data provided by the crane manufacturer should be used in selecting the maximum allowable bucket size. Table 11.7

Figure 11.8
Dragline Mounted on a Crawler Crane
Courtesy Link-Belt Construction Equipment Company

Figure 11.9
Components of a Dragline

S.W. Nunnally, *Construction
Methods and Management*, 4/e
© 1998. Reprinted by permission of
Prentice-Hall, Inc., Upper Saddle
River, NJ.

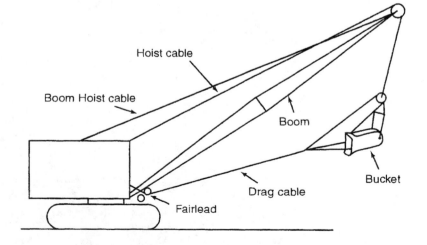

shows an example of such data for a Manitowoc 4000W VICON® crane. To ensure safe operation, the combined weight of bucket and load should not exceed 75% of the load that would cause the dragline to tip.

Figure 11.10
Dragline Bucket

S.W. Nunnally, *Construction
Methods and Management*, 4/e
© 1998. Reprinted by permission of
Prentice-Hall, Inc., Upper Saddle
River, NJ.

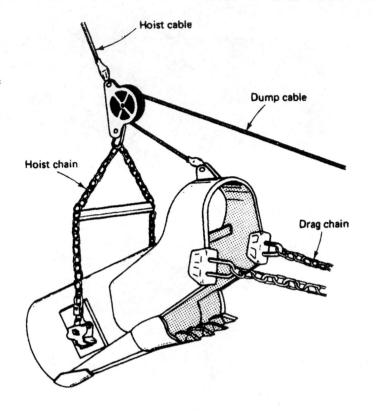

Table 11.7
Rated Dragline Lifting Capacity for Manitowoc 4000W VICON® Crane

Operating Radius	Boom Length			
	70 ft.	*80 ft.*	*90 ft.*	*100 ft.*
55 ft.	20,000 lb.	20,000 lb.		
60 ft.	20,000 lb.	20,000 lb.	20,000 lb.	
65 ft.	20,000 lb.	20,000 lb.	20,000 lb.	20,000 lb.
70 ft.	20,000 lb.	20,000 lb.	20,000 lb.	20,000 lb.
75 ft.		20,000 lb.	20,000 lb.	20,000 lb.
80 ft.		20,000 lb.	20,000 lb.	20,000 lb.
85 ft.			19,600 lb.	19,000 lb.
90 ft.				17,300 lb.
95 ft.				15,800 lb.

Data for this table was extracted from capacity charts for Manitowoc's Model 4000W VICON® crane.

Dragline buckets are rated at 90% of their struck volume, as illustrated in Figure 11.11, to compensate for the angle of repose of the loaded material. Dragline buckets are manufactured for light, medium, and heavy duty. Light-duty buckets generally are

Figure 11.11
Rated Capacity of Dragline
Buckets

Reprinted with Permission SAE J67
© 1994 Society of Automotive
Engineers, Inc.

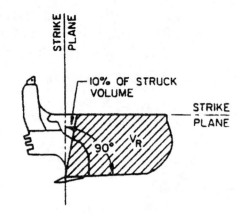

used for material rehandling, such as loading from a stockpile. Medium-weight buckets are used for excavating sand, clay, or other loose material. Heavy-duty buckets are used for tough digging to withstand the abrasion of rock. Table 11.8 provides representative weights for dragline buckets.

The digging reach and the operating radius of a dragline are considerably greater than for a front shovel or backhoe. This flexibility comes with reduced digging capability. The dragline relies on gravity to force the bucket into the material, while shovels and backhoes use hydraulic cylinders to force the bucket into the material. Consequently, draglines work best in loose material. They often are used for dredging operations and equipped with perforated buckets to allow the water to drain out of the holes in the bucket. Although the dragline bucket cannot be positioned as accurately as front shovels and backhoe buckets, a good operator can load trucks efficiently. Because of their greater productivity, hydraulic backhoes generally have replaced the smaller draglines on construction projects, unless the material to be excavated is very soft or wet.

Table 11.8
Representative Dragline Bucket Sizes and Weights

Rated Volume	Medium-Duty Bucket	Heavy-Duty Bucket
1/2 cu. yd.	1,175 lb.	
1 cu. yd.	2,150 lb.	
1 1/2 cu. yd.	3,175 lb	
2 cu. yd.	3,850 lb.	6,300 lb.
2 1/2 cu. yd.	4,875 lb.	6,600 lb.
3 cu. yd.	5,450 lb.	6,950 lb.
3 1/2 cu. yd.	6,025 lb.	8,725 lb.
4 cu. yd.		10,450 lb.
5 cu. yd.		14,050 lb.

Dragline productivity is a function of the same factors considered in estimating productivity for front shovels. They are the following:

- Type of material being excavated
- Depth of cut
- Angle of swing
- Size of dragline bucket
- Skill of operator
- Operating conditions

Productivity is estimated in a manner similar to that used in estimating productivity for front shovels. The first step is to estimate the ideal productivity, and then make adjustments for actual operating conditions. Ideal productivity can be estimated using Table 11.9. The table data is for *100% efficiency, excavation at the optimal depth,* and a *swing angle of 90° between digging and dumping.* For draglines equipped with buckets larger than 3 cubic yards, estimate the ideal productivity using Equation 11–4:

$$\text{Ideal Productivity} = \frac{\text{(Bucket Capacity)}}{\text{Ideal Cycle Time}} \qquad (11\text{–}4)$$

Under ideal conditions, the *cycle time for a dragline should be between 25 and 35 seconds.* If the dragline is being used to excavate nongranular material under water, the cycle time should be increased 40% to 50%.

The optimum excavating depth for a dragline is the minimum distance the bucket must be moved through the material to be excavated to obtain a full bucket. Optimum depths for various bucket sizes can be estimated from Table 11.10.

Once the ideal productivity has been estimated for a dragline, *we must correct for the actual digging depth and actual angle of swing.* The appropriate correction factor can be determined for Table 11.11.

Next, we need to determine an operating factor that accounts for job site conditions, operator skill, and management conditions. This factor can be determined either from Table 11.4 or by estimating the number of minutes the machine will work per hour.

Table 11.9
Ideal Dragline Productivity in Bank Cubic Yards per Hour

Bucket Capacity	$3/4$ cu. yd.	1 cu. yd.	$1^1/4$ cu. yd.	$1^1/2$ cu. yd.	$1^3/4$ cu. yd.	2 cu. yd.	$2^1/2$ cu. yd.	3 cu. yd.
Material								
Moist loam; light sandy clay	130	160	195	220	245	265	305	350
Sand and gravel	125	155	185	210	235	255	295	340
Common earth	105	135	165	190	210	230	265	305
Hard, tough clay	90	110	135	160	180	195	230	270
Wet, sticky clay	55	75	95	110	130	145	175	210

Table 11.10

Optimal Depth of Cut for Various Sizes of Dragline Buckets

Bucket Capacity	½ cu. yd.	¾ cu. yd.	1 cu. yd.	1¼ cu. yd.	1½ cu. yd.	1¾ cu. yd.	2 cu. yd.	2½ cu. yd.
Material								
Moist loam; light sandy clay	5.5 ft.	6.0 ft.	6.6 ft.	7.0 ft.	7.4 ft.	7.7 ft.	8.0 ft.	8.5 ft.
Sand and gravel	5.5 ft.	6.0 ft.	6.6 ft.	7.0 ft.	7.4 ft.	7.7 ft.	8.0 ft.	8.5 ft.
Common earth	6.7 ft.	7.4 ft.	8.0 ft.	8.5 ft.	9.0 ft.	9.5 ft.	9.9 ft.	10.5 ft.
Hard, tough clay	8.0 ft.	8.7 ft.	9.3 ft.	10.0 ft.	10.7 ft.	11.3 ft.	11.8 ft.	12.3 ft.
Wet, sticky clay	8.0 ft.	8.7 ft.	9.3 ft.	10.0 ft.	10.7 ft.	11.3 ft.	11.8 ft.	12.3 ft.

Data for this table was extracted from Robert L. Peurifoy, William B. Ledbetter, and Clifford J. Schexnayder, *Construction Planning, Equipment, and Methods,* 5th ed. (New York: McGraw-Hill, 1996), p. 195.

Table 11.11

Dragline Productivity Correction Factor
for Depth of Cut and Angle of Swing

Percent of Optimum Depth	Angle of Swing							
	30°	45°	60°	75°	90°	120°	150°	180°
20%	1.06	0.99	0.94	0.90	0.87	0.81	0.75	0.70
40%	1.17	1.08	1.02	0.97	0.93	0.85	0.78	0.72
60%	1.25	1.13	1.06	1.01	0.97	0.88	0.80	0.74
80%	1.29	1.17	1.09	1.04	0.99	0.90	0.82	0.76
100%	1.32	1.19	1.11	1.05	1.00	0.91	0.83	0.77
120%	1.29	1.17	1.09	1.03	0.98	0.90	0.82	0.76
140%	1.25	1.14	1.06	1.00	0.96	0.88	0.81	0.75
160%	1.20	1.10	1.02	0.97	0.93	0.85	0.79	0.73
180%	1.15	1.05	0.98	0.94	0.90	0.82	0.76	0.71
200%	1.10	1.00	0.94	0.90	0.87	0.79	0.73	0.69

S.W. Nunnally, *Construction Methods and Management,* 4/e © 1998. Reprinted by permission of Prentice-Hall, Inc., Upper Saddle River, NJ.

The actual dragline productivity is estimated by multiplying the ideal productivity by the appropriate correction factor from Table 11.11 and the operating factor. Let's look at an example to illustrate this concept.

Example 11.4

A contractor has a project to construct a large parking lot for a shopping center. One feature of the project is the construction of a large drainage ditch to collect and remove storm water runoff. The contractor has decided to use a crawler dragline with 1¾-cubic-yard bucket to excavate the ditch. The average depth of the cut is estimated to be 7.6 feet, and the excavated material will be loaded into dump trucks for removal from the project site. The angle of swing will be 120°. The material to be excavated is common earth. The job conditions are considered good, and the management conditions are considered excellent. What is the estimated productivity of the dragline in bank cubic yards per hour?

Solution

The estimated ideal productivity can be read directly from Table 11.9: the value under a $1^3/4$-cubic-yard bucket for common earth is 210 bank cubic yards per hour.

The optimum depth for the dragline can be estimated from Table 11.10: the value under a $1^3/4$-cubic-yard bucket for common earth is 9.5 feet. The percent of optimum depth for the excavating operation will be

$$\frac{(7.6 \text{ ft.})(100\%)}{9.5 \text{ ft.}} = 80\%$$

Using the percent of optimum depth (80%) and the angle of swing (120°), we can find the appropriate correction factor from Table 11.11 to be 0.90. The appropriate operating factor for good job conditions and excellent management conditions can be determined from Table 11.4 to be 0.78. Now we can estimate the dragline productivity to be

$$(210 \text{ BCY/hr.})(0.90)(0.78) = \textbf{147 BCY/hr.}$$

11.5   *Clamshells*

A clamshell essentially is a crane with a large hinged bucket suspended at the end of the boom as illustrated in Figure 11.12. The major components of a clamshell are identified in Figure 11.13. Clamshells are used for vertical excavation. They can dig vertically to considerable depths and can lift their loads well above the surface on which they are resting. The tagline is a spring-mounted cable attached to the bucket to keep it from rotating around the holding line. The tagline can be connected either to the end of the bucket or in the center on the side, depending on the digging orientation desired by the machine operator.

Since clamshells lack the positive digging force of a front shovel or backhoe, they are best suited for loose or soft-to-medium material. They typically are used for vertical excavation and to load trucks, conveyors, or overhead hoppers. A clamshell bucket is illustrated in Figure 11.14. The bucket is opened by releasing the tension on the closing line. The open bucket is dropped into the material to be excavated. The bucket is closed by pulling on the closing line, which causes the teeth to close rotating around the counterweight. Once the bucket is closed, it is raised by lifting on both the holding line and the closing line. The operator then swings to the dump site and releases the tension on the closing line, dumping the load. The operator then swings the machine back to the digging site for the next load.

Figure 11.12
Clamshell Dredging Granular Material

Courtesy Manitowoc Cranes, Inc.

Figure 11.13
Components of a Clamshell

S.W. Nunnally, *Construction Methods and Management*, 4/e © 1998. Reprinted by permission of Prentice-Hall, Inc., Upper Saddle River, NJ.

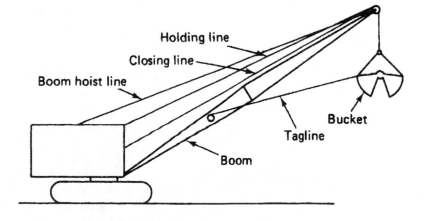

Figure 11.14
Clamshell Bucket

S.W. Nunnally, *Construction Methods and Management*, 4/e
© 1998. Reprinted by permission of Prentice-Hall, Inc., Upper Saddle River, NJ.

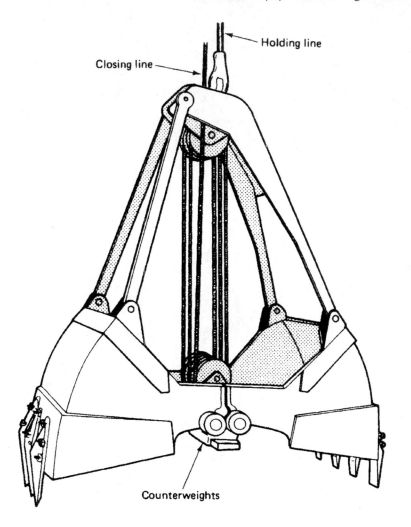

Clamshell buckets are available in various sizes, with or without removable teeth. They come in three weights: heavy weight for digging rock/soil mixtures and hard clay, medium weight for general purpose work, and light weight for handling light material. Buckets without teeth are used for rehandling material, such as loading from a loose stockpile. The capacity of a bucket usually is rated in loose cubic yards. Industry standard is to rate buckets by heaped volume, as illustrated in Figure 11.15. Representative clamshell bucket sizes and weights are shown in Table 11.12 for Owen buckets.

Just as with draglines, the maximum size bucket that can be used safely on a clamshell depends on the size of the engine, the boom length, the size of the counterweight, and the weight of the material being excavated. The clamshell lifting capacity data provided by the crane manufacturer should be used in selecting the maximum allowable bucket size. An example of such information is illustrated in Table 11.13 for a Manitowoc 4000W VICON® crane. To ensure safe operation, the combined weight of

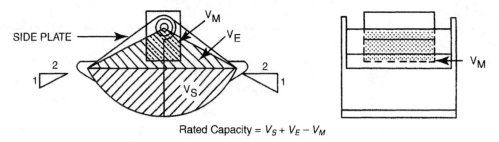

$$\text{Rated Capacity} = V_S + V_E - V_M$$

Figure 11.15
Rated Heaped Capacity of Clamshell Buckets

Reprinted with Permission SAEJ67 © 1994 Society of Automotive Engineers, Inc.

Table 11.12
Representative Clamshell Bucket Sizes and Weights

Rated Volume	General-Purpose Bucket	Heavy-Duty Bucket
$1/2$ cu. yd.	2,750 lb.	2,980 lb.
$3/4$ cu. yd.	4,140 lb.	4,620 lb.
1 cu. yd.	4,360 lb.	4,900 lb.
$1^1/2$ cu. yd.	6,540 lb.	7,480 lb.
2 cu. yd.	7,050 lb.	7,870 lb.
$2^1/2$ cu. yd.	8,315 lb.	10,255 lb.
3 cu. yd.	8,815 lb.	10,650 lb.
$3^1/2$ cu. yd.	12,960 lb.	14,260 lb.
4 cu. yd.	13,820 lb.	14,960 lb.
5 cu. yd.	16,795 lb.	19,295 lb.
6 cu. yd.	19,245 lb.	21,645 lb.

Data for this table was extracted from literature published by Anvil Attachments, Inc., for Owen clamshell buckets.

the bucket and load should not exceed the maximum lifting capacity for that length of boom and operating radius. Industry standards limit the maximum load to 67.5% of the load that would cause the machine to tip.

Clamshell productivity is a function of the same factors considered in estimating productivity for draglines. They are the following:

- Type of material being excavated
- Depth of cut
- Angle of swing
- Size of clamshell bucket
- Skill of operator
- Operating conditions

Productivity is estimated in a manner similar to that used in estimating productivity for draglines. The first step is to estimate the ideal productivity and then make adjustments

Table 11.13
Rated Clamshell Lifting Capacity for Manitowoc 4000W VICON® Crane

Operating Radius	Boom Length					
	70 ft.	*80 ft.*	*90 ft.*	*100 ft.*	*110 ft.*	*120 ft.*
55 ft.	28,000 lb.	28,000 lb.	28,000 lb.	28,000 lb.	28,000 lb.	28,000 lb.
60 ft.	28,000 lb.	28,000 lb.	28,000 lb.	28,000 lb.	28,000 lb.	28,000 lb.
65 ft.	28,000 lb.	27,700 lb.	27,200 lb.	26,600 lb.	26,200 lb.	25,600 lb.
70 ft.	25,400 lb.	24,800 lb.	24,300 lb.	23,700 lb.	23,300 lb.	22,700 lb.
75 ft.		22,300 lb.	21,900 lb.	21,200 lb.	20,800 lb.	20,200 lb.
80 ft.		20,200 lb.	19,700 lb.	19,100 lb.	18,600 lb.	18,100 lb.
85 ft.			17,900 lb.	17,200 lb.	16,800 lb.	16,200 lb.
90 ft.			16,200 lb.	15,600 lb.	15,100 lb.	14,500 lb.
95 ft.				14,100 lb.	13,700 lb.	13,100 lb.
100 ft.				12,800 lb.	12,400 lb.	11,800 lb.
105 ft.					11,200 lb.	10,600 lb.
110 ft.						9,600 lb.

Data for this table was extracted from capacity charts for Manitowoc's Model 4000W VICON® crane.

for actual operating conditions. Ideal productivity can be estimated using Table 11.14. The table data is for 100% efficiency and a swing angle of 90° between digging and dumping. For clamshells equipped with buckets larger than $2^1/2$ cubic yards, estimate the ideal productivity with Equation 11–4. Under ideal conditions, the cycle time for a clamshell should be between 25 and 35 seconds. If the clamshell is being used to excavate nongranular material under water, the cycle time should be increased 50% to 60%.

Once the ideal productivity has been estimated for the clamshell, *we must correct for the actual angle of swing*. The appropriate correction factor can be determined from Table 11.15.

Table 11.14
Ideal Clamshell Productivity in Bank Cubic Yards per Hour

Bucket Capacity	$1/2$ cu. yd.	$3/4$ cu. yd.	1 cu. yd.	$1^1/4$ cu. yd.	$1^1/2$ cu. yd.	$1^3/4$ cu. yd.	2 cu. yd.	$2^1/2$ cu. yd.
Material								
Moist loam or sandy clay	65	95	120	140	155	170	190	225
Sand and gravel	60	85	110	130	140	160	175	205
Common earth	55	70	95	115	125	145	160	185

Walker's Building Estimator's Reference Book, 25th ed. (Lisle, IL: Frank R. Walker Company, 1995), p. 2.37.

Table 11.15
Clamshell Productivity Correction Factor for Angle of Swing

Angle of Swing

30°	45°	60°	75°	90°	120°	150°	180°
1.32	1.19	1.11	1.05	1.00	0.91	0.83	0.77

Next, we need to determine an operating factor that accounts for the job site conditions, operator skill, and management conditions. This factor can be determined either from Table 11.4 or by estimating the average number of minutes the machine will work per hour.

The actual clamshell productivity is estimated by multiplying the ideal productivity by the appropriate correction factor from Table 11.15 and the operating factor. Let's now look at an example to illustrate this concept.

Example 11.5

A contractor has decided to use a 2-cubic-yard clamshell mounted on a crawler crane to excavate for the footing foundations for three concrete piers for a small highway bridge. The excavated material will be dumped in stockpiles for later use in backfilling the completed piers. The material being excavated is common earth, and the average angle of swing will be 120°. Both the job and management conditions are considered good. What is the estimated productivity of the clamshell in bank cubic yards per hour?

Solution

The estimated ideal productivity of 160 bank cubic yards per hour can be read from Table 11.14 by selecting the value under 2-cubic-yard bucket for common earth.

The correction factor for angle of swing can be determined from Table 11.15 by selecting the factor for 120°. The factor is 0.91. The operating factor for good job and management conditions can be found in Table 11.4 to be 0.75. Now, we can estimate the actual clamshell productivity to be

$$(160 \text{ BCY/hr.})(0.91)(0.75) = 109 \text{ BCY/hr.}$$

11.6   Cost and Time Analysis

To estimate the cost of performing a construction task with an excavator, it is first necessary to estimate the hourly ownership and operating cost using the techniques discussed in Chapter 4, the cost references discussed in Chapter 5, or historical cost data. The costs can be used in conjunction with the machine productivity estimated by the techniques discussed in this chapter to estimate the unit cost for using the excavator to perform a specific construction task. When using excavators to load trucks, it is necessary to adjust estimated machine productivity if the excavator must sit idle waiting for a truck to load. Techniques for estimating appropriate productivity for truck-loading operations will be discussed in Chapter 12. Unit cost data for the specific task is needed to determine a cost estimate for the task. Machine productivity also is needed to determine the time required to perform the task. This information is needed to determine the activity duration for a construction schedule. Let's now look at an example.

Example 11.6

The contractor of Example 11.2 estimates his hourly ownership and operating costs for the Link Belt 4300 tracked hydraulic backhoe excavator to be as follows:

Ownership cost	$25.75 per hour
Operating cost	$32.00 per hour
Operator wages	$28.50 per hour

a. What is the estimated unit cost in dollars per bank cubic yard to excavate for the parking garage assuming that there are sufficient dump trucks so that the excavator never sits idle? Determine unit cost for the excavator only.
b. The contractor reviewed the plans for the parking garage and determined the dimensions of the required excavation to be 20 feet deep, 75 feet wide, and 120 feet long. How many days will it take to complete the excavation if the productivity of the excavator is the determining factor? Assume the contractor will work 8 hours per day.

Solution

a. The total hourly cost for the excavator is

$$\$25.75/\text{hr.} + \$32.00/\text{hr.} + \$28.50/\text{hr.} = \$86.25/\text{hr.}$$

In Example 11.2 the hourly production rate of the excavator was determined to be 214 BCY/hr. The estimated unit cost is

$$\frac{\$86.25/\text{hr.}}{214 \text{ BCY/hr.}} = \mathbf{\$0.40/BCY} \text{ for the excavator only}$$

Hauling cost must be added to determine the total unit cost.

b. The total volume to be excavated is

$$\frac{(20 \text{ ft.})(75 \text{ ft.})(120 \text{ ft.})}{27 \text{ cu. ft./cu. yd.}} = 6{,}667 \text{ BCY}$$

The total time required to complete the excavation is

$$\frac{6{,}667 \text{ BCY}}{(214 \text{ BCY/hr.})(8 \text{ hr./day})} = \mathbf{4 \text{ days}}$$

11.7 Problems

1. A contractor has a project involving the construction of a small manufacturing plant. The site drawings for the project indicate that a 2-foot compacted fill is required to support a concrete slab foundation for the plant. The contractor has selected a borrow site and has decided to use dump trucks to haul the needed fill material. The contractor has decided to use a Hitachi EX 750 hydraulic excavator with a shovel attachment to load the trucks. The excavator is equipped with a 5.2-cubic-yard bottom-dump general-purpose bucket. The optimal digging depth for the machine is 15 feet. The material to be loaded is common earth with a swell estimated to be 25%. When compacted to the design density, the shrinkage of the fill material is estimated to be 10%. Analysis of the borrow site indicates that the average angle of swing will be 90° and that the average depth of dig will be 18 feet. Estimated job and management conditions will be good. What is the estimated productivity of the shovel in compacted cubic yards per hour if the ideal cycle time is estimated to be 24 seconds?

2. A contractor has a contract for the construction of a high-rise office building with an underground parking garage. The size of the excavation required for the parking garage is 100 feet long, 45 feet wide, and 25 feet deep. The contractor plans to use a Caterpillar 5080 tracked hydraulic front shovel to excavate the soil and load 15-cubic-yard dump trucks. The rated heaped capacity of the shovel bucket is 6.8 cubic yards and the optimum digging depth for the shovel is 15.5 feet. The material to be excavated is bank clay with a swell of 35%. The contractor plans to excavate the foundation in two 12.5-foot layers and has determined the average angle of swing will be 120°.

   a. What is the estimated productivity of the excavator in bank cubic yards per hour if the ideal cycle time is 24 seconds and the operational efficiency is 40 minutes per hour?

   b. If an adequate number of dump trucks is used to eliminate excavator idle time, how long will it take to complete the excavation for the parking garage?

3. A contractor has decided to use a Case 9010B hydraulic backhoe to excavate a 24-inch-wide trench for the construction of a water line. The backhoe has a general-purpose bucket with a rated heaped capacity of 19 cubic feet. The average depth of the 400-foot trench is about 6 feet. The soil to be excavated is tough clay with a swell of 33%. Operational efficiency is estimated at 45 minutes per hour.

   a. What is the estimated productivity of the backhoe in bank cubic yards per hour if job conditions are considered average?

   b. How long will it take to excavate the trench?

4. A contractor is planning to use a backhoe to excavate for the foundation of a bank building she is constructing. The 10-foot-deep foundation will be 60 feet long by 40 feet wide in size. To meet her construction schedule, the contractor needs to excavate the foundation in 2 days. She has determined the swell for the sandy clay soil to be 16%. What size backhoe (bucket size) should she select for this job, if job conditions are considered average and the machine operates 50 minutes per hour and 8 hours per day?

5. A contractor has a contract to install 1,000 feet of pressurized water line and is planning to use a Caterpillar 322L tracked excavator (backhoe) to excavate the trench for

the construction of the pipe and to set the pipe in the trench. The required trench will be 4 feet wide and 10 feet deep. The material excavated will be stockpiled along the open trench and used to backfill the completed water line. The soil to be removed is a hard, tough clay weighing 100 pounds per bank cubic foot with a swell of 30%. The contractor plans to work 8 hours per day and estimates the operational efficiency for the excavating operation will be about 30 minutes per hour, with the remainder of the time being used to set the pipe. The maximum digging depth of the backhoe is 19 feet and the rated heaped capacity of the bucket is 39 cubic feet. Job conditions are considered below average.

   a. What is the estimated productivity of the excavator in linear feet of trench per hour?

   b. If it costs the contractor $125 per hour to rent and operate the excavator, how much do you estimate the excavation portion of the project will cost?

6. A contractor has decided to use a dragline to excavate a ditch to drain storm water runoff from her construction site. The dragline bucket and fairlead are to be mounted on a 40-ton crawler crane with 70-foot boom. The material to be excavated is a hard, tough clay weighing 3,000 pounds per bank cubic yard with a swell of 22%. Given the density of the material to be loaded, the contractor has determined that the largest heavy-duty dragline bucket that can be safely mounted on the crane has a rated capacity of 2 cubic yards.

   a. What is the estimated production rate of the dragline in bank cubic yards per hour if the average depth of the dig is 12 feet and the average angle of swing is 120°? The contractor plans to operate the machine about 40 minutes per hour.

   b. Rental and operating costs for the dragline come to $55.75 per hour, and the operator's wage is $25.40 per hour plus 35% for fringes. What is the estimated unit cost per bank cubic yard for excavating the ditch?

   c. If the ditch to be constructed is 5 feet wide, 18 feet deep, and 700 feet long, how many days will it take the dragline to complete the excavation, if the contractor works 8 hours per day?

7. A contractor is dredging sand out of the bottom of a river channel to be used in his concrete plant. He is using a 40-ton crane with a 2-cubic-yard clamshell bucket to excavate the sand. The average angle of swing is 120°. He is using dump trucks to haul the sand to the concrete plant and estimates that the clamshell will actually operate about 40 minutes per hour. What is the estimated production rate for the clamshell in bank cubic yards per hour?

8. A contractor has rigged a crawler crane with a 3-cubic-yard clamshell bucket and a tagline to load a stockpile of dry common earth into 12-cubic-yard dump trucks. The average angle of swing is 90°, and the ideal cycle time is estimated to be 26 seconds. Job conditions are considered good; management conditions are considered excellent.

   a. What is the estimated productivity of the clamshell in loose cubic yards per hour?

   b. How long will it take the clamshell to load one dump truck?

   c. The ownership and operating costs for the clamshell are estimated to be $105 per hour, and the operator earns $25.75 per hour plus 40% for fringes. What is the estimated unit cost per loose cubic yard to load the stockpile if the clamshell does not sit idle waiting for a truck to load?

12

Trucks and Haulers

12.1   *Introduction*

Trucks and haulers are flexible pieces of construction equipment that are used to carry bulk construction materials such as soil, sand, gravel, rock, or asphalt. The cost of hauling with these units generally is quite economical, because they are able to traverse haul roads at relatively high speeds. Trucks and haulers usually are the most cost-effective types of hauling equipment when the haul distances are greater than about 2 miles. At shorter distances, scrapers may be more economical, because of the high cost of loading trucks and haulers. Trucks also are used on urban construction projects, because scrapers generally are not allowed on paved roads or in urban settings. Since trucks and haulers are not self-loading, they must be loaded by another piece of equipment. The most common types of loading equipment are loaders (either wheeled or tracked), front shovels, excavators, clamshells, and draglines. Key contractor decisions include selection of the type and size of truck or hauler, the type and size of loading equipment, and the number of trucks to use on a specific construction task. As will be illustrated in this chapter, proper fleet balancing is critical to minimizing the cost of a loading and hauling operation.

12.2   *Types and Uses of Trucks and Haulers*

Trucks and haulers usually are either end dumping or bottom dumping. Some specialized trucks may be side dumping. The term *truck* usually refers to a single-chassis vehicle, while the term *hauler* usually refers to a truck tractor pulling one or more end-dumping or bottom-dumping trailers. Bottom-dumping haulers are used in applications where the hauled material is to be distributed in layers. Wet, cohesive soil does not work well in bottom-dumping haulers, because it tends to bulk up and not spread well. If the material to be hauled is rock or wet clay, end-dump trucks should be used.

Trucks and haulers may be classified according to the following:

- On-highway or off-highway
- Load capacity (volume and weight)
- Type of drive (two-wheel, four-wheel, or six-wheel)
- Method of dumping

On-highway trucks and haulers comply with gross vehicle weight, axle loading, and width limitations imposed by state highway departments. On-highway end-dump trucks typically have load capacities of 5 to 12 loose cubic yards. On-highway bottom-dump haulers may have load capacities up to 30 loose cubic yards. Off-highway trucks and haulers are larger than on-highway types and do not comply with state-imposed restrictions for highway use. As with scrapers, the condition of the haul road will significantly affect the productivity of off-highway trucks and haulers. Large trucks and haulers have less labor costs per cubic yard moved than small trucks, but tend to be harder on haul roads and require more maneuvering space at loading and dumping sites. Figure 12.1 shows a typical on-highway dump truck, Figure 12.2 shows a typical off-highway rigid-frame dump truck, Figure 12.3 shows a typical off-highway articulated dump truck, Figure 12.4 shows a typical end-dump hauler, and Figure 12.5 shows a typical bottom-dump hauler.

Figure 12.1
Typical On-Highway Dump Truck

Figure 12.2
Typical Off-Highway Rigid-Frame Dump Truck

Courtesy TEREX Americas

Figure 12.3
Typical Off-Highway Articulated Dump Truck

Courtesy TEREX Americas

Figure 12.4
Typical End-Dump Hauler
Courtesy Trail King Industries

Figure 12.5
Typical Bottom-Dump Hauler
Courtesy Trail King Industries

Table 12.1
Load-Carrying Capabilities of Off-Highway Dump Trucks

Model	Empty Weight	Maximum Load	Heaped Capacity
Caterpillar (Rigid-Frame)			
769D	34.5 tons	40.5 tons	30.7 cu. yd.
773D	44.3 tons	57.7 tons	44.6 cu. yd.
777D	71 tons	106 tons	78.6 cu. yd.
785B	106 tons	169 tons	102 cu. yd.
Caterpillar (Articulated)			
D25D	21.4 tons	25 tons	18 cu. yd.
D30D	23.7 tons	30 tons	21.6 cu. yd.
D250E	22.2 tons	25 tons	18 cu. yd.
D300E	24.2 tons	30 tons	21.6 cu. yd.
D350E	30.7 tons	35 tons	25.1 cu. yd.
D400E	32.0 tons	40 tons	28.8 cu. yd.
Euclid (Rigid-Frame)			
R40C	35 tons	42 tons	31 cu. yd.
R60C	46 tons	66 tons	47 cu. yd.
R65C	48 tons	71 tons	67 cu. yd.
R90C	77 tons	100 tons	75 cu. yd.
Volvo (Articulated)			
A25C	19.6 tons	25 tons	17.7 cu. yd.
A30C	23 tons	30 tons	21.6 cu. yd.
A35C	28.3 tons	35 tons	25 cu. yd.
A40	33.2 tons	40 tons	29 cu. yd.

Data for this table was extracted from technical literature produced by Caterpillar, Inc., and Volvo
Construction Equipment North America, Inc.

Table 12.1 provides the load-carrying capacities of Caterpillar, Euclid, and Volvo off-highway end-dump trucks. Articulated trucks often are used where job site conditions are adverse.

12.3   *Production Estimation*

Truck and hauler productivity can be estimated by determining the vehicle hauling capacity, the cycle time, and the operational efficiency. The hauling capacity can be determined by weight or volume. Manufacturers of trucks and haulers specify a rated load for their products, as illustrated in Table 12.1, and the size of the truck or hauler bed limits the volume to be carried.

Manufacturers' technical data usually specify the volume capacity two ways: struck capacity and heaped capacity. **Struck capacity** is the capacity when filled level with the sides of the bed. ***Heaped capacity*** is the capacity when the material in the bed is piled above the top of the bed in the center and tapered down to the top edge of the bed. Rated volume capacity usually is specified in loose cubic yards or loose cubic meters. Truck and hauler capacity for dense material, such as rock, usually is determined by weight. For lighter materials, the volume constraint typically governs truck and hauler capacity.

The cycle time has two components, a fixed time and a variable time. The fixed time consists of the loading time, the dumping time, and the time to spot the truck or hauler under the loading equipment for the next load. The variable time consists of the travel time (loaded) and the return time (empty). Cycle time can be estimated as follows:

$$CT = FT + VT \qquad (12\text{--}1)$$

where FT is the fixed time, which is equal to the sum of the loading time, the dumping time, and the spotting time

        VT is the variable or travel time

The loading time is a function of the capacity and cycle time of the loading equipment, the capacity of the truck or hauler, and the skill of the loading operator. The dumping time is a function of the type and condition of the material (wet or dry), the method of dumping or spreading, and the type and maneuverability of the truck. The spotting time is a function of the organization of the loading site and the maneuverability of the truck or hauler. The haul and return times are a function of the haul road profile (grade resistance), the surface condition of the haul road (rolling resistance), the distance to be traveled, the altitude of the project site, and the performance characteristics of the truck or hauler.

The loading time is estimated by multiplying the number of loading cycles needed to load the truck or hauler by the cycle time for the loading machine. The number of loading cycles required is estimated by the following equation:

$$\text{Number of Loader Cycles Required to Load Truck} = \frac{\text{Volume Capacity of Truck}}{\text{Volume Capacity of Loader}} \quad (12\text{--}2)$$

Truck capacity and loader capacity must be on the same basis (bank, loose, or compacted). *The answer to Equation 12.2 should be rounded up to a whole number, as partial load cycles are not possible.* The loading time can now be estimated by the following equation:

$$LT = (\text{Number of Loader Cycles Required})(\text{Loader Cycle Time}) \qquad (12\text{--}3)$$

The term *loader* in Equations 12–2 and 12–3 means the loading machine. It could be a front shovel, backhoe, dragline, clamshell, or a loader.

Dumping time and spotting time are determined by actually measuring both on similar projects or by estimating them with the use of Table 12.2.

Travel and return times for on-highway trucks and haulers must be estimated by considering the haul distance and the traffic conditions. Travel speeds generally are determined by traffic conditions and not by the performance characteristics of the truck or hauler. Travel and return times for off-highway trucks and haulers are calculated by determining the required rimpull for each segment of the haul road and determining the

Table 12.2

Fixed Times for Trucks and Haulers

Job Conditions	Turn and Dump Time		Spotting Time	
	End Dump	*Bottom Dump*	*End Dump*	*Bottom Dump*
Favorable	1.0 min.	0.4 min.	0.15 min.	0.15 min.
Average	1.3 min.	0.7 min.	0.30 min.	0.50 min.
Unfavorable	1.5–2.0 min.	1.0–1.5 min.	0.80 min.	1.00 min.

Data for this table was extracted from James J. O'Brien, John A. Havers, and Frank W. Stubbs, Jr., eds., *Standard Handbook of Heavy Construction,* 3rd ed. (New York: McGraw-Hill, 1996), p. B7-24.

maximum truck or hauler speed from the manufacturer's data, such as that illustrated in Figure 12.6. The minimum rimpull required is equal to the total resisting force for each haul road segment and can be determined as follows:

$$F_R = [(R_{RR})(Wt)] \pm [(\% \text{ grade})(20 \text{ lb./ton per } \% \text{ grade})(Wt)] \qquad (12\text{–}4)$$

where F_R is the total resisting force and the minimum rimpull required

R_{RR} is the rolling resistance in lb./ton

Wt is the vehicle weight in tons (either loaded or empty)

If a manufacturer's performance chart is not available, the maximum speed can be estimated from the following equation, which is the same as Equation 7–15 in Chapter 7:

$$\text{Maximum Speed (mph)} = \frac{(375)(HP)(\text{Gear Train Efficiency})}{\text{Required Rimpull (lb.)}} \qquad (12\text{–}5)$$

where HP is the rated horsepower

The gear train efficiency is between 0.70 and 0.85 for most construction equipment. If it is unknown, use 0.8.

Many off-highway trucks are equipped with variable hydraulic retarders that are used to limit speeds when descending a grade without using the vehicle's service brake. Retarder performance charts, such as Figure 12.7, are published by equipment manufacturers to show the speeds that can be maintained while descending grades that have slopes such that the negative grade resistance is greater than the rolling resistance.

The truck or hauler will not operate at its maximum speed for the entire segment of the haul road. It will be accelerating or decelerating during some of its travel time. To account for these lower speeds, the average travel time for each segment is estimated by adjusting the maximum speed with a speed factor as shown in Equation 12–6:

$$\text{Average Speed} = (\text{Maximum Speed})(\text{Speed Factor}) \qquad (12\text{–}6)$$

Appropriate speed factors are shown in Table 12.3. Speed factors for segment lengths not shown can be estimated by linear interpolation.

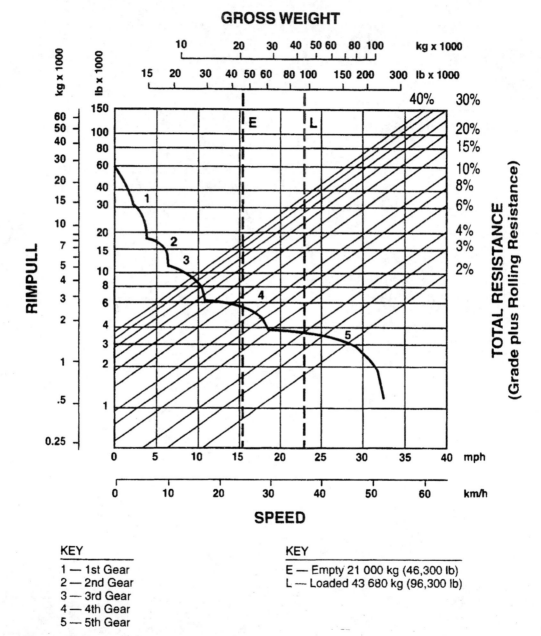

Articulated Trucks | D250E Rimpull-Speed-Gradeability
                      | ● 23.5R25 Tires

KEY

1 — 1st Gear
2 — 2nd Gear
3 — 3rd Gear
4 — 4th Gear
5 — 5th Gear

KEY

E — Empty 21 000 kg (46,300 lb)
L — Loaded 43 680 kg (96,300 lb)

Figure 12.6

Performance Chart for Caterpillar D250E Articulated Dump Truck

Courtesy Caterpillar Inc.

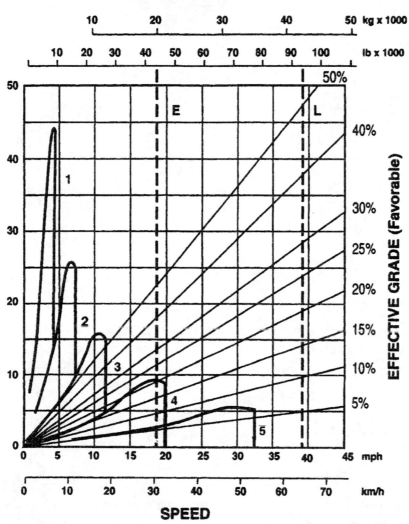

D250E Brake/Retarder Performance Curve
● 23.5R25 Tires

Articulated Trucks

Figure 12.7
Retarder Performance Chart for Caterpillar D250E Articulated Dump Truck
Courtesy Caterpillar Inc.

Table 12.3
Speed Factors for Trucks and Haulers

Length of Segment	Starting from Standstill or Coming to a Stop*	Maximum Speed Compared to Previous Segment	
		Increasing	*Decreasing*
100 ft.	0.45	0.65	1.75
150 ft.	0.55	0.73	1.62
200 ft.	0.62	0.76	1.51
300 ft.	0.68	0.80	1.39
400 ft.	0.74	0.83	1.33
500 ft.	0.77	0.85	1.28
700 ft.	0.83	0.87	1.23
1,000 ft.	0.86	0.89	1.19
2,000 ft.	0.92	0.93	1.12
3,000 ft.	0.94	0.95	1.07
4,000 ft.	0.95	0.96	1.05
5,000 ft.	0.96	0.97	1.04

*If the truck stops at both ends of a segment, divide the segment length into two parts and determine a speed factor for each part.

Data for this table is from David A. Day and Neal B. H. Benjamin, *Construction Equipment Guide*, 2nd ed. (New York: John Wiley & Sons, 1991), p. 172. Reprinted by permission of John Wiley & Sons, Inc.

The travel time can be determined for each segment of the haul road by dividing the distance by the average speed. The total variable time is equal to the sum of the travel times for all haul road segments.

Truck or hauler productivity can be estimated by Equation 12–7:

$$\text{Productivity} = \frac{(\text{Volume Hauled})(\text{Operational Efficiency})}{\text{Cycle Time}} \qquad (12\text{–}7)$$

Let's now look at an example to illustrate these concepts.

Example 12.1

A contractor has been awarded a contract for the construction of a regional shopping center. As part of the project, the contractor must construct a large structural fill for the shopping center parking lot. He has identified a suitable borrow source for fill material that is about 2 miles from the construction site. He has decided to use Caterpillar D250E articulated end-dump trucks to haul the fill material and to use a Hitachi EX 750 hydraulic excavator with front shovel attachment to load the trucks. Soil tests on the fill material indicate a density of 121 pounds per bank cubic foot. The swell for the rock-earth fill material is estimated to be 20%, and the shrinkage, when compacted to the design density, is estimated to be 12%. The 10,000-foot haul road has an uphill grade of 5% for the first 4,000 feet, a downhill grade of 1% for the next 3,000 feet, and is fairly level for the last 3,000 feet when traveling from the borrow site to the fill site. The rolling resistance of the haul road is estimated to be 60 pounds per ton, and the coefficient of traction is estimated to be 0.6. The Hitachi front shovel is equipped with a 5.5-cubic-yard bottom-dump general-purpose bucket with an estimated cycle time of 24 seconds per bucket load of fill material. The contractor obtained the following information from the manufacturer's literature for the dump truck:

	Weight Distribution	
	Empty	
Rated heaped capacity: 18 cu. yd.	Front axle	58%
Empty weight: 44,400 lb.	Center axle	21%
	Rear axle	21%
Maximum load: 25 tons	***Loaded***	
Type of drive: Center and rear axles	Front axle	32%
	Center axle	34%
	Rear axle	34%

What is the estimated productivity of 1 dump truck in compacted cubic yards per hour if it does not wait in a queue at the loading site and the contractor operates 50 minutes per hour?

Solution

The first step is to determine the maximum load the dump truck can carry safely without exceeding the load weight constraint. The heaped capacity of the truck in bank cubic yards is

$$\frac{18 \text{ LCY}}{1.20 \text{ LCY/BCY}} = 15 \text{ BCY}$$

The weight of the load when filled to heaped capacity is

$$(15 \text{ BCY})(121 \text{ lb./bank cu. ft.})(27 \text{ cu. ft./cu. yd.}) = 49{,}005 \text{ lb.}$$

which is less than the maximum load of 25 tons or 50,000 pounds. Therefore, the truck safely can carry 18 loose cubic yards, or 15 bank cubic yards of fill material.

Next, we need to estimate the cycle time for the dump truck. To determine the fixed time, we first need to estimate the number of shovel cycles that are needed to load a single truck using Equation 12–2. The volume capacity of the shovel is found by multiplying its rated capacity by an appropriate fill factor. We can estimate the fill factor by taking the average value for rock-earth mixtures from Table 11.2, which is 1.1. The shovel bucket capacity can now be estimated to be

$$(5.5 \text{ LCY})(1.1) = 6.0 \text{ LCY}$$

The number of shovel cycles needed to load 1 dump truck is

$$\frac{18 \text{ LCY}}{6 \text{ LCY}} = 3 \text{ cycles}$$

The truck loading time now can be estimated by multiplying the number of shovel cycles needed to load one truck by the cycle time for the shovel. The resulting estimated loading time for the truck is

$$\frac{(3 \text{ cycles})(24 \text{ sec./cycle})}{60 \text{ sec./min.}} = 1.2 \text{ min.}$$

We will assume the job conditions to be average and estimate the turn and dump time to be 1.3 minutes and the spotting time to be 0.3 minutes from Table 12.2. The total fixed time is estimated to be

$$1.2 \text{ min.} + 1.3 \text{ min.} + 0.3 \text{ min.} = 2.8 \text{ min.}$$

To determine the variable time, we must estimate the maximum speed the dump truck can traverse each haul road segment. We also must determine the maximum rimpull that can be generated without the wheels spinning. This involves multiplying the coefficient of traction by the weight on the rear two driving axles. The maximum rimpull that can be generated when the truck is empty is

$$(0.6)(0.42)(44,400 \text{ lb.}) = 11,188 \text{ lb.}$$

The maximum rimpull that can be generated when the truck is loaded is

$$(0.6)(0.68)(44,400 \text{ lb.} + 49,005 \text{ lb.}) = 38,109 \text{ lb.}$$

The total weight when fully loaded is 93,405 pounds, or 46.7 tons. The total resisting force when traveling fully loaded on the first segment of the haul road is

$$F_R = [(60 \text{ lb./ton})(46.7 \text{ ton})] + [(5\%)(20 \text{ lb./ton per } \% \text{ slope})(46.7 \text{ ton})]$$
$$= 2,802 \text{ lb.} + 4,670 \text{ lb.} = 7,472 \text{ lb.}$$

Since the required rimpull (7,472 lb.) is less than the maximum that can be generated without the wheels slipping (38,109 lb.), we will have no problems with traction.

The total resisting force when traveling fully loaded on the second haul road segment is

$$F_R = [(60 \text{ lb./ton})(46.7 \text{ ton})] - [(1\%)(20 \text{ lb./ton per } \% \text{ slope})(46.7 \text{ ton})]$$
$$= 2,802 \text{ lb.} - 934 \text{ lb.} = 1,868 \text{ lb.}$$

Again, we have no problems with traction. The total resisting force when traveling fully loaded on the last haul road segment is 2,802 pounds, because there is no grade resistance. Likewise, the total resisting force when traveling empty on the first return haul road segment is

$$F_R = (60 \text{ lb./ton})(22.2 \text{ ton}) = 1,332 \text{ lb.}$$

because there is no grade resistance.

The total resisting force when traveling empty on the second return haul road segment is

$$F_R = [(60 \text{ lb./ton})(22.2 \text{ ton})] + [(1\%)(20 \text{ lb./ton per } \% \text{ slope})(22.2 \text{ ton})]$$
$$= 1,332 \text{ lb.} + 444 \text{ lb.} = 1,776 \text{ lb.}$$

The total resisting force when traveling empty on the last return haul road segment is

$$F_R = [(60 \text{ lb./ton})(22.2 \text{ ton})] - [(5\%)(20 \text{ lb./ton per \% slope})(22.2 \text{ ton})]$$
$$= 1,332 \text{ lb.} - 2,220 \text{ lb.} = -888 \text{ lb.}$$

Checking the required rimpull for the return segments with the maximum rimpull that can be generated when empty indicates that we will have no problems with traction.

Now we can estimate the maximum speed that the dump truck can traverse each haul road segment from Figure 12.6 for positive total resisting forces and from Figure 12.7 for negative total resisting forces. Reading Figure 12.6 is similar to reading the performance charts for scrapers that we used in Chapter 10. Read vertically up the left axis to the desired rimpull, read across horizontally to the performance curve, and then read down to read the maximum speed. Reading Figure 12.7 is more complicated. First the effective grade must be determined using the following formula:

$$\text{Effective Grade} = \frac{\text{Favorable Rimpull (lb.)}}{(20 \text{ lb./ton per \% slope})(\text{Wt. in tons})}$$

which is

$$\frac{888 \text{ lb.}}{(20 \text{ lb./ton per \% slope})(22.2} = 2\%$$

Next, find the truck weight on the top horizontal axis, which is 44,400 pounds for the empty truck. This is the vertical dashed line marked E. Read down line E until you intersect the effective grade diagonal line. Since our effective grade is 2%, we must interpolate between zero and 5%. At the intersection of the weight and the effective grade, read horizontally to intersect the performance curve. Read down from the point of intersection with the performance curve to determine the maximum speed, which for this example is 32 miles per hour in fifth gear, or 20 miles per hour in fourth gear. Let's use fifth gear, since the truck is empty. Now we can complete the following table to determine the variable time:

Distance	Resisting Force	Max. Speed	Speed Factor	Average Speed	Time
4,000 ft. (loaded)	7,472 lb.	11 mph	0.95	10.4 mph	4.4 min.
3,000 ft. (loaded)	1,868 lb.	32 mph	0.95	30.4 mph	1.1 min.
3,000 ft. (loaded)	2,802 lb.	30 mph	0.94	28.2 mph	1.2 min.
3,000 ft. (empty)	1,332 lb.	32 mph	0.94	30.1 mph	1.1 min.
3,000 ft. (empty)	1,776 lb.	32 mph	1.00	32 mph	1.1 min.
4,000 ft. (empty)	−888 lb.	32 mph	0.95	30.4 mph	1.5 min.

The average speed is determined by selecting the appropriate speed factor from Table 12.3 for each segment and applying Equation 12–6. Since the truck will stop at each end of the haul road, the appropriate speed factor for starting from a standstill or coming to a stop should be used for segments one and three. The speed factor for the middle loaded segment comes from the increasing column, and a speed factor of 1.0 was selected for the middle segment when empty because there is no difference in speed. Travel time is determined by dividing the travel distance by the average speed. The total variable or travel time now can be estimated by adding the travel times for each haul road segment, which is 10.4 minutes.

The total cycle time for the dump truck is

$$CT = FT + VT = 2.8 \text{ min.} + 10.4 \text{ min.} = 13.2 \text{ min.}$$

Using Equation 12–7, the productivity of the truck now can be estimated to be

$$\frac{(15 \text{ BCY})(0.88 \text{ CCY/BCY})(50 \text{ min./hr.})}{13.2 \text{ min.}} = \textbf{50 CCY/hr.}$$

Because we desire the productivity in compacted cubic yards, we must use the percent shrinkage to convert the truck volume from bank cubic yards.

As discussed in Chapter 7, when operating at high altitudes, truck or hauler productivity will be decreased because of a reduction in engine performance. Manufacturers generally provide derating factors for their trucks in their technical literature. If such information is not available, a good way to estimate the reduction in productivity is to reduce engine performance by 3% per 1,000 feet above 1,000 feet in elevation if the engine is naturally respirated. If the engine is turbocharged, there generally is no loss in power up to about 10,000 feet. Derating factors for turbocharged engines operating above 10,000 feet should be obtained from the engine manufacturer. Since most modern off-highway trucks are equipped with turbocharged engines, derating factors for altitude generally are not required. Let's look at an example of a truck with a naturally respirated engine to illustrate the use of altitude derating factors.

Example 12.2

A contractor is planning to use 12-cubic-yard, 200-horsepower end-dump trucks to remove material being excavated for the foundation for a new office building. The project site is located at an elevation of 4,000 feet, and the dump truck engines are naturally respirated. The contractor plans to load the dump trucks with a 3-cubic-yard hydraulic backhoe excavator that has a cycle time estimated to be 22 seconds. The material being excavated is sandy clay weighing 2,700 pounds per bank cubic yard with a swell of 30%. The mile-long haul road has an uphill grade of 3% when traveling from the loading site. The rolling resistance of the haul road is estimated to be 100 pounds per ton, and the coefficient of traction is estimated to be 0.4. The weight of an empty dump truck is 20 tons, and the maximum load is 15 tons. The weight distribution is

Empty	Front axle	56%
	Drive axle	44%
Loaded	Front axle	33%
	Drive axle	67%

The maximum speed for the truck is 35 miles per hour. What is the estimated productivity of 1 dump truck in bank cubic yards per hour if it does not sit in a queue at the loading site waiting to be loaded and the contractor operates 45 minutes per hour?

Solution

The first step is to determine the maximum load that the truck can carry without exceeding the weight constraint. The heaped capacity of the truck in bank cubic yards is

$$\frac{12 \text{ LCY}}{1.3 \text{ LCY/BCY}} = 9.2 \text{ BCY}$$

The weight of the load when filled to heaped capacity is

$$(9.2 \text{ BCY})(2{,}700 \text{ lb./BCY}) = 24{,}840 \text{ lb.}$$

which is less than the maximum load of 15 tons or 30,000 pounds. Therefore, the dump truck safely can carry 12 loose cubic yards or 9.2 bank cubic yards of the excavated material.

The truck loading time can be estimated by determining the number of loading cycles the excavator needs to fill the truck. The fill factor for the excavator can be determined from Table 11.5 to be 1.05 by using the average value for sandy clay. The number of excavator cycles needed to load the truck is

$$\frac{12 \text{ LCY}}{(3 \text{ LCY})(1.05)} = 3.8 \text{ cycles}$$

which must be rounded up to 4 cycles. The estimated truck loading time can now be determined to be

$$\frac{(4 \text{ cycles})(22 \text{ sec./cycle})}{60 \text{ sec./min.}} = 1.5 \text{ min.}$$

We will estimate the job conditions at the dump site to be favorable and average at the loading site. Using Table 12.2, we can estimate the turn and dump time to be 1.0 minute and the spotting time to be 0.3 minute. The total fixed time is estimated to be

$$1.5 \text{ min.} + 1.0 \text{ min.} + 0.3 \text{ min.} = 2.8 \text{ min.}$$

To determine the variable or travel time, we must estimate the maximum speed at which the trucks can traverse the haul road. We must also determine the maximum rimpull that can be generated without the wheels slipping. The maximum rimpull that can be generated when the dump truck is empty is

$$(0.4)(0.44)(40{,}000 \text{ lb.}) = 7{,}040 \text{ lb.}$$

The maximum rimpull that can be generated when the truck is fully loaded is

$$(0.4)(0.67)(40{,}000 \text{ lb.} + 24{,}840 \text{ lb.}) = 17{,}377 \text{ lb.}$$

The total resisting force when traveling loaded is

$$F_R = [(100 \text{ lb./ton})(32.4 \text{ ton})] + [(3\%)(20 \text{ lb./ton per } \% \text{ slope})(32.4 \text{ ton})]$$
$$= 3{,}240 \text{ lb.} + 1{,}944 \text{ lb.} = 5{,}184 \text{ lb.}$$

The total resisting force when traveling empty is

$$F_R = [(100 \text{ lb./ton})(20 \text{ ton})] - [(3\%)(20 \text{ lb./ton per } \% \text{ slope})(20 \text{ ton})]$$
$$= 2{,}000 \text{ lb.} - 1{,}200 \text{ lb.} = 800 \text{ lb.}$$

The required rimpull in both cases is less that the maximum rimpull that can be generated, so there will be no problem with traction.

The maximum speed can now be estimated with Equation 12–5. Since the project site is at 4,000 feet, the rated horsepower must be derated before we can use the equation. The derating factor is

$$\frac{(0.03)(4,000 \text{ ft.} - 1,000 \text{ ft.})}{1,000 \text{ ft.}} = 0.09$$

which means that the truck can generate only 91% of the rated horsepower or

$$(200 \text{ HP})(0.91) = 182 \text{ HP}$$

With Equation 12–5, the maximum speed when loaded can now be estimated to be

$$\frac{(375)(182 \text{ HP})(0.8)}{5,184 \text{ lb.}} = 10.5 \text{ mph}$$

Since we do not know the gear train efficiency, we will assume a value of 0.8.

The maximum speed when empty is estimated to be

$$\frac{(375)(182 \text{ HP})(0.8)}{800 \text{ lb.}} = 68 \text{ mph}$$

which exceeds the maximum rated speed, so the maximum speed, when empty, will be 35 miles per hour.

To determine the average speed, we must determine the appropriate speed factor from Table 12.3. Since the truck will stop at each end of the haul road, we will divide the haul road distance in half and determine a speed factor for 2,640 feet from the "Starting from Standstill or Coming to a Stop" column. By linear interpolation, we estimate the speed factor to be 0.93. The average travel speed when loaded will be

$$(0.93)(10.5 \text{ mph}) = 9.8 \text{ mph}$$

The average travel speed when empty will be

$$(0.93)(35 \text{ mph}) = 32.5 \text{ mph}$$

The travel time can now be estimated to be

$$\frac{(1 \text{ mi.})(60 \text{ min./hr.})}{9.8 \text{ mph}} + \frac{(1 \text{ mi.})(60 \text{ min./hr.})}{32.5 \text{ mph}} = 6.1 \text{ min.} + 1.8 \text{ min.} = 7.9 \text{ min.}$$

The total cycle time for the truck is estimated to be

$$CT = FT + VT = 2.8 \text{ min.} + 7.9 \text{ min.} = 10.7 \text{ min.}$$

With Equation 12–7, we can estimate the productivity of the truck to be

$$\frac{(9.2 \text{ BCY})(45 \text{ min./hr.})}{10.7 \text{ min.}} = 38.7 \text{ BCY/hr.}$$

12.4 *Balancing Loading and Hauling Productivity*

Most contractors want to balance their hauling capacity with their loading capacity to minimize equipment idle time, which costs money and produces no revenue. Because of time or cost considerations, the number of pieces of loading equipment or the number of trucks or haulers may determine the size of fleet selected for a specific construction task. The size of trucks or haulers that can be used on a project may be limited by maneuver space restrictions at the load or dump site or overhead restrictions on the haul road.

For efficient operation, the trucks or haulers selected for a project should have hauling capacities about four to five times the bucket capacity of front shovels, backhoes, or loaders. If draglines or clamshells are used for loading, the truck or hauler capacity should be larger (five to eight times the bucket capacity), because these machines lack positive bucket control and require larger dump targets.

The number of trucks or haulers that should be used per piece of loading equipment can be determined using Equation 12–8:

$$N_H = \frac{CT_H}{T_L} \tag{12–8}$$

where N_H is the number of trucks or haulers

CT_H is the cycle time for the truck or hauler

T_L is the truck or hauler cycle time at load site (which is loading time + spotting time)

Let's look at an example to illustrate this concept.

Example 12.3

The contractor of Example 12.1 wants to determine the number of dump trucks he needs to maximize his fleet productivity. How many dump trucks should he use if he uses only one front shovel to load them?

Solution

We can determine the answer by using Equation 12–8. The cycle time for each truck was estimated to be 13.2 minutes in Example 12.1. The loading time was estimated to be 1.2 minutes, and the spotting time was estimated to be 0.3 minute. Thus, the truck cycle time at the load site is estimated to be 1.5 minutes. The number of trucks needed is

$$\frac{13.2 \text{ min.}}{1.5 \text{ min.}} = 8.8 \text{ trucks}$$

To maximize productivity, the contractor should use **9 dump trucks.** This will ensure that the front shovel does not sit idle waiting for trucks to load. If the contractor wants to select the most cost-effective fleet, he should evaluate both an 8-truck fleet and a 9-truck fleet and select the one that is more cost-effective. We will do this in Example 12.4.

12.5   *Cost and Time Analysis*

To estimate the cost of performing a construction task with trucks or haulers, it is first necessary to estimate the hourly ownership and operating cost for the trucks or haulers and the loading equipment. The techniques discussed in Chapter 4, the cost references discussed in Chapter 5, or historical data should be used to estimate these hourly costs. The costs are then used in conjunction with the overall productivity of the fleet of equipment to estimate the unit cost of performing the hauling operation. This information will be needed by a contractor in developing an overall cost estimate for the project. If it is cost-effective to reduce the rolling resistance of the haul road, haul road maintenance costs also should be included. Dividing the total volume of work to be performed by the overall productivity of the fleet of equipment provides an estimate of the time required to complete the hauling operation. This information will be required in developing a construction schedule for the project. Let's now look at an example as an illustration.

Example 12.4

The contractor of Example 12.1 estimates the hourly cost data for the Caterpillar D250E articulated dump truck and the Hitachi EX 750 front shovel to be as follows:

Equipment	Hourly Ownership Cost	Hourly Operating Cost	Effective Hourly Operator Cost
D250E truck	$24.00	$23.50	$24.00
EX 750 shovel	$60.00	$105.00	$32.00

The estimated volume of fill material required is 30,000 compacted cubic yards.

a. What is the estimated unit cost for loading and hauling the fill material if the contractor uses 8 dump trucks and 1 shovel?
b. What is the estimated unit cost for loading and hauling the fill material if the contractor uses 9 dump trucks and 1 shovel?
c. What is the estimated time to complete the fill operation using 8 or 9 dump trucks, whichever is more economical? Assume the loading and hauling productivity determines the productivity of the fill operation and that the contractor plans to work 8 hours per day.

Solution

a. The total hourly cost for 1 dump truck is

$$\$24.00/\text{hr.} + \$23.50/\text{hr.} + \$24.00/\text{hr.} = \$71.50/\text{hr.}$$

The total hourly cost for the shovel is

$$\$60.00/\text{hr.} + \$105.00/\text{hr.} + \$32.00/\text{hr.} = \$197.00/\text{hr.}$$

Since one shovel can load 8.8 trucks (determined in Example 12.3), the shovel will have some idle time with 8 dump trucks. Therefore, the productivity of the fleet will be determined by the productivity of the trucks, which is

$$(8)(50 \text{ CCY/hr.}) = 400 \text{ CCY/hr.}$$

The total hourly cost for the fleet is

$$[(8)(\$71.50)] + \$197.00 = \$769/hr.$$

The estimated unit cost is

$$\frac{\$769/hr.}{400 \text{ CCY/hr.}} = \$1.92/\text{CCY}$$

b. With 9 dump trucks, the productivity of the loading operation will determine the productivity of the overall loading and hauling operation, because the dump trucks will sit idle in the loading area for short periods of time waiting for the shovel. The productivity of the loading operation can be estimated using the following equation:

$$\text{Productivity} = \frac{(\text{Truck Capacity})(\text{Operational Efficiency})}{\text{Loading Time} + \text{Spotting Time}}$$

Inserting numerical values yields the following:

$$\text{Productivity} = \frac{(15 \text{ BCY})(0.88 \text{ CCY/BCY})(50 \text{ min./hr.})}{1.5 \text{ min.}}$$

$$= 440 \text{ CCY/hr.}$$

The hourly cost for the fleet is

$$[(9)(\$71.50)] + \$197.00 = \$840.50$$

The estimated unit cost is

$$\frac{\$840.50 \text{ per hr.}}{440 \text{ CCY/hr.}} = \$1.91 \text{ CCY}$$

c. Since the 9-truck fleet is more cost-effective, the estimated time to complete the fill operation is

$$\frac{30,000 \text{ CCY}}{(440 \text{ CCY/hr.})(8 \text{ hr./day})} = 8.5 \text{ days}$$

12.6   Problems

1. A contractor has been awarded a contract for the construction of a building complex that will be occupied by an automobile dealer. A major part of the site work for the project is the construction of a structural fill that will be paved and used to store new automobiles. Review of the contract drawings and specifications indicates that the compacted fill will average 15 inches in depth and cover an area 200 feet by 250 feet. The contractor has located a suitable source for the fill material that is 2 miles from the construction site. Compaction tests on fill material (rock-dirt mixture) indicate a unit weight of 114 pounds per compacted cubic foot at the design density, a shrinkage of 15%, and a swell of 20%. The contractor plans to use

four 18-cubic-yard end-dump trucks to haul the fill material to the construction site and has extracted the following information regarding the trucks from the manufacturer's literature:

	Weight Distribution (empty)	
Empty weight: 32,000 lb.		
Maximum load: 40,000 lb.	Front axle	67%
	Drive axle	33%
Flywheel power: 170 HP		
	Weight Distribution (loaded)	
Gear train efficiency: 78%	Front axle	45%
Maximum speed: 26 mph	Drive axle	55%

The haul road has an uphill grade of 2% for the first half mile, a downhill grade of 1% for the next mile, and an uphill grade of 4% for the last half mile when traveling from the borrow (load) site to the project (dump) site. The contractor plans to maintain the haul road and estimates the resulting rolling resistance will be about 80 pounds per ton and the coefficient of traction will be about 0.5. The contractor plans to load the dump trucks at the borrow site with a wheeled loader that has a 4.1-cubic-yard bucket and a cycle time estimated to be 45 seconds. The job conditions at the dump site are considered average and at the borrow site are considered favorable.

a. What do you estimate the cycle time to be for 1 dump truck?

b. What is the estimated productivity of 1 dump truck in compacted cubic yards per hour, if the contractor works 50 minutes per hour and the trucks do not wait in a queue to be loaded?

c. How many 8-hour days do you estimate it will take the contractor to haul the fill material needed to construct the parking area?

2. The contractor of Problem 1 has another project requiring the use of a large quantity of sand. He has located a good source of sand in a river that is 6,000 feet from the project site and has decided to dredge the sand with a 3-cubic-yard clamshell mounted on a crawler crane. He also has decided to use the type of dump trucks described in Problem 1 to haul the sand to the project site. The sand weighs 2,400 pounds per loose cubic yard, and the cycle time for the clamshell is estimated to be 40 seconds. The project site is located at an elevation of 5,000 feet, and the contractor determined the appropriate derating factor for the trucks from the manufacturer's literature to be 8%. The haul road has an uphill grade of 4% for the first 3,000 feet and a downhill grade of 2% for the last 3,000 feet when traveling from the river to the project site. The rolling resistance of the haul road is estimated to be 120 pounds per ton, and the coefficient of traction is estimated to be 0.4. Job conditions at both the load and dump site are considered average.

a. What is the estimated productivity of 1 dump truck in loose cubic yards per hour if the contractor's operational efficiency is about 45 minutes per hour and the trucks do not wait in a queue to be loaded?

b. How many dump trucks should the contractor use to maximize fleet productivity if he uses one clamshell?

   c. What is the estimated fleet productivity in loose cubic yards per hour if the contractor uses the number of trucks selected in (b) above?

3. A contractor has been awarded a contract for the construction of a 2-mile access road connecting a new residential development with a highway. The contractor needs to haul gravel (medium coarse stone) from a borrow source that is located 1 mile from the construction site. The contractor has decided to use Caterpillar D250E articulated end-dump trucks to haul the gravel and to use a John Deere 744E wheeled loader to load the trucks. The gravel weighs 3,100 pounds per bank cubic yard and has a swell of 14%. The John Deere loader is equipped with a 3.7-cubic-yard bucket and has a cycle time estimated to be 35 seconds. The average haul distance will be 1.5 miles. The haul road has a downhill grade of 2% for the first half-mile, an uphill grade of 3% for the second half-mile, and is generally level for the remaining half-mile when traveling from the load site to the dump site. The rolling resistance of the first mile of the haul road is estimated to be 100 pounds per ton and for the last half-mile to be 60 pounds per ton when traveling from the load site to the dump site. The coefficient of traction of the haul road is estimated to be 0.4. The contractor has extracted the following information regarding the dump truck from the manufacturer's literature:

Empty weight: 44,400 lb.

Maximum load: 50,000 lb.

Rated heaped capacity: 18 cu. yd.

Type of drive: Both rear axles

Maximum speed: 31.6 mph

Weight Distribution (empty)

Front axle	58%
Drive axle	42%

Weight Distribution (loaded)

Front axle	32%
Drive axle	68%

A performance chart for the dump truck is shown in Figure 12.6. The hourly ownership and operating cost (including operator wages) for the dump truck is estimated to be $73.00 and for the loader is estimated to be $58.00. Job site conditions at both the load and dump site are considered favorable.

   a. What is the estimated productivity of 1 dump truck in loose cubic yards per hour if the contractor works 50 minutes per hour and the truck does not wait in a queue to be loaded?

   b. How many dump trucks should the contractor use with one loader to minimize the loading and hauling cost?

   c. What is the estimated unit cost for loading and hauling the gravel with the number of trucks determined in (b) above?

4. A contractor has a project to construct a large parking garage at a regional airport. She has decided to use a Link Belt 5800 hydraulic backhoe excavator with a 3.1-cubic-yard bucket to excavate for the foundation of the parking garage and to use Caterpillar D250E articulated end-dump trucks to remove the excavated material. The material to be excavated is tough, hard clay weighing 107 pounds per bank cubic foot with a swell of 35%. The haul road is 7,000 feet long with a rolling

resistance estimated to be 80 pounds per ton and a coefficient of traction estimated to be 0.5. The first 1,000 feet of the haul road has an uphill grade of 3%, the next 4,000 feet has a downhill grade of 2%, and the last 2,000 feet has an uphill grade of 2% when traveling from the load site to the dump site. Manufacturer's information about the dump truck is provided in Problem 3, and a performance chart is shown in Figure 12.6. Job conditions at the dump site are considered average and at the load site are considered unfavorable. The cycle time of the backhoe is estimated to be 30 seconds. The hourly ownership and operating cost (including operator wages) for the dump truck is estimated to be $73.00 and for the backhoe is estimated to be $110.60.

    a. What is the estimated productivity of 1 dump truck in bank cubic yards per hour if the contractor works 45 minutes per hour and the truck does not wait in a queue to be loaded?

    b. How many dump trucks should the contractor use with one backhoe to minimize the excavating and hauling cost?

    c. What is the estimated unit cost for excavating and hauling the gravel with the number of trucks determined in (b) above?

5. A contractor has a contract for the construction of an industrial plant. One of the major site work tasks associated with the project is the construction of a compacted fill to support the concrete slab foundation for the plant. The contractor has located a suitable borrow source for the fill material that is 3 miles from the project site. The fill material is a rock-earth mixture weighing 3,000 pounds per bank cubic yard with a swell estimated to be 20%. When compacted to the design density, the fill material shrinkage is estimated to be 15%. The contractor has decided to use 16-cubic-yard end-dump trucks to haul the fill material and to use a Hitachi EX 450 hydraulic excavator with a front shovel attachment to load the trucks. The excavator is equipped with a 3.4-cubic-yard bottom-dump general purpose bucket, and the cycle time is estimated to be 24 seconds. Job conditions at both the load and dump site are considered average. The plans for the project indicate that the total volume of the required fill is 8,000 compacted cubic yards. The first mile of the haul road has an uphill grade of 3%, the second mile a downhill grade of 3%, and the last mile has a uphill grade of 1% when traveling from the load site to the dump site. The rolling resistance of the haul road is estimated to be 80 pounds per ton, and the coefficient of traction is estimated to be 0.4. The contractor has extracted the following information regarding the dump truck from the manufacturer's literature:

	Weight Distribution (empty)	
Empty weight: 27,000 lb.		
Maximum load: 36,000 lb.	Front axle	52%
	Drive axle	48%
Flywheel power: 160 HP		
	Weight Distribution (loaded)	
Type of drive: Rear axle	Front axle	28%
Maximum speed: 28 mph	Drive axle	72%

Following is a performance curve for the dump truck:

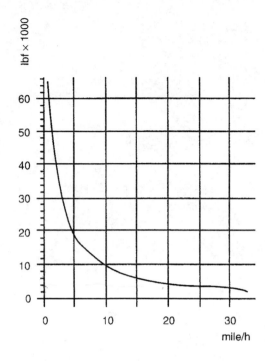

a. What is the estimated productivity of 1 dump truck in compacted cubic yards per hour if the contractor works 50 minutes per hour and the truck does not wait in a queue to be loaded?

b. How many dump trucks should the contractor use with 1 shovel to obtain maximum fleet productivity?

c. How many days will it take the contractor to complete the loading and hauling operation if he uses the number of trucks selected in (b) above and works 8 hours per day?

13

Graders

13.1   Introduction

A grader is a piece of construction equipment that has a long wheel base and a wide blade mounted midway between the front and rear axles, as illustrated in Figure 13.1. Graders are used to plane, mold, or grade the surface of the ground to the desired shape and elevation. As shown in Figure 13.2, some graders also are equipped with a scarifier and ripper that are used to loosen well-compacted soils so the grader can dig into the soil with the blade. The grader blade is called a *moldboard* and is equipped with replaceable cutting edges and end bits. Standard moldboard lengths vary from 10 to 16 feet.

13.2   Operation and Uses of Graders

A grader is a versatile piece of construction equipment. It can be used for the following construction tasks:

- Stripping light vegetation
- Rough grading
- Finish grading
- Backfilling
- Cutting ditches
- Sloping banks
- Scarifying
- Maintaining haul roads
- Blending soils

Rough grading involves leveling the surface of a fill as lifts are placed by scrapers or trucks. This aids in compacting the fill to the desired density. Once the fill is near the

Figure 13.1
Grader Shaping a Bank

Courtesy Caterpillar Inc.

Figure 13.2
Grader with Scarifier and Ripper

Courtesy John Deere

final elevation, the grader planes and smoothes the slopes and surface to the elevation specified in the plans and specifications. Blending soils involves pushing a windrow of soil back and forth to mix types of soil or to mix an additive, such as cement or asphalt, with the soil.

Grader blades can be rotated vertically into many positions. This is why graders are able to perform such a variety of tasks. The front wheels can be tilted up to 20°, as illustrated in Figure 13.3, which permits greater stability on sloping ground. Front wheels also may be leaned away from a cut to offset the force produced by the soil against an angled blade.

Graders are available with both straight and articulated frames. Articulated graders have greater maneuverability as illustrated in Figure 13.4. The articulated mode allows the grader to turn in a short radius. The crab mode permits the rear wheels of the grader to be offset so they remain on firm ground when cutting banks, side slopes, or ditches.

Figure 13.3
Grader with Tilted Front Wheels
Courtesy Caterpillar Inc.

Figure 13.4
Articulated Grader Positions

S.W. Nunnally, *Construction Methods and Management,* 4/e,©1998. Reprinted by permission of Prentice-Hall, Inc., Upper Saddle River, NJ.

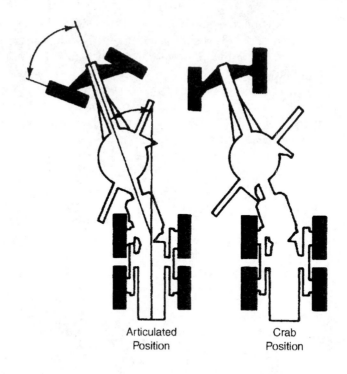

Articulated
Position

Crab
Position

Graders are used to grade haul roads to reduce the rolling resistance which will increase the productivity of scrapers or trucks using the road. The cost of haul road maintenance generally is significantly less than the cost of low productivity of hauling units.

13.3   *Productivity Estimation*

Grading operations tend to be either *linear*, such as a road, or *rectangular*, such as a parking lot. When grading a linear project, the grader operator usually grades in one direction, turns around at the end of the project, and grades in the other direction. Turn-around time is ignored in determining productivity for linear operations, because it is insignificant compared to the time spent grading. When grading a rectangular project, the grader operator uses either the *back-and-forth method* or the *looping method*. In the back-and-forth method, the grader operator grades in one direction, backs up with the grader blade raised, and then lowers the blade and makes a second pass. In the looping method, the grader operator raises the blade at the end of one pass, turns an arc, and grades in the reverse direction, as illustrated in Figure 13.5.

Grader productivity is expressed in an area measure per unit time, such as square yards or square feet per hour. Rough grading productivity may be estimated in cubic yards per hour to determine the number of graders required to match the productivity of a fleet of scrapers or trucks. The concept of fleet balancing will be discussed in Chapter 16.

Effective grading width is a term used to describe the width of each pass that the grader makes. This accounts for the blade being angled to discharge graded material to the side and for an overlap between passes to ensure complete coverage of the surface.

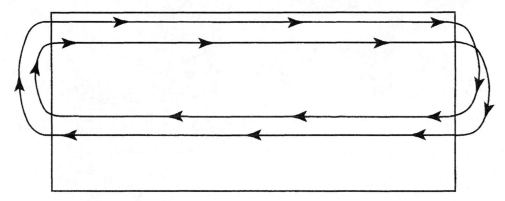

Figure 13.5
Area Grading Using the Looping Method

Grader productivity is a function of the effective grading width, the average grading speed, the number of passes required to achieve the desired smoothness, and the operational efficiency. It can be estimated by Equation 13–1:

$$\text{Productivity} = \frac{(V)(W)(OF)}{N} \quad (13\text{–}1)$$

where V is the average grading speed

   W is the effective grading width

   OF is the operating factor

   N is the number of passes required

Equation 13–1 provides the estimated productivity for *linear grader operations*, but does not work for rectangular operations, because it does not account for the time the grader is not grading.

To estimate grader productivity for *rectangular operations*, Equation 13–2 must be used:

$$\text{Productivity} = \frac{(\text{Area Graded per Cycle})(E)}{(CT)(N)} \quad (13\text{–}2)$$

where CT, the cycle time, is determined with either Equation 13–3 or 13–4

   E is the operational efficiency

   N is the number of passes required

The *cycle time for the back-and-forth method* is estimated with Equation 13–3:

$$CT = \frac{D_F}{V_F} + \frac{D_R}{V_R} \quad (13\text{–}3)$$

where D_F is the distance the grader travels when moving forward

   V_F is the average forward speed of the grader

D_R is the distance the grader travels in reverse

V_R is the average reverse speed of the grader

The *cycle time for the looping method* is estimated with Equation 13–4:

$$CT = \frac{D_F}{V_F} + \frac{D_T}{V_T}$$ (13–4)

where D_F is the distance the grader travels when moving forward

V_F is the average forward speed of the grader

D_T is the distance the grader travels when turning

V_T is the average turning speed of the grader

Now let's use these equations to estimate productivity in an example.

Example 13.1

A contractor has a project involving the construction of a compacted fill that will be used for storage of shipping containers. The fill will be constructed in 6-inch compacted lifts and measure 150 feet by 360 feet. The contractor plans to use scrapers to haul the fill material from a borrow site that is located 1 mile from the construction site. The contractor plans to use a Caterpillar 140G grader to grade the fill area as the scrapers spread the fill material. He also plans to use the grader to maintain the haul road to maximize scraper productivity. The grader is equipped with a 12-foot blade.

a. What is the estimated productivity of the grader when maintaining the haul road, if the effective grading width is 9 feet and the average grader speed when grading is 3 miles per hour? Assume an operational efficiency of 50 minutes per hour and that 2 passes of the road are required to achieve the desired smoothness.

b. What is the estimated productivity in compacted cubic yards per hour if the grader operator uses the back-and-forth method to grade the fill, with an average forward speed of 2.4 miles per hour and an average reverse speed of 6 miles per hour? Assume an operational efficiency of 50 minutes per hour and that 2 passes are required.

c. What is the estimated productivity in compacted cubic yards per hour if the grader operator uses the looping method to grade the fill with an average grading speed of 2.4 miles per hour and an average turning speed of 1.5 miles per hour? The minimum turning radius for the grader is 24 feet. Assume an operating efficiency of 50 minutes per hour and that 2 passes are required.

Solution

a. The grader productivity can be estimated with Equation 13–1 to be

$$\text{Productivity} = \frac{(3 \text{ mi./hr.})(5{,}280 \text{ ft./mi.})(9 \text{ ft.})(0.83)}{(9 \text{ sq. ft./sq. yd.})(2)}$$

$$= 6{,}574 \text{ sq. yd./hr.}$$

b. For this analysis, we will define one cycle as one pass grading across the long dimension of the fill and one reverse trip back to the starting point. With Equation 13–3, the grader cycle time can be estimated to be

$$CT = \frac{360 \text{ ft.}}{(2.4 \text{ mi./hr.})(88 \text{ ft./min. per mi./hr.})} + \frac{360 \text{ ft.}}{(6 \text{ mi./ mi./hr.})(88 \text{ ft./min. per mi./hr.})}$$

$$= 1.7 \text{ min.} + 0.7 \text{ min.} = 2.4 \text{ min.}$$

With Equation 13–2, the grader productivity can now be estimated to be

$$\text{Productivity} = \frac{(360 \text{ ft.})(9 \text{ ft.})(50 \text{ min./hr.})}{(9 \text{ sq. ft./sq. yd.})(2)(2.4 \text{ min.})}$$

$$= 3,750 \text{ sq. yd./hr.}$$

Since each lift thickness is 6 inches (compacted), the grader productivity in a volume measure is

$$\text{Productivity} = \frac{(3,750 \text{ sq.yd./hr.})(6 \text{ in.})}{36 \text{ in./yd.}}$$

$$= \mathbf{625 \text{ CCY/hr.}}$$

c. For this analysis, we will define one cycle as one pass grading across the long dimension of the fill and turning one arc in preparation for the next pass. The grader cycle time can be estimated with Equation 13–4. The distance the grader travels when turning is (π)(the arc radius) or $(3.14)(24 \text{ ft.})$, which is 75 feet.

$$CT = \frac{360 \text{ ft.}}{(2.4 \text{ mi./hr.})(88 \text{ ft./min. per mi./hr.})} + \frac{75 \text{ ft.}}{(1.5 \text{ mi./ mi./hr.})(88 \text{ ft./min. per mi./hr.})}$$

$$= 1.7 \text{ min.} + 0.6 \text{ min.} = 2.3 \text{ min.}$$

With Equation 13–2, the grader productivity can now be estimated to be

$$\text{Productivity} = \frac{(360 \text{ ft.})(9 \text{ ft.})(50 \text{ min./hr.})}{(9 \text{ sq. ft./sq. yd.})(2)(2.3 \text{ min.})}$$

$$= 3,913 \text{ sq. yd./hr.}$$

Since each lift thickness is 6 inches (compacted), the grader productivity in a volume measure is

$$\text{Productivity} = \frac{(3,913 \text{ sq. yd./hr.})(6 \text{ in.})}{36 \text{ in./yd.}}$$

$$= \mathbf{652 \text{ CCY/hr.}}$$

13.4 Cost and Time Analysis

To estimate the direct cost of performing a construction task with a grader, first estimate the hourly ownership and operating costs using the techniques discussed in Chapter 4, the cost references discussed in Chapter 5, or historical cost data. These costs can be used in conjunction with the productivity estimated with either Equation 13–1 or 13–2 to determine the unit cost for using a grader to perform the task. Multiplying the unit cost by the total quantity of work to be performed yields an estimate of the total cost for the task. Dividing the total volume of work to be performed by the productivity yields an estimate of the time required to complete the task. Let's now look at an example.

Example 13.2

The contractor of Example 13.1 estimates the hourly ownership cost for the Caterpillar 140G grader to be $12.50, the hourly operating cost to be $22.75, and the effective hourly operator's salary to be $28.00.

a. What is the unit cost per compacted cubic yard to grade the fill, if the contractor selects the more economical method of grading?
b. What is the total cost of grading the haul road? Assume the haul road is 24 feet wide.
c. How long does it take 1 grader to grade each lift of the fill?

Solution

a. The total hourly ownership and operating cost for the grader is estimated to be

$$\$12.50/hr. + \$22.75/hr. + \$28.00/hr. = \$63.25/hr.$$

Example 13.1 shows that the looping method of grading provides the greater productivity for this project. Therefore, we will use 652 compacted cubic yards per hour as the grader productivity. The estimated unit cost is

$$\frac{\$63.25/hr.}{625\ CCY/hr.} = \textbf{\$0.10 CCY}$$

b. Since the effective grading width of the grader is 9 feet, it must make 3 trips to cover the 24-foot-wide haul road. Since 2 passes are required, the grader must make a total of 6 trips. Therefore, the total area to be graded is

$$\frac{(5,280\ ft.)(9\ ft.)(6\ trips)}{9\ sq.\ ft./sq.\ yd.} = 31,680\ sq.\ yd.$$

The productivity of the grader was determined in Example 13.1 to be 6,574 square yards per hour. The total time to complete the grading operation is

$$\frac{31,680\ sq.\ yd.}{6,574\ sq.\ yd./hr.} = \textbf{4.8 hours}$$

c. The surface area of each lift is

$$\frac{(150\ ft.)(360\ ft.)}{9\ sq.\ ft./sq.\ yd.} = 6,000\ sq.\ yd.$$

In Example 13.1 the grader productivity for the looping method was determined to be 3,913 square yards per hour. The time to grade each lift is estimated to be

$$\frac{6{,}000 \text{ sq. yd.}}{3{,}913 \text{ sq. yd./hr.}} = 1.5 \text{ hours}$$

13.5   Problems

1. A grader is being used to maintain a 10-mile, 24-foot-wide haul road between a gravel pit and a construction site. The grader has a 14-foot-long blade. Assume an effective grading width of 10 feet. The operator will grade in second gear at a speed of 3.3 miles per hour to give him good control of the blade.
    a. What is the estimated productivity of the grader in square yards per hour, if the operational efficiency is 45 minutes per hour and one pass is required to achieve the desired smoothness?
    b. How long will it take to make one pass over the entire road if the operational efficiency is 45 minutes per hour?
2. A contractor has been awarded a contract for the construction of a shopping center. Part of the building site contained contaminated soil that has been removed, and the contractor must construct a structural fill before starting the building foundation. Site work drawings for the project indicate a compacted fill measuring 108 feet wide by 160 feet long by 10 feet deep. The contractor has identified a source for suitable fill material that is located 5 miles from the construction site. The contractor plans to use a grader to grade the fill as dump trucks bring in the fill material to help with the compaction of the soil. The fill will be constructed in compacted 8-inch lifts, and 3 passes of the grader are required for each lift. The grader has a 12-foot blade that will be angled to provide a 9.5-foot effective grading width. The grader will grade each pass in first gear at 2 miles per hour and then back across the fill at an average speed of 5 miles per hour. What is the estimated productivity of 1 grader in compacted cubic yards per hour if the operational efficiency is 50 minutes per hour?
3. A contractor has been awarded the contract for the construction of a parking lot for a regional hospital. The parking lot is to be 1,000 feet by 500 feet with a depth of 3 feet. The fill is to be constructed in 9-inch compacted lifts. The contractor plans to use scrapers to bring the fill to the project site. He has decided to use graders to shape the fill as the scrapers spread the fill material. The contractor has selected graders with 12-foot blades that have a minimum turning radius of 22 feet. The effective grading width will be 8.5 feet, and the operational efficiency will be 50 minutes per hour. The graders will grade in second gear at a average speed of 3 miles per hour and turn at an average speed of 1.2 miles per hour. The contractor has decided to use the looping method to grade the surface of the fill. What is the estimated productivity of the grader in compacted cubic yards per hour if 2 passes are required to achieve the desired smoothness?
4. A Caterpillar 120G grader is being used to grade the surface of a parking lot in preparation for the placement of asphalt pavement. Granular material is being

placed in 6-inch compacted lifts to provide adequate support for the pavement. The parking lot is rectangular, 400 feet by 100 feet. The grader will grade at an average speed of 3.6 miles per hour and back up at an average speed of 9 miles per hour. Assume it takes 4 passes to adequately grade the fill material and that the effective grading width is 10 feet. Ownership and operating costs for the grader average $27.50 per hour and the operator earns $22.00 per hour. The contractor plans to use the back-and-forth method of grading and to operate about 45 minutes per hour. What is the estimated unit cost in dollars per compacted cubic yard for the grading operation?

5. A contractor plans to use Caterpillar 631E Series II scrapers to move 50,000 bank cubic yards of soil to a construction site. The half-mile haul road is in poor condition with a rolling resistance estimated to be 200 pounds per ton. The contractor has decided to use a Champion 720A VHP grader to grade the haul road twice per day to reduce the rolling resistance to an estimated 70 pounds per ton. The haul road is 26 feet wide, and the effective grading width of the grader will be 9 feet. The operator will grade in second gear at an average speed of 3.5 miles per hour. Two passes will be required to achieve the desired smoothness. The hourly ownership cost for the grader is estimated to be $9.00, the hourly operating cost is estimated to be $20.65, and the grader operator earns $20.75 per hour plus 25% for fringe benefits. Operational efficiency is estimated to be 50 minutes per hour.
   a. What is the estimated grader productivity in square yards per hour?
   b. What is the estimated daily cost for grading the haul road?

6. A contractor is constructing a fill that will be used as the foundation for a concrete bus parking area. The plans for the parking area indicate a 800-foot-by-540-foot surface for the 2-foot compacted fill. The contractor has decided to use a John Deere 672B grader to final grade the surface of the fill prior to placement of the concrete pavement. The grader is equipped with a 12-foot blade and has a minimum turning radius of 22.5 feet. Four passes are required to achieve the desired smoothness. The average grading speed is estimated to be 3 miles per hour. The effective grading width will be limited to about 75% of the length of the grader blade, and turns will be executed in first gear at an average speed of 1 mile per hour.
   a. What is the estimated productivity of the grader in square yards per hour if the contractor uses the looping method of grading and an operational efficiency of 50 minutes per hour?
   b. How long will it take the grader to complete the final grading?

14

Soil Compaction and Stabilization

14.1   Introduction

Soils are major components of many construction projects. They may be natural, or *in situ*, soils, or they may be imported soils that have been processed in some manner. To successfully complete project activities involving site work, it is essential that you understand soil characteristics and their influence on project execution. In Chapter 7 we examined the basic structure of soil and discussed the concepts of moisture content, swell, and shrinkage. In this chapter we are going to examine soil classification and gradation and learn which types of soils are best as construction materials. We then will discuss compaction and learn how the soil moisture content influences the amount of compactive effort that is required to achieve the desired soil density. Last, we will examine methods for stabilizing soil by adding lime, cement, or asphalt to increase its strength.

14.2   Soil Properties

Soil properties have a direct effect on the ease or difficulty of handling earth, selection of construction equipment, and production rates of the equipment. We discussed both swell and shrinkage in Chapter 7 and learned that the amount of swell and shrinkage varies with different types of soil. We also learned how swell affects the load weight and the productivity of excavating and hauling equipment in bank cubic yards per hour. In Chapter 15 we will discuss how the soil type influences the selection of appropriate compaction equipment. In this section, we will discuss the classification of soil and the selection of good soils for construction operations.

The basic types of soils are

- Gravel
- Sand
- Clay
- Silt
- Organic

Sand and gravel generally are easy to identify visually because of their size and shape. Gravel is an excellent construction material, particularly if fine particles are present to fill the void areas between the larger particles. Sand can be used for construction purposes, but needs to be confined to prevent lateral movement when loaded. Generally, organic soil also is easy to identify by its dark color, texture, and sometimes by its odor. Silt and clay are more difficult to identify. Two visual methods are described in Table 14.1. Silt and organic soils are very poor construction materials, because silts have very little strength and organic soils will decompose, creating voids in the soil matrix. Clay is an acceptable construction material, particularly when mixed with gravel.

Two important characteristics of soil are gradation and plasticity. *Gradation* is a measure of the distribution of particle sizes in the soil. A well-graded soil is composed of particles of all sizes. A uniformly graded soil is composed primarily of particles of the same size. This is illustrated in Figure 14.1. Gradation curves, such as those shown in Figure 14.2, are developed by placing samples of soil on a series of screens, called *sieves*, starting with large openings and then using progressively smaller openings, as illustrated in Figure 14.3. The curves are created by measuring the amount of material retained on each sieve and plotting the cumulative amount that passed each one. Well-graded soils have diagonal curves, such as (A) in Figure 14.2, while uniformly graded soils have vertical curves, such as (B). Well-graded soils are stronger than uniformly graded soils, because there is better interlocking of soil particles and the void areas are filled with the smaller particles. If uniformly graded soils are all that are available for a compacted fill, contractors often blend small-particled soils with large-particled soils to improve the gradation of the soil and increase its strength.

Plasticity is a measure of the amount of water that a soil will absorb. Soil can exist in a solid, semisolid, plastic, or liquid state, depending on the amount of water that has

Table 14.1
Visual Methods for Identifying Silts and Clays

Method	Results
Rub particles between fingers	Gritty texture: silt Smooth texture: clay
Allow soil to dry and squeeze in hand	Powder: silt Hard to break: clay

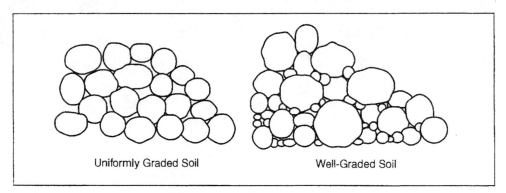

Figure 14.1
Soil Gradation

Marotta/Herubin, *Basic Construction Materials*, 5/e © 1997. Reprinted by permission of
Prentice-Hall, Inc. Upper Saddle River, NJ.

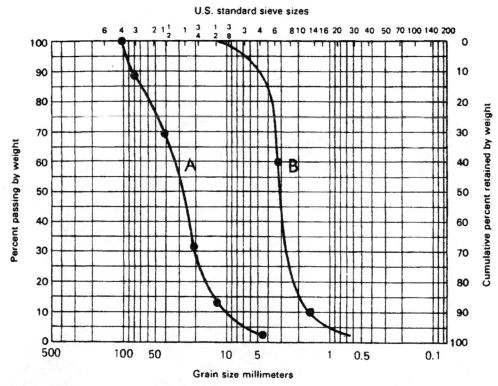

Figure 14.2
Soil Gradation Curves

Marotta/Herubin, *Basic Construction Materials*, 5/e © 1997. Reprinted by permission of
Prentice-Hall, Inc., Upper Saddle River, NJ.

Figure 14.3

Sieve Analysis

Courtesy the Asphalt Institute

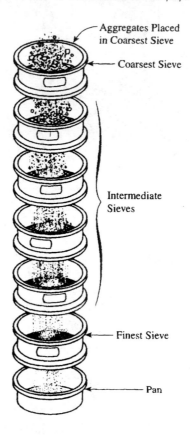

Aggregates Placed
in Coarsest Sieve

Coarsest Sieve

Intermediate
Sieves

Finest Sieve

Pan

been added to the soil. The amount of water in soil is characterized by the moisture content, which is defined as

$$\text{Moisture Content \%} = \frac{(\text{Wet Unit Weight} - \text{Dry Unit Weight})(100\%)}{\text{Dry Unit Weight}} \quad (14\text{--}1)$$

This is the same as Equation 7–1 in Chapter 7. Plasticity is measured by the *plasticity index (PI)*, which is the difference between the liquid limit and the plastic limit. The *liquid limit (LL)* is the moisture content at the plastic-liquid boundary, as illustrated in Figure 14.4. The *plastic limit (PL)* is the moisture content at the semisolid-plastic boundary. The *shrinkage limit (SL)* is the moisture content at the solid-semisolid boundary. Specific testing procedures for determining the plastic limit and liquid limit have been published by the American Society for Testing and Materials (Standard D4318). They have also published a testing procedure for determining the shrinkage limit (Standard D427). The plasticity index can be used to classify the fine particles in soil as either clay or silt.

There are several soil classification systems used in the United States. One of the most commonly used is the *Unified Soil Classification System* developed in the 1940s by Arthur Casagrande of Harvard University for the United States Army Corps of Engineers.[1] A key

---

[1] A complete description of the Unified Soil Classification System is published as Standard D2487 by the American Society for Testing and Materials.

Figure 14.4

Determination of Soil Plasticity

Schroeder/Dickenson, *Soils in Construction*, 4/e © 1996. Reprinted by permission of Prentice-Hall, Inc., Upper Saddle River, NJ.

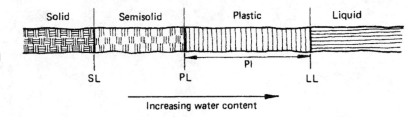

PLASTICITY CHART

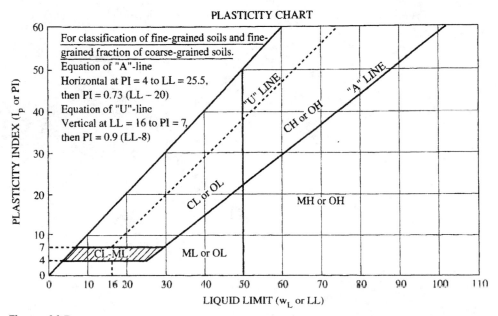

For classification of fine-grained soils and fine-grained fraction of coarse-grained soils.

Equation of "A"-line
Horizontal at PI = 4 to LL = 25.5,
then PI = 0.73 (LL – 20)

Equation of "U"-line
Vertical at LL = 16 to PI = 7,
then PI = 0.9 (LL-8)

Figure 14.5

Unified Soil Classification System Plasticity Chart

Harold N. Atkins, *Highway Materials, Soils, and Concrete*, 3/e © 1997. Reprinted by permission of Prentice-Hall, Inc., Upper Saddle River, NJ.

element of this classification system is the plasticity chart shown in Figure 14.5. By knowing both the liquid limit and the plasticity index, you can classify the fine particles as silt or clay. The letter *C* in Figure 14.5 stands for clay, the letter *M* for silt, and the letter *O* for organic. The second letter means either high plasticity (H) or low plasticity (L). Thus soil particles with a liquid limit of 60% and a plasticity index of 30% would be classified as highly plastic clay (CH).

14.3   Optimum Moisture Content and Compaction

The primary types of failure that occur in soil are shear and settlement. As we learned in Chapter 7, soil expands or swells when excavated, increasing its air content and making it more susceptible to shear and settlement failure. To counter this weakening of the soil, it is compacted to increase its strength and reduce future settlement. Compactive force

Figure 14.6
Nuclear Testing of Soil Density

Courtesy Troxler Electronic
Laboratories, Inc.

applied to the surface of the soil mass results in soil densification by forcing air out of the soil structure. To ensure that constructed fills possess the desired strength, a minimum compacted dry density is required by contract specifications. These specified densities are determined in a laboratory using standardized compaction tests.[2] The standard test, known as a *Proctor test* (named after the originator of the test), involves filling a 1/30-cubic-foot cylinder in three equal layers. Each layer is compacted by dropping a 5.5-pound hammer 25 times from a height of 1 foot. Field tests of soil compaction generally are made with nuclear moisture-density gauges (similar to the one illustrated in Figure 14.6) to ensure conformity with contract specifications.

The amount of compactive effort required to achieve the design density varies with the moisture content of the soil. This can be seen in Figure 14.7, which demonstrates that the resulting dry density varies with moisture content for a given compactive effort. As the moisture content of the soil is increased from zero, the dry density increases because the water lubricates the soil particles, allowing them to consolidate into a denser mass. At some point the amount of water exceeds the amount needed to lubricate the soil particles, and the excess water occupies space previously occupied by solid particles. The result is that the dry density starts to decline and continues to decline as the moisture content is

---

[2]For a detailed description of compaction testing procedures, readers should refer to Standard D698 published by the American Society for Testing and Materials.

Figure 14.7

Variation of Dry Density with Moisture Content

Harold N. Atkins, *Highway Materials, Soils, and Concrete*, 3/e © 1996. Reprinted by permission of Prentice-Hall, Inc., Upper Saddle River, NJ.

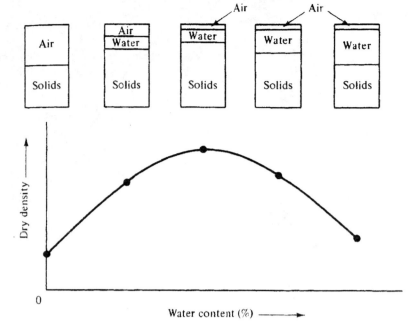

increased. The moisture content that results in the maximum dry density is called the *optimum moisture content.*

Keeping the soil moisture content near the optimum moisture content allows the contractor to obtain maximum compaction efficiency, because the required dry density can be achieved with the least compactive effort. Swell will decrease as the moisture content is increased to optimum; then it will remain relatively constant as the moisture content is increased. The optimum moisture content will vary with type of soil and generally is determined for each project in a laboratory. Once the optimum moisture content is known, the natural moisture content is determined. If the natural moisture content is higher than optimum, the soil must be dried. If the natural moisture content is less than optimum, moisture is added before the soil is compacted. Sometimes contractors add the moisture at the borrow site, but more often, they add the water at the fill site. Determining the amount of water needed and selecting the number and size of water trucks become important contractor decisions. Let's now look at an example to illustrate.

Example 14.1

A contractor has a contract for the construction of a branch bank building in a new shopping center complex. A part of the project is the construction of a paved parking area for bank customers. Project drawings indicate that a 1-foot compacted fill is required for the parking area. The contractor has located a suitable borrow source for the fill material that is 2 miles from the project site. The contractor plans to haul the fill material in dump trucks and load them at the borrow site with a hydraulic excavator. Tests on the fill material indicate a wet unit weight of 2,300 pounds per loose cubic yard at a natural moisture content of 2%. Compaction tests on the soil indicate that its optimum moisture content is 6%. The fleet of dump trucks deliver fill to the project site at a rate of 250 loose cubic yards per hour. How many gallons of water must the contractor deliver to the project site per hour if he wants to increase the moisture content of the fill material to optimum? He wants the productivity of the water delivery to be equal to that of the dump trucks.

Solution

The first step is to determine the dry unit weight of the fill material. The moisture content was defined in Equation 14.1 to be

$$\frac{(\text{Wet Unit Weight} - \text{Dry Unit Weight})(100\%)}{\text{Dry Unit Weight}}$$

Solving for the dry unit weight yields the following equation:

$$\text{Dry Unit Weight} = \frac{(100\%)(\text{Wet Unit Weight})}{(100\% + \text{Moisture Content})}$$

Substituting the numerical values yields

$$\text{Dry Unit Weight} = \frac{(100\%)(2,300 \text{ lb./LCY})}{(100\% + 2\%)} = 2,255 \text{ lb./LCY}$$

Since the natural moisture content is 2% and the optimum moisture content is 6%, we need to increase the moisture content by 4%. The weight of the water we need to add is

$$(0.04)(2,255 \text{ lb./LCY}) = 90.2 \text{ lb./LCY}$$

Since water weighs 8.33 pounds per gallon, we can determine the volume of water required to be

$$\frac{90.2 \text{ lb./LCY}}{8.33 \text{ lb./gal.}} = 10.8 \text{ gal./LCY}$$

Now we can determine the required water delivery rate to be

$$(10.8 \text{ gal./LCY})(250 \text{ LCY/hr.}) = \mathbf{2,700 \text{ gal./hr.}}$$

The number of water trucks needed to deliver water at this rate depends on the productivity of each truck. Water truck productivity is a function of the capacity of the truck (in gallons); the length of the spray bar; whether or not a pump is used to discharge the water from the truck; and the time it takes an empty truck to travel to the water loading site, refill, and return to the project site.

14.4   *Soil Stabilization*

Sometimes the strength of the soil is not adequate for it to carry the loads we intend to impose. We have several choices. We can

- Replace the soil with stronger soil
- Overlay the soil with stronger material to reduce the loading on the soil
- Increase the strength of the soil

Figure 14.8
Rotary Mixer Stabilizing Soil with Lime
Courtesy CMI Corporation

This third alternative is called soil stabilization.[3] Soil stabilization is done by mixing a stabilizing agent or additive with the soil. Stabilization allows the use of otherwise unsuitable natural soils. It eliminates the cost of excavating and removing the unsuitable soil and replacing it with suitable material. Three of the more common methods of stabilization used today are

- Lime stabilization
- Cement stabilization
- Asphalt stabilization

Specific mix designs for stabilized soils are determined in laboratories using actual soil samples and provided to contractors in contract specifications. Rotary mixers, such as illustrated in Figure 14.8, are used to pulverize the soil, mix the desired additive, and spread the resulting mixture. The model illustrated can cut and blend the soil to a depth of 16 inches. The operation of a rotary mixer is illustrated in Figure 14.9. It consists of a carrier whose large engine drives a rotor that rotates in a mixing chamber. The rotor cuts, pulverizes, and mixes the soil with the stabilizing agent.

---

[3]For in-depth discussion of soil stabilization, readers should consult *A Practical Guide to Soil Stabilization and Road Reclamation Techniques* (Oklahoma City, OK: CMI Corporation, 1994).

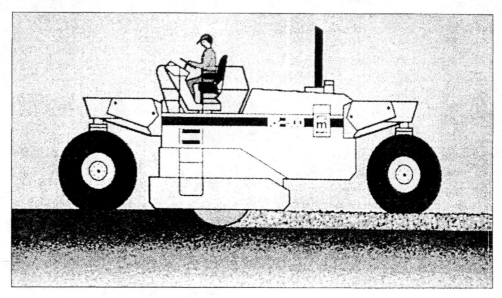

Figure 14.9
Operation of Rotary Mixer
Courtesy CMI Corporation

Lime often is used with soils that have a high clay content. Quicklime (calcium oxide) or hydrated lime (calcium hydroxide) reacts chemically with the clay, causing small particles to combine and form larger particles. It also reacts with available silica and alumina in the soil to cement soil components into a hardened matrix. The clay should have a plasticity index of at least 10%, or it will not react readily with the lime. Mixing lime with plastic soils results in a reduction in the plasticity index of the soil and an increase in its strength. It also will make the soil more resistant to water penetration. Mix designs for lime stabilization usually require the lime to be added to the soil in quantities of 2% to 4% by weight. The construction process for lime stabilization consists of these steps:

1. Loosen and pulverize the soil to be stabilized.
2. Spread the lime on the soil to be stabilized.
3. Mix the lime with the soil.
4. Spread the soil/lime mixture to the desired thickness.
5. Wet the soil/lime mixture.
6. Compact the wet soil/lime mixture.
7. Cure the soil/lime mixture for 3 to 7 days.

While lime is used to stabilize high-clay-content soils, cement is used to stabilize both granular soils and fine-grain soils. There are two types of cement-and-soil mixtures: (1) soil-cement and (2) cement-modified soil. Soil-cement contains sufficient cement to form a hardened mixture. It is compacted to a high density and cures into a hardened slablike structural material. Soil should have a plasticity index of less than 10% for the soil to be a good candidate for soil-cement. Cement-modified soil may be a hardened or semi-hardened mixture, depending on the amount of cement added. The cement reduces the soil's plasticity and increases its strength, much like lime does. Fine-grain soils with plasticity indexes greater than 10% can be stabilized with cement to form cement-modified soil, but generally are not good materials for soil-cement. The amount of cement required to form soil-cement varies from 3% to 8% by weight for sand and gravel to 8% to 15% for fine-grain soils containing clay or silt. The amount of cement required for cement-modified soil usually ranges from 3% to 6% by weight. The construction process for cement-stabilized soil is similar to that listed previously for lime-stabilized soil. The only difference is that after the desired density is achieved, soil-cement is finished with a smooth compactor before the mixture is allowed to cure. Soil-cement should be kept moist and cured for at least 7 to 8 days to achieve desired strength.

Asphalt can be added to granular soils, such as sand or gravel, to produce a more durable, stable soil. The amount of asphalt required usually is 1% to 3% of the dry weight of the soil. The moisture content of the soil should not exceed 3%. If it is higher, the soil should be aerated to reduce the moisture content to no more than 3%. The construction process for asphalt-stabilized soil consists of the following steps:

1. Loosen and pulverize the soil to stabilized.
2. Apply the required amount of asphalt.
3. Mix the asphalt with the soil.
4. Spread the asphalt-soil mixture to the desired thickness.
5. Compact the asphalt-soil mixture.
6. Finish the surface of the asphalt-soil mixture.

Let's now look at an example problem involving determination of the quantity of cement required to stabilize the soil for a construction project.

Example 14.2

A regional port authority has awarded a contractor a contract for the construction of a large paved area that will be used for storage of shipping containers. The project design calls for the construction of 10 inches of soil-cement covered with 6 inches of asphalt. The contract specifies that the cement content of the soil-cement is to be 8% of the soil dry unit weight. The granular fill material that is to be used for the soil-cement weighs 2,400 pounds per loose cubic yard at a moisture content of 3%. How much cement should the contractor add to each loose cubic yard of fill material to achieve the content specified in the contract?

Solution

The first step is to determine the dry unit weight of the soil, as we did in Example 14-1. The dry unit weight is

$$\frac{(100\%)(2{,}400 \text{ lb./LCY})}{(100\% + 3\%)} = 2{,}330 \text{ lb./LCY}$$

Now we can determine the amount of cement required to be

$$(0.08)(2{,}330 \text{ lb./LCY}) = \textbf{186.4 lb./LCY}$$

Once you have determined the quantity of stabilizing agent to use, you need to select the equipment to stabilize the soil. Stabilization costs will depend on the productivity of the stabilizing equipment and the hourly cost of owning and operating it. The productivity of a rotary mixer may be determined on an area basis or a volume basis. The productivity on an area basis can be estimated using Equation 14–2:

$$\text{Productivity} = (S)(W)(OF) \tag{14–2}$$

where S is the speed of the machine

W is the cutting width

OF is the operating factor

The productivity on a volume basis can be estimated using Equation 14–3:

$$\text{Productivity} = (S)(W)(D)(OF) \tag{14–3}$$

where S is the speed of the machine

W is the cutting width

D is the cutting depth

OF is the operating factor

Let's look at an example to illustrate.

Example 14.3

The contractor of Example 14.2 has decided to use a Caterpillar SS-250 rotary mixer to mix the cement with the soil. The cutting width of the machine is 8 feet, and the cutting depth is 10 inches. The average travel speed of the machine while stabilizing the soil will be 30 feet per minute. The contractor plans an operational efficiency of 50 minutes per hour.

a. What is the estimated productivity of the rotary mixer in square yards per hour?
b. What is the estimated productivity of the rotary mixer in bank cubic yards per hour?
c. What is the estimated unit cost in dollars per bank cubic yard for the rotary mixer to stabilize the soil, if the hourly ownership and operating cost (including operator's wages) is $95?

Solution

a. With Equation 14–2, the area-measure productivity can be estimated to be

$$\text{Productivity} = \frac{(30 \text{ ft./min.})(8 \text{ ft.})(0.83)(60 \text{ min./hr.})}{9 \text{ sq. ft./sq. yd.}}$$

$$= 1{,}328 \text{ sq. yd./hr.}$$

b. With Equation 14–3, the volume-measure productivity can be estimated to be

$$\text{Productivity} = \frac{(30 \text{ ft./min.})(8 \text{ ft.})(10 \text{ in.})(0.83)(60 \text{ min./hr.})}{(12 \text{ in./ft.})(27 \text{ cu. ft./cu. yd})}$$

$$= 369 \text{ BCY/hr.}$$

c. The unit cost is estimated to be

$$\frac{\$95/hr.}{369\ BCY/hr.} = \textbf{\$0.26 BCY}$$

14.5   *Problems*

1. A contractor is constructing streets for a residential project. She has decided to use scrapers to excavate, haul, and spread fill material to construct the subgrade for the streets. Soil tests on the fill material indicate a wet unit weight of 115 pounds per bank cubic foot and a dry unit weight of 110 pounds per bank cubic foot. Compaction tests indicate that the optimum moisture content for the fill material is 8%. The scrapers can deliver the fill material to the project site at the rate of 150 loose cubic yards per hour. Swell for the fill material is estimated to be 20%, and shrinkage is estimated to be 12% when compacted to the design density. How many gallons of water must the contractor deliver to the project site per hour if she wants to increase the moisture content to 8% and keep up with the productivity of the scrapers? (Note: Water weighs 8.33 pounds per gallon.)

2. A contractor is excavating fill material weighing 2,996 pounds per bank cubic yard with a loader and hauling the material in dump trucks to a fill area 4 miles away. Soil tests indicate that the dry unit weight of a bank cubic yard of fill material is 2,800 pounds.
   a. What is the in situ moisture content of the soil the contractor is excavating?
   b. Compaction tests indicate that the optimum moisture content of the soil is 10%. How many gallons of water per bank cubic yard of soil should be added to raise the moisture content to 10%? (Note: Water weighs 8.33 pounds per gallon.)
   c. How many gallons of water should be added to each loose cubic yard of soil as it is being spread on the fill site to bring the moisture content up to the desired 10%? Soil tests indicate that the soil swell is about 28%.
   d. How many truck tractors with 5,000-gallon water trailers should be used to apply the water if they can apply water at a rate of 8 gallons per minute and the dump trucks can spread the fill material at a rate of 300 loose cubic yards per hour?

3. A contractor has a contract for the construction of a shopping center and a large parking lot. Soil tests indicate the natural soil has a high clay content, requiring either stabilization or replacement to make an acceptable subgrade for the parking lot pavement. The in situ soil weighs 2,900 pounds per bank cubic yard at a moisture content of 5%. Tests indicate that adding 3% lime by dry unit weight of the soil would stabilize the soil adequately. How much lime (in pounds) should the contractor purchase if an 8-inch layer of soil is to be stabilized and the parking lot measures 150 feet by 390 feet?

4. A contractor has a contract for the construction of a new runway for a regional airport. The contract specifications require cement stabilization of the natural soil to a depth of 8 inches before an aggregate base course is placed. Soil tests on the existing soil indicate a wet unit weight of 107 pounds per bank cubic foot and a dry unit

weight of 103 pounds per bank cubic foot. The contract specifies that the cement content required for the stabilized subgrade is 4% of the soil dry unit weight.

a. What is the moisture content of the existing soil?

b. How much cement (in pounds) should the contractor add to each bank cubic yard of existing soil to achieve the cement content specified in the contract?

5. A contractor has a contract for the construction of a new post office. Part of the project involves the construction of a large paved truck storage area. The contract requires that the storage area receive an asphalt concrete surface placed on an asphalt-stabilized base course. The granular base course material being trucked in to the construction site weighs 2,800 pounds per bank cubic yard at a moisture content of 2%. The contract specifies that the asphalt content in the compacted base course be 2% of the dry weight of the soil. Soil tests taken on the base course material indicate a swell of 12% and a shrinkage of 8% when compacted to the design density. The contractor estimates that 2,000 loose cubic yards of base course material are required for the storage area. How many gallons of asphalt should the contractor order for the base course if one gallon of asphalt weighs 8 pounds?

6. The contractor of Problem 3 has decided to use a CMI RS-500B rotary mixer to stabilize the soil with lime. The mixing width will be 96 inches, the mixing depth will be 8 inches, and the mixing speed is estimated to be 20 feet per minute. The operational efficiency is estimated to be 45 minutes per hour.

a. What is the estimated productivity of the rotary mixer in bank cubic yards per hour?

b. How long (in hours) will it take the contractor to stabilize the parking lot subgrade with the rotary mixer?

15

Soil Compactors

15.1   *Introduction*

Compaction is the mechanical densification of soil. It is accomplished by forcing the soil particles together, expelling air from the soil structure. Soil is compacted to improve its strength and minimize settlement. The amount of compactive effort required to achieve the desired density varies, depending on the moisture content of the soil and the type of soil. Compacting near the optimum moisture content results in the most efficient compaction operation. When compacted, soil shrinks (that is, its density increases beyond that of its natural bank state). The amount of shrinkage depends on the soil type, the soil moisture content, and the amount of compactive effort applied.

To ensure earth fills meet design strength criteria, specific compacted densities generally are required by contract specifications. Contractors usually construct test strips with the fill material to determine the amount of compactive effort required to achieve the desired design density. The compactive effort is a function of the following:

- Weight and type of compactor to be used
- Number of passes the compactor will make over each section of the fill
- Thickness of the material being compacted

Many types of compactors are available, and contractors should select compaction equipment that is most effective for the type of material to be compacted. Once the equipment has been selected, the number of passes necessary to achieve the required density is determined through field testing with the fill material that is to be used.

If the natural moisture content of the soil is not near the optimum value, water should be added to or removed from the fill material as it is being spread and compacted. Contractors determine the required water delivery rate by the methods discussed in Chapter 14. Water delivery capability and compaction productivity generally are selected to exceed the delivery capability of the trucks or scrapers to maximize overall fleet efficiency. We will discuss this in more detail in Chapter 16.

15.2   *Types and Uses of Compactors*

There are many types of compaction equipment manufactured. They can be grouped into the following four types or classifications:

- Pneumatic-tire
- Smooth steel-drum
- Tamping-foot
- Vibratory

The primary compacting methods are

- Static weight (or pressure)
- Kneading (or manipulation)
- Vibration (or shaking)
- Impact (or sharp blow)

A *pneumatic-tire compactor* is illustrated in Figure 15.1. This type of compactor uses its static weight and the kneading action of the tires for compaction and is effective

Figure 15.1
Pneumatic-Tire Compactor

Courtesy Svedala Industries, Inc.–
Dynapac Compaction and Paving

with clay and granular soils. These compactors have an odd number of wheels—commonly 7, 9, 11, or 13—so that the rear tires track over the spaces between the front tires. Some pneumatic compactors have bent axles so the tires "wobble," increasing the kneading action. Most pneumatic-tire compactors have an empty space between the axles for ballast to increase the static weight. Pneumatic-tire compactors typically weigh between 10 and 35 tons and can compact lifts of 6 to 12 inches.

A *smooth steel-drum compactor* is illustrated in Figure 15.2. This type of compactor uses its static weight for compaction and is effective on all types of soils. Some models are made with hollow cylinders or drums that can be filled with ballast to increase the machine's weight. This compactor also is used to finish or seal the surface of a fill to inhibit water penetration. Smooth steel-drum compactors typically weigh between 3 and 18 tons and can compact lifts of 5 to 8 inches.

A *tamping-foot compactor* uses a compaction drum equipped with protruding feet, as illustrated in Figure 15.3. Older versions of this type of compactor were known as *sheepsfoot* compactors. The tamping-foot compactor uses its static weight and kneading action for compaction and is effective with clay and silty clay soils. The feet sink into the loose material, kneading and tamping the soil at the bottom of the lift. As passes are made, the feet penetrate less on each pass until the compactor is said to have "walked out" of the lift. Tamping-foot compactors typically weigh between 15 and 40 tons and work best if the lift thickness is limited to 6 to 10 inches.

Vibratory compactors are manufactured in a variety of sizes and types. Most utilize eccentric weights mounted on the compactor axles to create the vibration. This type of

Figure 15.2

Smooth Steel-Drum Compactor

Courtesy Svedala Industries, Inc.–
Dynapac Compaction and Paving

Figure 15.3
Tamping-Foot Compactor
Courtesy Caterpillar Inc.

compactor uses its static weight, vibration, and impact to achieve compaction. The result is that vibratory compactors are able to achieve deeper penetration of compactive effort than comparable static or nonvibratory compactors are able to achieve. Large vibratory smooth steel-drum compactors can compact rock lifts up to 3 feet effectively. A vibratory smooth steel-drum compactor is illustrated in Figure 15.4, and a vibratory tamping-foot compactor is illustrated in Figure 15.5. Small vibratory compactors, such as the one illustrated in Figure 15.6, are used to compact backfill placed in utility trenches. Hand-operated vibratory rammers, such as the one illustrated in Figure 15.7, and vibratory plate compactors, such as the one illustrated in Figure 15.8, are used to compact in confined spaces. Vibratory rammers can compact up to 16 inches and travel at speeds of 30 to 50 feet per minute. Vibratory plate compactors can compact to a depth up to 1 foot and travel at speeds of 70 to 80 feet per minute.

Table 15.1 provides the best type of compactor to use for different types of soil. The size to use depends on an economic analysis of the specific project and the productivity of other construction equipment being used on the project. We will discuss fleet sizing in Chapter 16.

Figure 15.4
Vibratory Smooth Steel-Drum Compactor

Courtesy Caterpillar Inc.

Figure 15.5
Vibratory Tamping-Foot Compactor

Courtesy Caterpillar Inc.

Figure 15.6
Walk-Behind Vibratory Tamping-Foot Trench Compactor
Courtesy Multiquip, Inc.

Figure 15.7
Vibratory Ram Compactor
Courtesy Multiquip, Inc.

Figure 15.8

Vibratory Plate Compactor

Courtesy Multiquip, Inc.

Table 15.1

Most Efficient Compactor for Different Types of Material

Material	Type Compactor
Rock fill	Heavy-duty vibratory smooth steel-drum
Sand and gravel	Medium-weight vibratory smooth steel-drum
Silty soil	Medium-weight and heavy vibratory smooth steel-drum
Clay soil	Vibratory tamping-foot

15.3 *Productivity Estimation*

Compactor productivity usually is expressed in compacted cubic yards per hour. The loose fill material is spread by trucks or by scrapers in lifts or layers that are deeper than the final compacted state. The compactor applies pressure on the fill material, increasing its density and reducing its thickness. The reason for using compacted cubic yards per hour is that the contract drawings describe the dimensions of the fill in its final compacted state.

Compactor productivity is a function of the following:

- Effective compaction width
- Average compactor speed
- Thickness of the compacted lift

- Number of passes required to achieve the desired density
- Operational efficiency

It can be estimated using Equation 15–1:

$$\text{Productivity} = \frac{(W)(S)(L)(OF)}{P} \tag{15–1}$$

where W is the effective compaction width

S is the average compactor speed

L is the thickness of the lift to be compacted

OF is the operating factor

P is the number of passes required

The effective compaction width will be less than the length of the compactor drum or the width of the tires on a pneumatic-tire compactor, because the operator will overlap each pass to ensure all areas are fully compacted. *The average compaction speed for most compactors is between 3 and 8 miles per hour.* If the average speed is unknown, 5 miles per hour is a good estimate. Let's now look at an example problem.

Example 15.1

A contractor is constructing a compacted fill that will be used to support concrete slab foundations for a complex of large warehouses. The contractor is using scrapers to haul and spread the sandy clay fill material and has decided to use a Dynapac CA 51 PD vibratory tamping-foot compactor to compact the fill to the density required by the contract specifications. The compactor has a compaction drum that is 7 feet long and will compact at an average speed of 5 miles per hour. The contractor has decided to compact the fill in 8-inch compacted lifts and has determined that 6 passes are required to achieve the required density. To ensure adequate compaction, the contractor plans to use a 1-foot overlap between adjacent passes. What is the estimated productivity of the compactor in compacted cubic yards per hour if the contractor works 50 minutes per hour?

Solution

Since the contractor plans an overlap of 1 foot between adjacent passes and the length of the compaction drum is 7 feet, the effective compaction width for this operation is 6 feet. The operating factor is 50 min./60 min. or 0.83. We can estimate the compactor productivity by use of Equation 15–1.

$$\text{Productivity} = \frac{(6 \text{ ft.})(5 \text{ mi./hr.})(5,280 \text{ ft./mi.})(8 \text{ in.})(0.83)}{(12 \text{ in./ft.})(27 \text{ cu.yd./cu. ft.})(6)}$$

$$= 541 \text{ CCY/hr.}$$

15.4   *Cost and Time Analysis*

To estimate the direct cost of a compaction operation, first estimate the hourly owner-ship and operating costs using the techniques discussed in Chapter 4, the cost refer-ences discussed in Chapter 5, or historical cost data. These costs can be used in con-junction with the compactor productivity estimated with Equation 15–1 to estimate the unit cost for the compaction operation. If fill material is hauled and spread by trucks or scrapers and their productivity is less than that of the compactors, the overall fleet pro-ductivity must be used to estimate the direct unit cost of the operation. We will discuss this in more detail in Chapter 16. Multiplying the unit cost by the total quantity of work to be performed yields the estimated cost for the task. Dividing the quantity of work by the overall productivity yields an estimate of the time required to complete the task. Let's look at an example as an illustration.

Example 15.2

The contractor of Example 15.1 is using 2 scrapers to haul and spread the fill material. The swell of the sandy clay soil is estimated to be 30%, and the shrinkage when compacted to the required density is estimated to be 10%. The productivity of each scraper is estimated to be 290 loose cubic yards per hour. The hourly ownership and operating cost (including operator's wages) is estimated to be $170 for each scraper and $80 for the compactor.

a. What is the overall productivity of the compaction operation?
b. What is the estimated unit cost in dollars per compacted cubic yard to haul and com-pact the fill?
c. If the required amount of fill is 15,000 compacted cubic yards, how many 8-hour days will it take the contractor to complete the fill operation?

Solution

a. In Example 15.1, the compactor's productivity was estimated to be 541 compacted cubic yards per hour. The productivity of the scrapers is estimated to be

$$\frac{(2)(290 \text{ LCY/hr.})(0.9 \text{ CCY/BCY})}{(1.3 \text{ LCY/BCY})} = 401 \text{ CCY/hr.}$$

Since the productivity of the scrapers is less than that of the compactor, the overall productivity of the fill operation is determined by the scraper productivity, which is **401 compacted cubic yards per hour.**
b. The total hourly ownership and operating cost for the 2 scrapers and 1 compactor is

$$(2)(\$170)/\text{hr.} + \$80/\text{hr.} = \$420 \text{ per hour}$$

The total unit cost is estimated to be

$$\frac{\$420/\text{hr.}}{401 \text{ CCY/hr.}} = \$1.05/\text{CCY}$$

c. The duration for the fill operation is estimated to be

$$\frac{15,000 \text{ CCY}}{(401 \text{ CCY/hr.})(8 \text{ hr./day})} = \textbf{4.7 days}$$

15.5   *Problems*

1. A contractor is using a Caterpillar 815B tamping-foot compactor on a parking lot fill. The actual compacting width per pass with the machine is 6.5 feet, but the contractor wants to overlap each pass by 8 inches to ensure adequate compaction. The average speed of the compactor is 4 miles per hour, and the thickness of the each compacted lift is 8 inches. The contractor prepared a test strip and determined that 4 passes would achieve the required density. What is the estimated productivity of the compactor in compacted cubic yards per hour if the contractor works 45 minutes per hour?

2. A contractor is using a HAMM 2520 D vibratory smooth steel-drum compactor to compact the gravel base course for asphalt pavement. The width of the compacting cylinder is 7.2 feet and the average compacting speed is 3 miles per hour. The contract specifications require 6 inches of well-compacted granular base. The contractor is using dump trucks to haul and spread the gravel and plans a 6-inch overlap between adjacent compactor passes to ensure adequate compaction. The contractor determined from a test strip that 5 passes are required to achieve the required density. What is the estimated productivity of the compactor in compacted cubic yards per hour if the contractor has an operational efficiency of 50 minutes per hour?

3. A contractor is using a Wacker VPA 1350W vibratory plate compactor to compact the backfill being placed around a new 8-inch water line. The width of the compacting surface (base plate) is 19.5 inches. The average compacting speed for the compactor is 70 feet per minute. The contractor is compacting in 10-inch lifts and overlaps each adjacent pass by 3 inches to ensure adequate compaction. The contractor determined from a test strip that 3 passes are required to achieve the required density. The hourly ownership and operating cost for the compactor (including the operator's wages) is $35. What is the estimated unit cost in dollars per compacted cubic yard to compact the backfill if the contractor has an operational efficiency of 40 minutes per hour?

4. Seven scrapers are hauling 1,600 bank cubic yards of excavated material per hour to a fill area to be compacted with BOMAG vibratory tamping-foot compactors. The width of the compacting drum on the compactors is 6.9 feet. The compacted lift thickness is 6 inches. Tests performed on the compacted material indicate that the material shrinks to about 85% of its bank volume when compacted. One-foot overlap between adjacent passes is required to ensure adequate compaction. The contractor determined from a test strip that 5 passes are required to achieve the specified density.

    a. How many compacted cubic yards of the fill material do you estimate a single compactor can compact per hour at an average compacting speed of 3 miles per hour and an operational efficiency of 50 minutes per hour?

b. How many compactors should be used to compact the fill and maintain a production rate at least equal to that of the scrapers?

5. A contractor is using dump trucks to deliver fill material to a construction project. The sandy clay is to be used to backfill behind a retaining wall to construct a building site for a motel. Because of the cohesive nature of the fill material, the contractor has decided to rent a HYPAC C822A vibratory tamping-foot compactor to compact the backfill to the required density. The dump trucks are able to deliver and spread fill material at the project site at a rate of 500 loose cubic yards per hour. The contractor plans to construct the backfill in 8-inch compacted lifts. The width of the compacting drum on the compactor is 4.8 feet. One foot of overlap between adjacent passes is required to ensure adequate compaction. The fill material weighs 2,825 pounds per bank cubic yard and has a swell of 33%. Tests indicate that 6 passes of the compactor are required to achieve the required density, and shrinkage is estimated to be 12%.

a. At a compactor speed of 3 miles per hour, how many compactors should the contractor use to achieve the production rate of the dump trucks, if the operational efficiency is 45 minutes per hour?

b. If compactors rent for $195 per day, the hourly operating cost is $21, and operators earn $29.00 per hour plus 25% for fringes, how much do you estimate it will cost per compacted cubic yard to compact the backfill?

16

Operation Analysis

16.1 Introduction

Operation analysis involves determining all of the tasks involved in completing each site work construction activity. Such tasks may include combinations of the following:

- Clearing and grubbing
- Excavating
- Loading
- Hauling
- Backfilling
- Grading
- Compacting

Once the individual tasks have been identified, specific items of equipment are selected to perform each task. Specific choices may be limited to those owned by the contractor or those available from a local equipment dealer if the equipment is to be leased or rented. Once the specific items of equipment have been selected, the last step is to determine the number of each required for efficient performance of the construction activity. After the equipment has been selected and its productivity estimated, operation analysis is completed by estimating the overall direct unit cost for the construction activity.

In this chapter we will examine operational analysis and apply the concepts we learned in Chapters 8 through 15. Operational analysis is a critical step in developing cost estimates and schedules for construction projects.

16.2   *Equipment Selection*

Equipment selection involves selection of the correct type of equipment for each task and determination of the number of each type required. The most economic fleet for a site work construction activity generally is one in which the productivity of each type of equipment is similar to that of the others, so no equipment sits idle for extended periods of time. This involves balancing the fleet to match the productivity of the various types of equipment that will be used. Let's look at an example to illustrate.

Example 16.1

A contractor is preparing a bid for the construction of a small shopping center and adjacent parking lot. The parking lot requires a compacted fill 900 feet by 150 feet with an average depth of 3 feet. The only available material is moist loam weighing 2,800 pounds per bank cubic yard with a swell estimated to be 25%. The shrinkage at the design compacted density is estimated to be 15%. The source of the fill material is 2 miles from the project site. The first mile of the haul road has an uphill grade of 4% and the second mile has an uphill grade of 2% when traveling from the borrow source to the shopping center site. The coefficient of traction for the haul road is estimated to be 0.5, and the rolling resistance is estimated to be 90 pounds per ton.

a. The contractor owns a fleet of 12-cubic-yard end-dump trucks that he plans to use to haul the required fill material. To load the trucks, the contractor has decided to use his own 4-cubic-yard articulated wheeled loader. In reviewing the technical literature for the loader, the contractor determined that its static tipping load is 20,000 pounds. The contractor investigated the borrow site and estimates that the average haul distance for the loader (one-way) will be 45 feet. He estimates that the average loader speed will be 1.5 miles per hour and that the average fixed time will be 30 seconds. What is the estimated time to load 1 dump truck?

b. The gear train efficiency of the 12-cubic-yard, 210-horsepower dump trucks is estimated to be 0.8. The maximum load is 16 tons, and the empty weight is 18 tons. The load distribution for the truck is as follows:

      Empty: Front wheels 55%   *Loaded:* Front wheels 35%
                 Drive wheels 45%   Drive wheels 65%

The maximum rated speed for the truck is 40 miles per hour. Operational efficiency of the trucks and loader is estimated to be 50 minutes per hour. How many trucks should the contractor use on this project, if he wants to maximize fleet productivity?

c. To grade and spread the fill material in 8-inch uncompacted lifts, the contractor has selected graders with 12-foot moldboards. The effective grading width is estimated to be 10 feet, and the minimum turning radius is 24 feet. The grader will grade at an average speed of 2.5 miles per hour, and it will turn at an average speed of 1 mile per hour or back across the fill at 4 miles per hour. Which method, looping or back and forth, should the contractor use on this project to maximize grader productivity? How many graders should the contractor use on this project if 3 passes are required and operational efficiency is estimated to be 50 minutes per hour?

d. The contractor has selected vibratory tamping compactors to compact the fill to the specified density. The effective compacting width will be 6 feet, and the average compactor speed is estimated to be 3 miles per hour. Four passes are required to achieve the desired density. How many compactors should the contractor use on the project, if the operational efficiency is 50 minutes per hour?

Solution

a. The first step is to determine an appropriate fill factor for the wheeled loader. Referring to Table 9.1, we find the fill factor for moist loam to be 1.00 to 1.10. Selecting the average value, we estimate the fill factor to be 1.05. Next, we need to determine the maximum safe load for the loader. The heaped capacity is equal to the rated capacity times the fill factor, which is

$$(4 \text{ LCY})(1.05) = 4.2 \text{ LCY}$$

The maximum load weight is estimated to be

$$\frac{(4.2 \text{ LCY})(2{,}800 \text{ lb./BCY})}{1.25 \text{ LCY/BCY}} = 9{,}408 \text{ lb.}$$

Since the maximum load weight (9,408 lb.) is less than the tipping load (20,000 lb.), the maximum volume the loader can carry is 4.2 LCY. The number of loader cycles required to load 1 dump truck is

$$\frac{12 \text{ LCY}}{4.2 \text{ LCY}} = 2.9$$

which must be rounded up to 3 cycles.

Now we need to estimate the cycle time for the loader. The average travel distance will be 90 feet, and the average speed 1.5 miles per hour, so the variable time can be estimated to be

$$\frac{90 \text{ ft.}}{(1.5 \text{ mi./hr.})(88 \text{ ft./min. per mi./hr.})} = 0.7 \text{ min.}$$

The cycle time can now be estimated by adding the fixed time, which is 30 seconds.

$$CT = 0.5 \text{ min.} + 0.7 \text{ min.} = 1.2 \text{ min.}$$

The time required to load 1 dump truck can now be estimated to be

$$(3 \text{ cycles})(1.2 \text{ min./cycle}) = \textbf{3.6 min.}$$

b. First, we need to determine the maximum load the dump trucks can safely carry. The weight of the heaped volume is

$$\frac{(12 \text{ LCY})(2{,}800 \text{ lb./BCY})}{1.25 \text{ LCY/BCY}} = 26{,}880 \text{ lb.}$$

which is less than the maximum rated load of 32,000 pounds, so the trucks can carry 12 LCY safely.

We will assume the job conditions to be average and estimate the turn and dump time to be 1.3 minutes and the spotting time to be 0.3 minutes from Table 12.2. By adding these times to the loading time, we can estimate the total fixed time for the trucks to be

$$3.6 \text{ min.} + 1.3 \text{ min.} + 0.3 \text{ min.} = 5.2 \text{ min.}$$

To determine the variable time, we must estimate the maximum speed the truck can traverse each haul road segment. We also must determine the maximum rimpull that can be generated without the wheels spinning. This involves multiplying the coefficient of traction by the weight on the driving axles. Since the rear wheels are the driving wheels, we will check them for traction. The maximum rimpull that can be generated when the trucks are empty is

$$(0.5)(0.45)(36,000 \text{ lb.}) = 8,100 \text{ lb.}$$

The maximum rimpull that can be generated when the trucks are loaded is

$$(0.5)(0.65)(36,000 \text{ lb.} + 26,880 \text{ lb.}) = 20,436 \text{ lb.}$$

The total weight when fully loaded is 62,880 pounds or 31.4 tons. The total resisting force when traveling fully loaded on the first segment of the haul road is

$$F_R = [(90 \text{ lb./ton})(31.4 \text{ ton})] + [(4\%)(20 \text{ lb./ton per } \% \text{ slope})(31.4 \text{ ton})]$$
$$= 2,826 \text{ lb.} + 2,512 \text{ lb.} = 5,338 \text{ lb.}$$

Since the required rimpull (5,338 lb.) is less than the maximum that can be generated without the wheels slipping (20,436 lb.), we will experience no problems with traction. The total resisting force when traveling fully loaded over the second segment of the haul road is

$$F_R = [(90 \text{ lb./ton})(31.4 \text{ ton})] + [(2\%)(20 \text{ lb./ton per } \% \text{ slope})(31.4 \text{ ton})]$$
$$= 2,826 \text{ lb.} + 1,256 \text{ lb.} = 4,082 \text{ lb.}$$

Again, we will have no problems with traction. The total resisting force when traveling empty over the first return segment of the haul road is

$$F_R = [(90 \text{ lb./ton})(18 \text{ ton})] - [(2\%)(20 \text{ lb./ton per } \% \text{ slope})(18 \text{ ton})]$$
$$= 1,620 \text{ lb.} - 720 \text{ lb.} = 900 \text{ lb.}$$

Comparing the required rimpull (900 lb.) with the maximum that can be generated when empty without the wheels spinning (8,100 lb.) indicates that there will be no problem with traction. The total resisting force when traveling over the second return segment of the haul road is

$$F_R = [(90 \text{ lb./ton})(18 \text{ ton})] - [(4\%)(20 \text{ lb./ton per } \% \text{ slope})(18 \text{ ton})]$$
$$= 1,620 \text{ lb.} - 1,440 \text{ lb.} = 180 \text{ lb.}$$

Again, there will be no problems with traction. We will estimate the maximum speed the trucks will traverse each haul road segment by using the following equation that we discussed in Chapter 7:

$$\text{Maximum Speed (mi./hr.)} = \frac{(375)(HP)(\text{Gear Train Efficiency})}{\text{Required Rimpull (lb.)}}$$

Now we can complete the following table to determine the variable time for the trucks.

Distance	Resisting Force	Maximum Speed	Speed Factor	Average Speed	Travel Time
1 mi. (loaded)	5,338 lb.	11.8 mph	0.96	11.3 mph	5.3 min.
1 mi. (loaded)	4,082 lb.	15.4 mph	0.96	14.8 mph	4.1 min.
1 mi. (unloaded)	900 lb.	40.0 mph	0.96	38.4 mph	1.6 min.
1 mi. (unloaded)	180 lb.	40.0 mph	0.96	38.4 mph	1.6 min.

Since each truck will stop at each end of the haul road, the appropriate speed factor for each segment can be found from Table 12.3 by selecting the factor for starting from a standstill or coming to a stop. Travel time is estimated by dividing the segment distance by the average speed for each haul road segment. The variable time can now be estimated by adding the travel times for a total of 12.6 minutes. The truck cycle time can now be estimated by adding the fixed time and the variable time, which is 17.8 minutes (12.6 min. + 5.2 min.). The number of trucks that should be used can be determined by dividing the truck cycle time by the time the truck is at the loading site. The time the truck is at the loading site is equal to the loading time plus the spotting time, which is

$$3.6 \text{ min.} + 0.3 \text{ min.} = 3.9 \text{ min.}$$

The number of trucks needed is

$$\frac{17.8 \text{ min.}}{3.9 \text{ min.}} = 4.6 \text{ trucks}$$

Therefore, **5 trucks** are needed if the contractor wants to maximize fleet productivity.

c. Before determining the grader productivity, we should first determine the productivity of the hauling operation. Since 5 trucks are to be used, the fleet productivity will be determined by the productivity of the loader, as trucks will wait at the loading site to be loaded. The required time to load 1 truck is the loading time plus the spotting time, which is 3.9 minutes. The productivity of the loading operation can be estimated by the following equation:

$$\text{Productivity} = \frac{(\text{Truck Volume})(\text{Operational Efficiency})}{(\text{Time Required to Load 1 Truck})}$$

The productivity of the hauling operation, therefore, can be estimated to be

$$\frac{(12 \text{ LCY})(50 \text{ min./hr.})}{3.9 \text{ min.}} = 153.8 \text{ LCY/hr.}$$

To determine which grading technique maximizes grader productivity, we will estimate the cycle time for a single pass by both methods. The technique providing the shortest cycle time will provide the greater productivity. We will assume the grader will grade along the long axis of the fill, which is 900 feet. With Equation 13–3, we can estimate the cycle time for the back-and-forth method to be

$$= \frac{900 \text{ ft.}}{(2.5 \text{ mi./hr.})(88 \text{ ft./min. per mi./hr.})} + \frac{900 \text{ ft.}}{(4 \text{ mi./hr.})(88 \text{ ft./min. per mi./hr.})}$$

$$= 4.1 \text{ min.} + 2.6 \text{ min.} = 6.7 \text{ min.}$$

With Equation 13–4 we can estimate the cycle time for the looping method to be

$$= \frac{900 \text{ ft.}}{(2.5 \text{ mi./hr.})(88 \text{ ft./min. per mi./hr.})} + \frac{24 \pi \text{ ft.}}{(1 \text{ mi./hr.})(88 \text{ ft./min. per mi./hr.})}$$

$$= 4.1 \text{ min.} + 0.9 \text{ min.} = 5.0 \text{ min.}$$

Thus the **looping method** has the smaller cycle time and will maximize grader productivity. The area to be graded per single pass is

$$\frac{(900 \text{ ft.})(10 \text{ ft.})}{9 \text{ sq. ft./sq. yd.}} = 1{,}000 \text{ sq. yd.}$$

With Equation 13–2, we can estimate the productivity of the grader to be

$$\frac{(1{,}000 \text{ sq. yd.})(50 \text{ min./hr.})}{(5 \text{ min.})(3 \text{ passes})} = 3{,}333 \text{ sq. yd./hr.}$$

The uncompacted lift thickness is 8 inches, so the productivity of the grader is estimated to be

$$\frac{(3{,}333 \text{ sq. yd./hr.})(8 \text{ in.})}{(36 \text{ in./yd.})} = 740 \text{ LCY/hr.}$$

Since the grader productivity (740 LCY/hr.) is greater than the productivity of the hauling operation (153.8 LCY/hr.), only **1 grader** is required.

d. With Equation 15–1, we can estimate the productivity of the compactor to be

$$\frac{(6 \text{ ft.})(3 \text{ mi./hr.})(5{,}280 \text{ ft./mi.})(8 \text{ in.})(0.83)}{(4 \text{ passes})(12 \text{ in./ft.})(27 \text{ cu. ft./cu. yd.})} = 487 \text{ LCY/hr.}$$

Since the compactor productivity (487 LCY/hr.) is greater than the productivity of the hauling operation (153.8 LCY/hr.), only **1 compactor** is required.

16.3   Cost Analysis

To estimate the equipment cost of performing a specific operation, first estimate the hourly ownership and operating cost for each type of equipment required using the techniques discussed in Chapter 4, the cost references discussed in Chapter 5, or historical cost data. These costs can be used in conjunction with the overall productivity of the fleet of equipment being used to estimate the unit cost for the operation. Dividing the total quantity of work to be performed by the overall fleet productivity will provide an estimate of the time required to complete the operation. Let's look at an example as an illustration.

Example 16.2

The contractor of Example 16.1 has determined the following cost data for the equipment to be used in constructing the fill for the parking lot:

Equipment	Ownership Cost	Operating Cost	Labor Cost
Loader	$28.00/hr.	$35.00/hr.	$27.75/hr.
Dump truck	$15.00/hr.	$18.00/hr.	$25.60/hr.
Grader	$20.00/hr.	$19.00/hr.	$30.25/hr.
Compactor	$25.00/hr.	$20.00/hr.	$25.30/hr.

a. What is the estimated unit cost in dollars per compacted cubic yard to construct the fill?

b. How many days should it take the contractor to complete the fill if he works 8 hours per day?

Solution

a. First, we will determine the total hourly cost for each piece of equipment. The total hourly cost for the loader is

$$\$28.00/\text{hr.} + \$35.00/\text{hr.} + \$27.75/\text{hr.} = \$90.75/\text{hr.}$$

The total hourly cost for each dump truck is

$$\$15.00/\text{hr.} + \$18.00/\text{hr.} + \$25.60/\text{hr.} = \$58.60/\text{hr.}$$

The total hourly cost for the grader is

$$\$20.00/\text{hr.} + \$19.00/\text{hr.} + \$30.25/\text{hr.} = \$69.25/\text{hr.}$$

The total hourly cost for the compactor is

$$\$25.00/\text{hr.} + \$20.00/\text{hr.} + \$25.30/\text{hr.} = \$70.30/\text{hr.}$$

The total hourly cost for 1 loader, 5 dump trucks, 1 grader, and 1 compactor is

$$\$90.75/\text{hr.} + [(5)(\$58.60/\text{hr.})] + \$69.25/\text{hr.} + \$70.30/\text{hr.} = \$523.30/\text{hr.}$$

The overall productivity of the equipment fleet was estimated in Example 16.1 to be 153.8 loose cubic yards per hour. To convert to compacted cubic yards per hour, we must divide by 1 plus the percent swell and multiply by 1 minus the percent shrinkage, which is

$$\frac{(153.8 \text{ LCY/hr.})(0.85 \text{ CCY/BCY})}{1.25 \text{ LCY/BCY}} = 104.6 \text{ CCY/hr.}$$

The unit cost can now be estimated to be

$$\frac{\$523.30/\text{hr.}}{104.6 \text{ CCY/hr.}} = \textbf{\$5.00/CCY}$$

b. The total volume of the fill is

$$\frac{(900 \text{ ft.})(150 \text{ ft.})(3 \text{ ft.})}{27 \text{ cu. ft./cu. yd.}} = 15,000 \text{ CCY}$$

The number of days required to complete the fill can be estimated at

$$\frac{15,000 \text{ CCY}}{(104.6 \text{ CCY/hr.})(8 \text{ hr./day})} = \textbf{18 days}$$

16.4   Problems

1. A contractor is preparing a bid for the construction of a small office building and plans to use a 2.4-cubic-yard crawler-mounted, hydraulically-operated backhoe to excavate for the building foundation. He plans to remove the excavated material from the job site with 15-cubic-yard end-dump trucks that he owns.

   a. The backhoe cost $290,000 to purchase and has an expected useful life of 12,000 operating hours. Fuel, oil, and minor maintenance are estimated to cost about $17.35 for each hour the backhoe is used. Major maintenance and repair costs are estimated to be about 55% of the annual straight-line depreciation value. The contractor estimates that he will use the backhoe about 1,000 hours per year and realize a salvage value after 12,000 hours of about 25% of the acquisition cost. The backhoe operator earns $20.00 per hour including fringe benefits. Insurance, interest, and taxes cost about 16%. What is the estimated cost per hour for the contractor to use the backhoe on the project?

   b. The dump trucks each cost $140,000 to purchase. Fuel, oil, and minor maintenance are estimated to cost about $12.75 for each hour a truck is used. Tires cost $2,500 to replace (estimated to occur at every 3,600 hours of use). Major maintenance and repair are estimated to be about 45% of the annual straight-line depreciation value. The contractor estimates the trucks will be used about 1,200 hours per year. He plans to replace the trucks after 12,000 hours of use and anticipates a salvage value of about 12% of the purchase price. Truck drivers earn $14.50 per hour including fringe benefits. What is the estimated cost per hour for the contractor to use 1 dump truck on the project?

   c. The contractor estimates that the average cycle time for the backhoe will be 45 seconds, and that its operational efficiency will be 50 minutes per hour. He determined from the project drawings that the size of the foundation will be 70 feet by 30 feet and 12 feet deep. The material to be excavated is sandy clay with a swell estimated to be 20% and a unit weight of 2,600 pounds per bank cubic yard. The disposal site for the excavated material is 2 miles from the project site. The haul road has an average uphill grade of 3% when traveling from the excavation site to the disposal site. The rolling resistance of the haul road is estimated to be 65 pounds per ton, and the coefficient of traction is estimated to be 0.5. Operational efficiency of the trucks is estimated to be 50 minutes per hour, and job conditions are considered average. The gear train efficiency of the 250-horsepower dump trucks is estimated to be 0.75. The maximum load that can be carried safely in the trucks is 17.5 tons, and an empty truck weighs 35,000 pounds. The weight distribution for the trucks is

   | Loaded: | 60% on rear drive axle | Empty: | 40% on rear drive axle |
   | | 40% on front axle | | 60% on front axle |

   The maximum rated speed for the trucks is 35 miles per hour. How many trucks should the contractor use for this hauling operation to minimize his cost?

   d. The contractor estimates that he will need a truck tractor and trailer for 1.5 hours to haul the backhoe to the project site and another 1.5 hours to return the backhoe to his equipment storage yard. How much should the contractor estimate as his total cost for this excavation and hauling operation? The hourly ownership and operating costs (including operator's wages) for the truck tractor and trailer are estimated to be $85.00 per hour.

2. A contractor is preparing a bid for the construction of a branch bank building and requires a compacted fill 900 feet by 160 feet with an average depth of 4 feet. The only available material is a moist earth and gravel mixture, weighing 3,500 pounds per bank cubic yard, with an estimated swell of 20%. The shrinkage at the compacted design density is estimated to be 15%. The source of the fill material is 1.4 miles from the project site. The first 0.6 miles of the haul road has an uphill grade of 5% when traveling from the material source to the project site, and the last 0.8 miles has an uphill grade of 3%. The coefficient of traction for the haul road is estimated to be 0.4, and the rolling resistance is estimated to be 110 pounds per ton. The contractor is planning to use 7 Caterpillar 631E Series II single-engine scrapers to excavate, haul, and spread the needed fill material. Job conditions are considered unfavorable. Manufacturer's performance data for the scrapers is shown in Figure 10.10. Other characteristics are shown below:

	Weight Distribution
Rated heaped capacity: 31 cu. yd.	*Empty*
Empty weight: 96,880 lb.	Drive axle 67%
Maximum load: 75,000 lb.	Rear axle 33%
	Loaded
Maximum speed: 33 mph	Drive axle 53%
	Rear axle 47%

The scrapers are to be push loaded to their maximum rated capacity.

a. How many compacted cubic yards of fill can be excavated, hauled, and spread by the scrapers per hour if their operational efficiency is 50 minutes per hour? How many pusher tractors should the contractor use to support the 7 scrapers?

b. The contractor needs a grader to shape the fill material as it is being spread in 8-inch compacted lifts by the 7 scrapers. The grader will use the back-and-forth method of grading and be operated at a forward speed of 2.2 miles per hour when grading with a 12-foot blade. Because of the angle of the blade and the need to overlap passes, the effective grading width will be 8 feet. The grader will be operated in reverse at an average speed of 4.7 miles per hour. Two passes are required to achieve the desired smoothness. How many compacted cubic yards per hour can be graded with 1 grader if the operational efficiency is 45 minutes per hour? How many graders should the contractor use on the project to maintain a grader production rate that at least equals the scraper production rate?

c. The contractor plans to use vibratory compactors to achieve the specified density. The compactors have 10-foot-wide drums and compact at an average speed of 1.8 miles per hour. Six passes are required, and a 1-foot overlap will be used to ensure adequate compaction. How many compacted cubic yards of fill will a single compactor compact per hour, if the operational efficiency is 50 minutes per hour? How many compactors should the contractor use on the project to maintain a compactor production rate that at least equals the scraper production rate?

d. The contractor has determined the following hourly cost data for each type of equipment to be used on the project:

Equipment	Ownership Cost	Operating Cost	Labor Cost
Scraper	$32.00/hr.	$70.00/hr.	$33.75/hr.
Pusher tractor	$15.70/hr.	$31.70/hr.	$27.65/hr.
Grader	$16.70/hr.	$19.50/hr.	$29.40/hr.
Compactor	$12.50/hr.	$13.00/hr.	$25.50/hr.

What is the estimated cost for constructing the fill?

Lifting and Loading Equipment

17.1   Introduction

Lifting and loading equipment have been used on construction projects for centuries. Without such equipment, we would be unable to construct vertical structures. The basic operational concept for lifting and loading is to lift a load vertically, move it horizontally to the desired location, and set it in the desired position. Productivity is not the primary consideration in selecting lifting and loading equipment for specific projects. Instead, the primary selection criteria are the following:

- Maximum load to be moved
- Vertical distance load is to be moved
- Horizontal distance load is to be moved

Manufacturers produce a variety of lifting and loading equipment designed for many different purposes. Contractors select the specific type and size based on an analysis of project requirements. In addition to the weight of the loads to be moved and the distances they are to be moved, contractors also must consider the layout of the job site and the job site surface conditions.

In this chapter, we will discuss several types of lifting and loading equipment and learn how to use manufacturers' literature to select the appropriate type for specific construction tasks.

17.2   Forklifts

Forklifts are used to transport construction materials around project sites and to load and unload trucks and rail cars. The primary identifying feature of a forklift is the twin horizontal arms that support the load and raise or lower it along a vertical mast. The arm

Figure 17.1
Forklift Transporting Construction Material

Courtesy Case Corporation

spacing is adjustable on most forklifts to accommodate the load to be moved. A typical forklift is illustrated in Figure 17.1. The horizontal arms or forks are cantilever beams that are supported by a cross frame that rides up and down the mast. The mast is mounted on the front of a two-axle tractor while the engine is mounted over the rear axle, serving as a counterweight to the load. The front wheels, which carry the load, are larger than the rear wheels, which are primarily for steering. Forklifts may have either two- or four-wheel drive. Some units have telescoping masts, while others have fixed masts. Most can tilt the mast forward for load removal and tilt the mast to the rear to prevent the load from falling off while in transit. The maximum forward tilt for most machines is about 30°, and the maximum rearward tilt is about 10°.

The lift capacity of a forklift depends on the height the load is to be lifted. The higher the load is to be lifted, the lower the rated capacity of the forklift, as illustrated in Table 17.1. Forklifts generally are used for material handling on construction projects, rather than supporting the erection of vertical structures.

17.3   *Telescopic Material Handlers*

Telescopic material handlers are similar to forklifts but use telescopic booms to support the forks rather than vertical masts, as illustrated in Figure 17.2. These material handlers

Table 17.1
Rated Lift Capacity for Case 585E
Forklift with 28-Foot Mast

Height	Rated Capacity
12 ft.	5,000 lb.
15 ft.	4,000 lb.
21 ft.	2,500 lb.
28 ft.	1,000 lb.

Data for this table was extracted from
technical literature published by the
Case Corporation.

have greater lift capacity and longer reach (both vertical and horizontal) than forklifts. As with forklifts, the fork spacing is adjustable to accommodate the load to be moved. The machines have four-wheel drive and operate in three steering modes, as illustrated in Figure 17.3. With a tight turning radius and compact dimensions, these material handlers operate efficiently in the confined spaces that are typical on most construction sites.

Figure 17.2
Telescopic Material Handler
Courtesy Caterpillar Inc.

Figure 17.3
Alternative Steering Modes of
Telescopic Material Handler

Courtesy Caterpillar, Inc.

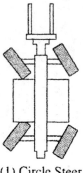 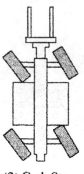 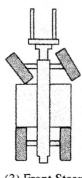

(1) Circle Steer   (2) Crab Steer   (3) Front Steer

The lift capacity of telescopic material handlers is greatest at short boom lengths and decreases as the boom is extended, as illustrated in Figure 17.4. Larger material handlers can safely lift up to 5 tons at short boom lengths and can reach in excess of 40 feet. The safe loading capacity of the machine in a given situation is a function of both the vertical and horizontal reach. Let's look at an example to illustrate.

Example 17.1

A contractor has a project to construct a three-story office building and plans to use a Caterpillar TH103 telescopic handler to lift needed roofing material. The front wheels of the material handler are 10 feet from the wall of the new building, and the vertical reach needed is 38 feet. What is the maximum safe load that the handler can lift?

Solution

We can determine the maximum safe load from the performance characteristics shown in Figure 17.4. First, we find the vertical line indicating a horizontal distance of 10 feet. Then we read vertically until we intersect a horizontal line indicating a vertical distance of 35 feet. Interpolating between 35 and 40 feet, we can read the maximum safe load to be **6,000 pounds.**

17.4   *Lift Trucks*

Another type of lifting and loading equipment is the lift truck, which is illustrated in Figure 17.5. This type of equipment consists of a rotating telescoping boom mounted on a flatbed truck. Small models are used for material handing, while larger models may be used for material handling or building component erection. The great advantage of a lift truck is its quick set-up time and rapid mobility when traveling between project sites. The high-lift boom generally is mounted on a turntable support mechanism next to the cab to distribute the load to all axles of the truck. Lift trucks are manufactured in many sizes with lift capacities from 6 to 35 tons. Larger models can extend their booms up to

Figure 17.4
Rated Lift Capacity for Caterpillar
TH103 Telescopic Material
Handler

Courtesy Caterpillar Inc.

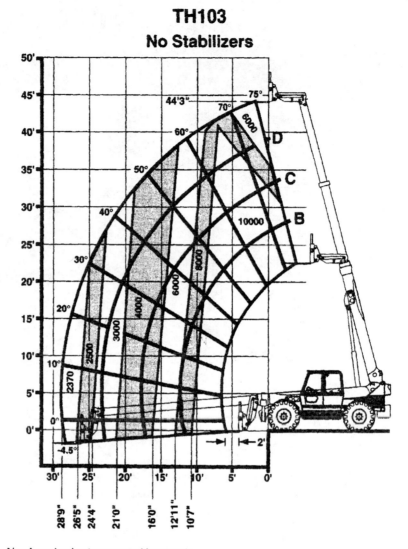

TH103
No Stabilizers

Numbers in chart measured in pounds.

100 feet. As with other lifting and loading equipment, the rated lifting capacity decreases as the boom length is increased, as illustrated in Table 17.2.

17.5   *Hydraulic Cranes*

Hydraulic cranes are manufactured in two basic types, both with telescopic self-contained booms. One type, illustrated in Figure 17.6, uses a single engine for both the lifting mechanism and ground mobility. The other, illustrated in Figure 17.7, has two

Figure 17.5
Lift Truck

Table 17.2
Rated Lift Capacity for National N-135
Truck-Mounted Articulating Crane

Boom Length	Capacity
7'	19,000 lb.
15' 10"	8,700 lb.
27' 10"	4,750 lb.
34' 6"	3,650 lb.
48'	3,000 lb.

Data for this table was extracted from technical literature published by the National Crane Corporation.

separate engines, one to power the crane and the other to power the carrier. Single-engine hydraulic cranes are mounted on two-axle carriers with all-wheel drive and large wheels for good job site mobility. They can operate safely on highways and streets, but most have maximum speeds of only about 30 miles per hour. Most contractors, therefore, use low-bed trailers to move them when they must be moved long distances. The two-engine models

Figure 17.6
Single-Engine Hydraulic Crane

Figure 17.7
Two-Engine Hydraulic Crane
Courtesy Grove U.S. L.L.C.

Figure 17.8
Fully Extended Outriggers on Truck-Mounted Hydraulic Crane

Courtesy Link-Belt Construction Equipment Company

have good highway mobility and are capable of operating at normal highway speeds. Single-engine hydraulic cranes are manufactured with lifting capacities of 15 to 100 tons, while two-engine models are manufactured with lifting capacities of 15 to 150 tons. Crane capacity is limited by the weight restrictions imposed by state highway agencies to protect highway surfaces. The major advantage hydraulic cranes have over lattice-boom cranes is their ability to arrive at the job site with boom mounted and ready for work with minimum set-up required.

Hydraulic cranes move loads vertically by raising and lowering a hook mounted on a cable and horizontally by swinging the upper structure. The major factor controlling the safe load of a crane is the *operating radius* (the horizontal distance from the center of rotation of the boom to the hook). It is a function of the length of the boom and the *boom angle* (the vertical angle between the boom and the horizontal plane). Industry standards limit the maximum safe load to 75% of the load that would cause the crane to start to tip.[1] The safe lifting capacity of hydraulic cranes can be increased by using *outriggers* (beams mounted on ground-bearing pedestals that widen the effective base of the crane), as illustrated in Figure 17.8. Crane manufacturers produce charts, such as the one shown in Table 17.3, that provide the safe loading capacity for various operating conditions.

---

[1]*Mobile Power Crane and Excavator and Hydraulic Crane Standards*, PCSA Standard No. 4, Power Crane and Shovel Association, May 1988.

Table 17.3
Rated Lift Capacity for Link-Belt RTC-8030 Hydraulic Crane

Operating Radius	Rated Capacity with Outriggers Extended	Rated Capacity with Outriggers Retracted
10 ft.	60,000 lb.	33,800 lb.
12 ft.	55,300 lb.	24,200 lb.
15 ft.	36,900 lb.	16,500 lb.
20 ft.	21,000 lb.	10,100 lb.
25 ft.	14,100 lb.	6,700 lb.
30 ft.	10,400 lb.	4,800 lb.
35 ft.	8,400 lb.	3,500 lb.
40 ft.	6,900 lb.	2,600 lb.
45 ft.	5,600 lb.	1,900 lb.
50 ft.	4,800 lb.	1,300 lb.
55 ft.	3,900 lb.	
60 ft.	3,300 lb.	
70 ft.	2,600 lb.	
80 ft.	2,000 lb.	
90 ft.	1,300 lb.	
95 ft.	1,000 lb.	

Data for this table was extracted from technical literature published by Link-Belt Construction Equipment Company.

17.6   *Lattice-Boom Cranes*

Lattice-boom cranes are mounted on either a crawler chassis, as illustrated in Figure 17.9, or a truck chassis, as illustrated in Figure 17.10. The lattice boom is a lightweight, open structure that is suspended from the crane with cable. The reduction in boom weight means that the crane can safely lift heavier loads than it could if the boom were solid. The disadvantage of lattice-boom cranes is the set-up time required to install the boom, since the cranes generally are moved between project sites with the boom removed. Truck-mounted lattice-boom cranes are manufactured with lifting capacities of between 35 and 250 tons, and crawler-mounted lattice-boom cranes are manufactured with lifting capacities of 40 to 600 tons. Crawler units of less than a 100-ton capacity have good lifting capacity and are capable of duty-cycle work, such as handling concrete buckets or clamshells. Units with capacities greater than 100 tons generally are manufactured for lift and do not have the rugged components necessary for duty-cycle work.

The basic components of a crawler crane with a lattice boom are illustrated in Figure 17.11. For each crane size there is a base length of boom. To extend the crane's reach, additional sections may be added to the boom, or a jib may be installed. Boom extension sections typically are 10, 20, or 40 feet in length. For heavy lift situations, additional counterweights may be added to the rear of the crane. The maximum safe boom angle for lattice-boom cranes is about 80° above horizontal to keep the boom from falling back across the cab of the crane.

Figure 17.9
Crawler-Mounted Lattice-Boom
Crane

Courtesy Link-Belt Construction
Equipment Company

Figure 17.10
Truck-Mounted Lattice-Boom
Crane

Courtesy Grove U.S. L.L.C.

Figure 17.11

Components of Crawler-Mounted Lattice-Boom Crane

S.W. Nunnally, *Construction Methods and Management*, 4/e © 1998. Reprinted by permission of Prentice-Hall, Inc., Upper Saddle River, NJ.

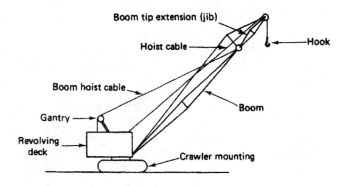

As with hydraulic cranes, the major factor controlling the load that can be lifted safely is the operating radius. Industry standards limit the maximum safe load to 75% of the load that would cause the crane to start to tip.[2] The safe lifting capacity of truck-mounted cranes can be increased by extending outriggers. Crawler-mounted cranes can increase their lift capacity by using wider tracks or by increasing the distance between the tracks. Several manufacturers build cranes with mechanisms than extend the distance between the tracks for lift stability and retract the tracks when the crane is to be moved. Crane manufacturers produce charts, such as the one shown in Table 17.4, that

Table 17.4

Rated Lifting Capacity for American 599C Crawler Crane

Operating Radius	Boom Length					
	40 ft.	*60 ft.*	*80 ft.*	*100 ft.*	*120 ft.*	*140 ft.*
10 ft.	80,000 lb.					
15 ft.	44,480 lb.	44,310 lb.				
20 ft.	29,580 lb.	29,370 lb.	29,050 lb.	28,720 lb.		
25 ft.	21,910 lb.	21,660 lb.	21,330 lb.	20,980 lb.	20,610 lb.	
30 ft.	17,220 lb.	16,960 lb.	16,620 lb.	16,260 lb.	15,870 lb.	15,500 lb.
35 ft.	14,060 lb.	13,800 lb.	13,440 lb.	13,080 lb.	12,690 lb.	12,300 lb.
40 ft.	11,780 lb.	15,510 lb.	11,160 lb.	10,790 lb.	10,390 lb.	10,000 lb.
50 ft.		8,440 lb.	8,080 lb.	7,710 lb.	7,310 lb.	6910 lb.
60 ft.		6,460 lb.	6,110 lb.	5,740 lb.	5,330 lb.	4,930 lb.
70 ft.			4,730 lb.	4,360 lb.	3,950 lb.	3,550 lb.
80 ft.			3,700 lb.	3,340 lb.	2,940 lb.	2,540 lb.
90 ft.				2,560 lb.	2,160 lb.	1,760 lb.
100 ft.				1,930 lb.	1,530 lb.	1,130 lb.
110 ft.					1,030 lb.	

Data for this table was extracted from the Lifting Capacities Chart for the 599C Crane published by American Crane Company.

---

[2]*Mobile Power Crane and Excavator and Hydraulic Crane Standards*, PCSA Standard No. 4, Power Crane and Shovel Association, May 1988.

provide the safe loading capacity for various operating conditions. The minimum operating radius for each boom length occurs at the maximum safe boom angle of 80°. As with other lifting and loading equipment, the safe lifting capacity of the crane is a function of both the vertical and horizontal reach. Let's look at an example to illustrate.

Example 17.2

A contractor has a project to construct a large industrial plant and has decided to use an American 599C crawler crane to support steel erection. The contractor has analyzed his lift requirements and determined that the longest operating radius required will be 50 feet and the highest reach required will be 65 feet. The maximum vertical reach was selected to ensure clearance of the hook and load above the structure being constructed. The bottom of the boom is mounted on the crane superstructure 5 feet above the ground, and the hook and slings required to move the steel elements weigh 1,000 pounds.

a. What length of boom should the contractor mount on the crane for this project?
b. With the boom selected in (a), what is the maximum load the crane can lift safely at an operating radius of 50 feet?

Solution

a. When the boom is lowered to an operating radius of 50 feet, it is the hypotenuse of a right triangle. The base of the triangle is 50 feet, and the vertical side is 60 feet (65 feet less the 5-foot distance that the base of the boom is above the ground). The length of the boom can now be determined by taking the square root of the sum of the squares of the two sides of the right triangle. The minimum boom length is

$$\sqrt{(50)^2 + (60)^2} = \sqrt{6,100} = 78 \text{ ft.}$$

Thus, the minimum required boom length is **80 feet,** because boom sections are made in increments of 10 feet.

b. We can read the maximum safe load for 80 feet of boom at an operating radius of 50 feet to be 8,080 pounds from Table 17.4. Since the hook and slings weigh 1,000 pounds, the maximum safe load at an operating radius of 50 feet is

$$8,080 \text{ lb.} - 1,000 \text{ lb.} = \textbf{7,080 lb.}$$

17.7   Tower Cranes

Unlike the other types of lifting and loading equipment discussed in this chapter, tower cranes generally operate from fixed positions. First developed in Europe to facilitate urban reconstruction following World War II, they commonly are used to support building construction projects throughout the world. Tower cranes have tall vertical, latticed masts or towers and horizontal or moveable booms, called *jibs*. They are used extensively in urban construction, because they require minimal ground area, have a long operating radius, and have almost unlimited height capability.

Figure 17.12
Horizontal Jib Tower Crane

The most common type of tower crane used is the *horizontal jib* crane illustrated in Figure 17.12. The crane features a long horizontal jib that supports the load and a short second jib to the rear of the mast that carries the counterweight. The hook block is suspended from a trolley that moves back and forth under the working jib. The crane operator is housed on the mast just under the jib.

A special type of horizontal jib crane is known as the *self-erecting* crane illustrated in Figure 17.13. This type of crane has a single horizontal jib that is secured by cables to the counterweight mounted at the base of the vertical mast.

Another type of tower crane is the *luffing jib* crane illustrated in Figure 17.14. The jib is mounted with a pivot to rotate the jib in a vertical direction. This type of crane is used in areas of restricted clearance where horizontal jib cranes with their fixed jibs are not suitable. It resembles a mobile crane in operation, in that the hook block is suspended at the end of the moveable jib. The crane's operating radius is adjusted by altering the jib angle.

The last type of tower crane manufactured is the *articulated jib* crane illustrated in Figure 17.15. Articulated jib cranes basically are luffing jib cranes with a pivot point in the middle of the jib.

Tower cranes are manufactured either with a swing circle mounted at the top of the tower, or they have a swing circle located at the base. Three types of tower base mount-

Figure 17.13
Self-Erecting Tower Crane

Figure 17.14
Luffing Jib Tower Crane

Courtesy Morrow Equipment Co.,
L.L.C.

Figure 17.15
Articulated Jib Tower Crane

Courtesy Morrow Equipment Co.,
L.L.C.

ings are used. The most common is a fixed mounting secured to a strong foundation. A second type of mounting is a traveling base consisting of bogies that ride on steel rails. The third type is a climbing mounting used when cranes are installed inside buildings under construction.

Tower cranes are rated in terms of the length of the jib used and the operating radius. Table 17.5 provides the maximum rated load for a horizontal jib crane under various operating conditions, and Table 17.6 provides similar data for a luffing jib crane.

17.8   *Problems*

1. A contractor has a contract for the construction of a two-story elementary school. He plans to use a Case 585E forklift to unload pallets of brick from flatbed trucks and spot the pallets around the exterior of the school walls to support the brick layers. Performance characteristics of the forklift are shown in Table 17.1.
   a. What is the maximum pallet weight the forklift can lift safely from the trucks if their beds are 4 feet above the ground?
   b. What is the maximum pallet weight the forklift can lift safely to the second floor if it is 16 feet above the ground?
2. A contractor has a project to construct a three-story apartment complex. To support construction, she has decided to use a Caterpillar TH103 telescoping material handler. To ensure adequate clearance, the front wheels of the machine will be 8 feet from the exterior wall.

Table 17.5
Rated Lifting Capacity for Pecco SK 280-20 Horizontal Jib Tower Crane

Operating Radius	Maximum Hook Radius for Length of Jib				
	124 ft.	*143 ft.*	*162 ft.*	*180 ft.*	*200 ft.*
98 ft.	22,050 lb.	22,050 lb.	21,600 lb.	20,700 lb.	19,000 lb.
108 ft.	20,300 lb.	20,100 lb.	19,400 lb.	18,600 lb.	17,000 lb.
118 ft.	18,400 lb.	18,100 lb.	17,600 lb.	16,800 lb.	15,400 lb.
124 ft.	17,500 lb.	17,300 lb.	16,700 lb.	16,000 lb.	14,700 lb.
128 ft.		16,500 lb.	16,000 lb.	15,300 lb.	14,000 lb.
134 ft.		15,600 lb.	15,100 lb.	14,500 lb.	13,300 lb.
138 ft.		15,200 lb.	14,700 lb.	14,000 lb.	12,900 lb.
143 ft.		14,700 lb.	14,200 lb.	13,600 lb.	12,400 lb.
151 ft.			13,200 lb.	12,600 lb.	11,600 lb.
157 ft.			12,600 lb.	12,100 lb.	11,000 lb.
162 ft.			12,200 lb.	11,700 lb.	10,700 lb.
167 ft.				11,200 lb.	10,200 lb.
174 ft.				10,700 lb.	9,700 lb.
180 ft.				10,300 lb.	9,300 lb.
187 ft.					9,000 lb.
193 ft.					8,600 lb.
200 ft.					8,300 lb.

Data for this table was extracted from the Lifting Capacities Chart for the SK 280-20 Pecco Crane produced by Morrow Equipment Company, L.L.C.

a. What is the maximum weight of lumber that can be lifted safely 13 feet to support framing the second floor?

b. What is the maximum weight of lumber that can be lifted safely 26 feet to support framing the third floor?

c. What is the maximum weight of roofing material that can be lifted safely 39 feet?

3. A contractor has rented a four-wheel rough-terrain crane to use for the construction of a tilt-up warehouse. She plans to use the crane to erect the concrete wall panels and construct the roof. The completed building will be 40 feet wide and 150 feet long. The crane will be sited about 15 feet from the edge of the building with outriggers fully extended.

a. To install the wall panels, the contractor has decided to extend the telescopic boom to 36 feet. The safe loading capacity of this length of boom is shown below for various operating radii. If the hook block and slings weigh 450 pounds, what is the maximum load that can be lifted safely at the edge of the building?

Operating Radius	10 ft.	12 ft.	15 ft.	20 ft.	25 ft.	30 ft.
Maximum Safe Load	36,000 lb.	30,600 lb.	27,700 lb.	23,050 lb.	18,450 lb.	15,250 lb.

Table 17.6

Rated Lifting Capacity for Pecco SN 141 Luffing Jib Tower Crane

Operating Radius	Radius of Hook at End of Jib				
	91 ft.	110 ft.	128 ft.	147 ft.	166 ft.
10 ft.	17,600 lb.	17,600 lb.	17,600 lb.	17,600 lb.	17,600 lb.
20 ft.	17,600 lb.	17,600 lb.	17,600 lb.	17,600 lb.	17,600 lb.
30 ft.	17,600 lb.	17,600 lb.	17,600 lb.	17,600 lb.	17,600 lb.
40 ft.	17,600 lb.	17,600 lb.	17,600 lb.	17,600 lb.	17,600 lb.
50 ft.	17,600 lb.	17,600 lb.	17,600 lb.	17,600 lb.	15,500 lb.
60 ft.	17,600 lb.	17,600 lb.	17,600 lb.	15,200 lb.	13,400 lb.
70 ft.	17,600 lb.	15,600 lb.	14,800 lb.	12,800 lb.	11,200 lb.
80 ft.	15,000 lb.	13,200 lb.	12,300 lb.	10,800 lb.	9,500 lb.
91 ft.	12,800 lb.	11,200 lb.	10,600 lb.	9,300 lb.	8,200 lb.
100 ft.		9,900 lb.	9,300 lb.	8,400 lb.	7,100 lb.
110 ft.		8,800 lb.	8,200 lb.	7,500 lb.	6,200 lb.
120 ft.			7,100 lb.	6,600 lb.	5,500 lb.
128 ft.			6,400 lb.	6,000 lb.	5,100 lb.
140 ft.				5,300 lb.	4,400 lb.
147 ft.				4,900 lb.	4,200 lb.
160 ft.					3,500 lb.
166 ft.					3,300 lb.

Data for this table was extracted from the Lifting Capacities Chart for the SN 141 Pecco Crane produced by Morrow Equipment Company, L.L.C.

b. To install the roof components, the contractor has decided to extend the boom to 48 feet. The safe loading capacity of this length of boom is shown below for various operating radii. If the hook block and slings weigh 350 pounds, what is the maximum load that can be lifted safely at the center of the building?

Operating Radius	15 ft.	20 ft.	25 ft.	30 ft.	35 ft.	40 ft.
Maximum Safe Load	29,500 lb.	23,050 lb.	18,450 lb.	15,250 lb.	12,080 lb.	9,630 lb.

4. A contractor has a contract for the construction of a small airplane hanger. He has decided to use an American 599C crawler crane to erect the structural components. He has analyzed his lift requirements and determined that his maximum load weighs 3 tons and the highest reach required is 85 feet above the ground. The hook block and slings required to secure the structural components weigh 680 pounds. The bottom of the boom is mounted 5 feet above the ground, and the maximum horizontal reach will be 50 feet.

a. What length of boom should the contractor mount on the crane for this project?

b. Can the crane safely lift the maximum load at an operating radius of 50 feet with the boom selected in part (a)?

5. A contractor has a project to construct a high-rise office building located on a confined urban site. The contractor has analyzed the project site and selected a location to erect a Pecco SK 280-20 horizontal jib tower crane. She has determined the maximum load to weigh 5.5 tons and that the longest reach will be 150 feet. Slings to support the load weigh 500 pounds. Can the crane safely pick up the maximum load at an operating radius of 150 feet? The weight of the trolley and hook have already been accounted for in developing the data in Table 17.5.

18

Pile-Driving Equipment

18.1   Introduction

Pile foundations have been used in building construction for centuries. They are used where natural soil conditions will not support shallow foundations. Piles are driven into the ground to transmit structural loads through weak soil formations onto stronger formations. Two types of piles are manufactured: *bearing* piles and *sheet* piles. Bearing piles are used to support vertical loads, while sheet piles are used to resist horizontal pressures, such as holding back earth embankments or the sides of open excavations.

Bearing piles may be *end-bearing* or *friction* piles. End-bearing piles transmit their loads onto strong strata by resting or bearing on the strata. Friction piles transmit their loads to the supporting strata through the skin friction between the pile surface and the surrounding material. Bearing piles may be driven into the ground vertically or at an angle. Piles driven at an angle often are referred to as *batter* piles and are designed to withstand both horizontal and vertical loading.

Sheet piling is driven vertically using either interlocking flat or Z-sections. Z-sections are stiffer than flat sections and more resistant to bending. Sheet piling driven in a straight line generally is supported with metal or concrete structural frames to keep the top sections from bending under the pressure of the soil placed behind the piling. Cofferdams typically are constructed with sheet piling driven in a series of circular sections without internal support frames.

In this chapter we will discuss the types of piles commonly used, the types of equipment used to drive them, and, finally, cost and time analysis for pile-driving operations.

18.2 *Pile Construction*

Bearing piles typically are constructed of wood, steel, or concrete. Wood piles may be treated or untreated, and steel piles are either H-shaped or round. Concrete piles may be cast in place or precast. Cast-in-place piles are constructed by driving a metal shield into the ground and either filling it with concrete or filling the hole with concrete as the shield is extracted. Shields may be cylindrical or tapered with smooth or corrugated exterior surfaces. Cast-in-place piles may or may not include steel reinforcement. Precast piles generally are prestressed and cast in square, round, or octagonal shapes. They tend to be brittle, requiring special care during driving. Composite piles, which are made of two materials in separate sections, may be specified. For example, the top section may be made of precast concrete and the bottom section of steel H-pile.

Piles are driven with hammers mounted on cranes. Individual piles are moved into position by the crane, and the hammer is used to drive them to the desired depth. Several sections may be spliced together to form long piles where needed to provide the desired load-carrying capacity. Templates often are used when piles are driven close together to construct single structural elements such as piers for bridges. The purpose of the template is to ensure that each pile is driven in exactly the correct position. Once the piles are driven to the desired depth, the tops are cut off to the elevation specified in the project drawings.

Predicting the load-carrying capacity of piling is difficult. Several dynamic formulas have been developed that relate pile capacity to the distance the pile moves when a certain impact load (number of blows) is applied. None is a very good predictor of pile capacity. The best method for determining the load-carrying capacity of a pile is to use a load test. There are several techniques used for load testing. One of the more common is to drive reaction piles around the pile to be tested. A reaction frame is secured to the reaction piling and constructed across the pile to be tested, as illustrated in Figure 18.1. Load is applied to

Figure 18.1

Typical Set-Up for Pile Testing

Courtesy American Construction Company

the pile by placing a jack between the pile and the reaction frame. Load is applied with the jack and movement is measured with gauges installed on the pile. Once the load-carrying capacity of the pile is verified, others can be driven to the same depth.

18.3   *Pile-Driving Equipment*

Piles are driven with hammers that are mounted on cranes. The oldest type of hammer is the drop hammer, which is a heavy metal weight that is lifted 10 to 20 feet and dropped on top of a pile. To ensure proper alignment of the pile and hammer, leads are mounted on the end of the crane boom, as illustrated in Figure 18.2. The crane selected for driving a pile must have adequate lifting capability to support the weight of the pile, the hammer, and the leads. Pile caps are placed on the top of the pile to center the pile under the hammer and protect the end of the pile. A cushion block, usually made of wood or composite material, is placed between the pile and the pile cap to reduce impact damage to

Figure 18.2
Crawler Crane Rigged with Drop Hammer for Driving Pile

S.W. Nunnally, *Construction Methods and Management*, 4/e © 1998. Reprinted by permission of Prentice-Hall, Inc., Upper Saddle River, NJ.

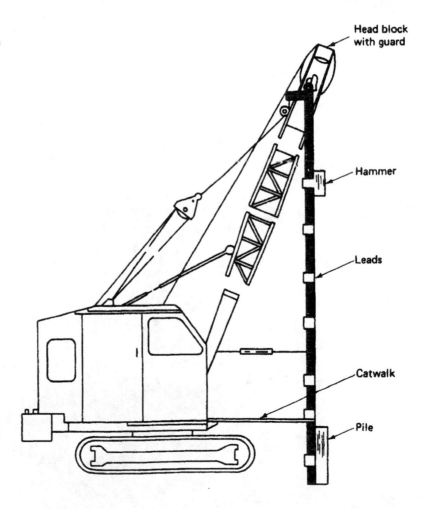

the pile. Driving a pile with a drop hammer is a slow operation, limited to about 5 to 8 blows per minute. For efficient driving, the weight of the hammer should be about one-third of the weight of the pile.

Powered hammers have a movable ram that moves up and down on a metal frame. Single-action hammers use steam, compressed air, or hydraulic fluid to lift the ram, which then falls under the force of gravity. They are characterized by heavy rams that move short distances, from 1 to 4 feet. Double-action hammers use steam or compressed air to drive pistons at both ends of the cycle. One piston lifts the ram, and the other drives it down against the pile. These hammers are characterized by lightweight rams that move short distances at relatively high speeds. Since powered hammers are self-contained, they may be used without leads, as illustrated in Figure 18.3.

Figure 18.3
Driving Circular Steel Piling

Courtesy Pileco, Inc.

Diesel hammers also are manufactured as single- or double-acting. The hammer is powered by a one-piston, two-cycle engine that fires when the hammer strikes the top of the pile. The explosive force that results from the combustion of the fuel-air mixture both helps drive the pile and forces the ram up for the next blow. Single-action hammers rely on the force of gravity to drive the hammer down against the pile. The height of drop for single-action diesel hammers is 12 to 15 feet. Double-action diesel hammers compress air in a cylinder during the upward movement of the ram. The combined action of the air and gravity drive the ram down onto the pile. The height of drop for double-action diesel hammers is 5 to 7 feet. A pile driver using a diesel hammer to drive precast concrete piling is illustrated in Figures 18.4 and 18.5.

Figure 18.4

Driving Concrete Pile with a Diesel Hammer

Courtesy American Construction Company

Figure 18.5

Close-up of Diesel Hammer

Courtesy American Construction
Company

Table 18.1 shows a comparison of the weights and productivity of hammers typically used to drive bearing piles. Drop hammers are slow and infrequently used today. Single-action hammers with their heavy weights work well on stiff, dense soil, while double-action hammers with their lighter weights, but faster cycle time, are used on medium or soft soils.

The last type of hammer used in driving piling is a vibratory hammer. These hammers have internal vibrating mechanisms powered by electric or hydraulic engines. For driving, they are attached to the end of the pile and suspended from a crane without

Table 18.1

Comparison of Pile Hammers

Hammer Type	Weight of Striking Parts	Number of Blows per Minute
Drop	500–3,000 lb.	5–8
Air/Steam		
Single-action	5,000–200,000 lb.	40–60
Double-action	500–5,000 lb.	80–140
Diesel		
Single-action	1,000–70,000 lb.	40–60
Double-action	1,000–7,000 lb.	80–95

Data for this table was extracted from James J. O'Brien, John A. Havers, and Frank W. Stubbs, Jr., Standard Handbook of Heavy Construction, 3rd ed. (New York: McGraw-Hill, 1996), pp. D3-26 through D3-29.

leads, as illustrated in Figure 18.6. The combined action of the hammer weight and the vibration of the pile cause the pile to slide into the soil. The vibrating action breaks down the frictional resistance between the pile surface and the soil, and the force of gravity acting on the hammer causes the pile to sink. Vibratory hammers typically weigh from 2 to 20 tons and are used for driving both bearing and sheet piling. They also are used to extract sheet piling, such as a temporary structure used to support the sides of an open excavation.

Figure 18.6

Driving Sheet Piling with a Vibratory Hammer

Courtesy American Construction Company

18.4   ***Productivity Estimation***

The productivity of a pile-driving operation depends on the type of equipment used, the type of piling being driven, and the subsurface soil conditions. Understanding the soil conditions and their impact on pile driving is essential in the selection of the appropriate equipment to use. The type of pile to be used is determined by the contract specifications. The contractor must select the type and size of hammer to use, the length of leads required (if they are to be used), the length of crane boom required, and the size of crane to use. Large cranes with heavy double-action hammers may be the most efficient for driving piling, but they are the most difficult to move and set up.

Operational efficiency for a pile driver may be only 30 to 40 minutes per hour because of the time required to move the crane and equipment to the location of each pile and set up everything for driving. Once a pile has been driven, the crane and other equipment must be moved to another location and set up. The time required to drive a single pile depends on the cross-sectional area of the pile, its length, and the subsurface soil conditions. Rough estimates of driving time for wood piles and steel H-piles can be made using Table 18.2.

18.5   ***Cost and Time Analysis***

Pile-driving cost estimation is a function of a time and motion study of the project. You must study the organization of the site and estimate the time required to drive each pile and the time required to move from one driving site to another and set up the pile-driving equipment. Costs are estimated by figuring the mobilization costs, the time required on the project site, and the demobilization costs. A typical pile-driving crew consists of the following:

- One foreman
- One pile-driver operator
- One oiler
- Two workers on pile driver
- Four laborers

Table 18.2

Typical Number of Piles Driven per Hour for
Wood and Steel H-Piles

Length of Pile	Wood Pile	Steel H-Pile
20 ft.	4.4 piles	3.8 piles
30 ft.	2.9 piles	3.0 piles
40 ft.	2.2 piles	2.5 piles
50 ft.	2.0 piles	2.1 piles
60 ft.	1.7 piles	1.8 piles

Table 18.3
Hourly Rental or Ownership and Operating Costs for
Powered Pile-Driving Hammers

Hammer Type	Total Hourly Cost
Single-action diesel	$50–$340/hr.
Double-action diesel	$40–$100/hr.
Single-action pneumatic	$60–$250/hr.
Double-action pneumatic	$30–$60/hr.
Vibratory	$40–$200/hr.

Data for this table was extracted from *Contractor's Equipment Cost Guide.* (San Jose, CA: PRIMEDIA Information, Inc., 1996), pp. 15-1 through 15-4.

Initial project mobilization typically takes one or two days, and demobilization usually requires another one or two days. Hammer rental or ownership and operating costs can be estimated with Table 18.3.

Labor and equipment costs for driving piles usually are estimated by multiplying an hourly or daily rate by the estimated time the people and equipment will be required on the project site. Let's look at an example as an illustration.

Example 18.1

A contractor has a project to construct a three-story office building. The contract drawings show that the building is to have a deep foundation consisting of 50 precast, prestressed concrete piles with an estimated length of 80 feet. The contractor analyzed the soil report for the project site and determined the soil to be fairly soft. She therefore selected a pneumatic (compressed air) double-action hammer to drive the piling. She also selected the other driving equipment and has estimated the following daily rental and operating cost for each:

Type Equipment	Estimated Cost
Crane with boom	$750 per day
Double-action hammer	$300 per day
Pile-driver leads	$75 per day
Air compressor	$290 per day
Air hoses	$32 per day

The contractor has selected the following pile-driving crew at the labor rates indicated:

Crew Member	Number	Labor Rate
Foreman	1	$30 per hour
Operator	1	$27 per hour
Oiler	1	$23 per hour
Pile driver worker	2	$20 per hour
Laborer	4	$19 per hour

Set-up time is estimated to be 1 day, and demobilization time is estimated to be 1 day. Operational efficiency of the pile driver is estimated to be 30 minutes per hour, and the driving rate is estimated to be 50 feet per hour. Transportation costs to bring the equipment to the project site are estimated to be $2,000, and the cost to return the equipment to the rental agency is estimated to be $2,000.

a. How many days do you estimate it will take to drive the 50 piles if the contractor works 8 hours per day?

b. What is the estimated cost to install the piles (not including the cost of the piles)?

Solution

a. The productivity of the driving operation can be estimated by multiplying the estimated driving rate by the operating factor, which is

$$(50 \text{ ft./hr.})(0.5) = 25 \text{ ft./hr.}$$

The time required to drive the 50 piles is estimated to be

$$\frac{(50 \text{ piles})(80 \text{ ft./pile})}{(25 \text{ ft./hr.})(8 \text{ hr./day})} = 20 \text{ days}$$

The total time can be estimated by adding the set-up and demobilization time, which is

$$20 \text{ days} + 2 \text{ days} = \textbf{22 days}$$

b. The hourly cost for labor is

$$\$30/\text{hr.} + \$27/\text{hr.} + \$23/\text{hr.} + [(2)(\$20/\text{hr.})] + [(14)(\$19/\text{hr.})]$$

The daily labor cost is

$$(8 \text{ hr./day})(\$196/\text{hr.}) = \$1,568/\text{day}$$

The daily equipment cost is

$$\$750/\text{day} + \$300/\text{day} + \$75/\text{day} + \$290/\text{day} + \$32/\text{day} = \$1,447/\text{day}$$

The total estimated equipment and labor cost for driving the piling is

$$(22 \text{ days})(\$1,568/\text{day} + \$1,447/\text{day}) = \$66,330$$

Adding the transportation cost, we estimate the total equipment and labor cost for driving the piling to be

$$\$66,330 + \$2,000 + \$2,000 = \textbf{\$70,330}$$

18.6   Problems

1. A contractor has a project to construct a highway bridge for a rural highway. The abutments and piers for the bridge are to be founded on wood piling. The contractor estimates that he can drive 550 feet of piling per day at an operational efficiency of 40 minutes per hour. The project plans indicate that 48 piles are to be driven and

that the estimated length for each is 60 feet. The contractor estimates that 8 hours will be required to set up the pile driving equipment and that 6 hours will be required for demobilization. How many 8-hour days do you estimate it will take the contractor to drive the 48 piles?

2. A contractor has a project to construct a secondary school. The contract drawings indicate that the school gymnasium is to have a deep foundation of 14-inch steel H-piles. A total of 90 piles are required, and the depth of each is estimated to be 85 feet. The contractor has decided to use a single-action pneumatic hammer to drive the piles. She has also selected the other driving equipment and estimates the following rental and operating cost for each:

Type Equipment	Estimated Cost
Crane with boom	$900 per day
Single-action hammer	$750 per day
Pile-driver leads	$80 per day
Air compressor	$360 per day
Air hoses	$30 per day

Set-up time is estimated to be 12 hours, and demobilization time is estimated to be 10 hours. Operational efficiency of the pile driver is estimated to be 24 minutes per hour, and the driving rate of the hammer is estimated to be 120 feet per hour.

a. How many 8-hour days do you estimate it will take the contractor to drive the 90 piles?

b. What is the estimated equipment cost for driving the piles?

3. A contractor has a project to construct an industrial plant. The contract drawings show the plant foundation to be 16-inch octagonal, precast, prestressed concrete piles. The foundation plans show that 136 piles are required and that the estimated length of each pile is 65 feet. The contractor has decided to use a single-action diesel hammer to drive the piling. He also has selected the other driving equipment and estimates the following rental and operating cost for each:

Type Equipment	Estimated Cost
Crane with boom	$860 per day
Diesel hammer	$650 per day
Pile driver leads	$78 per day

Operational efficiency of the pile driver is estimated to be 36 minutes per hour, and the driving rate of the hammer is estimated to be 95 feet per hour. Set-up time is estimated to be 8 hours, and demobilization time is estimated to be 6 hours. Labor costs for the pile-driving crew are estimated to be $240 per hour. Total transportation costs to move the equipment to the project site and return it to the rental agency are estimated to be $5,000.

a. How many 8-hour days do you estimate it will take the contractor to complete driving the piling for this project?

b. What is the estimated total equipment and labor cost to drive the piling?

19

Concrete Equipment

19.1   Introduction

Concrete is a flexible construction material that can be used to create structural components of many shapes or to create strong pavements that withstand surface abrasion. This flexibility, combined with its availability, cost, strength, and durability, make concrete a widely used construction material.

Concrete is produced by mixing portland cement, water, and aggregate. Sometimes *admixtures* are added to the mixture to improve the workability or other properties of the concrete mix. The cement and water react chemically to form a paste that binds the aggregate into a rocklike mixture as the paste hardens. The chemical reaction that produces the hardened paste is known as *hydration*. Concrete typically is composed of 60% to 75% aggregate and 25% to 40% paste. Because aggregates make up such a significant portion of the mixture, their properties greatly influence the properties of the finished concrete. Sound, well-graded aggregates produce the most economical mixes. Since the paste must coat all the surfaces of the aggregates and fill all void spaces, a mixture containing various sized aggregates will minimize the void volume to be filled with paste. Rounded aggregates have less surface area than rough, angular aggregates, and, therefore, require less paste per unit volume of aggregate.

In its liquid state, concrete possesses little strength and requires formwork to contain the fluid mixture in the desired shape. As it cures and the hydration of the cement continues, concrete gains strength. The hydration generally is considered to be complete after 28 days of curing. Cured concrete is strong in compression, but weak in tension. Consequently, reinforcing steel is added to most structural elements to carry tensile loads.

In this chapter we will discuss the production and handling of concrete, the major types of equipment used in working with concrete, and, finally, cost and time estimation for concrete work.

19.2   *Concrete Production*

The type of cement, the source of aggregates, the type or types of admixtures, and the mix proportions usually are stated in the contract specifications.[1] Admixtures typically used in concrete are shown in Table 19.1. Heavy construction contractors often mix their own concrete, but most commercial and residential contractors purchase concrete from concrete companies, that deliver the mixed concrete to the construction sites.

The process of proportioning the ingredients of the concrete mix, either by weight or volume, is called *batching*. To produce concrete of uniform high quality, each ingredient must be accurately proportioned. Most specifications require a batching accuracy of 1% to 3%. To meet these rigid accuracy requirements, concrete is batched at central batch plants that measure the ingredients for each mix. Some central plants mix the concrete, while others only batch the ingredients. Mixer trucks are used to transport the mixed concrete or to mix and transport the concrete to the project site. These trucks have rotating drums to keep the concrete from setting up while in transit. Mixer trucks that are being used to transport concrete that was mixed at a central plant rotate at slower rates than those that are used to mix concrete that is only batched at a central plant. Trucks carrying mixed concrete can carry about 30% more than similar-sized units that are used to mix water with the dry ingredients.

The strength of the concrete is affected significantly by the water/cement ratio, as illustrated in Figure 19.1. The water/cement ratio is defined as the weight of the water divided by the weight of the cement in a unit volume of concrete. Not only does the strength of the concrete decrease as the water/cement ratio increases, its durability and water-tightness also decrease. Additionally, the higher the water/cement ratio, the greater the shrinkage. Therefore, it is imperative that additional water not be added at the project site to increase the workability of the concrete. Air entraining and superplasticizer admixtures often are added to increase the workability of the mix without reducing the strength of the finished concrete.

Table 19.1

Typical Concrete Admixtures

Admixture	Desired Effect
Accelerator	Accelerate strength development
Air entraining agent	Improve workability
Retarder	Retard setting time (usually used during hot weather)
Superplasticizer	Improve flow characteristics

---

[1] For a discussion of concrete mix design, refer to *Design and Control of Concrete Mixtures*, 13th ed. (Skokie, IL: Portland Cement Association, 1994).

Figure 19.1

Typical Concrete Strength—
Water/Cement Ratio Relationship

Andres/Smith, *Principles & Practices
of Heavy Construction*, 5/e © 1998.
Reprinted by permission of Prentice-
Hall, Inc., Upper Saddle River, NJ.

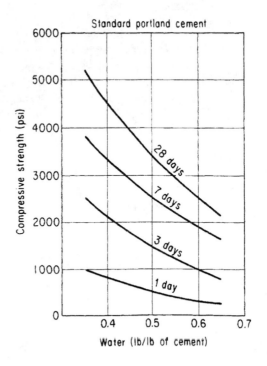

Figure 19.2

Concrete Slump Test

Building Construction Principles
G.M. Hardie, © 1995. Reprinted by
permission of Prentice-Hall, Inc.,
Upper Saddle River, NJ.

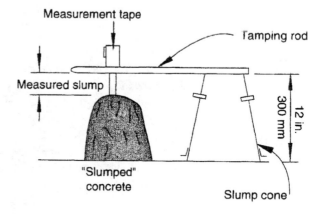

A common test that is used to measure the workability of the mixed concrete is
called the ***slump test***.[2] The test involves placing concrete inside an inverted metal cone
and consolidating it with a metal rod. The metal cone is lifted, and the amount of slump
is measured as illustrated in Figure 19.2. The maximum slump allowed for most purposes is about 3 inches.

---

[2]For a detailed description of slump test procedures, readers should refer to Standard C143 published by the
American Society for Testing and Materials.

19.3   *Structural Concrete*

Structural concrete is made by constructing strong forms that shape the fluid concrete into the dimensions required to accomplish the structural task. Structural concrete elements may be walls, slabs, beams, or columns. Steel reinforcement generally is required to carry any tensile loads imposed on the structural members. The size and amount of steel will be identified in the contract drawings and specifications. Form design, however, is the responsibility of the contractor, and is beyond the scope of this book.[3]

The basic tasks involved in structural concrete construction operations are the following:

- Batching
- Mixing
- Transporting
- Placing
- Consolidating
- Finishing
- Curing

Batching generally is performed at a central batch plant. *Mixing* may be performed at a central plant or in mixer trucks en route from the batch plant to the construction site. Batching, mixing, and transporting generally are the responsibility of the concrete supplier, as most contractors purchase ready-mixed concrete that the suppliers deliver to the project sites.

Concrete placement involves moving the concrete from the mixer truck to the spot where it is desired. Placement may be directly from the mixer truck into the form, may require the use of a concrete pump, may be accomplished with a concrete bucket mounted on a crane, or with wheelbarrows or motorized concrete buggies. Fresh concrete should be placed as near as possible to its final position. Placement should start at one end of the form with each new batch placed adjacent to previously placed concrete.

Consolidation is compacting the fresh concrete by eliminating entrapped air and molding the concrete in the form and around embedded reinforcing steel. Consolidation generally is done by either interior or exterior vibration.

Finishing is shaping the surface to the desired elevation and texture. Finishing involves screeding, floating, troweling, and maybe brooming. *Screeding* is striking off the surface of the fresh concrete to the desired elevation. *Floating* smoothes and compacts the surface while embedding the top layer of aggregate. *Troweling* provides a smooth finished surface. *Brooming* involves dragging a stiff broom across the surface to provide a textured finish that is skid-resistant.

Curing keeps the concrete moist until the hydration of the cement is completed. Methods used to retain water in the mix include covering it with wet burlap, ponding water on the surface, and spraying the surface with curing compound to retard the evaporation of water from the fresh concrete. Curing helps the concrete reach its maximum design strength.

---

[3] For a discussion of concrete form design, refer to Mary K. Hurd, *Formwork for Concrete*, 6th ed. (Detroit, MI: American Concrete Institute, 1995).

19.4   *Concrete Handling Equipment*

Types of equipment commonly used for handling concrete include wheelbarrows, buggies, chutes, conveyors, mixer trucks, buckets, and pumps. Care must be exercised in handling concrete to ensure that the mix ingredients do not segregate. In general, free fall of concrete should be limited to less than 5 feet to keep the coarse aggregate from separating from the fine aggregate and paste.

Concrete mixer trucks have inclined-axis, revolving drum assemblies that are used for mixing concrete ingredients or agitating mixed concrete. They may discharge the mixed concrete from the rear, as illustrated in Figure 19.3, or from the front, as illustrated in Figure 19.4. Mixer trucks typically have mixing capacities of from 6 to 15 cubic yards. They can be loaded to about 130% of their mixing capacity when used for agitating concrete that was mixed at a central plant. Typical agitating speeds are 2 to 6 revolutions per minute, and typical mixing speeds are 6 to 18 revolutions per minute. After a batch has been mixed (usually in 70 to 100 revolutions of the drum), the drum is slowed to the agitating speed. Concrete should be discharged from the mixer truck within 1.5 hours after the start of mixing or before the drum has rotated 300 times.[4]

Figure 19.3
Typical Rear-Discharge Concrete Mixer Truck

---

[4]*Specification for Ready-Mixed Concrete*, Standard C94-86 (Philadelphia: American Society for Testing and Materials, 1986).

Figure 19.4
Typical Front-Discharge Concrete Mixer Truck
Courtesy Oshkosh Truck Corporation

Concrete buckets are used in conjunction with cranes or helicopters to place concrete. They are manufactured in different shapes and sizes ranging from $1/2$ to 4 cubic yards for general purpose concrete construction. Large buckets, up to 12 cubic yards in capacity, are manufactured for special applications, such as mass concrete structures used in heavy construction. A typical concrete bucket is illustrated in Figure 19.5. Some concrete buckets have rectangular cross-sections, but most are circular. The concrete is placed in the bucket by a concrete mixer truck, the bucket is lifted and moved to the location the concrete is needed, and then the bucket is emptied by opening a gate that forms the bottom of the bucket, as illustrated in Figure 19.6.

Concrete pumps are used to transport concrete under pressure through rigid pipe, flexible hose, or a combination of both to its final destination. Concrete pumps are rated in terms of cubic yards of concrete delivered per hour and in capabilities of horizontal and vertical pumping distances. Manufacturers produce pumps that can deliver up to 200 cubic yards per hour at vertical distances of 170 feet or horizontal distances of 150 feet. A typical concrete pump in a travel configuration is shown in Figure 19.7, and a pump being used to deliver concrete is illustrated in Figure 19.8. Most concrete pumps use twin pistons to push the concrete from a receiving hopper through the pipe or hose. They operate on the same principle as a two-cylinder reciprocating engine. One piston draws concrete from the hopper during the return stroke while the other pushes it on the forward stroke. Pistons in both cylinders operate in opposite directions so there is constant pressure on the concrete in the pipe.

Figure 19.5
Typical Concrete Bucket

Courtesy Camlever

Figure 19.6
Placing Concrete in a Column with a Concrete Bucket

Figure 19.7
Concrete Pump in Travel Configuration
Courtesy Putzmeister America

Figure 19.8
Concrete Pumps Placing a Large
Slab
Courtesy Putzmeister America

    Concrete buggies are used on construction projects to move concrete from mixer trucks to the site where the fresh concrete is needed. A powered concrete buggy is shown in Figure 19.9. Such buggies have capacities of 10 to 30 cubic feet and can travel at speeds up to 15 miles per hour. They are manufactured in two basic types: one characterized by the operator walking behind it, and the other by the operator riding on the buggy, as illustrated in Figure 19.9.

    Concrete vibrators are used to consolidate concrete. Most internal vibrators consist of a vibratory head that is immersed vertically into the fresh concrete, such as those illustrated in Figure 19.10. The head contains an unbalanced weight connected to a shaft that rotates at a high speed. Such vibrators can be powered by electricity, gasoline, or compressed air. Vi-

Figure 19.9

Placing Concrete with a
Powered Concrete Buggy

Courtesy Amida Industries, Inc.

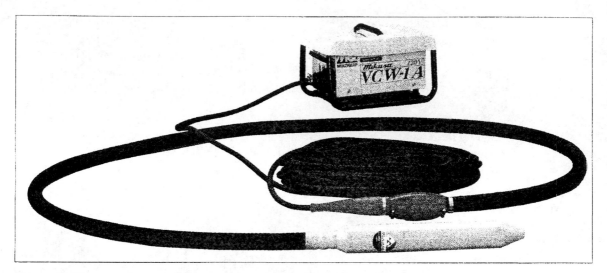

Figure 19.10
Concrete Vibrators
Courtesy Multiquip, Inc.

brator performance is affected by the dimensions of the head as well as the amplitude and frequency of its vibration. External vibrators are sometimes placed on the form work to consolidate the concrete adjacent to the form to produce smooth, finished concrete surfaces.

Power floats and *trowels* are used to embed the surface aggregate and smooth the surface of the concrete. Some are walk-behind as illustrated in Figure 19.11, while others are riding as illustrated in Figure 19.12.

Figure 19.11
Walk-Behind Power Trowel
Courtesy Multiquip, Inc.

Figure 19.12
Riding Power Trowel
Courtesy Multiquip, Inc.

19.5   *Concrete Pavements*

Concrete pavements are constructed in layers, as illustrated in Figure 19.13, to distribute the wheel loads over a wide area. Such pavements often are referred to as *rigid pavements*, because the concrete surface acts like a beam distributing the wheel loads roughly uniformly over the slab, as illustrated in Figure 19.14. The thickness of the concrete pavement, base material, and compacted subgrade are selected to support the design load and are specified in the construction contract.

Once the subgrade and base course have been placed and compacted, the concrete surface is placed. The concrete may be placed inside metal paving forms, or it may be

Figure 19.13
Typical Concrete Pavement
Structure

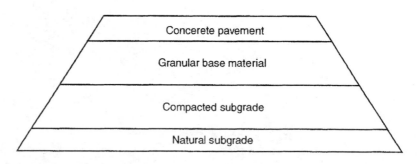

Figure 19.14
Load Distribution in Concrete
Pavement Structure

Harold N. Atkins, *Highway Materials,
Soils, and Concrete*, 3/e © 1997.
Reprinted by permission
of Prentice-Hall, Upper Saddle
River, NJ.

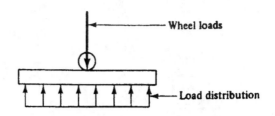

placed with a *slip-form paver.* Once the concrete has been placed, it must be consolidated, finished, and cured. Modern slip-form pavers consolidate and finish the concrete, so all that remains is to cure the concrete properly.

19.6   *Concrete Paving Equipment*

Slip-form pavers, such as the one illustrated in Figure 19.15, are used to distribute the concrete across the surface to be paved, and then to vibrate, screed, and finish the concrete. Stiff concrete (slump less than 1 inch) is used so it will retain its shape after fin-

Figure 19.15
Concrete Highway Construction with Slip-Form Paver
Courtesy GOMACO Corporation

Figure 19.16
Constructing Concrete Curb with a Slip-Form Paver
Courtesy GOMACO Corporation

ishing without the support of forms. Typical slip-form pavers are capable of placing concrete pavements up to 18 inches thick and 25 feet wide at speeds up to 18 feet per minute. Small slip-form pavers are used to construct concrete curbs and gutters, such as the one illustrated in Figure 19.16.

19.7   *Productivity Estimation*

Concrete construction involves the use of several types of equipment. The contractor may choose to use a concrete pump, a crane with concrete bucket, or concrete buggies to transport the concrete from the mixer trucks to the desired placement location at the project site. Most contractors purchase ready-mixed concrete that is delivered to project sites by concrete suppliers. The rate at which concrete can be delivered may determine the overall placement productivity. Generally, contractors order sufficient trucks so the pump, crane, or buggies never wait for concrete to maximize placement productivity. The productivity of a concrete pump can be estimated from the manufacturer's technical literature. The productivity of a crane with a concrete bucket can be estimated with Equation 19–1:

$$\text{Productivity} = \frac{(\text{Bucket Volume})(\text{Operational Efficiency})}{\text{Cycle Time}} \qquad (19\text{–}1)$$

The productivity of concrete buggies can be estimated with the following two equations:

$$\text{Cycle Time} = \text{Load Time} + \text{Travel Time} + \text{Dump Time} \qquad (19\text{–}2)$$

$$\text{Productivity} = \frac{(\text{Buggy Volume})(\text{Operational Efficiency})}{\text{Cycle Time}} \qquad (19\text{–}3)$$

Let's look at an example as an illustration.

Example 19.1

A contractor has a project involving the construction of a 90-foot-by-120-foot concrete slab that is to be 10 inches thick. The contractor can rent concrete buggies that carry 16 cubic feet of concrete or a 2-cubic-yard concrete bucket. The contractor estimates that it will take 1.7 minutes to load and dump each concrete buggy, which can travel at an average speed of 1.5 miles per hour when loaded and 2.5 miles per hour when empty. The average travel distance (one way) is estimated to be 250 feet. The contractor can rent a hydraulic crane to transport the bucket; he estimates the cycle time would be about 8 minutes. The contractor estimates that the operational efficiency will be 50 minutes of productive work per hour.

a. What is the estimated productivity of 1 concrete buggy?
b. What is the estimated productivity of the crane with the concrete bucket?

Solution

a. The cycle time for one concrete buggy can be estimated with Equation 19–2 to be

$$\text{Cycle Time} = 1.7 \text{ min.} +$$

$$\frac{250 \text{ ft.}}{(1.5 \text{ mi./hr.})(88 \text{ ft./min. per mi./hr.})} + \frac{250 \text{ ft.}}{(2.5 \text{ mi./hr.})(88 \text{ ft./min. per mi./hr.})}$$

$$= 1.7 \text{ min.} + 1.9 \text{ min.} + 1.1 \text{ min.} = 4.7 \text{ min.}$$

The productivity of one buggy can be estimated with Equation 19–3 to be

$$\text{Productivity} = \frac{(16 \text{ cu. ft.})(50 \text{ min./hr.})}{(27 \text{ cu. ft./cu. yd.})(4.7 \text{ min.})} = \textbf{6.3 cu. yd./hr.}$$

b. The productivity of the crane with the concrete bucket can be estimated with Equation 19–1 to be

$$\text{Productivity} = \frac{(2 \text{ cu. yd.})(50 \text{ min./hr.})}{8 \text{ min.}} = \textbf{12.5 cu. yd./hr.}$$

19.8   **Cost and Time Analysis**

To estimate the direct equipment cost of a concrete operation, it is first necessary to estimate the hourly ownership or rental cost and the hourly operating cost for each item of equipment to be used. This can be done using either the cost references discussed in Chapter 5, rental quotations from equipment dealers, or historical cost data. These costs can be used in conjunction with the overall productivity of the concrete operation to estimate the equipment cost. The other major costs will be the material cost of the concrete, steel reinforcement, and form work and the labor cost to support the operation. Once these latter costs have been estimated, you can estimate the total cost for the concrete operation. The time required to complete the concrete operation can be estimated by dividing the total volume of concrete required by the estimated productivity of the set of equipment to be used. Let's look at an example.

Example 19.2

The contractor of Example 19.1 can rent concrete buggies for $76 per day. Hourly operating costs are estimated to be $1.50, and the hourly wage for the operator will be $20.50. The contractor can rent the hydraulic crane for $232 per day and the concrete bucket for $24 per day. Hourly operating costs are estimated to be $15, and the hourly wage for the crane operator will be $30. The contractor plans to work 8 hours per day.

a. What is the estimated cost in dollars per cubic yard if the contractor places the concrete with the crane and bucket?
b. What is the estimated cost in dollars per cubic yard if the contractor places the concrete with buggies?
c. What is the estimated time required to place the concrete slab if the contractor uses 3 concrete buggies?

Solution

a. The total hourly cost for the crane and concrete bucket can be estimated by dividing the daily rental cost by 8 and adding the hourly operating and operator costs. The estimated hourly cost is

$$\frac{\$232/\text{day}}{8 \text{ hr./day}} + \frac{\$24/\text{day}}{8 \text{ hr./day}} + \$15/\text{hr.} + \$30/\text{hr.} = \$77.00/\text{hr.}$$

The estimated unit cost for placing the concrete with the crane and bucket is

$$\frac{\$77.00 \text{ per hour}}{12.5 \text{ cu. yd./hr.}} = \textbf{\$6.16/cu. yd.}$$

b. In a similar manner, the hourly rental, operating, and operator costs for the buggies is estimated to be

$$\frac{\$76/\text{day}}{8 \text{ hr./day}} + \$1.50/\text{hr.} + \$20.50/\text{hr.} = \$31.50/\text{hr.}$$

The estimated unit cost for placing the concrete with a buggy is

$$\frac{\$31.50 \text{ per hour}}{6.3 \text{ cu. yd./hr.}} = \$5.00/\text{cu. yd.}$$

c. The total volume of concrete required is

$$\frac{(90 \text{ ft.})(120 \text{ ft.})(10 \text{ in.})}{(12 \text{ in./ft.})(27 \text{ cu. ft./cu. yd.})} = 333.3 \text{ cu. yd.}$$

The total time required to place the concrete with 3 buggies is estimated to be

$$\frac{333.3 \text{ cu/ yd.}}{(3)(6.3 \text{ cu. yd./hr.})} = 17.6 \text{ hours}$$

19.9   Problems

1. A contractor has a project to construct a warehouse complex. Each warehouse is to have a 10-inch thick concrete slab foundation measuring 70 feet by 140 feet. The contractor wants to place the slab for each building in a single 8-hour workday. He plans to place each slab with motorized concrete buggies that can carry 12 cubic feet of ready-mixed concrete. The average travel distance (one way) for the buggies is estimated to be 90 feet, and the time required to load and unload each buggy is estimated to be 1.5 minutes. The average buggy speed when loaded is estimated to be 1 mile per hour and when empty is estimated to be 2 miles per hour. Operational efficiency is estimated to be about 45 minutes per hour. How many concrete buggies should the contractor use to be able to complete each slab in 1 day?

2. A contractor has a project to construct a manufacturing plant. One of the construction tasks on the project involves the placement of a 12-inch concrete slab that measures 65 feet by 115 feet. The contractor plans to purchase ready-mixed concrete from a local concrete supplier. To place the concrete, she can procure a 140-cubic-yard-per-hour concrete pump with operator for $195 per hour. To support the pumping operation, she will need to hire a laborer at $19.50 per hour. Operational efficiency of the concrete pump is estimated to be 45 minutes per hour. As an alternative, the contractor can rent motorized concrete buggies that can carry 20 cubic feet of fresh concrete for $50 per day. Hourly operating cost of each buggy is estimated to be $1.80, and the operator's wage will be $22.50 per hour. Average travel distance for the buggy is estimated to be 100 feet (one way), and the time to load and unload each buggy is estimated to be 1.8 minutes. Average travel speed for the buggy is estimated to be 1.4 miles per hour when loaded and 2.5 miles per hour when empty. Operational efficiency of each buggy is estimated to be 50 minutes per hour, and the contractor plans to work 8 hours per day.

   a. What is the estimated unit cost in dollars per cubic yard to place the concrete with the pump?

   b. What is the estimated unit cost in dollars per cubic yard to place the concrete with the buggies?

c. How many buggies would the contractor need to rent to have the same placement productivity as the concrete pump?

d. Should the contractor rent the buggies or procure the pump?

3. A contractor has a project to construct a six-story office building. The floor of each story is to be a cast-in-place concrete slab. The contractor has decided to purchase ready-mix concrete delivered on site from a local concrete supplier. To place the concrete, the contractor can procure a concrete pump with operator for $186 per hour. The rated capacity of the pump is 115 cubic yards per hour, and its maximum vertical reach is 120 feet. A laborer is required to support the pump at a cost of $18.75 per hour. Operational efficiency of the concrete pump is estimated to be 45 minutes per hour. As an alternative, the contractor can rent a crane for $350 per day and a 4-cubic-yard concrete bucket for $35 per day. The crane operator earns $28 per hour, and a laborer to support the crane operation earns $18.75 per hour. The crane cycle time is estimated to be 8 minutes, and its operational efficiency is estimated to be 50 minutes per hour. The contractor plans to work 8 hours per day.

a. What is the estimated unit cost in dollars per cubic yard to place the concrete with the pump?

b. What is the estimated unit cost in dollars per cubic yard to place the concrete with the crane?

c. How many cranes would the contractor need to rent to have the same placement productivity as the concrete pump?

d. Should the contractor rent the crane and bucket or procure the pump?

4. A contractor has a project to construct a ten-story office building and has decided to erect a tower crane to support construction operations. She has decided to use a concrete pump to place all concrete slabs and a concrete bucket to place all concrete columns for the building. The contractor plans to purchase ready-mixed concrete from a local concrete supplier. The supplier will deliver the concrete to the project site in 8-cubic-yard concrete mixer trucks. The load time and the travel time for each truck are estimated to be 25 minutes. Operational efficiency of the mixer trucks is estimated to be 50 minutes per hour. To place the floor slabs, the contractor plans to procure a 90-cubic-yard-per-hour concrete pump with operator at a cost of $150 per hour. Operational efficiency of the pump is estimated to be 45 minutes per hour. To place the columns, the contractor plans to use a 3-cubic-yard concrete bucket that she owns. The cycle time for the crane and bucket is estimated to be 12 minutes, and the operational efficiency of the crane is estimated to be 50 minutes per hour.

a. How many concrete mixer trucks should be used to support the concrete pump when the contractor is placing floor slabs? The contractor does not want the pump to sit idle waiting for concrete trucks.

b How many concrete trucks should be used to support the crane when the contractor is placing columns? The contractor does not want the crane to sit idle waiting for concrete trucks.

c. How much time should the contractor schedule for the placement of each floor slab if they measure 85 feet by 118 feet and are 8 inches thick?

Pumping Equipment

20.1   Introduction

Many construction projects require the use of water pumps. Pumps may be used to provide water needed to support the construction or may be used to remove unwanted water from the construction site. Typical construction tasks requiring the use of water pumps are the following:

- Dewatering excavations of surface water
- Dewatering excavations of ground water
- Dewatering cofferdams
- Providing construction water
- Providing water for fire protection

Pump selection is based on analysis of the situation and determination of the required volume of water to be pumped per hour. Construction pumps often must operate under adverse conditions, handling water that may be muddy or contain trash. In some situations, pumps may be operated intermittently, while in others they may be required continuously. Costs associated with pumping operations include the ownership and operating costs for the pumps and associated equipment and the cost of installing and removing the pumping system.

Pumps can be critical items on many construction projects. The best solution to a pumping requirement is to select equipment that will provide the needed pumping capability at the least cost and provide redundancy in the event of a pump failure. In this chapter, we will discuss the types of pumps contractors use, the selection of pumps for different situations, and methods for estimating pumping costs.

20.2   *Types of Pumps*

There are four types of pumps that contractors typically use:

- Centrifugal pumps
- Diaphragm pumps
- Submersible pumps
- Trash pumps

Centrifugal, diaphragm, and trash pumps generally are driven by either air-cooled or water-cooled gasoline or diesel engines, while submersible pumps are driven by electric motors.

Centrifugal pumps use centrifugal force to pump water. Each pump has an impeller, such as the one illustrated in Figure 20.1, with an intake at its center. Water entering the impeller is rotated and discharged by centrifugal force into the casing that surrounds the impeller and discharged from the pump. Centrifugal pumps are well suited for large-capacity pumping requirements. They have good efficiency (generally greater than 70%) and can pump water with small quantities of solid material. These pumps are manufactured in sizes from $1^{1}/_{2}$ inch through 12 inches and have pumping capacities up to 7,000 gallons per minute. A typical centrifugal pump is illustrated in Figure 20.2.

Diaphragm pumps contain flexible circular disks, called diaphragms, that are pushed back and forth, alternately increasing and decreasing the size of the pump chambers. The movement of the diaphragm in conjunction with appropriate valves allows the pump to suck in water and then discharge it. Diaphragm pumps are capable of pumping water containing a large percentage of solid material and large volumes of air. They are well suited for dewatering excavations containing large quantities of mud or trash or where there is an unsteady inflow of water. These pumps are manufactured in sizes of 2-, 3-, and 4-inches and have pumping capacities of up to 150 gallons per minute. A typical diaphragm pump is illustrated in Figure 20.3.

Submersible pumps are centrifugal pumps that have their impellers closely connected to electric motors in a single housing that normally operates below the surface of the water. They require no suction hose and are designed to operate when partly or fully submerged. Submersible pumps are widely used for dewatering foundations, sumps, and cofferdams. They typically have lower efficiency than nonsubmersible centrifugal

Figure 20.1
Typical Centrifugal Pump
Impeller

Courtesy The Gorman-Rupp
Company

Figure 20.2
Typical Centrifugal Pump

Courtesy The Gorman-Rupp Company

Figure 20.3
Typical Diaphragm Pump

Courtesy The Gorman-Rupp
Company

Figure 20.4
Typical Submersible Pump

Courtesy The Gorman-Rupp
Company

pumps (generally less than 60%). These pumps are manufactured in sizes from $1^1/_2$ inch through 14 inches and have pumping capacities of up to 900 gallons per minute. A typical submersible pump is illustrated in Figure 20.4.

Trash pumps are centrifugal pumps that are manufactured with special, open-type impellers that are capable of handling large quantities of suspended solids with little or no wear on the pump. They are manufactured in sizes from $1^1/_2$ inch through 10 inches and have pumping capacities up to 3,500 gallons per minute. Most manufacturers also produce submersible pumps that can pump water containing trash.

20.3   *Pump Selection*

The appropriate type of pump to select for a specific construction task depends on the characteristics of the job site and the quality of the water to be pumped. Table 20.1 can be used as an aid in selecting an appropriate pump type.

To select a pump that is suitable for a particular construction application, you need to estimate the following:

- The amount of water that must be handled in terms of volume per unit of time
- The static head between the intake surface and the discharge height
- The height of the pump above the surface of the water that is to be pumped
- The size and length of pipe and/or hose needed to carry the water
- The fittings and valves needed for the piping system
- The elevation of the pump above sea level
- The quality of the water to be pumped (that is, does it contain any foreign matter?)

Table 20.1
Pump Selection Table

Use	Pump Type
Dewatering	
Clear water	Centrifugal, diaphragm, submersible, and trash
Water with high solid content	Diaphragm, submersible, and trash
Well points	Centrifugal and diaphragm
Cofferdams	Centrifugal and submersible
Water Supply	
Concrete mixing	Centrifugal and submersible
Concrete curing	Centrifugal and submersible
Construction water for earthmoving operations	Centrifugal and submersible

Data from *Selection Guidebook for Portable Dewatering Pumps*, used courtesy of Contractors Pump
Bureau of the Construction Industry Manufacturers Association.

Pumps must work against gravity when moving water from one elevation to another.
The vertical difference in elevation is called the ***static head*** and usually is expressed in
feet. Water flowing through a pipe, pipe fittings, or a hose meets resistance, primarily
due to friction. This friction resistance can be converted to a potential force or ***friction
head*** required to cause the water to flow. This friction head is the equivalent vertical
height at which the inlet must be above the outlet to cause the required flow. The friction head varies with the size of the pipe and the rate of flow through the pipe. The total
effective head a pump must work against is the sum of the static head and the friction
head.

Another factor in pump performance is the ***static suction lift,*** which is the vertical
height of the pump above the water surface being pumped. The maximum static suction
lift for most centrifugal and diaphragm pumps is about 25 feet. Pump discharge—that is,
volume of water per unit of time—decreases as the static suction lift is increased.

Before looking at an example problem, we need to discuss a method for estimating
the friction head. The first step is to determine the equivalent length of pipe for each
pipe fitting and valve. This can be done using Table 20.2.

Next, we determine the friction head for the total equivalent length of pipe, which
is the sum of the actual pipe length and the equivalent pipe length of the fittings and
valves. This can be done with Table 20.3.

Sometimes hoses are used instead of pipe. To determine the effective friction head
of a length of hose, use Table 20.4.

Let's now look at an example to illustrate the use of these tables.

Example 20.1

A contractor wants to remove water from an excavation at a rate of 400 gallons per
minute. The pump will be located 10 feet above the water. Suction will be taken through

Table 20.2
Equivalent Length in Feet of Straight Pipe for Various Fittings and Valves

Fitting or Valve	Nominal Pipe Diameter								
	1 in.	2 in.	3 in.	4 in.	5 in.	6 in.	8 in.	10 in.	12 in.
Angle valve	24	30	42	59	70	85	115	150	170
Check valve	12	18	20	26	34	40	53	67	80
Foot valve	38	46	64	75	76	76	76	76	76
Gate valve	0.9	1.2	1.7	2.5	2.9	3.5	4.6	6.0	7.0
Globe valve	45	58	85	104	145	170	230	290	340
45° elbow	2.8	3.6	5.3	7.0	9.0	10	13	17	20
90° elbow	4.5	5.5	8.3	12	14	17	21	26	34
Tee with side outlet	9.0	12	17	23	28	34	45	58	68

Data from *Selection Guidebook for Portable Dewatering Pumps*, used courtesy of Contractors Pump Bureau of the Construction Industry Manufacturers Association.

Table 20.3
Equivalent Friction Head in Feet per 100 Feet of Pipe

Flow in gal./min.	Nominal Pipe Diameter								
	1 in.	2 in.	3 in.	4 in.	5 in.	6 in.	8 in.	10 in.	12 in.
10	0.93	0.31							
20	3.38	1.18							
30	7.15	2.45	0.35						
40	12.2	4.29	0.59	0.14					
50	18.5	6.43	0.90	0.22					
60	26.6	9.05	1.3	0.32					
70	35.1	11.9	1.7	0.41	0.14				
80	44.8	15.4	2.3	0.58	0.18				
90	55.5	18.9	2.7	0.68	0.22				
100	66.3	23.3	3.2	0.79	0.27	0.09			
125		35.1	4.9	1.2	0.42	0.18			
150		49.4	6.8	1.7	0.57	0.21			
200			11.6	2.9	0.96	0.40			
250			17.7	4.4	1.5	0.60	0.15		
300			24.7	6.1	2.0	0.84	0.21		
400				10.4	3.5	1.4	0.35		
500				15.6	5.3	2.2	0.53	0.18	0.08
600				22.4	6.2	3.1	0.74	0.25	0.10
700				30.4	9.9	4.1	1.0	0.34	0.14
800						5.2	1.3	0.44	0.18
900						6.6	1.6	0.54	0.22
1,000						7.8	2.0	0.65	0.27
1,200						10.8	2.7	0.95	0.37
1,400						14.7	3.6	1.2	0.48
1,600							4.7	1.6	0.65

Note: For old or rough pipes, add 50% to friction values.

Data from *Selection Guidebook for Portable Dewatering Pumps*, used courtesy of Contractors Pump Bureau of the Construction Industry Manufacturers Association.

Table 20.4
Equivalent Friction Head in Feet per 100 Feet of Smooth Bore Hose

Flow in gal./min.	Nominal Pipe Diameter						
	1 in.	2 in.	3 in.	4 in.	5 in.	6 in.	8 in.
10	1.0	0.2					
20	3.9	0.9					
30	8.5	2.0	0.3				
40	14.3	3.5	0.5				
50	21.8	5.2	0.7				
60	30.2	7.3	1.0				
70	40.4	9.8	1.3				
80	52.0	12.6	1.7				
90	64.2	15.7	2.1	0.5			
100	77.4	18.9	2.6	0.6			
125		28.6	4.0	0.9			
150		40.7	5.6	1.3			
200		68.5	9.6	2.3	0.8	0.32	
250			14.8	3.5	1.2	0.49	
300			20.3	4.9	1.7	0.69	
400				8.4	2.9	1.1	0.28
500				12.7	4.3	1.7	0.43
600				17.8	6.1	2.4	0.60
700				23.7	8.1	3.3	0.80
800					10.3	4.2	1.1
900					12.8	5.2	1.3
1,000					15.6	6.4	1.6
1,200						9.2	2.3
1,400						11.9	3.0
1,600							3.7

Data from *Selection Guidebook for Portable Dewatering Pumps,* used courtesy of Contractors Pump Bureau of the Construction Industry Manufacturers Association.

15 feet of 4-inch hose with a strainer at its end. Water will be discharged through 250 feet of 4-inch pipe to a point 15 feet above the pump. Two 90° elbows, one gate valve, and one check valve will be used in installing the piping for the pump. What is the total effective head that the pump must work against?

Solution

The first step is to determine the equivalent length of 4-inch pipe for the pipe fittings and valves using Table 20.2.

Fitting/Valve	Equivalent Length	Quantity	Total Equivalent Length
90° elbow	12 ft.	2	24.0 ft.
Gate valve	2.5 ft.	1	2.5 ft.
Check valve	26 ft.	1	26.0 ft.

Total Equivalent Length of Pipe for Fittings and Valves = 52.5 ft.

Actual Length of Pipe = 250.0 ft.

Total Equivalent Length of Pipe for Pipe, Fittings, and Valves = 302.5 ft.

Now we can determine the friction head for the total equivalent length of pipe from Table 20.3. First, we find the equivalent friction head per 100 feet of 4-inch pipe for a flow rate of 400 gallons per minute to be 10.4 feet. Next, we calculate the friction head of the 302.5 feet of 4-inch pipe to be

$$\frac{(302.5 \text{ ft. of pipe})(10.4 \text{ ft. of head})}{(100 \text{ ft. of pipe})} = 31.5 \text{ ft. of head}$$

From Table 20.4, the equivalent friction head for the 4-inch hose can be determined in a similar manner:

$$\frac{(15 \text{ ft. of hose})(8.4 \text{ ft. of head})}{(100 \text{ ft. of hose})} = 1.3 \text{ ft. of head}$$

The static head for the pump is equal to the sum of the vertical distance between the pump and the surface of the water being pumped and the vertical distance between the pump and the point of discharge. For this example, the static head is 10 feet (distance between the pump and the water being pumped) plus 15 feet (distance between the pump and the discharge point) or 25 feet. The total effective head is equal to the sum of the static head and the two friction heads (one for the pipe and one for the hose), which is

25 ft. + 31.5 ft. + 1.3 ft. = **57.8 ft.**

Now that we have determined the total effective head, we can select an appropriate pump for the construction task. The Contractors Pump Bureau of the Construction Industry Manufacturers Association has published performance standards for the following three categories of centrifugal pumps:

- M-rated pumps are designed to pass solids up to 10 percent by volume and to pass spherical solids equal to 25 percent of the nominal inlet diameter of the pump.
- MT-rated pumps are heavy-duty trash pumps constructed of cast iron.
- MTC-rated pumps are lightweight, compact trash pumps.

Table 20.5 provides performance standards for M-rated pumps, Table 20.6 provides performance standards for MT-rated pumps, and Table 20.7 provides performance standards for MTC-rated pumps. These tables provide the maximum discharge rate in gallons per minute for the various pumps when pumping against a range of effective heads for different suction distances between the pump and the surface of the water being pumped. Linear interpolation may be used to estimate pump discharge capacities for effective head values and pump heights not shown in the tables. Let's now look at an example to illustrate the use of these tables.

Table 20.5

Performance Standards for M-Rated Centrifugal Pumps

Model 8-M (2-inch)
Pump Discharge in Gallons per Minute

Total Effective	Height of Pump Above Water				
Head	5 ft.	10 ft.	15 ft.	20 ft.	25 ft.
5 ft.	140	117	102	82	58
10 ft.	137	117	102	82	58
20 ft.	135	117	102	82	58
25 ft.	133	116	102	82	58
30 ft.	132	116	102	82	58
40 ft.	123	105	100	80	58
50 ft.	109	92	90	76	55
60 ft.	90	70	70	70	55
70 ft.	66	40	40	40	40
80 ft.	40	40	40	40	40

Model 12-M (2-inch)
Pump Discharge in Gallons per Minute

Total Effective	Height of Pump Above Water				
Head	5 ft.	10 ft.	15 ft.	20 ft.	25 ft.
5 ft.	200	167	140	110	75
10 ft.	196	167	140	110	75
20 ft.	190	167	140	110	75
25 ft.	185	166	140	110	75
30 ft.	174	165	140	110	75
40 ft.	158	158	140	110	75
50 ft.	145	145	130	106	70
60 ft.	126	126	117	97	68
70 ft.	102	102	100	85	60
80 ft.	74	74	74	68	48
90 ft.	40	40	40	40	32

Model 18-M (3-inch)
Pump Discharge in Gallons per Minute

Total Effective	Height of Pump Above Water				
Head	5 ft.	10 ft.	15 ft.	20 ft.	25 ft.
5 ft.	300	259	210	200	160
10 ft.	295	259	210	200	160
20 ft.	277	259	210	200	160
30 ft.	260	250	210	200	160
40 ft.	241	241	207	177	160
50 ft.	225	225	202	172	140
60 ft.	197	197	197	169	140
70 ft.	160	160	160	160	138
80 ft.	125	125	125	125	125
90 ft.	96	96	96	96	96

(continued on the next page)

Table 20.5
(continued)

Model 20-M (3-inch)
Pump Discharge in Gallons per Minute

Total Effective Head	Height of Pump Above Water			
	10 ft.	*15 ft.*	*20 ft.*	*25 ft.*
30 ft.	333	280	235	165
40 ft.	315	270	230	162
50 ft.	290	255	220	154
60 ft.	255	235	205	143
70 ft.	212	209	184	130
80 ft.	165	165	157	114
90 ft.	116	116	116	94
100 ft.	60	60	60	60

Model 40-M (4-inch)
Pump Discharge in Gallons per Minute

Total Effective Head	Height of Pump Above Water			
	10 ft.	*15 ft.*	*20 ft.*	*25 ft.*
30 ft.	660	575	475	355
40 ft.	645	565	465	350
50 ft.	620	545	455	345
60 ft.	585	510	435	335
70 ft.	535	475	410	315
80 ft.	465	410	365	280
90 ft.	375	325	300	220
100 ft.	250	215	195	145
110 ft.	65	60	50	40

Model 90-M (6-inch)
Pump Discharge in Gallons per Minute

Total Effective Head	Height of Pump Above Water			
	10 ft.	*15 ft.*	*20 ft.*	*25 ft.*
30 ft.	1,480	1,280	1,050	790
40 ft.	1,430	1,230	1,020	780
50 ft.	1,350	1,160	970	735
60 ft.	1,225	1,050	900	690
70 ft.	1,050	900	775	610
80 ft.	800	680	600	490
90 ft.	450	400	365	300
100 ft.	100	100	100	100

Table 20.5
(continued)

| Model 125-M (8-inch) Pump Discharge in Gallons per Minute | | | | |
| Total Effective Head | Height of Pump Above Water | | | |
	10 ft.	*15 ft.*	*20 ft.*	*25 ft.*
30 ft.	2,060	1,820	1,560	1,200
40 ft.	1,960	1,740	1,520	1,170
50 ft.	1,800	1,620	1,450	1,140
60 ft.	1,640	1,500	1,360	1,090
70 ft.	1,460	1,340	1,250	1,015
80 ft.	1,250	1,170	1,110	950
90 ft.	1,020	980	940	840
100 ft.	800	760	710	680
110 ft.	570	540	500	470
120 ft.	275	245	240	240

Data from *Selection Guidebook for Portable Dewatering Pumps,* used courtesy of Contractors Pump Bureau of the Construction Industry Manufacturers Association.

Table 20.6
Performance Standards for MT-Rated Centrifugal Pumps

| Model 11-MT (2-Inch) Pump Discharge in Gallons per Minute | | | | | |
| Total Effective Head | Height of Pump Above Water | | | | |
	5 ft.	*10 ft.*	*15 ft.*	*20 ft.*	*25 ft.*
5 ft.	185	164	132	105	75
10 ft.	183	164	132	105	75
20 ft.	178	164	132	105	75
30 ft.	169	164	132	105	75
40 ft.	164	164	132	105	75
50 ft.	150	150	132	105	75
60 ft.	135	135	132	105	75
70 ft.	88	88	88	88	68
80 ft.	40	40	40	40	40

(continued on the next page)

Table 20.6
(continued)

Model 18-MT (3-inch)
Pump Discharge in Gallons per Minute

Total Effective Head	Height of Pump Above Water			
	10 ft.	*15 ft.*	*20 ft.*	*25 ft.*
20 ft.	310	265	200	115
30 ft.	305	265	200	115
40 ft.	300	265	200	110
50 ft.	275	260	200	105
60 ft.	215	215	200	100
70 ft.	170	170	170	100
80 ft.	87	87	87	87
90 ft.	25	25	25	25

Model 33-MT (4-inch)
Pump Discharge in Gallons per Minute

Total Effective Head	Height of Pump Above Water			
	10 ft.	*15 ft.*	*20 ft.*	*25 ft.*
30 ft.	550	460	350	240
40 ft.	540	455	350	240
50 ft.	500	430	340	230
60 ft.	450	395	320	220
70 ft.	370	360	300	210
80 ft.	275	275	260	180
90 ft.	190	190	190	150
100 ft.	100	100	100	100

Model 35-MT (4-inch)
Pump Discharge in Gallons per Minute

Total Effective Head	Height of Pump Above Water			
	10 ft.	*15 ft.*	*20 ft.*	*25 ft.*
30 ft.	585	500	350	240
40 ft.	585	500	350	240
50 ft.	585	500	350	240
60 ft.	545	500	350	240
70 ft.	495	480	350	240
80 ft.	430	420	340	240
90 ft.	320	320	260	220
100 ft.	100	100	100	100

Table 20.6
(continued)

Total Effective Head	Model 70-MT (5-inch) Pump Discharge in Gallons per Minute			
	Height of Pump Above Water			
	10 ft.	*15 ft.*	*20 ft.*	*25 ft.*
30 ft.	1,180	975	715	350
40 ft.	1,175	950	715	350
50 ft.	1,160	935	715	350
60 ft.	1,150	925	715	350
70 ft.	1,120	900	715	350
80 ft.	950	875	700	350
90 ft.	700	700	600	350
100 ft.	450	450	450	300
110 ft.	200	200	200	200

Data from *Selection Guidebook for Portable Dewatering Pumps,* used courtesy of Contractors Pump Bureau of the Construction Industry Manufacturers Association.

Table 20.7
Performance Standards for MTC-Rated Centrifugal Pumps

Total Effective Head	Model 10-MTC (2-inch) Pump Discharge In Gallons per Minute				
	Height of Pump Above Water				
	5 ft.	*10 ft.*	*15 ft.*	*20 ft.*	*25 ft.*
5 ft.	168	151	120	95	67
10 ft.	166	151	120	95	67
20 ft.	162	151	120	95	67
30 ft.	150	150	120	95	67
40 ft.	130	130	112	90	67
50 ft.	110	110	98	82	65
60 ft.	82	82	79	70	55
70 ft.	54	54	54	48	40

(continued on the next page)

Table 20.7
(continued)

Total Effective	Model 18-MTC (3-inch) Pump Discharge in Gallons per Minute				
	Height of Pump Above Water				
Head	*5 ft.*	*10 ft.*	*15 ft.*	*20 ft.*	*25 ft.*
5 ft.	300	275	240	212	140
10 ft.	294	275	240	212	140
20 ft.	275	275	240	212	140
30 ft.	274	274	240	212	140
40 ft.	240	240	212	156	101
50 ft.	180	180	180	152	100
60 ft.	130	130	130	125	96
70 ft.	75	75	75	75	72

Total Effective	Model 22-MTC (4-inch) Pump Discharge in Gallons per Minute			
	Height of Pump Above Water			
Head	*10 ft.*	*15 ft.*	*20 ft.*	*25 ft.*
20 ft.	440	378	312	205
30 ft.	430	378	312	205
40 ft.	350	350	310	205
50 ft.	250	250	250	203
60 ft.	125	125	125	125

Data from *Selection Guidebook for Portable Dewatering Pumps*, used courtesy of Contractors Pump. Bureau of the Construction Industry Manufacturers Association)

Example 20.2

The contractor of Example 20.1 has decided to use an MT-rated pump, because he is concerned that the water to be pumped may contain significant amounts of suspended solids. What is the smallest pump than can be used?

Solution

In Example 20.1, we determined the total effective head to be 57.8 feet. The desired discharge rate is 400 gallons per minute, and the height of the pump above the water is 10 feet. Looking at Table 20.6, we find that the Model 33-MT pump can pump 450 gallons per minute against a total effective head of 60 feet when the pump is 10 feet above the water. This is the smallest MT-rated pump that can meet the performance requirements, so select a **Model 33-MT pump.**

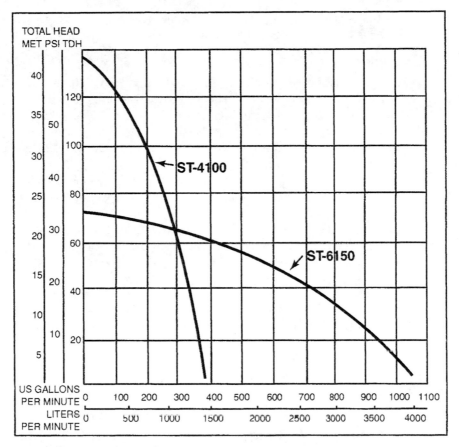

Note: MET refers to total head of water, PSI refers to total head in
pound per inch, and TDH refers to total head in feet of water.

Figure 20.5
Submersible Pump Performance Curve

Courtesy Multiquip, Inc.

Manufacturers of submersible pumps provide performance curves similar to the
one shown in Figure 20.5 for Multiquip ST-4100 and ST-6150 pumps. These curves relate pump discharge in gallons per minute to the total effective head. Since submersible
pumps are placed in the water to be pumped, we are not concerned with the distance
between the pump and the water surface. Let's look at an example.

Example 20.3

A contractor needs to remove storm runoff from an open excavation and has decided to
use 2 Multiquip ST-4100 submersible pumps that are each connected to 75 feet of 4-inch

smooth bore hose. The vertical distance from the submerged pumps to the point of discharge is 50 feet. What is the estimated combined discharge rate of the 2 pumps?

Solution

The first step is to estimate the discharge rate from Figure 20.5 and determine the friction head. Then we determine the total effective head by adding the friction head to the static head. Using the total effective head, we must check Figure 20.5 to determine if our estimated discharge rate was reasonable. If not, we must estimate a different discharge rate and repeat the process until we find the estimated rate is close to the rate we find that corresponds to the total effective head.

Looking at Figure 20.5, we see that the discharge rate for a head of 50 feet is about 320 gallons per minute. Since the total effective head will be greater than 50 feet, let's assume the discharge rate is 300 gallons per minute. From Table 20.4, we find that the equivalent friction head for a 4-inch hose carrying 300 gallons per minute is 4.9 feet per 100 feet of hose. The total friction head can now be determined to be

$$\frac{(4.9 \text{ ft.})(75 \text{ ft. of hose})}{(100 \text{ ft. of hose})} = 3.7 \text{ ft.}$$

The total effective head is 50 feet plus 3.7 feet or about 54 feet. The discharge rate for a ST-4100 pump against a total effective head of 54 feet can be read from Figure 20.5 to be about 300 gallons per minute. Therefore, our initial estimate of 300 gallons per minute is good. The total discharge rate of the two pumps is

$$(2)(300 \text{ gal./min.}) = \textbf{600 gal./min.}$$

20.4   The Effect of Altitude

When pumps are used at elevations above sea level, their performance is reduced. The reduced atmospheric pressure reduces the pump's ability to suck water. At elevations above sea level, the suction lift of the pump should be reduced to ensure the same quantity of water can get into the pump. Table 20.8 gives equivalent suction lifts for various elevations.

Table 20.8
Equivalent Suction Lifts for Various Elevations

Elevation	Suction Lift			
Sea level	10.0 ft.	15.0 ft.	20.0 ft.	25.0 ft.
2,000 ft.	8.8 ft.	13.2 ft.	17.6 ft.	22.0 ft.
4,000 ft.	7.8 ft.	11.7 ft.	15.6 ft.	19.5 ft.
6,000 ft.	6.9 ft.	10.4 ft.	13.8 ft.	17.3 ft.
8,000 ft.	6.2 ft.	9.3 ft.	12.4 ft.	15.5 ft.
10,000 ft.	5.7 ft.	8.6 ft.	11.4 ft.	14.3 ft.

Data from *Selection Guidebook for Portable Dewatering Pumps,* used courtesy of Contractors Pump Bureau of the Construction Industry Manufacturers Association.

Table 20.9
Correction Factors for Estimating Pump Performance
at Various Elevations

Elevation	Discharge	Effective Head
Sea level	1.00	1.00
2,000 ft.	0.97	0.95
4,000 ft.	0.95	0.91
6,000 ft.	0.93	0.87
8,000 ft.	0.91	0.83
10,000 ft.	0.88	0.78

Data from *Selection Guidebook for Portable Dewatering
Pumps*, used courtesy of Contractors Pump Bureau of the
Construction Industry Manufacturers Association.

The reduced air density above sea level reduces the horsepower output of the pump's gasoline engine which reduces pump speed, resulting in a loss of capacity and discharge head. Table 20.9 provides correction factors that should be used in estimating pump performance at elevations above sea level. Let's look at an example to illustrate the use of these tables.

Example 20.4

A contractor plans to use a Model 90-M centrifugal pump to fill water trucks from a stream. The height of the pump above the surface of the water is 15 feet, and the total effective head is 45 feet. The project site is located at an elevation of 4,000 feet. What is the estimated discharge rate of the pump?

Solution

From Table 20.8, we find that the equivalent suction lift at sea level for a suction lift of 15 feet at an elevation of 4,000 feet is 20 feet. From Table 20.9, we find that the discharge correction factor for an elevation of 4,000 feet is 0.95 and the head correction factor is 0.91. The equivalent head at sea level for a head of 45 feet at an elevation of 4,000 feet is

$$\frac{45 \text{ ft.}}{0.91} = 50 \text{ ft.}$$

From the Model 90-M performance standards in Table 20.5, we find the discharge at an effective head of 50 feet and a suction lift of 20 feet is 970 gallons per minute. Applying the altitude correction factor, we find the pump discharge to be

$$(970 \text{ gal./min.})(0.95) = \textbf{921 gal./min.}$$

20.5   *Well-Point Systems*[1]

Well-point systems are installed to lower the ground water table to allow excavations and underground construction to be performed under dry conditions. Individual well points are constructed by installing perforated tubes with well-point tips at the end of pipes, called *risers*, as illustrated in Figure 20.6. Individual well points generally are connected to horizontal header pipes in a ring around the construction site, as illustrated in Figure 20.7. A single pump or multiple pumps are connected to the header system to suck down the water table to allow all below-water-table construction to be completed under dry conditions. Once the construction is completed, the well-point system can be removed.

20.6   *Cost Analysis*

Pumps either are operated intermittently, such as for filling water trucks, or continuously, in the case of well-point systems. Ownership costs will be the same whether the pump is operated intermittently or continuously, but the operating costs will be different. Many contractors own a few pumps to support their construction operations, such as removing rain runoff from excavations or providing construction water. Well-point systems, how-

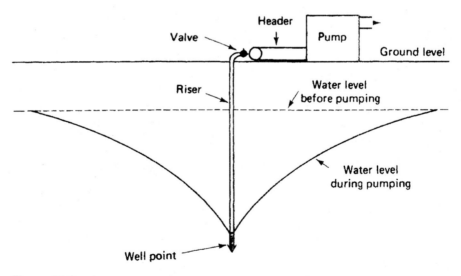

Figure 20.6
Typical Well Point

S.W. Nunnally, *Construction Methods and Management*, 4/e © 1998. Reprinted by permission of Prentice-Hall, Inc., Upper Saddle River, NJ.

---

[1] For a discussion of well-point system design, refer to *Construction Dewatering* by J. Patrick Powers (New York: John Wiley & Sons, 1981).

Figure 20.7
Typical Well-Point System

G.M. Hardie, *Building Construction: Principles* © 1995. Reprinted by permission of Prentice-Hall, Inc., Upper Saddle River, NJ.

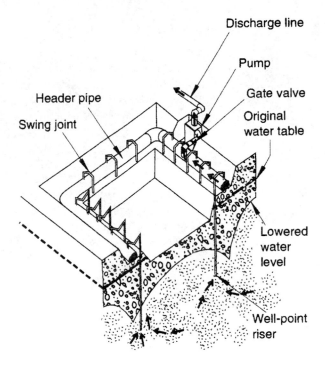

ever, generally are rented or installed and operated by specialty contractors. Hourly ownership and operating costs for contractor-owned pumps can be estimated with either the cost references discussed in Chapter 5 or from historical data. Rental costs must be obtained from equipment suppliers.

Pumping and dewatering costs are not determined based on the pump productivity, but on the total cost for each specific pumping task. For example, if a contractor is using a pump to load water trucks to support the construction of a compacted earth fill, he or she would estimate the time required to construct the fill, say 6 days, and the amount of time per hour that the pump would actually be in use, say 15 minutes per hour. If the contractor works 8 hours per day, the pump cost for the fill operation would be 48 hours times the hourly ownership cost plus 12 hours times the hourly operating cost, because the pump is in use only 25% of the time.

In estimating the cost of a well-point system, the following costs must be considered:

- Cost of rental of pump and piping system
- Cost of installing system
- Cost of operating system
- Cost of removing pump and piping system

If the system is to be installed by a specialty contractor, all of these costs would be included in the contractor's cost proposal. If the general contractor is going to rent the equipment, each cost must be estimated separately. Let's look at an example to illustrate.

Example 20.5

A contractor has determined that a well-point system is required to lower the ground water table on a construction project. Since the contractor does not own the equipment to install the dewatering system, he has decided to rent it. The contractor determined that a system of 20 well points is needed. To ensure a reliable system, he has decided to rent 2 self-priming centrifugal pumps, using one as a standby in the event the other fails to operate. The contractor has determined the following estimated cost data:

Pump rental cost	$1,500 per month
Well-point system rental cost	$800 per month
System installation cost	$2,000
Pump operating cost	$4 per hour for 2 pumps
Labor cost	$25 per hour
System removal cost	$1,500

The contractor has determined from his construction schedule that he will need the well-point system for 2 months. What is the estimated direct cost for this dewatering operation?

Solution

Once the well-point system is installed, it will be operated 24 hours per day, 7 days per week, to keep the construction site dry. The monthly pump operating cost is estimated to be

$$(30 \text{ days/mo.})(24 \text{ hr./day})(\$4/\text{hr.} + \$25/\text{hr.}) = \$20,880/\text{mo.}$$

The total pump rental and operating cost per month is

$$[(2 \text{ pumps})(\$1,500/\text{mo.})] + \$20,880/\text{mo.} + \$800/\text{mo.} = \$24,680/\text{mo.}$$

The total cost for the well-point system is estimated to be

$$[(2 \text{ mo.})(\$24,680/\text{mo.})] + \$2,000 + \$1,500 = \mathbf{\$52,860}$$

20.7   Problems

1. A contractor has determined that he needs water to cure concrete slabs on a construction project. He has decided to haul the water in a 2,500-gallon water truck from a nearby lake. The contractor has selected a Multiquip ST-6150 submersible electric pump with 60 feet of 6-inch hose to fill the water truck at the lake. The vertical distance between the surface of the lake and the top of the water truck is 39 feet. How long do you estimate it will take the pump to fill the truck?

2. A contractor wants the capability to remove water from an open excavation at a rate of 750 gallons per minute. She can rent Multiquip ST-4100 submersible electric pumps each for $50 per day and estimates her operating cost will be $1.25 per hour per pump. The vertical distance between the surface of the water to be removed and the point of discharge is 77 feet. The contractor can rent 100 feet of 4-inch hose for

each pump for $25 per day. She estimates that she will need the pumping capability for 6 weeks during the spring rainy season and will use the pumps about 2 hours per day.

   a. How many pumps should the contractor rent to provide a pumping capability of 750 gallons per minute?

   b. What is the estimated cost for the 6-week pumping operation if the pumps are operated every calendar day for the 6-week period?

3. A contractor needs construction water to increase the moisture content of the soil on an earth fill project. He plans to install a pump with associated piping at a stream near the project site to fill his water trucks. The contractor wants to be able to pump at a rate of at least 150 gallons per minute to minimize the time it takes to load the trucks. The pump will be placed 10 feet above the surface of the water. The suction line is a 3-inch rubber hose 25 feet long with a strainer at the inlet. The pump will discharge through 200 feet of 3-inch steel pipe to a point 30 feet above the pump with three standard 90° elbows and a globe valve. What is the smallest M-rated centrifugal pump that the contractor should select for this operation?

4. A contractor has installed a sump at one end of her project site to remove rain runoff from an open excavation. She estimates that dirty water flows into the sump at a rate of 500 gallons per minute. She wants to install a pump to remove water from the sump to keep the excavation dry. The pump will be located 15 feet above the surface of the water in the sump, and suction will be taken with 30 feet of 4-inch hose. Water will be discharged through 100 feet of 4-inch hose to a point 20 feet above the pump. What is the smallest MT-rated centrifugal pump that the contractor should select for this dewatering operation?

5. A contractor is constructing a large underground utility system and is experiencing ground water seepage into an open trench. He has decided to use a Model 18-MTC centrifugal pump to remove the dirty water. The pump will sit 15 feet above the surface of the water to be pumped. The suction line is 25 feet of 3-inch rubber hose. The water will be discharged through 100 feet of 3-inch steel pipe with one standard 90° elbow and one check valve to a vertical height of 11 feet above the pump. What is the estimated discharge rate of the pump in gallons per minute?

6. A contractor has a contract for the construction of a large shopping center on a site that previously contained a service station. The underground fuel tanks used by the service station leaked, contaminating the soil. The contractor must remove all contaminated soil and replace it with a compacted fill. To support the fill operation, the contractor has installed a pumping system at a nearby pond to fill water trucks. The pumping system consists of one Model 20-M centrifugal pump connected to a steel piping system. The intake side of the pump is connected to 30 feet of 3-inch steel pipe with a foot valve and one standard 90° elbow. The discharge side of the pump is connected to 115 feet of 3-inch steel pipe with three standard 90° elbows and one check valve. The pump sits 22 feet above the surface of the pond, and the vertical distance between the pump and the point of discharge is 69 feet. How long will it take to fill a 1,000-gallon water truck if the project site is located at an elevation of 2,000 feet?

7. A contractor needs to install a pumping system to dewater an open excavation. She can rent each Model 11-MT trash pump for $75 per week or each Model 18-MT

pump for $125 per week. Hourly operating cost are estimated to be $0.40 per hour for one Model 11-MT pump and $1.15 per hour for one Model 18-MT pump. The piping system required for each Model 11-MT pump is 125 feet of 2-inch steel pipe, three standard 90° elbows, and one check valve. The piping system required for each Model 18-MT pump is 125 feet of 3-inch steel pipe, three standard 90° elbows, and one check valve. The pumps will sit 20 feet above the surface of the water to be pumped and will pump the water to a vertical height of 20 feet above the pump. Following are material and labor costs for purchasing and installing both pumping systems:

System	Material	Labor
2-inch	$1,200	$ 875
3-inch	$2,250	$1,200

These costs are for the piping system required for one pump. Labor costs to operate the pumping system, which are estimated to be $26 per hour, are the same for either system. Only one operator is required no matter how many pumps are used. The contractor estimates that she needs a pumping capacity of 400 gallons per minute and will require the pumping system for 6 weeks.

a. What is the estimated cost of installing and operating the pumping system with Model 11-MT pumps if the pumping system is operated continuously for 6 weeks?

b. What is the estimated cost of installing and operating the pumping system with Model 18-MT pumps if the pumping system is operated continuously for 6 weeks?

Asphalt Equipment

21.1   Introduction

Asphalt is a bituminous product that is produced from crude oil by a distillation process. It is mixed with aggregate to produce a waterproof, smooth-wearing surface that is resilient and will resist pressures exerted by wheeled loads. The asphalt binds the aggregate particles together in a matrix and waterproofs the mixture. The aggregate provides the load-bearing capacity of the mixture and resists abrasion to the surface. Because of their plastic nature, asphalt pavements often are referred to as *flexible pavements.*

Sound, well-graded aggregates are needed to produce quality asphalt. They will occupy 90 to 95 percent of the mix volume. The strength of an asphalt pavement is influenced by the ability of the individual aggregate particles to lock together under load. Rough, angular aggregates produce stronger pavements than smooth, rounded aggregates. Aggregate blending generally is required to produce the pavement mix gradation needed for successful pavement performance.

Asphalt pavements and wearing surfaces are used on many construction projects. Some contractors subcontract all asphalt work to specialty contractors, while others perform the work themselves. Quality asphalt work depends on good subgrade and base course preparation and quality control during asphalt placement and compaction. In this chapter, we will discuss the major types of asphalt pavements used in construction, the types of equipment used in constructing these pavements, and, finally, cost and time estimation for asphalt work.

21.2   *Asphalt Pavements*[1]

Asphalt pavement structures are constructed in layers, as illustrated in Figure 21.1, to improve the load-carrying capacity of natural soils. They distribute wheel loads over a cone-shaped area under the wheel, as illustrated in Figure 21-2, to reduce the induced loading of the subgrade. The composition and thickness of each layer are selected to support the design load. The compacted subgrade may be imported material or natural material stabilized with cement or lime. The base course or layer generally is well-graded granular material. The asphalt pavement provides a wearing surface and water-proofs the structure to prevent surface water infiltration and subsequent weakening of the subgrade. The asphalt pavement also carries the design load and distributes it so it can be carried by the base material.

Asphalt pavements are constructed by mixing liquid asphalt with aggregate either at a central mixing plant or on the job site. Asphalt paving material that is mixed in a central plant often is referred to as *plant mix* or *hot mix*. Asphalt paving material that is mixed on the job site usually is referred to as *mixed-in-place* or *cold mix*.

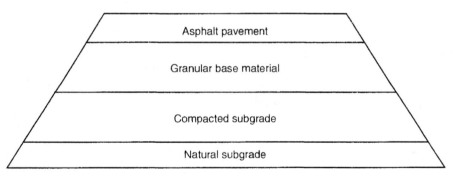

Figure 21.1
Typical Asphalt Pavement Structure

Figure 21.2
Load Distribution in Asphalt
Pavement Structure

Harold N. Atkins, *Highway Materials, Soils, and Concrete*, 3/e © 1997. Reprinted by permission of Prentice-Hall, Inc., Upper Saddle River, NJ.

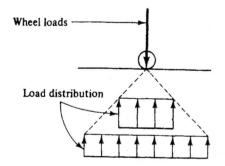

[1]For a discussion of pavement design, consult *The Asphalt Handbook* (College Park, MD: The Asphalt Institute, 1989).

Plant mix is made by mixing heated asphalt cement and heated aggregates (hence the term *hot mix*) in a central plant. Three sizes of aggregate are blended to minimize the amount of void space that must be filled with asphalt:

- Coarse aggregate
- Fine aggregate
- Mineral dust, called *mineral filler*

Asphalt cement is a solid or semisolid substance that is the residual product from the distillation of crude oil. It must either be heated or modified to be used for construction purposes. Because it is not workable at normal temperatures, temperature control is a critical quality-control concern in plant mix operations. Plant mix is trucked from a central plant to the project site in dump trucks or bottom-dump haulers and spread with an asphalt paver. The pavement is compacted and finished while hot and then allowed to cool.

Mixed-in-place asphalt pavements are mixed on the project site with graders or rotary mixers. Modified asphalt cement is used because the mix is not heated (hence the name *cold mix*). Either *asphalt cutbacks* or *emulsions* are used. An asphalt cutback is produced by dissolving asphalt cement in a solvent, while an asphalt emulsion is produced by suspending asphalt cement in water. Medium-cure (MC) cutbacks use kerosene as the solvent, while rapid-cure (RC) cutbacks use gasoline or naphtha. The liquid asphalt cutback or emulsion is sprayed on the cold aggregate and mixed. The mixture is spread with a grader and compacted to achieve the desired density. After the pavement is constructed, the solvent or water evaporates, leaving asphalt cement.

21.3 *Asphalt Construction Techniques*

Asphalt pavements are made by mixing asphalt with aggregate, spreading the mixture over the surface to be paved, compacting the mixture to the desired density, and finishing the pavement surface. Once the subgrade and base have been placed and compacted, the base is primed with a coat of liquid asphalt and allowed to cure for about 24 hours. The application rate generally is between 0.1 and 0.5 gallons per square yard.[2] The purpose of this prime coat is to seal the surface of the base and provide a bond between the base and the pavement. Once the prime coat has cured, plant mix is transported to the construction site in trucks that dump the hot mixture into an asphalt paving machine, which spreads the mixture across the surface to be paved, provides an initial compaction, and grades the surface. The paving machine is followed immediately by heavy smooth steel-drum or pneumatic-tire compactors to compact the pavement mix to the desired density before it cools. After the pavement has been compacted, it is finished with a smooth steel-drum compactor to provide a smooth-wearing surface. Mixed-in-place asphalt pavement is mixed either with graders or rotary mixers. Once the desired mix has been achieved, the mix is spread with a grader. Smooth steel-drum or pneumatic-tire compactors are used to compact the mix, and a smooth drum compactor is used to finish the pavement.

---

[2] *Principles of Construction of Hot-Mix Asphalt Pavements*, Manual Series No. 22 (College Park, MD: The Asphalt Institute, 1983), p. 185.

Sometimes contract specifications call for **surface treatments** which are alternating layers of sprayed asphalt and aggregate. Unlike pavements, surface treatments do not add to the strength of the subgrade, because their thickness generally is less than an inch. Surface treatments are used to waterproof the surface and provide a wearing surface. Single surface treatment often are called *seal coats*. They are made by spreading a layer of liquid asphalt cutback or emulsion and spreading small aggregate over the wet asphalt. The aggregate is then compacted into the wet asphalt. Double-surface treatments are constructed by spreading a layer of liquid asphalt cutback or emulsion and spreading a layer of course aggregate over the wet asphalt. The coarse aggregate is compacted, a second layer of liquid asphalt cutback or emulsion is sprayed over it, and a layer of fine aggregate is spread over the wet asphalt. A smooth drum compactor is then used to force the fine aggregate particles down into the void spaces between the coarse aggregate particles.

21.4   *Types of Asphalt Equipment*

Asphalt plants are used to make plant or hot mix. They blend, heat, and mix aggregate with asphalt cement to produce a uniform mix. There are two types of asphalt plants that are used: batch plants and drum-mix plants. In both plant types, cold aggregates are fed into a rotating drum dryer to remove any moisture and heat the aggregates to the desired mixing temperature. In batch plants, the heated aggregates are then screened into several sizes and fed into hot bins. The heated aggregates are then dropped into the mixing chamber in the proportion desired to achieve the specified gradation, and hot, liquid asphalt cement is added. The volume of aggregate and heated asphalt inserted into the mixing chamber is that required to fill one truck. The drum-mix plant is a continuous-flow plant that mixes asphalt with the aggregate in the same drum that is used for drying and heating it. Aggregate gradation is controlled at the cold feed rather than at hot bins. Once the aggregates are dried and heated in the mixing chamber, liquid asphalt is sprayed on them. While being mixed, the aggregate/asphalt mixture slowly moves to the end of the inclined rotating drum and is discharged into waiting trucks. Figure 21.3 shows a schematic diagram of a batch asphalt plant. A schematic diagram of a drum-mix plant is shown in Figure 21.4. Asphalt plants are capable of producing up to about 800 tons of asphalt mixture per hour.

Paving machines are used to spread and compact plant mix pavements. A typical paving machine is illustrated in Figure 21.5. These machines can produce pavements in widths from 6 to 32 feet and in thickness from 1 to 10 inches. A paving machine is a self-propelled machine mounted either on tracks or rubber tires that spreads the pavement mixture to the desired thickness and provide the initial compaction. Receiving hoppers mounted in front and a system of conveyors, or bar feeders, and augers, or spreading screws, spread the asphalt mixture in front of the screed, as illustrated in Figure 21.6. The screed strikes off the surface at the desired thickness and provides initial compaction to the pavement. Some paving machines have vibratory screeds, while others have tamping bars immediately in front of the screed to provide the initial compaction. The screed is heated to keep the asphalt mix from adhering to it. Typical operating speeds for paving machines are 10 to 70 feet per minute.

Dump trucks are able to dump directly into the hopper, while a pickup machine is needed if the pavement mix is delivered with bottom-dump haulers. A pickup machine

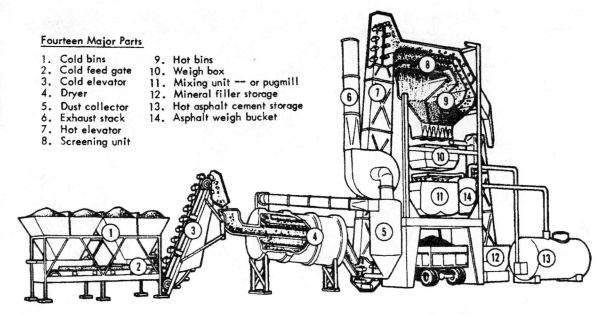

Fourteen Major Parts

1. Cold bins
2. Cold feed gate
3. Cold elevator
4. Dryer
5. Dust collector
6. Exhaust stack
7. Hot elevator
8. Screening unit
9. Hot bins
10. Weigh box
11. Mixing unit -- or pugmill
12. Mineral filler storage
13. Hot asphalt cement storage
14. Asphalt weigh bucket

Figure 21.3
Typical Batch-Type Asphalt Plant
Courtesy The Asphalt Institute

has an elevated system of paddles, similar to that used in elevating scrapers, to pick up the mix, elevate it, and dump it into the receiving hopper. Pickup machines are more productive than hopper machines because they rarely stop. Hopper machines must stop every time the dump truck is empty and must be replaced.

Paver productivity can be estimated using Equation 21-1:

$$\text{Productivity} = (\text{Speed})(\text{Screed Length})(\text{Operating Factor}) \qquad (21\text{-}1)$$

Asphalt distributors are trucks with tanks and spray bars, as illustrated in Figure 21.7, that apply liquid asphalt to a surface. They are equipped with burners for heating the liquid asphalt to the proper application temperature and a pump to force the liquid

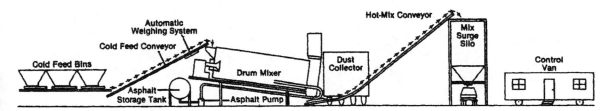

Figure 21.4
Typical Drum-Mix Asphalt Plant
Courtesy The Asphalt Institute

Figure 21.5
Asphalt Paving Machine
Courtesy Caterpillar Inc.

asphalt through the spray bar under pressure. The spray bar has evenly spaced nozzles that can be set at various angles to ensure uniform distribution of the liquid asphalt. The spray bar can be set at different heights to provide single, double, or triple coverage. The rate at which the asphalt is distributed depends on the following:

- The length of the spray bar
- The vehicle travel speed
- The pump output

The required application rate usually is expressed in gallons per square yard. Travel speed is measured by a wheel that is mounted below the distributor, or on some distributors, by a radar device. Pump output is measured in gallons per minute by the pump tachometer. The required speed can be determined from Equation 21–2:

$$\text{Speed} = \frac{\text{Pump Output}}{(\text{Spray Bar Length})(\text{Application Rate})} \qquad (21\text{–}2)$$

The productivity of the distributor can be estimated by using Equation 21–3:

$$\text{Productivity} = (\text{Speed})(\text{Spray Bar Length})(\text{Operating Factor}) \qquad (21\text{-}3)$$

Figure 21.6
Material Flow in an Asphalt Paver
Courtesy The Asphalt Institute

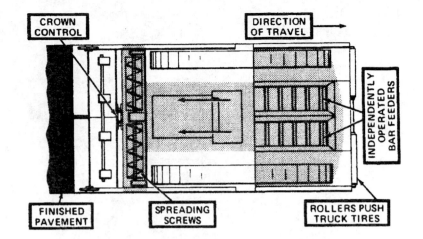

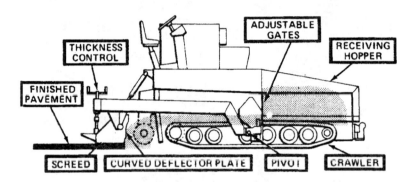

Figure 21.7
Typical Asphalt Distributor
Courtesy E. D. Etnyre & Co.

    Aggregate spreaders are used to spread aggregate during the construction of surface treatments. There are several types of spreaders used, ranging from mechanical spreaders mounted on the rear of backing dump trucks to self-propelled spreaders, such as the type illustrated in Figure 21.8. Self-propelled models are hitched to the dump trucks and pull the trucks in reverse while spreading a uniform layer of aggregate.

    Compactors are used to compact the asphalt pavement to the desired density and smooth the surface. The compactor that immediately follows the paver often is referred to as the *breakdown roller*. Its function is to compact the pavement to the desired density. Steel-drum and pneumatic-tire compactors generally are used for breakdown rolling, as illustrated in Figure 21.9. Finish rolling removes compactor marks

Figure 21.10

Finish Rolling with Steel-Drum Compactor

Courtesy Compaction America, Inc.

from the surface and is done with tandem steel-drum compactors, as illustrated in Figure 21.10.

The number of passes required by the breakdown roller to achieve the desired pavement density usually is determined by constructing a test strip. In many asphalt paving projects, a third compactor is used between the breakdown roller and the finish roller. This intermediate roller is used to reduce the number of passes required by the breakdown roller. Both the breakdown and the intermediate compactors are used to achieve the required pavement density. To ensure adequate compaction of pavement, all compaction needs to be completed before the mix cools to 185° F. This means that all compaction must occur soon after the hot pavement is laid, as illustrated in Figure 21.11. Nuclear density gauges similar to the one illustrated in Figure 14.6 are used for field testing of compaction.

Compactor productivity can be estimated by the following equation:

$$\text{Productivity} = \frac{(W)(S)(OF)}{P} \tag{21–4}$$

where W is the effective compaction width

           S is the average compactor speed

           OF is the operating factor

           P is the number of passes required

The other pieces of equipment used in asphalt operations have been discussed in previous chapters. On-highway dump trucks and bottom-dump haulers typically are used to transport asphalt plant mix. Cycle times are determined by estimating the travel

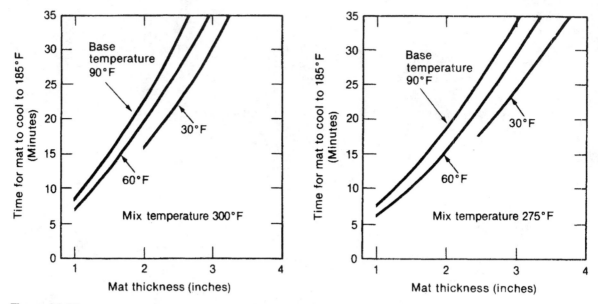

Figure 21.11
Time Allowed for Compaction, Based on Temperature and Thickness of Pavement
Mat and Temperature of Underlying Base

Courtesy The Asphalt Institute

time between the job site and the asphalt plant. Heavy tarpaulins often are used to cover open trucks to maintain the temperature of the mix. Grader productivity can be estimated by the methods discussed in Chapters 13.

21.5   *Productivity Estimation*

Construction of asphalt pavements requires the use of multiple types of construction equipment. Trucks and haulers are used to haul the hot asphalt mix, pavers are used to place and shape the pavement, and compactors are used to provide the desired density and surface finish. In most paving operations the overall productivity is determined by the productivity of the paver. Sufficient trucks or haulers are used so that the paver never waits for loaded trucks, and adequate compactors are used to equal or exceed the paver productivity. Let's look at an example as an illustration.

Example 21.1

A contractor has been awarded a contract for the construction of a shopping center and adjacent parking area. The contract drawings indicate that the parking area will measure 1,200 feet by 900 feet. Contract specifications require the parking area to be surfaced with 4 inches of asphalt pavement compacted to a density of 145 pounds per cubic foot.

The contractor has decided to use a Barber-Greene 245B track-mounted paver with a 10-foot screed to lay the asphalt pavement. The paver speed is estimated to be 45 feet per minute while laying the pavement. The contractor plans to use 12-cubic-yard dump trucks to haul the hot asphalt mix from an asphalt plant located 10 miles from the project site. Cycle time for the trucks is estimated to be 35 minutes. Each truck can carry safely 10 cubic yards of hot mix weighing 112 pounds per cubic foot. Because the paver must stop to change trucks each time a truck is empty, the operational efficiency of the paver is estimated to be 30 minutes per hour. The contractor plans to use pneumatic-tire compactors to obtain the desired pavement density. The effective compaction width of these compactors will be 6 feet, and they will compact at an average speed of 2.5 miles per hour. The contractor determined from a test strip that 4 passes of the pneumatic-tire compactors are required to achieve the specified density. The contractor also has selected a tandem steel-drum compactor to finish the pavement. This compactor will compact at an average speed of 2 miles per hour at an effective compaction width of 4 feet. Only 1 pass will be required to finish the surface of the pavement. Operational efficiency of the trucks and compactors is estimated to be 50 minutes per hour.

a. What is the estimated productivity of the paver in square yards per hour?
b. How many dump trucks should the contractor use to keep up with the paver?
c. How many compactors should the contractor use to keep up with the paver?

Solution

a. The paver productivity can be estimated with Equation 21.1 to be

$$\text{Productivity} = \frac{(45 \text{ ft./min.})(10 \text{ ft.})(30 \text{ min.})(60 \text{ min./hr.})}{(9 \text{ sq. ft./sq. yd.})(60 \text{ min.})}$$

$$= 1{,}500 \text{ sq. yd./hr.}$$

b. The total volume of compacted pavement that the paver can place per hour is estimated to be

$$\text{Volume} = \frac{(1{,}500 \text{ sq. yd./hr.})(4 \text{ in.})}{(36 \text{ in./yd.})} = 167 \text{ cu. yd./hr.}$$

The total weight of asphalt mix required per hour is

$$\text{Weight} = \frac{(167 \text{ cu. yd./hr.})(145 \text{ lb./cu. ft.})(27 \text{ cu. ft./cu. yd.})}{(2{,}000 \text{ lb./ton})}$$

$$= 327 \text{ tons/hr.}$$

The productivity of 1 dump truck can be estimated to be

$$\text{Productivity} = \frac{(\text{Load Weight})(\text{Operational Efficiency})}{(\text{Cycle Time})}$$

$$= \frac{(10 \text{ cu. yd.})(112 \text{ lb./cu. ft.})(27 \text{ cu. ft./cu. yd.})(50 \text{ min./hr.})}{(35 \text{ min.})(2{,}000 \text{ lb./ton})}$$

$$= 21.6 \text{ tons/hr.}$$

The number of trucks required can be determined by dividing the paver productivity by the productivity of 1 dump truck, which is

$$\frac{327 \text{ tons/hr.}}{21.6 \text{ tons/hr.}} = 15.1; \text{ therefore, we need } \textbf{16 dump trucks}$$

c. The productivity of the pneumatic-tire compactor is estimated with Equation 15–1 to be

$$\frac{(6 \text{ ft.})(2.5 \text{ mi./hr.})(5{,}280 \text{ ft./mi.})(50 \text{ min.})}{(4 \text{ passes})(9 \text{ sq. ft./sq. yd.})(60 \text{ min.})} = 1{,}800 \text{ sq. yd./hr.}$$

Similarly, the productivity of the tandem steel-drum compactor is estimated to be

$$\frac{(4 \text{ ft.})(2 \text{ mi./hr.})(5{,}280 \text{ ft./mi.})(50 \text{ min.})}{(1 \text{ pass})(9 \text{ sq. ft./sq. yd.})(60 \text{ min.})} = 3{,}900 \text{ sq. yd./hr.}$$

Since the productivity of each compactor exceeds that of the paver, the contractor will need **1 pneumatic-tire compactor** and **1 tandem steel-drum compactor.**

21.6   *Cost and Time Analysis*

To estimate the equipment cost of a paving operation, it is first necessary to estimate the hourly ownership and operating cost for each item of equipment to be used. This can be done using either the cost references discussed in Chapter 5 or historical cost data. These costs can be used in conjunction with the overall productivity of the paving operation to estimate the equipment cost. The other major costs will be the material cost of the asphalt mixture and the cost of labor needed to support the operation. Once these latter costs have been estimated, you can estimate the total cost for the paving operation. The time required to complete the paving operation can be estimated by dividing the total volume of pavement required by the estimated productivity of the set of equipment to be used. Let's now look at two examples.

Example 21.2

The contractor of Example 21.1 needs to prime the parking area base course before placing the asphalt pavement. He has selected an application rate of 0.4 gallons per square yard. The asphalt distributor spray bar is 10 feet long, and the pump output is 100 gallons per minute. Operational efficiency is estimated to be 40 minutes per hour.

a. What is the estimated time required to prime the base course?
b. The hourly ownership cost for the asphalt distributor is estimated to be $10, the hourly operating cost (less cost of operator) is estimated to be $26, and the operator earns $28 per hour. What is the estimated equipment cost per square yard for priming the base course?

Solution

a. The first step is to estimate the distributor speed using Equation 21–2:

$$\text{Speed} = \frac{(100 \text{ gal./min.})(9 \text{ sq. ft./yd.})}{(10 \text{ ft.})(0.4 \text{ gal./sq. yd.})} = 225 \text{ ft./min.}$$

Next, we can estimate the distributor productivity with Equation 21–3:

$$\text{Productivity} = \frac{(225 \text{ ft./min.})(10 \text{ ft.})(40 \text{ min.})}{(60 \text{ min.})} = 1,500 \text{ sq. ft./min.}$$

The total area to be primed is

$$(1,200 \text{ ft.})(900 \text{ ft.}) = 1,080,000 \text{ sq. ft.}$$

The time required to complete the priming operation is

$$\frac{(1,080,000 \text{ sq. ft})}{(1,500 \text{ sq. ft./min.})(60 \text{ min./hr.})} = 12 \text{ hr.}$$

b. The total hourly ownership and operating cost is

$$\$10/\text{hr.} + \$26/\text{hr.} + \$28/\text{hr} = \$64/\text{hr.}$$

The estimated equipment unit cost is

$$\frac{(\$64/\text{hr.})(9 \text{ sq. ft./sq. yd.})}{(1,500 \text{ sq. ft./min.})(60 \text{ min./hr.})} = \$0.006 \text{ sq. yd.}$$

Example 21.3

The contractor of Example 21.1 has determined the following cost data for the equipment he plans to use in the paving operation:

Item	Ownership Cost	Operating Cost	Operator's Wage
Paving machine	$80/hr.	$35/hr.	$28/hr.
Dump truck	$23/hr.	$15/hr.	$22/hr.
Pneumatic-tire compactor	$31/hr.	$18/hr.	$28/hr.
Steel-drum compactor	$24/hr.	$9/hr.	$28/hr.

a. What is the estimated equipment cost per square yard of asphalt pavement?
b. What is the estimated time required to lay and finish the asphalt pavement?

Solution

a. In Example 21.1, we determined that the amount of equipment needed for the paving operation is 1 paver, 16 dump trucks, 1 pneumatic-tire compactor, and 1 steel-drum compactor. The total hourly cost for each item of equipment is:

Paving machine $80/hr. + $35/hr. + $28/hr. = $143/hr
Dump truck $23/hr. + $15/hr. + $22/hr. = $60/hr.

Pneumatic-tire compactor   \$31/hr. + \$18/hr. + \$28/hr. =   \$77/hr.
Steel-drum compactor   \$24/hr. +   \$9/hr. + \$28/hr. =   \$61/hr.

The total hourly cost for the entire fleet of equipment is

$$\$143/hr. + [(16)(\$60/hr.)] + \$77/hr. + \$61/hr. = \$1,241/hr.$$

The fleet productivity is governed by the productivity of the paving machine, which we found in Example 21.1 to be 1,500 square yards per hour. The equipment cost per square yard can now be estimated to be

$$\frac{\$1,241/hr.}{1,500 \text{ sq. yd./hr.}} = \textbf{\$0.83 sq. yd.}$$

b. The time required to complete the paving operation is estimated to be

$$\frac{(1,200 \text{ ft.})(900 \text{ ft.})}{(9 \text{ sq. ft./sq. yd.})(1,500 \text{ sq.yd./hr.})} = \textbf{80 hr.}$$

21.7   *Problems*

1. A contractor has a project requiring the construction of a mile of paved access road. She owns a 1,000-gallon asphalt distributor that she plans to use to prime the base before laying the asphalt pavement. The width of the paved surface is to be 24 feet, and the prime coat application rate is to be 0.5 gallons per square yard. The distributor spray bar is 12 feet long, and the pump output is 124 gallons per minute. Operational efficiency is estimated to be 30 minutes per hour because of the time required to fill the distributor each time the tank is emptied.
   a. How many hours do you estimate it will take to complete the priming operation?
   b. How many gallons of asphalt will be required?
   c. The hourly ownership cost for the distributor is estimated to be \$9.40 per hour, the hourly operating cost (less the operator's wages) is estimated to be \$27.20 per hour, and the operator earns \$26.50 per hour. What is the total estimated cost for the priming operation (including the cost of the asphalt), if the asphalt costs \$2.00 per gallon?

2. A contractor has a project involving the paving of a large parking area that will be used by a trucking company to store large highway trucks. The size of the paved area is to be 900 feet by 400 feet. The pavement surface will be 6 inches of asphalt pavement compacted to a density of 140 pounds per cubic foot. The contractor has decided to use a Blaw-Knox PF-150 tracked paving machine with a 12-foot screed to lay the asphalt. Paver speed is estimated to be 27 feet per minute, and paver operational efficiency is estimated to be 40 minutes per hour. The contractor plans to use dump trucks that can carry 12 cubic yards of hot mix weighing 100 pounds per cubic foot. The contractor plans to use pneumatic-tire compactors to obtain the required pavement density. The effective compaction width of these compactors is 5 feet, and they will compact at an average speed of 2.4 miles per hour. The contractor has se-

lected tandem steel-drum compactors to finish the pavement. The finish compactors will compact at an average speed of 1.5 miles per hour and have effective compaction widths of 5 feet. Two passes are required to finish the pavement surface. Operational efficiency of the compactors is estimated to be 50 minutes per hour.

a. What is the estimated productivity of the paving machine in square yards per hour?

b. How many dump trucks should the contractor use to keep up with the paver? The average cycle time for the trucks is 40 minutes, and the operational efficiency is estimated to be 50 minutes per hour.

c. How many pneumatic-tire compactors should the contractor use to keep up with the paving machine? Test strip results indicate that 8 passes are required to achieve the required density.

d. How many finish compactors should the contractor use to keep up with the finish machine?

e. How many 8-hour days do you estimate it will take to complete this paving operation?

3. A contractor has a project that involves placing a single surface treatment on a 600-foot-by-900-foot area that will be used to store shipping containers. Following are the steps in constructing the surface treatment:

- Apply prime coat on base material
- Cure prime coat for 24 hours
- Apply liquid asphalt cutback binder
- Spread aggregate
- Compact aggregate

The contractor plans to use a 3,000-gallon asphalt distributor with a 12-foot spray bar. The prime coat application rate will be 0.25 gallons per square yard, and the pump output will be 110 gallons per minute. The surface treatment cutback binder application rate will be 0.35 gallons per square yard, and the pump output will again be 110 gallons per minute. Operational efficiency for the asphalt distributor is estimated to be 40 minutes per hour. To spread the aggregate, the contractor plans to use a self-propelled aggregate spreader. The spreader hopper is 12 feet long, and the spreader will travel at a speed of 300 feet per minute. The specified aggregate application rate is 30 pounds per square yard. Operational efficiency of the spreader is estimated to be 40 minutes per hour. The contractor plans to compact the aggregate with 3 tandem steel-drum compactors. The compactors will compact at an average speed of 2.5 miles per hour with an effective compaction width of 5 feet. Two passes are required to achieve the desired compaction. Operational efficiency of the compactors is estimated to be 50 minutes per hour.

a. How many hours do you estimate it will take to apply the prime coat on the base material?

b. How many hours do you estimate it will take the distributor to apply the asphalt cutback binder?

c. How many hours do you estimate it will take the aggregate spreader to spread the aggregate assuming the contractor uses sufficient dump trucks to haul the aggregate?

    d. How many hours do you estimate it will take the compactors to compact the aggregate?

    e. Estimate the quantity required for the following materials:
- Prime coat asphalt (gallons)
- Asphalt cutback binder (gallons)
- Aggregate (tons)

4. A contractor has a project involving the construction of 10 miles of paved road. The pavement width is to be 24 feet, and the specified compacted density of the 4-inch pavement is 142 pounds per cubic foot. The contractor plans to apply the prime coat to the base material with a 2,000-gallon asphalt distributor with a 12-foot spray bar. The required application rate is 0.3 gallons per square yard, and the distributor pump output is 96 gallons per minute. Operational efficiency of the distributor is estimated to be 40 minutes per hour. After the prime coat has cured for 24 hours, the contractor plans to lay the asphalt pavement with a wheeled paving machine with a 12-foot screed. The paver speed is estimated to be 30 feet per minute. Operational efficiency of the paver is estimated to be 30 minutes per hour. The contractor plans to use dump trucks to haul the hot asphalt mix from a central plant. Each truck can carry 12 cubic yards of hot mix weighing 108 pounds per cubic foot. The cycle time for each truck is estimated to be 45 minutes. Operational efficiency of the trucks is estimated to be 50 minutes per hour. The contractor plans to compact the pavement with 2 pneumatic-tire compactors and finish the surface of the pavement with 1 tandem steel-drum compactor.

    a. How many hours do you estimate it will take the distributor to apply the prime coat?

    b. How much do you estimate it will cost to purchase the asphalt for the prime coat if it costs $1.75 per gallon?

    c. What is the estimated productivity of the paving machine in square yards per hour?

    d. How many trucks should the contractor use to keep up with the paving machine?

    e. How many 8-hour days do you estimate it will take for the paving machine to lay the asphalt pavement if the contractor uses the number of trucks you determined in (d) above?

    f. How much do you estimate it will cost to purchase the hot mix if it costs $25 per ton?

    g. The contractor has determined the following cost data for the equipment to be used in the project:

Item	Ownership Cost	Operating Cost	Operator's Wage
Asphalt distributor	$10/hr.	$25/hr.	$25/hr.
Paving machine	$75/hr.	$30/hr.	$26/hr.
Dump truck$25/hr.	$16/hr.	$21/hr.	
Pneumatic-tire compactor	$34/hr.	$21/hr.	$26/hr.
Steel-drum compactor	$22/hr.	$10/hr.	$26/hr.

What is the estimated total equipment cost for applying the prime coat and laying the asphalt pavement?

Equipment Fleet Management

22.1   *Introduction*

Equipment represents a significant capital investment that must be managed wisely to ensure that it continues to contribute to the profitability of the construction company. Owning a large fleet of equipment may not be a good business decision unless a contractor has sufficient work to keep the equipment busy. Besides being used to earn money for the contractor, the equipment must be maintained properly to protect the investment. Some contractors establish their equipment fleets as profit centers and charge equipment use to individual projects. Others establish subsidiary companies to manage their equipment fleets. Whatever technique a contractor chooses, good equipment management is essential. The objective is to minimize operating, maintenance, and repair costs while maximizing productivity and return on investment.

To manage an equipment fleet properly, contractors should:

- Inspect each item of equipment regularly to determine its condition.
- Keep complete records on each item of equipment recording age, usage, fuel consumption, maintenance and repair costs, downtime, and time between component replacement.
- Implement a good preventive maintenance program.

In this chapter, we will discuss acquisition and disposal of equipment, methods of equipment financing, techniques for determining equipment rates, equipment maintenance, and equipment safety.

22.2   *Acquisition and Disposal of Equipment*

Contractors must continually review their equipment fleets to determine whether they need to purchase additional equipment, replace existing equipment, or dispose of underutilized equipment. Such decisions should be based on good cost and performance records and realistic forecasts of future company requirements. The best equipment to acquire are items that have good productivity and low life-cycle costs and are adaptable to performing a variety of tasks. The acquisition process begins with an evaluation of the needs of the company. Following are specific questions that should be asked:

- What type of equipment is needed?
- What features are needed?
- What size of equipment is needed?
- What is the anticipated usage?

Equipment is acquired through one of these methods:

- Purchase
- Lease
- Rental

The appropriate method depends on anticipated usage. Purchase is the least costly method of acquiring equipment, providing the equipment earns adequate revenue to cover its ownership and operating cost. Leasing equipment by the month or year usually costs more than owning the equipment but is less costly than renting it. Renting equipment by the hour, day, week, or month is the most costly method of acquisition and should be used only for short-term and unexpected equipment requirements. Contractors may use all three methods for obtaining needed equipment: renting equipment for one-time jobs, leasing equipment for medium-term requirements, and purchasing equipment for long-term requirements.

Purchasing equipment provides contractors a greater selection of equipment from which to choose, provides the option of accelerated depreciation to offset current profits, and may provide opportunities for negotiating significant discounts with dealers. Purchasing also allows contractors to standardize their equipment to minimize the variety of repair parts they need to stock and minimize training for operators and repair personnel. When selecting specific types, sizes, and manufacturers, contractors should consider the following:

- Equipment cost
- Equipment productivity
- Product features and attachments
- Dealer support (parts and service)

Most contractors with a relatively stable volume of work within a limited geographical area generally find it desirable and economical to own their own equipment.

Equipment may be leased with or without an option for future purchase. Leasing generally is the best option when a job calls for specialized equipment that requires significant investment but has only limited future use. Leased equipment often is used to provide additional assets during peak demand periods, and this eqipment is released when no longer required. A tower crane is an excellent example of equipment that typically is leased by a contractor. Leasing equipment offers some potential financial advantages to the contractor. It is a form of financing that is considered an operating expense, not a liability, on financial statements. Leasing can improve a contractor's working capital position by avoiding having funds tied up in fixed assets. It also requires no initial cash outlay (down payment), freeing working capital for other uses.

Although the direct cost of equipment rental may be substantially higher than for either leasing or purchasing, rental can have its advantages. It can be very efficient for low utilization equipment and for short-term needs such as short-term peak requirements, seasonal use, or replacements for equipment being repaired. Equipment is not rented for a guaranteed period and can be returned at any time. Rental is a good option for projects that are distant from the contractor's primary base of operations. Maintenance and repair of rental equipment are the responsibility of the rental dealer.

Equipment replacement decisions are based on the ownership and operating cost of currently owned equipment and projected costs of new equipment. The basic decision is whether to continue to use old technology or to upgrade to achieve better productivity. Some contractors choose to rebuild older machines rather than replace them. Replacement decisions are made by comparing the estimated ownership and operating costs for the various alternatives and selecting the lowest cost alternative.

Disposal decisions are made either as a consequence of replacement decisions or because the equipment is not earning sufficient revenue to cover the cost of owning and operating it. When equipment is being replaced, it might be traded in on the new equipment, sold to others, or salvaged as scrap. Excess equipment selected for disposal usually is sold but may be salvaged as scrap.

22.3   *Equipment Financing*

Contractors have several choices in deciding how to finance equipment acquisitions. One potential source is to use internally generated funds and pay cash. This is probably the most expensive alternative, and the one most contractors avoid. Paying cash reduces the working capital of the company and uses company assets to purchase equipment. Most construction companies earn 20% to 40% on equity, while external financing may cost 10% to 12%. For this reason, most contractors choose to use external financing to purchase equipment.

The primary sources of external financing are banks, commercial financing and leasing companies, and equipment dealers. Bankers typically use company balance sheet analysis to make their lending decisions and may require compensating deposits. Commercial financing and leasing companies, which typically require collateral before making loans, may be associated with specific dealers. These companies generally offer better rates for long-term loans than do banks, because they are not subject to the same regulations that banks are. The last method is to acquire financing directly from the dealers using a lease with option to purchase. There is no one best method of obtaining external financing. Contractors must analyze their cash flow requirements and relationships with potential lenders to make the best decisions for their companies.

Table 22.1
Average Primary Productive Lives of Construction Equipment

Equipment Type	Average Primary Productive Life
Asphalt paver	12 years
Compactor	13 years
Concrete slip-form paver	15 years
Grader	
Articulated	12 years
Rigid-frame	19 years
Hydraulic excavator	11 years
Loader	
Crawler	11 years
Wheeled	12 years
Scraper	
Conventional	15 years
Elevating	13 years
Tractor	
Crawler	11 years
Wheeled	12 years
Truck	
Articulated	8 years
Rigid-frame	14 years

This data was extracted from *Construction Equipment*, 82(3): 32–48.

22.4   *Equipment Costing and Control*

Another critical area of equipment management is the determination of hourly or daily rates to charge projects for use of the equipment. Rates are based on anticipated annual usage and annual ownership and operating costs. Both *operating* and *standby* rates are established to force project managers to manage their equipment assets. Rates initially are established by using the cost references discussed in Chapter 4. Actual cost data is collected by the company accounting system, and the rates are adjusted based on actual costs. Ownership costs are estimated by determining the anticipated productive life of the piece of equipment and the anticipated utilization per year and determining the hourly cost with the time value of money techniques discussed in Chapter 2. The typical productive lives of most construction equipment are shown in Table 22.1. Computers and automated databases are used by many contractors to keep track of usage and cost data for each piece of equipment. Other contractors use equipment time cards to record equipment use, fuel consumption, and repair costs. This data can be used to develop rates to charge projects and develop cost estimates. It can also be used to determine when to make disposal decisions.

22.5   *Equipment Maintenance*

Maintenance is servicing, adjusting, and repairing equipment. Contractors must be aware of the importance of proper equipment maintenance and the effect of equipment breakdowns on project costs and schedules. Effective maintenance programs will reduce equipment costs by minimizing failures, reducing downtime, and increasing equipment resale value. As discussed in Chapter 4, maintenance and repair costs typically increase as equipment ages. Good preventive maintenance programs can reduce repair costs and extend the useful lives of equipment.

The first step in establishing a good maintenance program is to follow the manufacturers' recommendations. They typically provide the following publications for each model they produce:

- Owner/operator manual
- Parts book
- Lubrication and service guide

The owner/operator manual describes daily maintenance inspections that should be made, both before and after operation; start-up and shut-down procedures; and proper techniques for using the machine. Most manuals also include checklists for the before- and after-operation inspections. The parts book lists all of the parts used in the piece of equipment, along with identifying part numbers. The lubrication and service guide provides service intervals and identifies the proper types of lubricant to use.

Following are the primary components of a good preventive maintenance program:

- Proper use of equipment
- Proper fuel handling
- Proper lubrication
- Periodic adjustment
- Scheduled replacement of air, fuel, and oil filters
- Periodic oil and coolant sampling

Oil and coolant analysis are used to diagnose failure without tearing down engine components. This allows early identification of problems and results in before-failure equipment overhaul.

Oil samples are taken at intervals recommended by the equipment manufacturer, usually at each oil change. The samples of used oil are analyzed to determine the presence of any metals or contaminants, such as water, fuel, or coolant. The purpose of the analysis is to compare the properties of the used oil with the properties of new unused oil to determine if anything unusual is occurring in the engine. The presence of unusual amounts of metal fragments indicates the potential for engine failure.

Coolant is essential to control engine operating temperatures. It is analyzed at each oil change to ensure it has the correct chemical properties to function properly. Twice per year, the coolant should be analyzed for the presence of contaminants. Coolant sampling is illustrated in Figure 22.1.

The frequency of preventive maintenance service should be increased when operating equipment under extremely adverse conditions. Filters and lubricants should be changed often under dusty conditions. To reduce maintenance costs, contractors often spray water on haul roads to control dust. Radiators should be kept free of dirt and debris so they will function properly.

Figure 22.1
Coolant Sampling
Courtesy Caterpillar Inc.

Tires on wheeled equipment should be inspected frequently for unusual wear and tire pressure. The tracks on crawler equipment also must be inspected frequently for wear and loose track bolts, and they should be adjusted to maintain the correct tension.

Contractors generally establish an inventory of common repair parts to expedite equipment repair. Stockage policies should be based on experience, manufacturers' recommendations, and job conditions. Stockage and repair of replacement components result in lower total maintenance costs. The downtime for a piece of equipment is less with component replacement than with component repair. The defective components are repaired after being replaced and stored until needed.

Another aspect of maintenance management is the development of maintenance policies. Daily routine maintenance can be performed by equipment operators, but most minor or major repairs should be performed by mechanics. Contractors often use mobile maintenance teams to repair equipment on site to minimize downtime. Major repairs, which require sophisticated shop tools, are performed either in contractor or dealer maintenance facilities.

Some contractors use automated equipment maintenance management. Several software packages are available commercially, and some contractors have developed their own systems. Data about a piece of equipment are entered when the item is acquired, and maintenance cost and usage data are collected until the item is selected for disposal. Preventive maintenance services are scheduled based on criteria selected by the contractor, usually hours of operation. Any problems with equipment performance or condition are input to be used in making repair decisions. The computer aids in producing work orders, which are sent to the maintenance facility. The maintenance personnel use the work orders to develop parts lists and order the parts. Work order cost data is charged against the item of equipment. Component replacement and fuel consumption are tracked for each item of equipment. These automated systems also can be used to manage the inventory of repair parts, often using bar-coding technology for part identification.

22.6 Equipment Safety

Construction equipment can be very dangerous if operated improperly. In addition, the equipment can be damaged during improper operation. Safety, therefore, is a significant concern in equipment management. Contractors should consider the following types of policies and procedures in developing their safety programs:

- Management
- Operator competence
- Maintenance

At a minimum, management policies and procedures should provide guidance for the following:

- Organization of job sites
- Selection and training of operators
- Installation of rollover protection on equipment
- Installation of backup alarms on equipment
- Enforcement of speed limits on haul roads

Operator policies and procedures should provide guidance for these issues:

- Wearing of safety equipment
- Conducting before-operation inspections
- Operating equipment safety
- Stopping equipment if operator loses sight of anyone working in area
- Shutting off engine before dismounting machine
- Not allowing others to ride on equipment unless proper seating is provided

Maintenance policies and procedures should address at least the following:

- Training of maintenance personnel
- Safe maintenance procedures
- Procedures and regulations for wearing safety equipment
- Proper jacking, hoisting, and blocking procedures

Glossary

Activity—An individual task that is required to complete a project.

Activity duration—Estimated time required to complete an activity.

Activity float—Amount of time an activity can be delayed without delaying completion of a project.

Admixture—An ingredient other than cement, aggregate, or water added to a concrete mix to improve workability or other properties of the mix.

Annual cost method—Comparing alternatives on an annual cost basis.

Annual depreciation amount—An amount that is subtracted from the book value of a piece of equipment at the beginning of a year to determine the book value at the end of the year.

Annual depreciation rate—Using the declining balance method of depreciation, a factor that is multiplied by the depreciable value or the book value to determine the annual depreciation amount.

Asphalt cutback—Asphalt that has been liquefied by dissolving it in a solvent.

Asphalt emulsion—Water containing suspended asphalt cement.

Bank measure—A determination of the density of a mass of soil in its natural state.

Base course—A compacted granular layer used in pavement structures to support either concrete or asphalt surfaces.

Book value—The initial cost of a piece of equipment less the total depreciation to date.

Boom angle—The vertical angle between a crane boom and the horizontal plane.

Coefficient of traction—A factor that is multiplied by the total load on a driving wheel or track to determine the maximum tractive force that can be applied to an operating surface just before slipping occurs.

Cold mix asphalt pavement—Asphalt pavement constructed with paving material mixed at a field site.

Compacted measure—A determination of the density of a mass of soil after it has been compacted.

Cost of facilities capital—A formula used to estimate the cost of borrowing funds to finance equipment: the average value of the equipment times the cost of money rate divided by the number of hours used per year.

Cost of money—The interest rate that must be paid on borrowed money.

Critical activity—An activity that has no float and cannot be delayed without delaying the completion of the project.

Critical path—The chain of activities that determine the project completion time.

Cycle time—Time required to complete a repetitive operation such as loading a truck, traveling to the dump site, dumping the load, and returning for another load.

Depreciable value—The purchase price of a piece of equipment less its estimated salvage value.

Depreciation—An artificial expense that spreads the depreciable value of a piece of equipment over the depreciation period.

Depreciation accounting—The allocation of a part of the cost of a piece of equipment over its estimated useful life.

Depreciation period—The number of years a piece of equipment is owned.

Derating factor—A factor that is multiplied by the available rimpull or drawbar pull at standard operating conditions to estimate the power available at higher altitudes.

Direct cost—Total cost of performing a construction task; includes labor, material, equipment, and subcontract costs.

Drawbar pull—The power available at the rear hitch of a piece of track-mounted equipment when operated under standard conditions.

Duration—The time required to complete an activity.

Early finish—Earliest time an activity can be completed.

Early start—Earliest time an activity can start.

Effective grade—A grade that would produce a grade resisting force that is equal to the total resisting force.

Equipment fuel factor—A factor that is multiplied by the flywheel horsepower to estimate the hourly fuel consumption.

Equipment productivity—A measure of the volume of load that can be carried or moved, or the area compacted or graded, per unit of time, usually per hour.

Equipment repair factor—A percentage multiplier that is applied to the hourly straight-line depreciation amount to estimate the hourly equipment maintenance and repair cost.

Equipment service cost factor—A percentage multiplier that is applied to the hourly fuel cost to estimate the hourly servicing (filter, oil, and grease) cost.

Equivalence—A concept that payments or receipts that differ in magnitude but are made at different times may be equivalent to each other.

Fill factor—A factor that is multiplied by the heaped capacity of a bucket to estimate its heaped load for various materials. Fill factors are used to account for the different bulking properties of different types of material.

Flexible pavement—An asphalt pavement that distributes wheel loads directly to the supporting base and depends on particle interlock for stability.

Float—The amount of time an activity can be delayed without delaying the overall completion of the project.

Friction head—The equivalent vertical height that the inlet of a pipe must be located at above the outlet to cause water to flow at the required rate. It is a measure of the friction resistance of the pipe to the movement of the water.

Gradation—A measure of the distribution of particle sizes in soil.

Grade assistance—The force of gravity that assists vehicle movement down a grade.

Grade resistance—The force of gravity that a piece of equipment must overcome when moving up a grade.

Heaped capacity—The volume contained in a bucket after being loaded with soil that is heaped above the edge of the bucket, or the volume contained in a truck or scraper when the material in the bed or bowl is piled above the sides in the center and tapered down to the top of the sides.

Hot mix asphalt pavement—Asphalt pavement constructed with paving material mixed in a central plant.

Indirect cost—Overhead cost added to project direct cost to cover company overhead, profit, taxes, insurance, and bonding.

In situ—In place, as natural, undisturbed soil.

Interest—The charge for borrowed money or the return expected from invested money.

Interest factor—A factor that is multiplied by a sum of money paid or received at a point in time to determine its equivalent value at a different time.

Interest rate—The cost of borrowing money or the return obtainable by investing it.

Late finish—Latest time an activity can be completed without delaying the completion of the project.

Late start—Latest time an activity can start without delaying the completion of the project.

Liquid limit—The moisture content at the plastic-liquid boundary of a sample of soil.

Liquidated damages—An amount specified in a contract to compensate an owner for damages incurred as a consequence of the contractor not completing a project within the time specified in the contract.

Loose measure—A determination of the density of a mass of soil after it has been excavated.

Minimum attractive rate of return—The effective interest rate that should be earned to recover the cost of capital (money) and any other equipment costs such as taxes, insurance, and license fees.

Mixed-in-place asphalt pavement—Asphalt pavement constructed with paving material that is mixed on the job site.

Moisture content—A percentage representing the weight of water in a sample of soil divided by the weight of the solids.

Operating factor—A percentage equal to the estimated number of minutes per hour the equipment is working and not idling, divided by 60.

Operating radius—The horizontal distance from the center of rotation of a crane boom to the hook.

Operational efficiency—The amount of estimated working time per hour.

Optimum moisture content—The moisture content that results in maximum dry density when a given compactive effort is applied.

Outriggers—Beams mounted on ground-bearing pedestals that are extended from a crane to extend the effective width of its support base.

Ownership costs—The cost of owning a piece of equipment including: depreciation, interest, taxes, insurance, storage, and license fees.

Plant mix asphalt pavement—Asphalt pavement constructed with paving material mixed in a central plant.

Plasticity—A measure of the amount of water that a soil will absorb.

Plastic limit—The moisture content at the semisolid plastic boundary of a sample of soil.

Present worth—The equivalent worth of a future sum of money at today's value.

Present worth method—Comparing alternatives on a present worth basis.

Prime coat—A coat of liquid asphalt sprayed on the base course to seal the surface of the base material and provide a bond between the base and the overlying asphalt pavement.

Proctor test—A standardized compaction test used to determine the compacted dry density of soil when compacted under a standard loading for various moisture contents.

Quantity take-off—A measure of the quantity of work to be performed in each task or activity.

Rate of return—The annual interest rate at which the sum of investment and expenditures equals total income from the investment.

Rigid pavement—A concrete pavement that acts as a beam distributing wheel loads roughly uniformly over a large area.

Rimpull—The power available at the rims of the driving wheels of a wheeled piece of equipment under standard operating conditions.

Rolling resistance—Resistance of the equipment operating surface to the forward or reverse movement of a piece of wheeled equipment.

Salvage value—The value of a piece of equipment at the time of disposal or retirement.

Shrinkage—Decrease in the volume of a mass of soil when compacted.

Shrinkage limit—The moisture content at the solid-semisolid boundary of a sample of soil.

Single payment compound amount factor—An interest factor that is used to determine the future worth of a present sum of money.

Single payment present worth factor—An interest factor that is used to determine the present worth of a future sum of money.

Slump test—A test to measure the workability of concrete. It involves placing concrete inside an inverted metal cone and consolidating it with a rod. The metal cone is lifted, and the amount of slump is measured.

Soil stabilization—Improving the strength of soil by mixing it with a stabilizing agent or additive.

Static head—The vertical distance that a pump is to move water.

Static suction lift—The vertical height of a pump above the surface of the water to be pumped.

Static tipping load—The minimum load placed in a loader bucket that causes the machine to rotate so the front rollers of a tracked loader clear the tracks or the rear wheels of a wheeled loader clear the ground.

Struck capacity—The volume contained in a bucket after being loaded level with the edges of the bucket, or the volume carried in a truck or scraper after being loaded level with the sides of the bed or bowl.

Subgrade—A compacted layer of imported or natural material used to support the base course in a pavement structure.

Surface treatment—A waterproof surface constructed of alternating layers of liquid asphalt and aggregate.

Swell—Increase in the volume of a mass of soil when excavated.

Time value of money—A recognition that the value of money increases with time because of the interest rate, which represents the cost of borrowing the money or the return obtainable by investing it.

Total resisting force—Total force acting against the forward or reverse movement of a piece of equipment. Equals the sum of the force due to rolling resistance and the force due to grade resistance.

Uniform series capital recovery factor—An interest factor that is used to determine a series of equal payments or receipts that is equivalent to a given present worth sum.

Uniform series compound amount factor—An interest factor that is used to determine the future worth of a series of equal payments or receipts.

Uniform series present worth factor—An interest factor that is used to determine the present worth of a series of equal payments or receipts.

Uniform series sinking fund factor—An interest factor that is used to determine a series of equal payments or receipts that is equivalent to a stated or required future sum.

Well point—A perforated pipe driven into the ground to permit pumping of ground water.

Work breakdown—Division of project scope of work into work packages and activities.

Work package—Element of work required to complete a project; usually consists of multiple activities.

Year-end convention—An approximation that considers that all cash that flows during an interest period flows at the end of the period.

Conversion Factors

To Convert From	To	Multiply By
acres	square yards	1,613
cubic feet	gallons	7.48
cubic yards	cubic feet	27
feet	meters	0.3048
gallons	liters	3.785
gallons of water	pounds of water	8.34
meters	feet	3.05
miles	feet	5,280
miles	kilometers	1.609
miles	yards	1,760
miles per hour	feet per minute	88
pounds per cubic foot	kilograms per cubic meter	16.018
pounds per cubic yard	kilograms per cubic meter	0.593
square meters	square yards	0.836
square yards	square feet	9

Interest Tables

	Cash Flow Factors		
Factor Name	*Converts*	*Symbol*	*Formula**
Single Payment Compound Amount	P to F	$(F/P, i, n)$	$(1 + i)^n$
Single Payment Present Worth	F to P	$(P/F, i, n)$	$\dfrac{1}{(1 + i)^n}$
Uniform Series Sinking Fund	F to A	$(A/F, i, n)$	$\dfrac{i}{(1 + i)^n - 1}$
Capital Recovery	P to A	$(A/P, i, n)$	$\dfrac{i(1 + i)^n}{(1 + i)^n - 1}$
Uniform Series Compound Amount	A to F	$(F/A, i, n)$	$\dfrac{(1 + i)^n - 1}{i}$
Uniform Series Present Worth	A to P	$(P/A, i, n)$	$\dfrac{(1 + i)^n - 1}{i(1 + i)^n}$

*For the mathematical derivation of the individual formulas, refer to a text on engineering economy, such as Eugene L. Grant, W. Grant Ireson, and Richard S. Leavenworth, *Principles of Engineering Economy* (New York: John Wiley & Sons, 1990), pp. 24–28.

1% Interest Rate

n	P/F	P/A	A/F	A/P	F/P	F/A
1	0.990	0.990	1.000	1.010	1.010	1.000
2	0.980	1.970	0.498	0.508	1.020	2.010
3	0.971	2.941	0.330	0.340	1.030	3.030
4	0.961	3.902	0.246	0.256	1.041	4.060
5	0.951	4.853	0.196	0.206	1.051	5.101
6	0.942	5.795	0.163	0.173	1.062	6.152
7	0.933	6.728	0.139	0.149	1.072	7.214
8	0.923	7.652	0.121	0.131	1.083	8.286
9	0.914	8.566	0.107	0.117	1.094	9.369
10	0.905	9.471	0.096	0.106	1.105	10.462
11	0.896	10.368	0.086	0.096	1.116	11.567
12	0.887	11.255	0.079	0.089	1.127	12.683
13	0.879	12.134	0.072	0.082	1.138	13.809
14	0.870	13.004	0.067	0.077	1.149	14.947
15	0.861	13.865	0.062	0.072	1.161	16.097
16	0.853	14.718	0.058	0.068	1.173	17.258
17	0.844	15.562	0.054	0.064	1.184	18.430
18	0.836	16.398	0.051	0.061	1.196	19.615
19	0.828	17.226	0.048	0.058	1.208	20.811
20	0.820	18.046	0.045	0.055	1.220	22.019
21	0.811	18.857	0.043	0.053	1.232	23.239
22	0.803	19.660	0.041	0.051	1.245	24.472
23	0.795	20.456	0.039	0.049	1.257	25.716
24	0.788	21.243	0.037	0.047	1.270	26.973
25	0.780	22.023	0.035	0.045	1.282	28.243
26	0.772	22.795	0.034	0.044	1.295	29.526
27	0.764	23.560	0.032	0.042	1.308	30.821
28	0.757	24.316	0.031	0.041	1.321	32.129
29	0.749	25.066	0.030	0.040	1.335	33.450
30	0.742	25.808	0.029	0.039	1.348	34.785
31	0.735	26.542	0.028	0.038	1.361	36.133
32	0.727	27.270	0.027	0.037	1.375	37.494
33	0.720	27.990	0.026	0.036	1.389	38.869
34	0.713	28.703	0.025	0.035	1.403	40.258
35	0.706	29.409	0.024	0.034	1.417	41.660
36	0.699	30.108	0.023	0.033	1.431	43.077
37	0.692	30.800	0.022	0.032	1.445	44.508
38	0.685	31.485	0.022	0.032	1.460	45.953
39	0.678	32.163	0.021	0.031	1.474	47.412
40	0.672	32.835	0.020	0.030	1.489	48.886
42	0.658	34.158	0.019	0.029	1.519	51.879
44	0.645	35.455	0.018	0.028	1.549	54.932
46	0.633	36.727	0.017	0.027	1.580	58.046
48	0.620	37.974	0.016	0.026	1.612	61.223
50	0.608	39.196	0.016	0.026	1.645	64.463

2% Interest Rate

n	P/F	P/A	A/F	A/P	F/P	F/A
1	0.980	0.980	1.000	1.020	1.020	1.000
2	0.961	1.942	0.495	0.515	1.040	2.020
3	0.942	2.884	0.327	0.347	1.061	3.060
4	0.924	3.808	0.243	0.263	1.082	4.122
5	0.906	4.713	0.192	0.212	1.104	5.204
6	0.888	5.601	0.159	0.179	1.126	6.308
7	0.871	6.472	0.135	0.155	1.149	7.434
8	0.853	7.325	0.117	0.137	1.172	8.583
9	0.837	8.162	0.103	0.123	1.195	9.755
10	0.820	8.983	0.091	0.111	1.219	10.950
11	0.804	9.787	0.082	0.102	1.243	12.169
12	0.788	10.575	0.075	0.095	1.268	13.412
13	0.773	11.348	0.068	0.088	1.294	14.680
14	0.758	12.106	0.063	0.083	1.319	15.974
15	0.743	12.849	0.058	0.078	1.346	17.293
16	0.728	13.578	0.054	0.074	1.373	18.639
17	0.714	14.292	0.050	0.070	1.400	20.012
18	0.700	14.992	0.047	0.067	1.428	21.412
19	0.686	15.678	0.044	0.064	1.457	22.841
20	0.673	16.351	0.041	0.061	1.486	24.297
21	0.660	17.011	0.039	0.059	1.516	25.783
22	0.647	17.658	0.037	0.057	1.546	27.299
23	0.634	18.292	0.035	0.055	1.577	28.845
24	0.622	18.914	0.033	0.053	1.608	30.422
25	0.610	19.523	0.031	0.051	1.641	32.030
26	0.598	20.121	0.030	0.050	1.673	33.671
27	0.586	20.707	0.028	0.048	1.707	35.344
28	0.574	21.281	0.027	0.047	1.741	37.051
29	0.563	21.844	0.026	0.046	1.776	38.792
30	0.552	22.396	0.025	0.045	1.811	40.568
31	0.541	22.938	0.024	0.044	1.848	42.379
32	0.531	23.468	0.023	0.043	1.885	44.227
33	0.520	23.989	0.022	0.042	1.922	46.112
34	0.510	24.499	0.021	0.041	1.961	48.034
35	0.500	24.999	0.020	0.040	2.000	49.994
36	0.490	25.489	0.019	0.039	2.040	51.994
37	0.481	25.969	0.019	0.039	2.081	54.034
38	0.471	26.441	0.018	0.038	2.122	56.115
39	0.462	26.903	0.017	0.037	2.165	58.237
40	0.453	27.355	0.017	0.037	2.208	60.402
42	0.435	28.235	0.015	0.035	2.297	64.862
44	0.418	29.080	0.014	0.034	2.390	69.503
46	0.402	29.892	0.013	0.033	2.487	74.331
48	0.387	30.673	0.013	0.033	2.587	79.354
50	0.372	31.424	0.012	0.032	2.692	84.579

3% Interest Rate

n	P/F	P/A	A/F	A/P	F/P	F/A
1	0.971	0.971	1.000	1.030	1.030	1.000
2	0.943	1.913	0.493	0.523	1.061	2.030
3	0.915	2.829	0.324	0.354	1.093	3.091
4	0.888	3.717	0.239	0.269	1.126	4.184
5	0.863	4.580	0.188	0.218	1.159	5.309
6	0.837	5.417	0.155	0.185	1.194	6.468
7	0.813	6.230	0.131	0.161	1.230	7.662
8	0.789	7.020	0.112	0.142	1.267	8.892
9	0.766	7.786	0.098	0.128	1.305	10.159
10	0.744	8.530	0.087	0.117	1.344	11.464
11	0.722	9.253	0.078	0.108	1.384	12.808
12	0.701	9.954	0.070	0.100	1.426	14.192
13	0.681	10.635	0.064	0.094	1.469	15.618
14	0.661	11.296	0.059	0.089	1.513	17.086
15	0.642	11.938	0.054	0.084	1.558	18.599
16	0.623	12.561	0.050	0.080	1.605	20.157
17	0.605	13.166	0.046	0.076	1.653	21.762
18	0.587	13.754	0.043	0.073	1.702	23.414
19	0.570	14.324	0.040	0.070	1.754	25.117
20	0.554	14.877	0.037	0.067	1.806	26.870
21	0.538	15.415	0.035	0.065	1.860	28.676
22	0.522	15.937	0.033	0.063	1.916	30.537
23	0.507	16.444	0.031	0.061	1.974	32.453
24	0.492	16.936	0.029	0.059	2.033	34.426
25	0.478	17.413	0.027	0.057	2.094	36.459
26	0.464	17.877	0.026	0.056	2.157	38.553
27	0.450	18.327	0.025	0.055	2.221	40.710
28	0.437	18.764	0.023	0.053	2.288	42.931
29	0.424	19.188	0.022	0.052	2.357	45.219
30	0.412	19.600	0.021	0.051	2.427	47.575
31	0.400	20.000	0.020	0.050	2.500	50.003
32	0.388	20.389	0.019	0.049	2.575	52.503
33	0.377	20.766	0.018	0.048	2.652	55.078
34	0.366	21.132	0.017	0.047	2.732	57.730
35	0.355	21.487	0.017	0.047	2.814	60.462
36	0.345	21.832	0.016	0.046	2.898	63.276
37	0.335	22.167	0.015	0.045	2.985	66.174
38	0.325	22.492	0.014	0.044	3.075	69.159
39	0.316	22.808	0.014	0.044	3.167	72.234
40	0.307	23.115	0.013	0.043	3.262	75.401
42	0.289	23.701	0.012	0.042	3.461	82.023
44	0.272	24.254	0.011	0.041	3.671	89.048
46	0.257	24.775	0.010	0.040	3.895	96.501
48	0.242	25.267	0.010	0.040	4.132	104.408
50	0.228	25.730	0.009	0.039	4.384	112.797

4% Interest Rate

n	P/F	P/A	A/F	A/P	F/P	F/A
1	0.962	0.962	1.000	1.040	1.040	1.000
2	0.925	1.886	0.490	0.530	1.082	2.040
3	0.889	2.775	0.320	0.360	1.125	3.122
4	0.855	3.630	0.235	0.275	1.170	4.246
5	0.822	4.452	0.185	0.225	1.217	5.416
6	0.790	5.242	0.151	0.191	1.265	6.633
7	0.760	6.002	0.127	0.167	1.316	7.898
8	0.731	6.733	0.109	0.149	1.369	9.214
9	0.703	7.435	0.094	0.134	1.423	10.583
10	0.676	8.111	0.083	0.123	1.480	12.006
11	0.650	8.760	0.074	0.114	1.539	13.486
12	0.625	9.385	0.067	0.107	1.601	15.026
13	0.601	9.986	0.060	0.100	1.665	16.627
14	0.577	10.563	0.055	0.095	1.732	18.292
15	0.555	11.118	0.050	0.090	1.801	20.024
16	0.534	11.652	0.046	0.086	1.873	21.825
17	0.513	12.166	0.042	0.082	1.948	23.698
18	0.494	12.659	0.039	0.079	2.026	25.645
19	0.475	13.134	0.036	0.076	2.107	27.671
20	0.456	13.590	0.034	0.074	2.191	29.778
21	0.439	14.029	0.031	0.071	2.279	31.969
22	0.422	14.451	0.029	0.069	2.370	34.248
23	0.406	14.857	0.027	0.067	2.465	36.618
24	0.390	15.247	0.026	0.066	2.563	39.083
25	0.375	15.622	0.024	0.064	2.666	41.646
26	0.361	15.983	0.023	0.063	2.772	44.312
27	0.347	16.330	0.021	0.061	2.883	47.084
28	0.333	16.663	0.020	0.060	2.999	49.968
29	0.321	16.984	0.019	0.059	3.119	52.966
30	0.308	17.292	0.018	0.058	3.243	56.085
31	0.296	17.588	0.017	0.057	3.373	59.328
32	0.285	17.874	0.016	0.056	3.508	62.701
33	0.274	18.148	0.015	0.055	3.648	66.210
34	0.264	18.411	0.014	0.054	3.794	69.858
35	0.253	18.665	0.014	0.054	3.946	73.652
36	0.244	18.908	0.013	0.053	4.104	77.598
37	0.234	19.143	0.012	0.052	4.268	81.702
38	0.225	19.368	0.012	0.052	4.439	85.970
39	0.217	19.584	0.011	0.051	4.616	90.409
40	0.208	19.793	0.011	0.051	4.801	95.026
42	0.193	20.186	0.010	0.050	5.193	104.820
44	0.178	20.549	0.009	0.049	5.617	115.413
46	0.165	20.885	0.008	0.048	6.075	126.871
48	0.152	21.195	0.007	0.047	6.571	139.263
50	0.141	21.482	0.007	0.047	7.107	152.667

			5% Interest Rate			
n	*P/F*	*P/A*	*A/F*	*A/P*	*F/P*	*F/A*
1	0.952	0.952	1.000	1.050	1.050	1.000
2	0.907	1.859	0.488	0.538	1.103	2.050
3	0.864	2.723	0.317	0.367	1.158	3.153
4	0.823	3.546	0.232	0.282	1.216	4.310
5	0.784	4.329	0.181	0.231	1.276	5.526
6	0.746	5.076	0.147	0.197	1.340	6.802
7	0.711	5.786	0.123	0.173	1.407	8.142
8	0.677	6.463	0.105	0.155	1.477	9.549
9	0.645	7.108	0.091	0.141	1.551	11.027
10	0.614	7.722	0.080	0.130	1.629	12.578
11	0.585	8.306	0.070	0.120	1.710	14.207
12	0.557	8.863	0.063	0.113	1.796	15.917
13	0.530	9.394	0.056	0.106	1.886	17.713
14	0.505	9.899	0.051	0.101	1.980	19.599
15	0.481	10.380	0.046	0.096	2.079	21.579
16	0.458	10.838	0.042	0.092	2.183	23.657
17	0.436	11.274	0.039	0.089	2.292	25.840
18	0.416	11.690	0.036	0.086	2.407	28.132
19	0.396	12.085	0.033	0.083	2.527	30.539
20	0.377	12.462	0.030	0.080	2.653	33.066
21	0.359	12.821	0.028	0.078	2.786	35.719
22	0.342	13.163	0.026	0.076	2.925	38.505
23	0.326	13.489	0.024	0.074	3.072	41.430
24	0.310	13.799	0.022	0.072	3.225	44.502
25	0.295	14.094	0.021	0.071	3.386	47.727
26	0.281	14.375	0.020	0.070	3.556	51.113
27	0.268	14.643	0.018	0.068	3.733	54.669
28	0.255	14.898	0.017	0.067	3.920	58.403
29	0.243	15.141	0.016	0.066	4.116	62.323
30	0.231	15.372	0.015	0.065	4.322	66.439
31	0.220	15.593	0.014	0.064	4.538	70.761
32	0.210	15.803	0.013	0.063	4.765	75.299
33	0.200	16.003	0.012	0.062	5.003	80.064
34	0.190	16.193	0.012	0.062	5.253	85.067
35	0.181	16.374	0.011	0.061	5.516	90.320
36	0.173	16.547	0.010	0.060	5.792	95.836
37	0.164	16.711	0.010	0.060	6.081	101.628
38	0.157	16.868	0.009	0.059	6.385	107.710
39	0.149	17.017	0.009	0.059	6.705	114.095
40	0.142	17.159	0.008	0.058	7.040	120.800
42	0.129	17.423	0.007	0.057	7.762	135.232
44	0.117	17.663	0.007	0.057	8.557	151.143
46	0.106	17.880	0.006	0.056	9.434	168.685
48	0.096	18.077	0.005	0.055	10.401	188.025
50	0.087	18.256	0.005	0.055	11.467	209.348

6% Interest Rate

n	P/F	P/A	A/F	A/P	F/P	F/A
1	0.943	0.943	1.000	1.060	1.060	1.000
2	0.890	1.833	0.485	0.545	1.124	2.060
3	0.840	2.673	0.314	0.374	1.191	3.184
4	0.792	3.465	0.229	0.289	1.262	4.375
5	0.747	4.212	0.177	0.237	1.338	5.637
6	0.705	4.917	0.143	0.203	1.419	6.975
7	0.665	5.582	0.119	0.179	1.504	8.394
8	0.627	6.210	0.101	0.161	1.594	9.897
9	0.592	6.802	0.087	0.147	1.689	11.491
10	0.558	7.360	0.076	0.136	1.791	13.181
11	0.527	7.887	0.067	0.127	1.898	14.972
12	0.497	8.384	0.059	0.119	2.012	16.870
13	0.469	8.853	0.053	0.113	2.133	18.882
14	0.442	9.295	0.048	0.108	2.261	21.015
15	0.417	9.712	0.043	0.103	2.397	23.276
16	0.394	10.106	0.039	0.099	2.540	25.673
17	0.371	10.477	0.035	0.095	2.693	28.213
18	0.350	10.828	0.032	0.092	2.854	30.906
19	0.331	11.158	0.030	0.090	3.026	33.760
20	0.312	11.470	0.027	0.087	3.207	36.786
21	0.294	11.764	0.025	0.085	3.400	39.993
22	0.278	12.042	0.023	0.083	3.604	43.392
23	0.262	12.303	0.021	0.081	3.820	46.996
24	0.247	12.550	0.020	0.080	4.049	50.816
25	0.233	12.783	0.018	0.078	4.292	54.865
26	0.220	13.003	0.017	0.077	4.549	59.156
27	0.207	13.211	0.016	0.076	4.822	63.706
28	0.196	13.406	0.015	0.075	5.112	68.528
29	0.185	13.591	0.014	0.074	5.418	73.640
30	0.174	13.765	0.013	0.073	5.743	79.058
31	0.164	13.929	0.012	0.072	6.088	84.802
32	0.155	14.084	0.011	0.071	6.453	90.890
33	0.146	14.230	0.010	0.070	6.841	97.343
34	0.138	14.368	0.010	0.070	7.251	104.184
35	0.130	14.498	0.009	0.069	7.686	111.435
36	0.123	14.621	0.008	0.068	8.147	119.121
37	0.116	14.737	0.008	0.068	8.636	127.268
38	0.109	14.846	0.007	0.067	9.154	135.904
39	0.103	14.949	0.007	0.067	9.704	145.058
40	0.097	15.046	0.006	0.066	10.286	154.762
42	0.087	15.225	0.006	0.066	11.557	175.951
44	0.077	15.383	0.005	0.065	12.985	199.758
46	0.069	15.524	0.004	0.064	14.590	226.508
48	0.061	15.650	0.004	0.064	16.394	256.565
50	0.054	15.762	0.003	0.063	18.420	290.336

	7% Interest Rate					
n	P/F	P/A	A/F	A/P	F/P	F/A
1	0.935	0.935	1.000	1.070	1.070	1.000
2	0.873	1.808	0.483	0.553	1.145	2.070
3	0.816	2.624	0.311	0.381	1.225	3.215
4	0.763	3.387	0.225	0.295	1.311	4.440
5	0.713	4.100	0.174	0.244	1.403	5.751
6	0.666	4.767	0.140	0.210	1.501	7.153
7	0.623	5.389	0.116	0.186	1.606	8.654
8	0.582	5.971	0.097	0.167	1.718	10.260
9	0.544	6.515	0.083	0.153	1.838	11.978
10	0.508	7.024	0.072	0.142	1.967	13.816
11	0.475	7.499	0.063	0.133	2.105	15.784
12	0.444	7.943	0.056	0.126	2.252	17.888
13	0.415	8.358	0.050	0.120	2.410	20.141
14	0.388	8.745	0.044	0.114	2.579	22.550
15	0.362	9.108	0.040	0.110	2.759	25.129
16	0.339	9.447	0.036	0.106	2.952	27.888
17	0.317	9.763	0.032	0.102	3.159	30.840
18	0.296	10.059	0.029	0.099	3.380	33.999
19	0.277	10.336	0.027	0.097	3.617	37.379
20	0.258	10.594	0.024	0.094	3.870	40.995
21	0.242	10.836	0.022	0.092	4.141	44.865
22	0.226	11.061	0.020	0.090	4.430	49.006
23	0.211	11.272	0.019	0.089	4.741	53.436
24	0.197	11.469	0.017	0.087	5.072	58.177
25	0.184	11.654	0.016	0.086	5.427	63.249
26	0.172	11.826	0.015	0.085	5.807	68.676
27	0.161	11.987	0.013	0.083	6.214	74.484
28	0.150	12.137	0.012	0.082	6.649	80.698
29	0.141	12.278	0.011	0.081	7.114	87.347
30	0.131	12.409	0.011	0.081	7.612	94.461
31	0.123	12.532	0.010	0.080	8.145	102.073
32	0.115	12.647	0.009	0.079	8.715	110.218
33	0.107	12.754	0.008	0.078	9.325	118.933
34	0.100	12.854	0.008	0.078	9.978	128.259
35	0.094	12.948	0.007	0.077	10.677	138.237
36	0.088	13.035	0.007	0.077	11.424	148.913
37	0.082	13.117	0.006	0.076	12.224	160.337
38	0.076	13.193	0.006	0.076	13.079	172.561
39	0.071	13.265	0.005	0.075	13.995	185.640
40	0.067	13.332	0.005	0.075	14.974	199.635
42	0.058	13.452	0.004	0.074	17.144	230.632
44	0.051	13.558	0.004	0.074	19.628	266.121
46	0.044	13.650	0.003	0.073	22.473	306.752
48	0.039	13.730	0.003	0.073	25.729	353.270
50	0.034	13.801	0.002	0.072	29.457	406.529

8% Interest Rate

n	P/F	P/A	A/F	A/P	F/P	F/A
1	0.926	0.926	1.000	1.080	1.080	1.000
2	0.857	1.783	0.481	0.561	1.166	2.080
3	0.794	2.577	0.308	0.388	1.260	3.246
4	0.735	3.312	0.222	0.302	1.360	4.506
5	0.681	3.993	0.170	0.250	1.469	5.867
6	0.630	4.623	0.136	0.216	1.587	7.336
7	0.583	5.206	0.112	0.192	1.714	8.923
8	0.540	5.747	0.094	0.174	1.851	10.637
9	0.500	6.247	0.080	0.160	1.999	12.488
10	0.463	6.710	0.069	0.149	2.159	14.487
11	0.429	7.139	0.060	0.140	2.332	16.645
12	0.397	7.536	0.053	0.133	2.518	18.977
13	0.368	7.904	0.047	0.127	2.720	21.495
14	0.340	8.244	0.041	0.121	2.937	24.215
15	0.315	8.559	0.037	0.117	3.172	27.152
16	0.292	8.851	0.033	0.113	3.426	30.324
17	0.270	9.122	0.030	0.110	3.700	33.750
18	0.250	9.372	0.027	0.107	3.996	37.450
19	0.232	9.604	0.024	0.104	4.316	41.446
20	0.215	9.818	0.022	0.102	4.661	45.762
21	0.199	10.017	0.020	0.100	5.034	50.423
22	0.184	10.201	0.018	0.098	5.437	55.457
23	0.170	10.371	0.016	0.096	5.871	60.893
24	0.158	10.529	0.015	0.095	6.341	66.765
25	0.146	10.675	0.014	0.094	6.848	73.106
26	0.135	10.810	0.013	0.093	7.396	79.954
27	0.125	10.935	0.011	0.091	7.988	87.351
28	0.116	11.051	0.010	0.090	8.627	95.339
29	0.107	11.158	0.010	0.090	9.317	103.966
30	0.099	11.258	0.009	0.089	10.063	113.283
31	0.092	11.350	0.008	0.088	10.868	123.346
32	0.085	11.435	0.007	0.087	11.737	134.214
33	0.079	11.514	0.007	0.087	12.676	145.951
34	0.073	11.587	0.006	0.086	13.690	158.627
35	0.068	11.655	0.006	0.086	14.785	172.317
36	0.063	11.717	0.005	0.085	15.968	187.102
37	0.058	11.775	0.005	0.085	17.246	203.070
38	0.054	11.829	0.005	0.085	18.625	220.316
39	0.050	11.879	0.004	0.084	20.115	238.941
40	0.046	11.925	0.004	0.084	21.725	259.057
42	0.039	12.007	0.003	0.083	25.339	304.244
44	0.034	12.077	0.003	0.083	29.556	356.950
46	0.029	12.137	0.002	0.082	34.474	418.426
48	0.025	12.189	0.002	0.082	40.211	490.132
50	0.021	12.233	0.002	0.082	46.902	573.770

			9% Interest Rate			
n	*P/F*	*P/A*	*A/F*	*A/P*	*F/P*	*F/A*
1	0.917	0.917	1.000	1.090	1.090	1.000
2	0.842	1.759	0.478	0.568	1.188	2.090
3	0.772	2.531	0.305	0.395	1.295	3.278
4	0.708	3.240	0.219	0.309	1.412	4.573
5	0.650	3.890	0.167	0.257	1.539	5.985
6	0.596	4.486	0.133	0.223	1.677	7.523
7	0.547	5.033	0.109	0.199	1.828	9.200
8	0.502	5.535	0.091	0.181	1.993	11.028
9	0.460	5.995	0.077	0.167	2.172	13.021
10	0.422	6.418	0.066	0.156	2.367	15.193
11	0.388	6.805	0.057	0.147	2.580	17.560
12	0.356	7.161	0.050	0.140	2.813	20.141
13	0.326	7.487	0.044	0.134	3.066	22.953
14	0.299	7.786	0.038	0.128	3.342	26.019
15	0.275	8.061	0.034	0.124	3.642	29.361
16	0.252	8.313	0.030	0.120	3.970	33.003
17	0.231	8.544	0.027	0.117	4.328	36.974
18	0.212	8.756	0.024	0.114	4.717	41.301
19	0.194	8.950	0.022	0.112	5.142	46.018
20	0.178	9.129	0.020	0.110	5.604	51.160
21	0.164	9.292	0.018	0.108	6.109	56.765
22	0.150	9.442	0.016	0.106	6.659	62.873
23	0.138	9.580	0.014	0.104	7.258	69.532
24	0.126	9.707	0.013	0.103	7.911	76.790
25	0.116	9.823	0.012	0.102	8.623	84.701
26	0.106	9.929	0.011	0.101	9.399	93.324
27	0.098	10.027	0.010	0.100	10.245	102.723
28	0.090	10.116	0.009	0.099	11.167	112.968
29	0.082	10.198	0.008	0.098	12.172	124.135
30	0.075	10.274	0.007	0.097	13.268	136.308
31	0.069	10.343	0.007	0.097	14.462	149.575
32	0.063	10.406	0.006	0.096	15.763	164.037
33	0.058	10.464	0.006	0.096	17.182	179.800
34	0.053	10.518	0.005	0.095	18.728	196.982
35	0.049	10.567	0.005	0.095	20.414	215.711
36	0.045	10.612	0.004	0.094	22.251	236.125
37	0.041	10.653	0.004	0.094	24.254	258.376
38	0.038	10.691	0.004	0.094	26.437	282.630
39	0.035	10.726	0.003	0.093	28.816	309.066
40	0.032	10.757	0.003	0.093	31.409	337.882
42	0.027	10.813	0.002	0.092	37.318	403.528
44	0.023	10.861	0.002	0.092	44.337	481.522
46	0.019	10.900	0.002	0.092	52.677	574.186
48	0.016	10.934	0.001	0.091	62.585	684.280
50	0.013	10.962	0.001	0.091	74.358	815.084

10% Interest Rate

n	P/F	P/A	A/F	A/P	F/P	F/A
1	0.909	0.909	1.000	1.100	1.100	1.000
2	0.826	1.736	0.476	0.576	1.210	2.100
3	0.751	2.487	0.302	0.402	1.331	3.310
4	0.683	3.170	0.215	0.315	1.464	4.641
5	0.621	3.791	0.164	0.264	1.611	6.105
6	0.564	4.355	0.130	0.230	1.772	7.716
7	0.513	4.868	0.105	0.205	1.949	9.487
8	0.467	5.335	0.087	0.187	2.144	11.436
9	0.424	5.759	0.074	0.174	2.358	13.579
10	0.386	6.145	0.063	0.163	2.594	15.937
11	0.350	6.495	0.054	0.154	2.853	18.531
12	0.319	6.814	0.047	0.147	3.138	21.384
13	0.290	7.103	0.041	0.141	3.452	24.523
14	0.263	7.367	0.036	0.136	3.797	27.975
15	0.239	7.606	0.031	0.131	4.177	31.772
16	0.218	7.824	0.028	0.128	4.595	35.950
17	0.198	8.022	0.025	0.125	5.054	40.545
18	0.180	8.201	0.022	0.122	5.560	45.599
19	0.164	8.365	0.020	0.120	6.116	51.159
20	0.149	8.514	0.017	0.117	6.727	57.275
21	0.135	8.649	0.016	0.116	7.400	64.002
22	0.123	8.772	0.014	0.114	8.140	71.403
23	0.112	8.883	0.013	0.113	8.954	79.543
24	0.102	8.985	0.011	0.111	9.850	88.407
25	0.092	9.077	0.010	0.110	10.835	98.347
26	0.084	9.161	0.009	0.109	11.918	109.182
27	0.076	9.237	0.008	0.108	13.110	121.100
28	0.069	9.307	0.007	0.107	14.421	134.210
29	0.063	9.370	0.007	0.107	15.863	148.631
30	0.057	9.427	0.006	0.106	17.449	164.494
31	0.052	9.479	0.005	0.105	19.194	181.943
32	0.047	9.526	0.005	0.105	21.114	201.138
33	0.043	9.569	0.004	0.104	23.225	222.252
34	0.039	9.609	0.004	0.104	25.548	245.477
35	0.036	9.644	0.004	0.104	28.102	271.024
36	0.032	9.677	0.003	0.103	30.913	299.127
37	0.029	9.706	0.003	0.103	34.004	330.039
38	0.027	9.733	0.003	0.103	37.404	364.043
39	0.024	9.757	0.002	0.102	41.145	401.448
40	0.022	9.779	0.002	0.102	45.259	442.593
42	0.018	9.817	0.002	0.102	54.764	537.637
44	0.015	9.849	0.002	0.102	66.264	652.641
46	0.012	9.875	0.001	0.101	80.180	791.795
48	0.010	9.897	0.001	0.101	97.017	960.172
50	0.009	9.915	0.001	0.101	117.391	1163.909

12% Interest Rate

n	P/F	P/A	A/F	A/P	F/P	F/A
1	0.893	0.893	1.000	1.120	1.120	1.000
2	0.797	1.690	0.472	0.592	1.254	2.120
3	0.712	2.402	0.296	0.416	1.405	3.374
4	0.636	3.037	0.209	0.329	1.574	4.779
5	0.567	3.605	0.157	0.277	1.762	6.353
6	0.507	4.111	0.123	0.243	1.974	8.115
7	0.452	4.564	0.099	0.219	2.211	10.089
8	0.404	4.968	0.081	0.201	2.476	12.300
9	0.361	5.328	0.068	0.188	2.773	14.776
10	0.322	5.650	0.057	0.177	3.106	17.549
11	0.287	5.938	0.048	0.168	3.479	20.655
12	0.257	6.194	0.041	0.161	3.896	24.133
13	0.229	6.424	0.036	0.156	4.363	28.029
14	0.205	6.628	0.031	0.151	4.887	32.393
15	0.183	6.811	0.027	0.147	5.474	37.280
16	0.163	6.974	0.023	0.143	6.130	42.753
17	0.146	7.120	0.020	0.140	6.866	48.884
18	0.130	7.250	0.018	0.138	7.690	55.750
19	0.116	7.366	0.016	0.136	8.613	63.440
20	0.104	7.469	0.014	0.134	9.646	72.052
21	0.093	7.562	0.012	0.132	10.804	81.699
22	0.083	7.645	0.011	0.131	12.100	92.503
23	0.074	7.718	0.010	0.130	13.552	104.603
24	0.066	7.784	0.008	0.128	15.179	118.155
25	0.059	7.843	0.007	0.127	17.000	133.334
26	0.053	7.896	0.007	0.127	19.040	150.334
27	0.047	7.943	0.006	0.126	21.325	169.374
28	0.042	7.984	0.005	0.125	23.884	190.699
29	0.037	8.022	0.005	0.125	26.750	214.583
30	0.033	8.055	0.004	0.124	29.960	241.333
31	0.030	8.085	0.004	0.124	33.555	271.293
32	0.027	8.112	0.003	0.123	37.582	304.848
33	0.024	8.135	0.003	0.123	42.092	342.429
34	0.021	8.157	0.003	0.123	47.143	384.521
35	0.019	8.176	0.002	0.122	52.800	431.663
36	0.017	8.192	0.002	0.122	59.136	484.463
37	0.015	8.208	0.002	0.122	66.232	543.599
38	0.013	8.221	0.002	0.122	74.180	609.831
39	0.012	8.233	0.001	0.121	83.081	684.010
40	0.011	8.244	0.001	0.121	93.051	767.091
42	0.009	8.262	0.001	0.121	116.723	964.359
44	0.007	8.276	0.001	0.121	146.418	1211.813
46	0.005	8.288	0.001	0.121	183.666	1522.218
48	0.004	8.297	0.001	0.121	230.391	1911.590
50	0.003	8.304	0.000	0.120	289.002	2400.018

14% Interest Rate

n	P/F	P/A	A/F	A/P	F/P	F/A
1	0.877	0.877	1.000	1.140	1.140	1.000
2	0.769	1.647	0.467	0.607	1.300	2.140
3	0.675	2.322	0.291	0.431	1.482	3.440
4	0.592	2.914	0.203	0.343	1.689	4.921
5	0.519	3.433	0.151	0.291	1.925	6.610
6	0.456	3.889	0.117	0.257	2.195	8.536
7	0.400	4.288	0.093	0.233	2.502	10.730
8	0.351	4.639	0.076	0.216	2.853	13.233
9	0.308	4.946	0.062	0.202	3.252	16.085
10	0.270	5.216	0.052	0.192	3.707	19.337
11	0.237	5.453	0.043	0.183	4.226	23.045
12	0.208	5.660	0.037	0.177	4.818	27.271
13	0.182	5.842	0.031	0.171	5.492	32.089
14	0.160	6.002	0.027	0.167	6.261	37.581
15	0.140	6.142	0.023	0.163	7.138	43.842
16	0.123	6.265	0.020	0.160	8.137	50.980
17	0.108	6.373	0.017	0.157	9.276	59.118
18	0.095	6.467	0.015	0.155	10.575	68.394
19	0.083	6.550	0.013	0.153	12.056	78.969
20	0.073	6.623	0.011	0.151	13.743	91.025
21	0.064	6.687	0.010	0.150	15.668	104.768
22	0.056	6.743	0.008	0.148	17.861	120.436
23	0.049	6.792	0.007	0.147	20.362	138.297
24	0.043	6.835	0.006	0.146	23.212	158.659
25	0.038	6.873	0.005	0.145	26.462	181.871
26	0.033	6.906	0.005	0.145	30.167	208.333
27	0.029	6.935	0.004	0.144	34.390	238.499
28	0.026	6.961	0.004	0.144	39.204	272.889
29	0.022	6.983	0.003	0.143	44.693	312.094
30	0.020	7.003	0.003	0.143	50.950	356.787
31	0.017	7.020	0.002	0.142	58.083	407.737
32	0.015	7.035	0.002	0.142	66.215	465.820
33	0.013	7.048	0.002	0.142	75.485	532.035
34	0.012	7.060	0.002	0.142	86.053	607.520
35	0.010	7.070	0.001	0.141	98.100	693.573
36	0.009	7.079	0.001	0.141	111.834	791.673
37	0.008	7.087	0.001	0.141	127.491	903.507
38	0.007	7.094	0.001	0.141	145.340	1030.998
39	0.006	7.100	0.001	0.141	165.687	1176.338
40	0.005	7.105	0.001	0.141	188.884	1342.025
42	0.004	7.114	0.001	0.141	245.473	1746.236
44	0.003	7.120	0.000	0.140	319.017	2271.548
46	0.002	7.126	0.000	0.140	414.594	2954.244
48	0.002	7.130	0.000	0.140	538.807	3841.475
50	0.001	7.133	0.000	0.140	700.233	4994.521

16% Interest Rate

n	P/F	P/A	A/F	A/P	F/P	F/A
1	0.862	0.862	1.000	1.160	1.160	1.000
2	0.743	1.605	0.463	0.623	1.346	2.160
3	0.641	2.246	0.285	0.445	1.561	3.506
4	0.552	2.798	0.197	0.357	1.811	5.066
5	0.476	3.274	0.145	0.305	2.100	6.877
6	0.410	3.685	0.111	0.271	2.436	8.977
7	0.354	4.039	0.088	0.248	2.826	11.414
8	0.305	4.344	0.070	0.230	3.278	14.240
9	0.263	4.607	0.057	0.217	3.803	17.519
10	0.227	4.833	0.047	0.207	4.411	21.321
11	0.195	5.029	0.039	0.199	5.117	25.733
12	0.168	5.197	0.032	0.192	5.936	30.850
13	0.145	5.342	0.027	0.187	6.886	36.786
14	0.125	5.468	0.023	0.183	7.988	43.672
15	0.108	5.575	0.019	0.179	9.266	51.660
16	0.093	5.668	0.016	0.176	10.748	60.925
17	0.080	5.749	0.014	0.174	12.468	71.673
18	0.069	5.818	0.012	0.172	14.463	84.141
19	0.060	5.877	0.010	0.170	16.777	98.603
20	0.051	5.929	0.009	0.169	19.461	115.380
21	0.044	5.973	0.007	0.167	22.574	134.841
22	0.038	6.011	0.006	0.166	26.186	157.415
23	0.033	6.044	0.005	0.165	30.376	183.601
24	0.028	6.073	0.005	0.165	35.236	213.978
25	0.024	6.097	0.004	0.164	40.874	249.214
26	0.021	6.118	0.003	0.163	47.414	290.088
27	0.018	6.136	0.003	0.163	55.000	337.502
28	0.016	6.152	0.003	0.163	63.800	392.503
29	0.014	6.166	0.002	0.162	74.009	456.303
30	0.012	6.177	0.002	0.162	85.850	530.312
31	0.010	6.187	0.002	0.162	99.586	616.162
32	0.009	6.196	0.001	0.161	115.520	715.747
33	0.007	6.203	0.001	0.161	134.003	831.267
34	0.006	6.210	0.001	0.161	155.443	965.270
35	0.006	6.215	0.001	0.161	180.314	1120.713
36	0.005	6.220	0.001	0.161	209.164	1301.027
37	0.004	6.224	0.001	0.161	242.631	1510.191
38	0.004	6.228	0.001	0.161	281.452	1752.822
39	0.003	6.231	0.000	0.160	326.484	2034.273
40	0.003	6.233	0.000	0.160	378.721	2360.757
42	0.002	6.238	0.000	0.160	509.607	3178.795
44	0.001	6.241	0.000	0.160	685.727	4279.546
46	0.001	6.243	0.000	0.160	922.715	5760.718
48	0.001	6.245	0.000	0.160	1241.605	7753.782
50	0.001	6.246	0.000	0.160	1670.704	10435.649

			18% Interest Rate			
n	P/F	P/A	A/F	A/P	F/P	F/A
1	0.847	0.847	1.000	1.180	1.180	1.000
2	0.718	1.566	0.459	0.639	1.392	2.180
3	0.609	2.174	0.280	0.460	1.643	3.572
4	0.516	2.690	0.192	0.372	1.939	5.215
5	0.437	3.127	0.140	0.320	2.288	7.154
6	0.370	3.498	0.106	0.286	2.700	9.442
7	0.314	3.812	0.082	0.262	3.185	12.142
8	0.266	4.078	0.065	0.245	3.759	15.327
9	0.225	4.303	0.052	0.232	4.435	19.086
10	0.191	4.494	0.043	0.223	5.234	23.521
11	0.162	4.656	0.035	0.215	6.176	28.755
12	0.137	4.793	0.029	0.209	7.288	34.931
13	0.116	4.910	0.024	0.204	8.599	42.219
14	0.099	5.008	0.020	0.200	10.147	50.818
15	0.084	5.092	0.016	0.196	11.974	60.965
16	0.071	5.162	0.014	0.194	14.129	72.939
17	0.060	5.222	0.011	0.191	16.672	87.068
18	0.051	5.273	0.010	0.190	19.673	103.740
19	0.043	5.316	0.008	0.188	23.214	123.414
20	0.037	5.353	0.007	0.187	27.393	146.628
21	0.031	5.384	0.006	0.186	32.324	174.021
22	0.026	5.410	0.005	0.185	38.142	206.345
23	0.022	5.432	0.004	0.184	45.008	244.487
24	0.019	5.451	0.003	0.183	53.109	289.494
25	0.016	5.467	0.003	0.183	62.669	342.603
26	0.014	5.480	0.002	0.182	73.949	405.272
27	0.011	5.492	0.002	0.182	87.260	479.221
28	0.010	5.502	0.002	0.182	102.967	566.481
29	0.008	5.510	0.001	0.181	121.501	669.447
30	0.007	5.517	0.001	0.181	143.371	790.948
31	0.006	5.523	0.001	0.181	169.177	934.319
32	0.005	5.528	0.001	0.181	199.629	1103.496
33	0.004	5.532	0.001	0.181	235.563	1303.125
34	0.004	5.536	0.001	0.181	277.964	1538.688
35	0.003	5.539	0.001	0.181	327.997	1816.652
36	0.003	5.541	0.000	0.180	387.037	2144.649
37	0.002	5.543	0.000	0.180	456.703	2531.686
38	0.002	5.545	0.000	0.180	538.910	2988.389
39	0.002	5.547	0.000	0.180	635.914	3527.299
40	0.001	5.548	0.000	0.180	750.378	4163.213
42	0.001	5.550	0.000	0.180	1044.827	5799.038
44	0.001	5.552	0.000	0.180	1454.817	8076.760
46	0.000	5.553	0.000	0.180	2025.687	11248.261
48	0.000	5.554	0.000	0.180	2820.567	15664.259
50	0.000	5.554	0.000	0.180	3927.357	21813.094

20% Interest Rate

n	P/F	P/A	A/F	A/P	F/P	F/A
1	0.833	0.833	1.000	1.200	1.200	1.000
2	0.694	1.528	0.455	0.655	1.440	2.200
3	0.579	2.106	0.275	0.475	1.728	3.640
4	0.482	2.589	0.186	0.386	2.074	5.368
5	0.402	2.991	0.134	0.334	2.488	7.442
6	0.335	3.326	0.101	0.301	2.986	9.930
7	0.279	3.605	0.077	0.277	3.583	12.916
8	0.233	3.837	0.061	0.261	4.300	16.499
9	0.194	4.031	0.048	0.248	5.160	20.799
10	0.162	4.192	0.039	0.239	6.192	25.959
11	0.135	4.327	0.031	0.231	7.430	32.150
12	0.112	4.439	0.025	0.225	8.916	39.581
13	0.093	4.533	0.021	0.221	10.699	48.497
14	0.078	4.611	0.017	0.217	12.839	59.196
15	0.065	4.675	0.014	0.214	15.407	72.035
16	0.054	4.730	0.011	0.211	18.488	87.442
17	0.045	4.775	0.009	0.209	22.186	105.931
18	0.038	4.812	0.008	0.208	26.623	128.117
19	0.031	4.843	0.006	0.206	31.948	154.740
20	0.026	4.870	0.005	0.205	38.338	186.688
21	0.022	4.891	0.004	0.204	46.005	225.026
22	0.018	4.909	0.004	0.204	55.206	271.031
23	0.015	4.925	0.003	0.203	66.247	326.237
24	0.013	4.937	0.003	0.203	79.497	392.484
25	0.010	4.948	0.002	0.202	95.396	471.981
26	0.009	4.956	0.002	0.202	114.475	567.377
27	0.007	4.964	0.001	0.201	137.371	681.853
28	0.006	4.970	0.001	0.201	164.845	819.223
29	0.005	4.975	0.001	0.201	197.814	984.068
30	0.004	4.979	0.001	0.201	237.376	1181.882
31	0.004	4.982	0.001	0.201	284.852	1419.258
32	0.003	4.985	0.001	0.201	341.822	1704.109
33	0.002	4.988	0.000	0.200	410.186	2045.931
34	0.002	4.990	0.000	0.200	492.224	2456.118
35	0.002	4.992	0.000	0.200	590.668	2948.341
36	0.001	4.993	0.000	0.200	708.802	3539.009
37	0.001	4.994	0.000	0.200	850.562	4247.811
38	0.001	4.995	0.000	0.200	1020.675	5098.373
39	0.001	4.996	0.000	0.200	1224.810	6119.048
40	0.001	4.997	0.000	0.200	1469.772	7343.858
42	0.000	4.998	0.000	0.200	2116.471	10577.355
44	0.000	4.998	0.000	0.200	3047.718	15233.592
46	0.000	4.999	0.000	0.200	4388.714	21938.572
48	0.000	4.999	0.000	0.200	6319.749	31593.744
50	0.000	4.999	0.000	0.200	9100.438	45497.191

25% Interest Rate

n	P/F	P/A	A/F	A/P	F/P	F/A
1	0.800	0.800	1.000	1.250	1.250	1.000
2	0.640	1.440	0.444	0.694	1.563	2.250
3	0.512	1.952	0.262	0.512	1.953	3.813
4	0.410	2.362	0.173	0.423	2.441	5.766
5	0.328	2.689	0.122	0.372	3.052	8.207
6	0.262	2.951	0.089	0.339	3.815	11.259
7	0.210	3.161	0.066	0.316	4.768	15.073
8	0.168	3.329	0.050	0.300	5.960	19.842
9	0.134	3.463	0.039	0.289	7.451	25.802
10	0.107	3.571	0.030	0.280	9.313	33.253
11	0.086	3.656	0.023	0.273	11.642	42.566
12	0.069	3.725	0.018	0.268	14.552	54.208
13	0.055	3.780	0.015	0.265	18.190	68.760
14	0.044	3.824	0.012	0.262	22.737	86.949
15	0.035	3.859	0.009	0.259	28.422	109.687
16	0.028	3.887	0.007	0.257	35.527	138.109
17	0.023	3.910	0.006	0.256	44.409	173.636
18	0.018	3.928	0.005	0.255	55.511	218.045
19	0.014	3.942	0.004	0.254	69.389	273.556
20	0.012	3.954	0.003	0.253	86.736	342.945
21	0.009	3.963	0.002	0.252	108.420	429.681
22	0.007	3.970	0.002	0.252	135.525	538.101
23	0.006	3.976	0.001	0.251	169.407	673.626
24	0.005	3.981	0.001	0.251	211.758	843.033
25	0.004	3.985	0.001	0.251	264.698	1054.791
26	0.003	3.988	0.001	0.251	330.872	1319.489
27	0.002	3.990	0.001	0.251	413.590	1650.361
28	0.002	3.992	0.000	0.250	516.988	2063.952
29	0.002	3.994	0.000	0.250	646.235	2580.939
30	0.001	3.995	0.000	0.250	807.794	3227.174
31	0.001	3.996	0.000	0.250	1009.742	4034.968
32	0.001	3.997	0.000	0.250	1262.177	5044.710
33	0.001	3.997	0.000	0.250	1577.722	6306.887
34	0.001	3.998	0.000	0.250	1972.152	7884.609
35	0.000	3.998	0.000	0.250	2465.190	9856.761
36	0.000	3.999	0.000	0.250	3081.488	12321.952
37	0.000	3.999	0.000	0.250	3851.860	15403.440
38	0.000	3.999	0.000	0.250	4814.825	19255.299
39	0.000	3.999	0.000	0.250	6018.531	24070.124
40	0.000	3.999	0.000	0.250	7523.164	30088.655
42	0.000	4.000	0.000	0.250	11754.944	47015.774
44	0.000	4.000	0.000	0.250	18367.099	73464.397
46	0.000	4.000	0.000	0.250	28698.593	114790.370
48	0.000	4.000	0.000	0.250	44841.551	179362.203
50	0.000	4.000	0.000	0.250	70064.923	280255.693

Index

Note: Tables are indicated with italicized page references.